ASPECTS OF GREEK AND ROMAN LIFE

General Editor: H. H. Scullard

* * *

FESTIVALS AND CEREMONIES OF THE ROMAN REPUBLIC

H. H. Scullard

FESTIVALS
AND CEREMONIES
OF THE
ROMAN REPUBLIC

H.H.Scullard

CORNELL UNIVERSITY PRESS
Ithaca, New York

First published 1981 by Cornell University Press
Second printing 1982

International Standard Book Number
0-8014-1402-4
Library of Congress Catalog Card Number
80-70447

Printed and bound in the United States of America

*The paper in this book is acid-free, and meets the
guidelines for permanence and durability of the Committee
on Production Guidelines for Book Longevity of
the Council on Library Resources.*

CONTENTS

LIST OF ILLUSTRATIONS

Sources of Illustrations

Alinari 14, 15, 16, 25, 32, 39; Deutsches Archäologisches Institut, Rome 4, 9, 31; Direzione dei Musei Capitolini 3, 23, 26, 28; Fototeca Unione 8, 10, 11, 12, 13, 17, 18, 22, 27, 29, 30, 33, 34, 35, 37, 38, 41 (32); Giraudon 1, 2, 7; Soprintendenza alle Antichità dell'Etruria Meridionale, Villa Giulia, Rome 20.

Coins in 40 and 41 from E.A. Sydenham, *The Coinage of the Roman Republic*, London 1952, have been reproduced by kind permission of Messrs Spink and Son, Ltd., London.

PREFACE

The aim of this book is to describe, day by day throughout the year, the public ceremonies which were held in Rome during the later Republic: in brief, to answer the question 'What's on in Town today?'. Most of these ceremonies were religious festivals or Games which were religious, at least in origin, and the dates of the majority were fixed in an official calendar. I have also included short descriptions of a few more secular occasions, such as political meetings, but even these had a religious background since many opened with an attempt to ascertain the will of the gods by 'taking the auspices' or, as we might say, 'by opening with prayer'. I have, therefore, included a preliminary sketch of Roman religious ideas and practices.

Although public life in the later Republic was full of festivals and Cicero could say of the Romans of his day that while 'we may be equal or inferior to other nations in other respects, in religion (*religio*), that is in reverence for the gods (*cultu deorum*), we are far superior', nevertheless the origin and significance of many of their rituals were unknown or only partially known even to educated men of that period, and a great scholar such as Varro can often provide much that is little more than antiquarian speculation. The roots of many of these practices go back into the Iron and Bronze Ages or earlier when the ancestors of the Romans were living in pre-urban conditions, yet many of these primitive ideas survived in rites which the conservative Romans were loath to abandon completely even when their meaning was obscured. Thus we shall have often to glance backward into more primitive realms of thought, but it is not the purpose of this book to seek to examine in any detail this shadowy world except in so far as it was of importance to the later Romans who naturally could not interpret it in terms made possible by the researches of modern anthropologists and sociologists. In the last resort our knowledge is, of course, strictly limited to what the ancient writers tell us, aided by archaeological and linguistic evidence. Students of comparative religion can only add to the probability that such and such a rite was correctly recorded, in the sense that they show that mankind has acted in a similar way in different times and places; they do, however, reveal processes of primitive thought which were foreign to the conscious thinking of the men of the Ciceronian age. Yet even the more sceptical of these latter-day Romans continued to maintain many old religious practices in the conviction that they were for the good of the State, even if their institutionalization had diminished their personal meaning for many individual city-dwellers; in the countryside older ideas retained a stronger hold.

I hope that while not aiming at completeness, I have provided adequate documentation of the ancient sources. In view of the immense volume of the modern literature I have kept references down to what, again I hope, is a reasonable minimum. There are some half a dozen indispensable books to which I have made frequent reference on specific points but I have not thought it necessary to list them all, with page references, on every topic to which they have contributed. The reader who wants more detailed information and views on individual deities and festivals should constantly bear in mind the contributions of G.Wissowa (*Religion und Kultus der Römer*), K.Latte (*Römische Religionsgeschichte*), W.Warde Fowler (*The Roman Festivals* and *The Religious Experience of the Roman People*), A.Degrassi (*Inscriptiones Italiae*,XIII,ii), G.De Sanctis (*Storia dei Romani*,IV,2,i) and Pauly-Wissowa's *Realencyclopaedie*. (Reference to these works is easy since the first five have adequate indices, De Sanctis lists his contents on p.ix f., and the articles in Pauly-Wissowa are, of course, arranged alphabetically.) Similarly, for detailed discussion of matters dealt with by Ovid in his *Fasti*, general reference should be made here to the commentaries by Sir James Frazer and by F.Bömer. My debt to all these writers is naturally immense, but I should mention Warde Fowler's *The Roman Festivals* in particular. This standard work is old and, as the author himself wrote in the reprint in 1916, 'to bring it fully up to date some parts of it would need not only revision but rewriting' (p.ix). I have not been so presumptuous as to attempt to provide an alternative: though much of the same ground is involved, my object has been different. My primary concern is not to examine the obscure origins of the old Roman festivals and deities in detail, but rather to describe the rituals that survived in the later Republic and to see throughout the year what they and some other forms of public ceremony offered to the inhabitants of Rome. They clearly occupied a very significant place in Roman society, though what they precisely meant to the individual Roman in religious or social terms, or how many Romans attended or took part in such rites, is unfortunately often far from clear. Thus, for instance, who can say what was in the mind of Ovid when, like a primitive shepherd, he leapt through the flames of the purificatory rite of the Parilia festival?

For translations of ancient authors I have gratefully made use of the Loeb Classical Library, with occasional minor adjustments.

March 1980   H.H.SCULLARD

Part One
RELIGION AND FESTIVALS

1 Prehistoric Beliefs

The Romans of the late Republic performed or witnessed many acts of religion and ritual whose origin they ascribed to the 'age of Romulus' or the 'time of Numa' – a period which we should now call that of the 'late Iron Age settlement'. Although their understanding of the early meaning and purpose of such rites may sometimes have been dim, at least they were conscious that they were following ancestral custom. But these practices of historical times had developed from prehistory, and when we ask what the inhabitants of the Iron Age huts on the Palatine hill may have thought about them, we are in a world of unlimited speculation, where we have to rely on the guesses of later Roman antiquarians and grammarians and on the aid provided by the work of modern philologists, archaeologists, anthropologists, students of comparative religion and myth, sociologists and psychologists. Where evidence, mainly literary, survives to show what was done, it does not always indicate why it was done, and even when explanations are offered, they may often be little more than informed or uninformed guesses: rites are easier to reconstruct than religious ideas. As H.J. Rose put it with brutal frankness: 'the laudable desire to get at the ideas behind ancient cult does not always lead to sound and well-founded theories.'[1] Since, however, this book is about the historical Romans rather than their prehistoric ancestors, it will suffice to indicate very briefly only some of the paths that have been cut through the dark forest that surrounded the minds of their ancestors. We can imagine how these pioneers cut out clearings in the forests for their settlements: it is less easy to speculate about their thoughts during such tasks, though some clues survive, as when Cato tells farmers, when thinning a grove, what sacrifice and prayers should be offered to the vague indwelling power, whether it be god or goddess (*Si deus, si dea es, quoium illud sacrum est*).

After the somewhat formal analysis of Roman religion by Mommsen and Wissowa in terms of institutions and cults, came the exciting influence of the study of primitive societies, and in particular the extraordinary range of human religious behaviour exposed by Sir James

Frazer's *Golden Bough* and the conception of *mana* as revealed among the Trobriand Islanders of Polynesia by the researches of Malinowski and others. Was there not, it was asked, an idea of 'power' like that of *mana* behind early Roman religion, a feeling that in man or physical objects unseen forces resided that were stronger than the individual and that might cause him good or evil? In other words, were not ideas of magic and taboo part of the primitive Roman tradition at a pre-deistic stage? What then of the gods and goddesses of Rome and the myths told about them? Was Wissowa right in his denial that there were any purely native Roman myths? Were they all either borrowed in later times from the rich source of Greek mythology or artificial literary creations designed to explain the origins of Rome and its early (legendary) history? On the other hand, if there were genuine Roman myths, were the characters in them personifications of natural forces or (as argued by F.Altheim and the Frankfort school) powerful beings such as were found in ideas of the broader Mediterranean world which were now shown to have influenced Italy in the days before Rome came into existence and which were modified by the Indo-European Romans? How indeed were the cults of the chthonic deities reconciled with those of the sky-gods? On the other hand, G.Dumézil and his followers have denied a pre-deistic stage in Roman religion and have stressed the Indo-European elements; they believe that the ancestors of the Romans brought with them into Italy religious beliefs and a mythology which they shared with others and especially with the Vedic Indians. This common Indo-European heritage was so strong that Rome inherited not only gods (especially the divine triad of Jupiter, Mars and Quirinus) but even a tripartite caste system of priestly rulers, warriors and farmers with presiding Roman deities who corresponded to their Indian counterparts. However, although an Indo-European element be admitted, Dumézil has, despite his immense learning, failed to convince many, and as to his application of his ideas to early Roman society it may suffice to quote A.Momigliano's verdict: 'not only is his evidence weak, but his theories are unnecessary'.[2]

In general, a 'primitivist' position, though perhaps not pressed as far as by H.J.Rose, seems a reasonable choice amid the bewildering welter of often mutually exclusive theories, but it is well to keep in mind the wise warning of A.D. Nock in regard to parallels in modern primitive societies: 'analogies will not teach us what happened in the past: they may help us to keep our reconstructions within limits consistent with what is known to happen'. He also sums up the dangers of the way: 'the key to all religions and to all mythologies has been sought in various theories – in an emphasis on the worship of ancestors, or on the worship of the heavenly bodies, or on the worship of the inanimate and even artificial bodies charged with power, or on the kinship of certain social units with animals or plants called totems, or again in the interpretation of all phenomena in terms of *mana*, the obscure magical force present in various objects, or again in the henotheistic ideas reported to be held among quite undeveloped tribes. Each time the key has opened certain doors, but no amount of filing has enabled it to open all the doors.'[3]

Some primitive ideas obviously survive into later times, but on the whole the Romans freed themselves from the cruder manifestations of magic and taboo, to some extent deliberately. Thus in the Twelve Tables of the mid-fifth century BC a law forbade the use of spells to 'steal' the fertility of a neighbour's land and 'the chanting of any evil charm': it was directed against anyone, *'qui fruges excantassit, qui malum carmen incantassit'*. However, men still continued to inscribe spells (*carmina*) and curses (*dirae*) on tablets (*tabellae defixionum*) to discomfort their private enemies and to use amulets (e.g. the *bullae* worn on necklaces by children) to avert dangers such as the evil eye. Little swinging figures (*oscilla*) were hung up at certain festivals (e.g. the Latin Festival: see p. 113) to protect the crops. But it is far from certain that these or the puppets that were thrown from a bridge into the Tiber at a procession of the Argei in the middle of May (p. 120) were surrogates for human sacrifice, a rite which the later Romans practised only in very exceptional circumstances. On the other hand, if it is (wrongly?) argued that these rites *did* involve substitutes and that therefore in earlier times human sacrifice *was* practised, all that can be said is that the idea was repugnant to the later Romans who regarded it as in no way a Roman rite (*minime Romanum sacrum*). Some milder forms of magic, however, did manage to survive in a few public ceremonies: the rite of *Aquaelicium*, when a stone (*lapis manalis*) was carried into the city in a procession from where it lay near the temple of Mars outside the Porta Capena, was a rain-making ceremony. The ceremonial whipping during the Lupercalia was a magical method of procuring fertility among women, and telepathic magic survived in the alleged power of the Vestal Virgins to stop runaway slaves leaving Rome by means of a spell. Beside such magical practices some belief in taboo continued, namely that certain objects were unclean or holy, with the consequential need for purification when such taboos were broken. Corpses, new-born infants, strangers, iron, certain places struck by lightning and certain days (see p. 45) were regarded as taboo, while the unfortunate priest of Jupiter (*flamen Dialis*) was subjected to a vast number of interdictions: for instance, he might not touch a horse, goat, dog, raw meat, a corpse, beans, ivy, wheat or leavened bread; his nails and hair must not be cut with an iron knife, and he must have no knot on his person. His wife, the *flaminica Dialis*, was also subject to certain taboos, but in general there were few survivals of these ideas which had generally disappeared before historical times.

A widespread but vague *mana* appears gradually to have been envisaged as localized impersonal forces, dwelling in stones, springs, rivers, groves or trees. These are often referred to nowadays as *numina*, though *numen* is not strictly identified with a deity until the Augustan period. However that may be, gradually presiding deities were thought to inhabit these natural places, and in time they began to acquire functional as well as local aspects.[4] In early days deities were invoked to help in all the numerous needs of home and farm, but slowly the process of subdivision of function was taken to ridiculous lengths. Thus these *indigites* presided over all the activities of man from the cradle (*Cunina*) to the grave (*Libitina*). Fabius Pictor recorded that the *flamen* (*Cerialis?*), when sacrificing to Tellus and Ceres, invoked no less than twelve 'deities', from Vervactor for the first ploughing to Promitor for the distribution of the corn. It is clear that the Roman priests developed elaborate lists (*indigitamenta*) of such *indigites*, probably inventing many, and the whole conception is sometimes regarded as a late creation. However, it goes back to Fabius in the third century BC and may well represent the inflation of a much more limited number of early beliefs. Thus farmers came to worship Ceres, who created growth (cf. *creare*), and Pomona, fruit, and then thought in terms of their functions: thus we hear of Lua Saturni (perhaps Saturn's power to expel disease) or the Salacia Neptuni (Neptune's power to provide springs of water), and since the meaning of some of these old titles is uncertain, they presumably provide evidence of an early stage of thought.

This brings us to the idea of the development of the idea of gods. Beside all these vague 'spirits', some forces emerged above the rest and transcended the limits of animism. These were deities such as Jupiter, the sky-god, who was part of the Romans' inheritance from their Indo-European origins, and Mars, an agricultural power who later developed into a war-god, while Quirinus, a deity of the settlement on the Quirinal, came to preside over all the assembled citizens. Further, gods, such as Janus and Vesta, were recognized as exercising influence first over domestic doorways and hearths, and then over wider areas than the private household. Thus early vague supernatural 'powers' approached more nearly to definite personalities, though not yet conceived in human form, and were honoured at simple rustic altars, not in temples of wood and stone.

2 Religion and the Family

Many of the State cults and festivals of Rome were in a sense family cults writ large, the projection for the wider needs of the community of the simple practices by which an individual tried to secure the safety and well-being of his household and land against the possible threat of supernatural powers. Thus we may glance briefly at some family ceremonies. Every important part of the house had its own spirit. The spirit of fire, Vesta, dwelt in the hearth, and during the chief meal each day a piece of sacred salted cake was thrown into the fire from a small sacrificial dish. Vesta was never fully personified like most deities, and her goodwill was needed if only because of the complication of rekindling a dead fire in ancient times (the later temple of Vesta contained no image and its fire was never allowed to go out). The store-cupboard (*penus*) also must be protected and its guardian spirits (Penates) propitiated. With them the Lares were closely connected. These, on one view, were originally deities of the farmland, who were later introduced into the house (probably through the *Lar familiaris*, who seems to have been the Lar of the servants); on another view they were the deified spirits of the dead ancestors of the family. At any rate each later Roman household had its Lararium or shrine and offered daily prayers to the Lares, with perhaps a gift of wine or incense. The Genius, 'the begetter', that is the procreative power on which the family depended for its continuance, was also worshipped: although, later at any rate, each man or woman had own *genius*, a kind of guardian angel, the family as a whole worshipped that of the *paterfamilias*. A most important part of the house was its door (*ianua*) which was the seat of Janus, who when conceived in the image of man faced both ways. It had to be guarded lest evil spirits might enter the house through it, and even dead members of the household had to be carried out by night feet first, lest they might find their way back and haunt the house. Janus' functions were gradually particularized: Janus Patulcius presided over opening the door, Janus Clusivius over its closing, while the threshold became the care of Limentinus, the hinge of Cardea, and the leaf of Forculus. If the divine members of the family were duly propitiated by family prayers at the beginning of the day and by the offering to Vesta, then, it was hoped, all would be well.

Besides his house, a man's fields had to be protected. Boundary stones (*termini*) had to be set up with due ceremony and became the object of an annual festival, the Terminalia, at which they were garlanded by the farmers whose lands adjoined (p. 79). The bounds also had to be beaten in order to purify, protect and fertilize the fields: at the Ambarvalia in May a

procession walked around them and offered prayer and the sacrifice of a
pig, sheep and bull (*suovetaurilia*; p. 124). The Lares, as deities of the fields,
were placated at the Compitalia at the places where the paths bounding
farms met, a cheerful ceremony in which slaves shared (p. 58). Thus in
various ways individual families tried to protect both land and home.

Each family was also concerned with the birth, marriage and death of
its members and observed certain *rites de passage*. Thus at the birth of a
child three men at night struck the threshold with an axe, pestle and
broom, agricultural instruments, to keep out the wilder spirits of the
fields, of whom the chief was later named Silvanus. At puberty a boy laid
aside his child's amulet (*bulla*) and exchanged his striped toga for the plain
toga of manhood in the presence of his family and friends. Marriage was
accompanied by many ceremonies. Thus after a bride left the protection of
her father's house and before she entered her husband's, she was in a
vulnerable position and so she wore certain articles of clothing, such as a
veil, for apotropaic purposes. Further, a bride coming from another
family might offend the household spirits as a potentially dangerous
stranger, so at the time of her entry she smeared the doorposts with wolf's
fat and oil, and then was carried over the threshold. The dead seem to have
been regarded as having little or no individuality but were identified with
the Di Manes, the Kindly Gods, who were perhaps originally chthonic
deities, but nevertheless it was considered necessary to perform certain
rites to ensure that they did not 'walk'. Hence at the festival of the
Lemuria in May (p. 118) the heads of each household did at the same time
what each individually had been accustomed to do privately after a death
in his household: in order to get rid of ghosts he clashed bronze vessels
(a relic of the Bronze Age?) and spitting out black beans from his mouth
he repeated nine times the formula, 'With these I redeem me and
mine', and when the ghosts had gathered up the beans behind him he
expelled them saying 'Ghosts of my fathers be gone' (*Manes exite paterni*).
In the more peaceful ceremony of the Parentalia a little earlier (p. 74) living
members decorated their family graves with flowers. With some of these
ceremonies we are passing from purely domestic rites to similar ceremonies which though still performed by individual families were also becoming the concern of the community as a whole.

3 The Gods, the State and Foreign Influences

The early Romans, whose views we have been trying to assess, were a
group of shepherds and farmers who were gradually uniting their villages

into a community. They were achieving this during the seventh century BC, and thus became one of the leading settlements in Latium, but the process was greatly accelerated during the next century when Rome was governed by Etruscan kings and became a powerful city. She was now mistress of a considerable territory and as strong as many of the Etruscan cities on her northern frontiers or the Greek cities in southern Italy. The object of early cult had been to secure the goodwill of the spirits or deities by certain rituals which if correctly performed were thought to guarantee the 'peace of the gods' (*pax deorum*). This notion was semi-legal and con- tractual: if the worshippers scrupulously did their part, it was hoped or even assumed that the deities would do theirs. Then the State stepped in to undertake this responsibility on behalf of the whole community. This meant the establishment or development of festivals similar to the simple private practices and an increase in the number of those officials responsi- ble for them. This organization of a priesthood is discussed below (p. 27), but we may note here that town-dwellers might gradually lose interest in the details of country festivals, while the calendar which prescribed their dates gradually got out of gear with the agricultural year. Thus State intervention tended to save the individual from anxiety, but soon led to some loss of interest on the part of an urbanized population.

The Romans, themselves Latins, naturally shared many beliefs with their Latin neighbours and indeed tended to assimilate any of their neigh- bours' deities which might respond to needs unanswered by their own. Thus Minerva, an Italian goddess of handicrafts, was imported to meet the requirements created by growing trade and industry in the regal period, while Diana of Aricia was installed on the Aventine for political motives (p. 173). Venus, originally the protectress of gardens, came perhaps from Ardea, and Fortuna, at first an agricultural deity, from Praeneste or Antium. But a much greater impetus came from the Etruscans, who went far to altering the form, if not the spirit, of Roman religion in many aspects. Their chief contribution was anthropomorphic: they introduced to the Romans the idea of gods and goddesses in human form, who should be depicted in statues and worshipped in temples of wood and stone rather than at simple open-air altars; a deity must have a cult-statue housed in a temple. The most famous of Rome's temples was that on the Capitol, begun by Tarquinius Priscus, completed by Tarquinius Superbus and dedicated in the first year of the Republic to the Etruscan triad, Tinia, Uni and Menrva under the Roman form of Jupiter, Juno and Minerva. It was one of the largest temples in all Italy and housed a terracotta statue of Jupiter made by the Etruscan artist Vulca, but its Etruscan connections were soon forgotten and it became the main shrine of Jupiter Optimus

Maximus, the presiding deity of the whole State. But as Etruscan influence waned after the expulsion of their dynasty from Rome, the Romans were slow to follow up these new ideas on a large scale: Mars and Hercules had long to be content with their altars in the Campus Martius and Forum Boarium, and cult-statues of native gods were at first not numerous. 'For more than 170 years' [i.e. from Rome's foundation in 753 BC], wrote Varro, 'the Romans worshipped their gods without images. Those who first made images of the gods both removed fear from their States and added error': thus familiarity might breed scepticism, if not contempt, among the less pious. The Romans, however, did not take to the more sinister aspects of Etruscan religion, with its preoccupation with death, but they did supplement their own practice of observing omens from the flight of birds or flashes of lightning with the Etruscans' more elaborate methods of divination (p. 29).

Etruscan religion, as well as Etruscan art, had been profoundly affected by Greek ideas, and another immense contribution of Etruria to Rome was to introduce her to the gods of Greece. But Etruria was not the only channel by which Greek influences reached Rome, since they also came via other Latin towns and later by direct intercourse with the Greek cities of southern Italy; in many cases it is not possible to trace the precise route by which a specific god or cult reached Rome. However the total effect was great. Hercules perhaps reached Rome from Latin Tibur: his worship as a patron of commerce was conducted at the Ara Maxima in the Forum Boarium in Greek fashion with unveiled head; until 312 BC it was a private, not a State, cult in the hands of two Roman families. The cult of Castor and Pollux came perhaps via Tusculum, traditionally in 499 BC, and they received a temple in the Forum. Apollo, as a healing god, received a precinct during the regal period and later, in 431 BC, a temple as the result of a plague. The Greek corn deities, Demeter, Dionysus and Kore, were given a temple on the Aventine, as Ceres, Liber and Libera, in 493, perhaps as a reaction to a famine. This was done after consulting a collection of Sibylline oracles kept in the temple of Jupiter Capitolinus under the care of *duoviri sacris faciundis* (increased in 367 BC to ten, *decemviri*) who consulted them in times of crisis to discover how the *pax deorum* might best be maintained; this led to their introducing other Greek gods, such as Mercury, Neptune and Aesculapius under their Latin names, together with Greek rites (*Graecus ritus*). Even more significant for the general public was an instruction from the Sibylline books in 399 BC that for eight days images of three pairs of gods should be exhibited on couches before tables laid with food and drink. This was a far cry from the ways of a few centuries earlier: no appeal was made to the older divine powers, but the whole population was summoned for eight days of holiday to share in the worship of Greek gods. Five such *lectisternia* were held in the fourth century, though generally in times of national difficulty. Separate from, but associated with, such *lectisternia*, ceremonies known as *supplicationes* might be decreed when the population went in procession around the temples of the city, the men garlanded and carrying laurel leaves, the women with streaming hair. At the temples they found statues or other emblems of the gods exposed on platforms (*pulvinaria*) where they could be adored by the kneeling worshippers. National need had broken through the formality of the State cult of the early Republic and forced a recognition of the more emotional needs of the ordinary individual to have a more personal part in the worship of the gods.

This tendency could not be reversed. In the tense days of the Hannibalic War a *lectisternium* of 217 displayed no less than twelve pairs of gods, Greek and Roman alike, while after the disaster at Cannae panic was allayed only by burying alive two Greeks and two Gauls in the Forum Boarium 'in no way a Roman rite' (*minime Romano sacro*). Another method of trying to calm and distract the people was the establishment of public Games, such as the Apollinares in 212; others soon followed, as we shall see in more detail later. A reaction to expel all private priests and prophets who were undermining the State religion by introducing foreign rites, was short-lived, since in 204 the first of the Oriental cults was introduced into Rome with the arrival of the cult-stone of the Great Mother of Phrygia: in 191 a temple was built on the Palatine for this Magna Mater, although it must be said that the Romans did not at first realize the orgiastic features of her cult, and when they did, they tried to control them. Although the worship of Dionysus or Bacchus had long been accepted in Rome as Liber, the wilder aspects of his cult only flared up in a wave of crime and immorality throughout Italy in 186 BC. This was too much for the Roman authorities who treated it as an offence against the State, not against religion, and legalized an extremely attenuated practice of the cult, with a death penalty for infringements. If a cult endangered public morality, or still more public safety, it must be checked, but otherwise the Roman did not persecute any non-monotheistic religion: why should he, since the worship of a few more gods made little difference in a polytheistic society? In the second century some weak efforts were made to check the spread to Rome from South Italy of Orphism, with its practice of initiation which offered the individual mystic purification and the hope of happiness in an afterlife, and of Pythagorean beliefs. No more effective was some feeble opposition to the spread of Greek philosophic ideas, which the more practical Romans tended to regard with some suspicion. However, encouraged by the speculations of Scipio Aemilianus and his friends, these Greek ideas gradually found a home in Rome, and Stoicism in particular exercised an immense influence in the Roman world at a time of religious sterility and bankruptcy in the last century of the Republic. Unlike the exotic cults of the East, the practical way of life laid down by the Stoic Sage provided a toughening of Rome's moral and spiritual fibre. (p. 32).

Long before this the overlaying of old Roman beliefs with Greek mythology had been completed, helped by the increasing influence of Latin literature which first made its appearance in the third century BC. Roman deities were identified with their Greek counterparts in the Olympian hierarchy, and the mythological foibles of the Greek gods were even shown on the Roman stage: thus the amours of Jupiter and the trickery of Mercury were exposed to a Roman audience in the *Amphitruo* of Plautus, while Ennius popularized the teaching of Euhemerus that the gods were merely outstanding human beings deified. This led to much scepticism, while the official State cults remained somewhat remote, so it is little wonder that many people sought relief in the wilder foreign cults or philosophical ideas. But, of course, throughout all these centuries the established festivals and Games were held each year and much later Ovid conceived the idea of writing a poem, the *Fasti,* in twelve books, describing the festivals month by month, linked often with mythological stories to explain their origins or some of the features that survived until his day. This poem, of which unfortunately we have only half, is a major source of our knowledge of the festivals, but before we consider them in detail, something must be said about religious practices, and the priesthoods, namely the methods and organization by which the *pax deorum* could be achieved.

4 Roman Cult

The chief methods of securing and maintaining the goodwill of the gods were sacrifice, prayer, expiation, purification and vows, while their will might perhaps be made known through portents and divination. Sacrifice (*sacrificium*) meant making anything *sacrum* ('holy') and the exclusive property of the deity, sometimes as a mark of honour, sometimes as a means of expiating an admitted offence or sin: it seldom, if ever, involved the idea of a sacramental entering into communion with the god. The offering had to contain some form of life. In family worship and in early days it would generally consist of food, such as salt meal (*mola salsa*) or spelt (*far*), or fruit, cheese or honey, or drink such as milk or wine. But in the State cult blood offerings were made from early times. The pig was the commonest victim; on important occasions sheep and oxen might be added. A formula in the accompanying prayer, '*macte esto*', 'be thou greater or stronger'. (cf. the root of *magnus, maior*), suggests that the underlying purpose was to transfer the 'life' in the offering to the god whose strength and glory would thereby be increased and thus he would be enabled to continue to look after the worshipper. The most vital parts of an animal, the liver, heart, kidneys and so forth, were burned on the altar for the god: the more edible parts were conveniently left over for the priest or worshipper to consume. This concept of sacrifice probably marks a stage between the earlier idea that the gods actually partook of the offering and the later view that the offering was merely an honorary gift. Further, some sacrifices were not free-will offerings, but expiatory, a *piaculum* or attempted atonement for an offence committed and thus an act of compensation to the god. The Romans were in fact so practically minded that they sometimes insured against anything going wrong in the proceedings (which would involve the expense of a repetition) by a prior piacular sacrifice which was to atone in anticipation. Thus when the Arval Brethren, a priesthood who suffered a taboo on iron, had to take an iron implement into their sacred grove, they offered a *piaculum* before-hand. (Pl. 1).

A blood sacrifice could be a messy business, as the Jews in their temple at Jerusalem must have realized. When a private Roman citizen had decided to what god he wanted to sacrifice – and it was very important to de-fine the god and even the aspect of the god that would correspond with his need – he, no less than the priests at the public festivals, had to proceed with extreme precision and caution, since minute details were laid down regarding the condition and behaviour of the victim. Male animals were sacrificed to gods, female to goddesses; the colour had to be right, white for Jupiter and Juno, black for deities of the underworld; size also mattered, sucking (*lactentes*) animals or adult (*maiores*) on different occasions. The priest or custodian (*aedituus*) of the relevant temple would supply the necessary information and arrange for the professional services of the men who actually killed the offering, and of a flute-player (*tibicen*) who had to play during the sacrifice in order to drown any ill-omened noises. If the worshipper was not a farmer who could provide his own beast, the animal had to be most carefully selected in the market, since its physical condition must be perfect. When the day came, the beast or beasts, with horns beribboned or even gilded, were led by the worshipper through the streets to the temple: if it proved very reluctant or tried to escape, a substitute might have to be acquired. The sacrifice itself was normally performed at an altar in front of the temple, not in the main building itself, though the doors would be left open to give a view of the statue of the god in his central chamber (*cella*) at the back of the temple. The celebrant would be accompanied by his friends, but women were excluded from some cults, and slaves from most; non-citizens, who might be dangerous aliens, were not encouraged: '*procul, o procul este profani*' (away, away, unhallowed ones) were the words placed by Virgil in the Sibyl's mouth when Aeneas sacrificed before entering the underworld. The priests washed their hands ceremoniously: hands and clothing must be pure. After a formal cry for silence (*favete linguis*) had been made, they covered their heads with folds of their togas, sprinkled flour on the horns of the animal and on the knife (*immolare*) and perhaps wine over its head. The animal was stripped of its decorations, prayers were offered and had to be precisely delivered. One attendant (*popa*), after calling out 'Am I to strike' (*agone?*), stunned the animal with a hammer-blow. Next the *cultarius*, after turning its head first to the sky and then down to earth, cut its throat; some of the blood was retained in vessels, some flowed on to the ground. The viscera were then examined, and, if not showing any fault that would have spoilt the ceremony, were placed on the burning altar. Some of the remaining meat might be eaten by the priests and worshippers. After State sacrifices banquets might be given to all the senators and other guests. (Pls 2; 401).

Sacrifices were treated as very solemn occasions. Every word and deed must conform exactly in every detail to the prescribed rules; if any slips were made, the whole proceedings had to be repeated (*instauratio*), together with a supplementary *piaculum*. Thus economy, if not religious feeling, demanded that due respect be shown throughout. Such sacrifices must have been common sights in Rome, whether at big public festivals or offered by private individuals in fulfilment of a vow or in hope of a blessing. A great many of the temples in the city had in fact been founded by victorious generals and others in fulfilment of vows made on the battle-field or elsewhere, and the date of the dedication of most of them is known. Not only on the day of the original foundation, but presumably annually on this day sacrifices would be offered: the dedicator would hardly neglect to draw attention to his benefaction during the rest of his lifetime, while we can well imagine that his descendants, with Rome's strong emphasis on the family, would keep up the ceremony in later generations. As we proceed to go through the various ceremonies of the year one by one, we may find some of the minor temples and cults of less interest, but it is not unlikely that had we been there, we should have found, say, a group of the Cornelii Lentuli sacrificing at the temple of Juno Sospita on 1 February, or of the Scipiones at the temple of the Tempestates on 1 June, or of the Claudii at Bellona's temple on 3 June, or of the Fulvii at the temple of Hercules Musarum on 30 June, or of the Acilii at the temple of Pietas on 13 November. Thus the deeds of their ancestors could be kept before the public and the glory of their house maintained. To us the days may seem formal entries in a calendar, but to contemporaries they offered an interesting spectacle and a reminder of the past.

Prayer, like sacrifice, was a matter for meticulous care. Those prayers preserved in the hymn (*carmen*) of the Arval Brethren (see p. 30) or in Cato's writings mark a transition between magic and religion. By their emphasis on the exact wording and their repetition they retain the characteristics of spells that bind the deity. But more generally the substance of prayer is petition rather than attempted compulsion. However, although the god may reject the request, if the right deity has been invoked with the correct formula then it would be thought unreasonable and contrary to his nature for him to withhold the request. Further, if the prayer was accompanied with a gift, a greater element of bargaining was introduced: *do ut des*, I am making this offering in order that you may give me what I ask – it was not quite a legal contract, but rather a suggestion that the god ought to reciprocate if he was worthy of his own nature.

Another method of approaching the gods was by a more formal vow (*votum*). Though often couched in legalistic language such vows do not bind both parties, but are prayers accompanied with the promise of an offering if they are answered. Thus a man or a woman might write a request on a wax tablet and tie it to the knee of the statue of the god, and then, if the request was granted, set up some small thank-offering (models of parts of the human body were particularly common offerings for restored health). On a larger scale a general before or during a battle might vow a temple which would be dedicated after a victory. Public vows, taken in the name of the State, were a later development, and to some extent a covenant in the name of the State.

But a prayer obviously could not be expected to succeed unless the right deity was invoked, so it might be addressed to a god with all his sub-titles included (even with an escape clause such as, 'Jupiter Optimus Maximus or by whatever other name you wished to be addressed': *'sive quo alio nomine te appellari volueris'*), or a list of other gods might be tacked on to the one first named, or the deity might be left vague (as *'si deus, si dea'*) or merely invoked like the 'unknown god' whose altar St Paul saw in Athens. Further, both in private and public prayers the exact legalistic formulae must be exactly repeated: if the speaker stumbled over a word, the whole procedure had to be repeated, and, as at sacrifices, so when public prayers were offered a flute-player might be employed to drown all ill-omened and distracting sounds. As an example of an early prayer, that made by a Roman farmer in clearing a wood, may be quoted: 'Be thou god or goddess to whom this grove is dedicated, as it is thy right to receive a sacrifice of a pig for the thinning of this sacred grove, and to this intent, I or one at my bidding do it, may it be rightly done. To this end, in offering this pig to thee I humbly beg that thou wilt be gracious and merciful to me, to my house and household, and to my children. Wilt thou deign to receive this pig which I offer thee to this end' (Cato, *Agr.* 139). Another example of a farmer's prayer is quoted on p. 84 below.

Finally, purification (*lustratio*) was virtually a form of piacular sacrifice. These ceremonies were designed to loose (*luere*) or free an area from hostile spirits by means of processional rites, which still survive in the ritual of the Roman Catholic Church, though changed in form and mean-ing. The processions marched round the boundaries of farm or village, and culminated in acts of sacrifice and prayer. Thus, as we shall see, the Ambarvalia was a lustration of the fields, and the Lupercalia of the early Palatine settlement; in the festival of the Amburbium the boundaries of the whole city were lustrated. Such a process of purification was extended from the boundary line of farm or city to the human beings within, to the whole population or to the army together with its weapons, such as the purification of the trumpets at the Tubilustrium in March. But many of these ceremonies gradually became over-formalized: the prayers were murmured and unheard by the people, and the lustration of the army deve-loped into a political census, but some, as the Lupercalia, retained their vitality throughout Republican times, while the political census, by which the list of Roman citizens was revised, ended in a lustration (*lustrum condere*) of the people who were marshalled outside the *pomerium* (the religious boundary of the city) in the Campus Martius (see p. 233).

The will of the gods could also be learnt from observing certain signs (*auspicia*). These might be unsought (*auspicia oblativa*), such as a chance flash of lightning, or definitely watched for (*auspicia inpetrativa*), as signs from the flight of birds (the original meaning of *auspicia: avis, specio*). They could also be either private or public. Any citizen could observe or invoke auspices without the help of a priest, and if he saw a strange sight or dreamed a strange dream, he was entitled to draw his own conclusions about their meanings (though he could, if he wished, consult a religious authority or even, in the late Republic, some relevant literature). But some portents or prodigies (such as a rainfall of stones or of blood) might affect the State and become the concern of the pontiffs. Further, it became customary to consult the gods before most public activities (such as elections or meetings of the *comitia*), so that taking the auspices became part of a magistrate's business. The dominant idea was not to seek to know the future, but to test the rightness of a preconceived plan by looking for a sign of divine encouragement or warning. This request for a simple 'yea' or 'nay' obviated the need for an elaborate priesthood, which alone could interpret the message. Thus the public *auspicia* could be left in the hands of magistrates (though many of these might in fact also be pontiffs or augurs) who could turn a blind eye or a deaf ear to any unsought auspices, unless they were formally reported by another magistrate (*obnuntiatio*) or by an augur. The requested *auspicia* (*inpetrativa*) took many forms, often phenomena in the sky, as thunder or lightning (particularly associated with Jupiter) or the flight or song of birds, or the movements or sound of quadrupeds: indeed some 'sacred' chickens were kept, whose behaviour while feeding provided the required 'sign' (*signa ex tripudiis*). Public auspices had to be taken on the same day and spot as the proposed action, and magistrates often started soon after midnight, and sometimes even carried through the act itself before daybreak in order to prevent any flaw (*vitium*) which would entail repeating the procedure (if it was only discovered later, it still operated: for example, in the case of the election of a magistrate, it necessitated his resignation). Thus all Roman public life was shot through with auspication. By the late Republic, though it had often become a mere formality or a weapon of political intrigue, many educated men, including Augustus, believed in it, while in earlier days at any rate, it would take a bold man to disregard the religious feeling of his contemporaries, as when Appius Claudius Pulcher had the sacred chickens drowned because they would not provide the signs he required: the superstitious might well have anticipated his subsequent naval defeat at Drepana in 249 BC. (Pl. 6).

5 *The Priests*

As the State on behalf of the whole community developed practices analogous to the religious rites of the family, it needed men to perform the ceremonies and take charge of the law governing the relations between the divine and human inhabitants, the *ius divinum*. Under the monarchy the king was the State-priest, the *paterfamilias* of the community, but with the establishment of the Republic his ceremonial duties devolved chiefly on a Pontifex Maximus and partly upon a Rex Sacrorum (or Sacrificulus) who retained his title, while his priestly helpers formed two major colleges of priests, the pontiffs and augurs. These priests, however, were not a professional class set apart, but men who took a prominent part in administering the State as magistrates. Laymen sufficed, since although in some respects Roman rites were complicated, there was no revealed religion or (before the introduction of the Sibylline oracles) sacred books (as in Etruria) which needed interpretation by full-time experts. In addressing the College of Pontiffs in 57 BC Cicero could say that among the divinely inspired elements of government none was more striking than that 'the worship of the gods and the vital interests of the State should be entrusted to the direction of the same individuals, to the end that the most distinguished and famous citizens might safeguard religion by good administration of the State, and safeguard the State by the wise interpretation of religion' (*Dom. 1*). Thus religion and politics went hand in hand, but in the later Republic the former was too often manipulated in the interests of the latter.

The *pontifices* may in origin have been connected with the magic rites of bridge-building, as their name suggests (unless *pons* once meant 'way'), but they became an advisory body (*collegium*) on religious affairs. Originally three, by the end of the Republic there were sixteen members, who held office for life and after 103 BC were chosen no longer by co-option but by a special assembly of seventeen of the thirty-five tribes into which all Roman citizens were divided. They controlled the religious calendar and arranged the holy days and intercalary months. Their leader, the Pontifex Maximus, gradually took over from the Rex Sacrorum control of the State religion; his official residence was the Regia in the Forum. He gained jurisdiction over all the other priests, and the pontifical college included the Vestals, the *flamines* and the Rex Sacrorum. The Vestal Virgins, young girls six in number and generally from patrician families, served for thirty years, tending the holy fire and cult of Vesta; they were not allowed to marry while in service, and unchastity could be punished by burial alive. The *flamines* were priests attached to the cult of individual gods and looked after their temples; this specialization made them more 'professional' than the pontiffs, and the office was less popular, especially that of the *flamen Dialis* who was subjected to a vast array of taboos (p. 15). The three major *flamines* were attached to Jupiter (*flamen Dialis*), Mars (*flamen Martialis*) and Quirinus (*flamen Quirinalis*). Of the other twelve, ten are known: *Volturnalis, Palatualis, Furrrinalis, Floralis, Falacer, Pomonalis, Volcanalis, Cerialis, Carmentalis* and *Portunalis*. The taboos surrounding the *flamen Dialis* and the obscurity of many of the deities they served (namely Volturnus, Pales, Furria, Flora, Falacer, Pomona, Volcanus,

Ceres, and Portunus) suggest a very early origin. The formal dress of the *flamines* was an *apex*, a *laena* and a laurel wreath. The *apex*, without which a *flamen* might not legally appear out of doors, was a conical or round cap on which was fixed a pointed piece of olive-wood surrounded at its base with a strand of wool. The *laena* was a thick woollen cloak, fastened with a bronze fibula. (Pls 3,4).

The College of Augurs, which also ultimately consisted of sixteen members, comprised official diviners who, as we have seen, by observation and interpretation of various signs (*auguria*) decided whether the gods approved or disapproved of certain proposed actions. But augurs did not officially go beyond this and attempt by divination to ascertain the future: Cicero (*Div.2.70*) is explicit when he says 'we Roman augurs are not the sort who foretell the future by observing the flight of birds and other signs' (*non . . . futura dicamus*). This type of divination was originally left to soothsayers (*haruspices*) from Etruria, who required specialized knowledge which was to be found in Etruscan religious teaching. The form most commonly practised was the examination of the vital organs of sacrificial animals, especially their livers (hepatoscopy). Their shape, colouring and markings had to be scrutinized and interpreted according to set rules, and models of livers were used for this purpose (the bronze liver from Piacenza is well known); if any irregularity appeared in any part of the real liver, it could be matched to the corresponding part of the bronze guide which would indicate the name of the deity who controlled that part of the sky that corresponded to the faulty part of the liver. Although the experts in this science, the *haruspices,* first came to Rome from Etruria, by Cicero's day a ·Roman citizen could become a *haruspex*. Although they were not official priests, they formed an *ordo* (however there were also many unofficial *haruspices* outside the *ordo*). They might also give advice on prodigies (such as deformed births) or phenomena such as thunderbolts or earthquakes. Though often discredited as frauds (Cato wondered how one *haruspex* could meet another without laughing), they were much in evidence in the later Republic and early Empire: thus C. Gracchus had kept a *haruspex* as a member of his household. (Pls 5, 7).

There were two lesser colleges of priests. One comprised two, then ten, and later (from 82 BC?) fifteen men for conducting sacrifices (*duoviri, decemviri,* and *quindecimviri sacris faciundis*). They were mainly responsible for keeping and, when required, consulting the Sibylline oracles (p. 20). These were a traditional collection of verses written in Greek. They were consulted at the bidding of the Senate and on their advice many Greek and foreign cults were introduced, including the first *lectisternium* in 399 BC.

Thus their keepers gained a general oversight of non-Latin cults. Secondly, a College of Epulones, 'Feast-organizers', was established in 196 BC and increased from three to ten members. They arranged and supervised the *epulum Iovi*, held for senators after the sacrifices at the festivals of Jupiter Optimus Maximus, and the public banquets which were held at several other festivals and Games, such as the Ludi Romani.

Besides the four major priesthoods, there were other groups (*sodales*) concerned with particular rituals, as the Arval Brethren, Salii, Luperci and Fetiales. The Fratres Arvales, twelve in number, held a festival in May in honour of the goddess Dea Dia to whom their sacred grove at the fifth milestone on the Via Campana outside Rome was dedicated. This was an ancient agricultural cult and their archaic song (*carmen*) has been preserved among the remains of their records (*Acta*), which unfortunately only survive from 21 BC. Their rite was either identical with, or similar to, the State ceremony of Ambarvalia (p. 124). The Salii (from *salire*, 'to dance') were priests of Mars who formed two groups, each twelve in number (p. 85). They wore archaic Italian armour, and held ritual processions through Rome, dancing and singing and beating their shields on 1 March and at the festivals of Quinquatrus (19 March) and the Armilustrium (19 October; see pp. 92, 195). The Luperci, who also comprised two groups (the Quinctiales and the Fabiani) on 15 February carried through an elaborate ceremony which was marked by their rushing half-naked around the Palatine (p. 77ff.).

The Fetiales formed a college of twenty members who conducted relations with Rome's neighbours, especially in declaring wars or arranging treaties. When faced with aggression by a neighbouring people the early Romans sent four Fetiales to demand restitution and threaten action if this was not made within about a month; one was called *pater patratus*, another the *verbenarius* who carried herbs and soil gathered on the citadel to give him magical protection outside his own land. Failing satisfaction, the Senate sent the Fetiales back to the enemy's borders where they formally declared war and hurled a magical spear into his land in order to cancel his power. There was much primitive ritual involved, as also when making a treaty the Fetiales killed a pig with a flint instrument (*lapis silex*), reflecting probably a stone-age weapon. When, however, Rome had to face enemies in more distant parts of Italy or overseas, this fetial procedure became inappropriate and the Fetiales were replaced by senatorial *legati*. However, in an attempt to retain something of the old rite, when war was declared on a distant enemy, a spear was thrown into a piece of land in front of the temple of Bellona in Rome, which by a legal fiction came to be regarded as enemy territory (see p. 146). This was first done in the war against

Pyrrhus (280 BC), and the practice long survived, since in AD 178 the emperor M. Aurelius himself cast the spear before going on a campaign on the northern frontier. Thus the Fetiales continued to exist, though they are not often mentioned in the later Republic; however, they were used in 136 BC when Rome repudiated a treaty with Numantia and this gave antiquarian writers a fresh interest in an old ritual, but we do not hear of them again until in 32 BC Octavian revived the procedure when declaring war on Cleopatra.[5]

Thus Rome in the late Republic had a considerable range of priests. Some, like the Fetiales and many of the *flamines*, were antiquarian survivals; others, like the Epulones, were recent creations to meet new needs, but the direction of the official religion of the State remained firmly in the hands of the Pontifex Maximus and the two Colleges of Pontiffs and Augurs. Before we turn to one of the chief pontifical concerns, namely the calendar which formed the framework in which the festivals of the gods were organized and made known, we must glance briefly at what the ordinary Roman may have thought about this religious background.

6 Religious Belief

Apart from affording a welcome break in the hard routine of everyday life, what did the festivals and rites of the State religion mean to the 'average' Roman of the later Republic? Such a question inevitably arises, but is so general as to be almost worthless and might equally elicit a general reply such as, *'quot homines, tot sententiae'*. One has only to think of the extraordinary range of belief within a specific religion such as Christianity, varying between the intellectual response of a Protestant Professor of theology and the unquestioning acceptance of a devout peasant worshipper in a Roman Catholic church in the heart of southern Italy, or the direct simplicity of a Quaker, while outside the circle of believers the attitude of agnostics, humanists or atheists varies from sympathy with some aspects to complete or hostile rejection. Since Roman 'religion' was not a revealed or received body of beliefs, reactions must be still harder to define. In fact belief was secondary and what was done was more important, but only in a ritualistic sense. No special ethical code was enjoined, but only a pedantically precise performance of certain acts by the individual or by the State on his behalf. The majority of people taking part presumably had a general feeling in the efficacy of such behaviour: it had worked in the past and it was part of the ancestral customs (*mos maiorum*) which had made Rome great, so there was little reason to question it. Although surviving literature throws some light on the religious attitude (and still more, of course, on the philosophical beliefs) of a few educated men, particularly Cicero, we can hardly pin down the views of 'the man in the street'; he probably accepted traditional practices without much thought, while some individuals might harbour ideas which extended from extreme and contemptuous scepticism to credulous superstition. However, despite the meagre evidence, we may glance at a few viewpoints.

After the ancestors of the Romans had passed beyond the stage when fear of the forces of nature had compelled them to try to placate these unseen powers by primitive and probably unquestioned rites, the farmers and the country dwellers no doubt for centuries continued to believe in the relatively simple rites of sacrifice and prayer by which they sought to protect their homes and crops from evil influences. With the growth of the city efforts were made to adapt rural practices to the needs of an urban population, but, as we have seen, some of these new State cults gradually lost their earlier appeal: if the State could maintain the *pax deorum*, the individual need not bother and was free to think as he liked. Thus, in the later centuries of the Republic, there was a real gap between the city and the countryside where older traditions continued to flourish: not all the nostalgic longings of the Roman poets for the simple rites of the country were directed to a vanished past, since much of the older lore lingered on, and indeed it was against the beliefs of the countryside that centuries later Christianity had to fight one of its sternest battles.

In Rome itself, as trade and conquest multiplied the number of foreign inhabitants, both slave and free, more foreign cults were accepted, without it would seem undermining the conservatism of older practices. As in other spheres of life, the Romans adopted a pragmatic approach; so long as alien cults could be controlled and the *pax deorum* be retained by traditional methods of worship, little harm would be done – indeed in retrospect we may surmise that by allowing men to find other forms of worship which might satisfy spiritual needs not met by the State cults, the Romans in fact provided a useful safety-valve. But they were very slow to abolish anything that had once been established, be it constitutional machinery or religious practice. So although a few old cults may have withered away by the end of the Republic (thus Varro complained that nobody remembered who the goddess Furrina was), yet many archaic customs managed to survive: thus we know from Cicero that when a procession of priests, including augurs, was passing by, yoked oxen had to be unyoked and moved aside in case they happened to excrete at that moment and thus provide a bad omen; one might have thought that so inconvenient a measure might have been allowed to fade away after centuries (an oblique reference to it may be contained in the *lapis niger* inscription of the sixth or fifth century BC). This chance reference by Cicero should make us wary of supposing that the Romans of a more rational age were necessarily less conservative than their ancestors. This may also be true of many at the less formal level of popular superstition: if Pliny had not happened to record the fact, who would have believed that the sceptical and hard-headed Julius Caesar, whose chariot had once met with an accident, there-after always recited a spell three times before getting into his chariot for a journey?[6]

The impact of rationalism on traditionalism is illustrated by the views of Polybius and Cicero. The rationalist Polybius, who came to Rome in the mid-second century BC at a time when Greek philosophical ideas were beginning to make some conservative Romans a trifle anxious about their impact on Roman society, provides an interesting view of how Roman religion struck a sceptical Greek: it appeared to him as the cement of the State and the dope of the people. He wrote (6.56), 'the quality in which the Roman Commonwealth is most distinctly superior is in my opinion their religious beliefs. I believe that what in other peoples is an object of reproach, I mean superstition (*deisidaimonia*), is the very thing that maintains the cohesion of the Roman State. These matters are clothed in such pomp and introduced to such an extent into their public and private life that nothing could exceed it, a fact that will surprise many. My own opinion at least is that their object is to use it as a check upon the common people . . . since every multitude is fickle, full of lawless de-sires and violent passion, it must be kept in check by invisible terrors and suchlike pageantry. So, to my mind, the ancients were not acting rashly or at haphazard when they introduced among the people ideas about the gods and belief in the terrors of hell, but the moderns are very rash and foolish in banishing such beliefs.' This somewhat cynical interpretation was not necessarily shared by Polybius' Roman friends, such as Scipio Aemilianus, C.Laelius and L.Furius Philus, who seem to have retained 'a desire to preserve and where necessary resuscitate the ancestral reli-gion'.[7] Though fully abreast of current Greek philosophical ideas, these men had been nurtured in a Roman tradition and may well have retained some belief in a religious system which was widely believed to have made Rome great. But whatever their inner religious convictions, many Romans, especially in the last century of the Republic, began to make greater use of the superstitions of the people and the religious machinery of the State for political and personal ends. Whether Aemilianus and his friends were among them remains uncertain.

These men, the so-called 'Scipionic Circle', were leaders in the intellectual discussions in which many Romans at this time began to examine the philosophical thought of Greece, and one of Scipio's friends, who stayed in his house for some time, was the Stoic philosopher, Panaetius of Rhodes. It would not be appropriate here to try to examine the tenets of either Stoicism or Epicureanism, beyond noting any effect they may have had on Roman religious thought. Zeno, the founder of Stoicism, was a pantheist: the unity behind all things could be identified with God, or Reason or Nature and was expressed in Fate and Divine Providence (*pronoia*). Since everything is divine, there was no need for religion in the form of temples and the deities of popular religion, but divination might be useful as a means through which Reason might reveal some of its purpose. But many of Zeno's views were modified by later disciples: thus Cleanthes wrote a hymn in praise of Zeus and held that after death all souls survived (until the next periodic conflagration of the universe), while Chrysippus believed that only the souls of the wise survived. Panaetius modified earlier teaching in many ways, softening its hard ethics and adapting them to the practical needs of statesmen, and rejecting divination and astrology (which Poseidonius later was to accept), but. believing in an immanent Spirit or Providence that controlled the world. In general the earlier view that religion should be more concerned with prayer and self-examination rather than with sacrifice and ritual, was modified, and mythology was explained allegorically: the various gods could represent different aspects of the activity of God, who was identical with the universe. The Romans were not unduly concerned about theological speculation, and many turned readily to this challenge to a new way of life once it had been modified sufficiently to avoid undue discordance with their ancestral customs.

Epicureanism taught that the mind of man must be freed first from fear of the gods, who existed in remote space (*intermundia*) and had no effect on human life – hence all the trappings of religion, such as sacrifice, prayer, omens, auguries, and ritual were irrelevant – and secondly from fear of death, since there was no survival of the soul. To achieve these goals, belief in a materialistic atomic theory provided the way. Thus Epicureanism totally rejected traditional Roman religion, although supplying a moral ideal of its own, the pursuit of the highest form of personal happiness which would lead to freedom from anxiety (*ataraxia*). This might even include worshipping the gods, but it was useless to seek anything from them. Lucretius seems to envisage some continuation of traditional worship when he says (6.68f) that unless you reject all erroneous ideas from your mind, 'you will not be able to approach the shrines of the gods with quiet heart' (*nec delubra deum placido cum pectore adibis*). However, a man should withdraw from the turmoil of political life and live simply with his friends. Despite the passionate advocacy of a Lucretius, this negative attitude to public life and traditional religion probably did not have a widespread influence on popular thought, but it did make a considerable impact on some groups of influential men, especially near the very end of the Republic.[8] But it ran counter to the grain of Roman thought: thus Cicero, at the beginning of his *De Natura Deorum*, asks (2) 'If they are right who deny that the gods have any interest in human affairs, how can *pietas*, *sanctitas*, *religio* exist?'

Cicero, though not a professional philosopher like Panaetius, expounded current philosophical ideas in a great number of books and did more than any other writer to 'popularize' these ideas throughout the Roman world. But despite such works as his three books on the Nature of the Gods (*De Natura Deorum*) and two on Divination (*De Divinatione*), it is far from easy to define his own philosophical and religious ideas.[9] In the first book of the *De Natura Deorum*, which is cast in the form of a dramatic conversation held in the house of C. Aurelius Cotta, consul in 75 BC and a pontiff, an Epicurean expounds his beliefs in the nature of the gods, and is answered indecisively by Cotta. In Book 2 another speaker puts forward the claims of Stoicism, on which Cotta comments in Book 3, not rejecting it completely but criticizing some aspects. Cotta was a follower of the Academy, to which Cicero adhered. At the end of the book Cicero gives away no more of his own position than saying that the Stoic speaker 'approximated more closely to an image of the truth'. He has, however, made Cotta the central figure because he embodied both traditional Roman religion as a pontiff, and a degree of scepticism as an Academic. Thus, at the end of Book 2 the Stoic speaker appeals to Cotta both as a leading citizen and as a pontiff not to commit the wicked impiety of arguing against the gods. Later (3.9) Cotta said that he was ready to accept the doctrine of divine existence simply because it was Roman tradition (*ita nobis maiores nostros tradidisse*); further argument was unnecessary. Cotta claimed that he always had and always would uphold the beliefs about the traditional immortal gods and rites, ceremonies and religious duties (*sacra caerimonias religionesque*; 3.5). He does not indicate any difficulty in reconciling this point of view with his personal sceptical philosophical opinions.

Cicero had little trouble in rejecting Epicureanism and believing in the existence of deity, but he was also an augur (and proud of this distinction); in his *De Republica* he supported the maintenance of augury, and in the first book of De *Divinatione* he places in the mouth of his brother Quintus arguments (many deriving from Stoicism) in favour of divination as a revelation of divine will. But in the second book he himself replies and in a strong attack exposes its unreasonableness and folly: it was a superstition that should be rooted out: 'I thought that I should be rendering a great service to myself and to my countrymen if I could tear this superstition up by the roots: *eam* (sc. *superstitionem*) *funditus sustulissemus*. For I want it to be distinctly understood that the destruction of superstition does not mean the destruction of religion. For I consider it part of wisdom to preserve the institutions of our forefathers by retaining their sacred rites and ceremonies. Furthermore, the beauty of the universe and the order of the heavens compel me to confess that there is some excellent and eternal Being (*naturam*) who deserves the respect and homage of men' (*Div*.3. 148). Thus Cicero seems to sum up his faith, while showing no discomfort at any apparent inconsistency – indeed why should he have felt any, when to the Roman mind religion and the State were so closely interlocked?[10]

The religious outlook of Varro appears not dissimilar from that attributed to Cotta by Cicero. Varro, who dedicated one of his works to Cicero, his contemporary, was among Rome's greatest scholars and an encyclopedic writer, only a tiny fraction of whose works survives. From the angle of Roman religion our greatest loss is the second half of his *Antiquitates* which dealt in sixteen books with *res divinae*, namely priests, temples, festivals and Games, *sacra*, and the gods. To his research and interest in religious antiquities we owe a very great part of our knowledge of Roman religious practice, since his works were widely used by later writers, and his habit of scholarly antiquarian research was continued by a freedman of the Augustan age, Verrius Flaccus, who also provided a mine of information for later writers. Both men were interested in language and etymology, and part of Varro's *De Lingua Latina* survives, though Verrius' *De Significatu Verborum* is lost; however an epitome of it was made by Festus (late second century BC) of which half survives, while Festus' own epitome was further epitomized by Paulus Diaconus (eighth century); a calendar which Verrius drew up is preserved in the Fasti Praenestini (p. 46).

The later writers who drew upon these rich sources included grammarians and also Church fathers who found in them illustrations of the folly of paganism. Thus St Augustine has much to say about Varro, who followed the Pontifex Maximus, Mucius Scaevola, in a tripartite classification of theology: the religion of the poets (*fabulosa theologia*, invented by them), the religion of the State (*civilis theologia*, created artifically by the State like its political institutions) and the religion of the philosophers (*naturalis theologia*). Ideally the last two should coincide, but in practice the State religion should at least share something of the philosophers' views. Varro wrote in order to preserve the State religion, fearing that the gods might perish not by the attacks of enemies but by the neglect of the Romans themselves (*civium neglegentia*). Thus he included accounts of all the minor spirits (*indigites*) in order that the precise deity might be known to meet every situation in life, and he assigned all the gods and deities to an ordered place in the universe. Thus he taught men to know what god should be invoked and for what reason (*quem cuiusque causa deum invocare atque advocare debeamus*). He himself appears to have been influenced by Stoicism and to have believed in one god, the soul of the universe, who may be identified with Jupiter Capitolinus, the other gods being his parts or virtues. Varro did not approve of animal sacrifice, image worship or the worship of Alexandrine gods in Rome. The gods should be respected, not least the old Italian deities whom he invoked with feeling in the preface to his work *De Re Rustica*, while the rites of the family should be maintained no less than those of the State. Thus despite his attachment to the thought of the New Academy, Varro remained very much a Roman traditionalist.[11]

While men were wrestling with the nature of the god or gods behind the faded shadows of the traditional deities of Graeco-Roman mythology, they also had to face the problem of death and survival. In earlier times any belief in personal survival was very vague: the Manes, the departed spirits, were regarded as surviving as a mass rather than as individuals, and they were worshipped at various festivals, the Feralia, Parentalia, and Lemuria, which we shall examine later. By the late Republic the dead were sometimes accorded greater individuality: thus Cicero (*in Pis*.16) referred to the shades of the Catilinarian conspirators (*coniuratorum manes*). But whatever ordinary folk may have thought, the writers and thinkers in general disbelieved in personal immortality: Catullus (5.6) referred to death as *nox est perpetua dormienda* ('one unending night to be slept through'); Caesar, as reported by Sallust (*Cat*.51.20), perhaps under Epicurean influence, said that 'death puts an end to all mortal ills and leaves no room for sorrow or joy', while Lucretius passionately expounded his master's doctrine of annihilation. But human longings and emotions sometimes broke through and personal loss led Cicero to feel some vague intimations of immortality. In 45 BC he suffered a crushing blow when his beloved daughter Tullia died – an attempt to seek distraction was one of the three reasons that led him to devote so much time to writing philosophic works. To ease his grief he planned to build a memorial to her: 'I want it to be a shrine (*fanum*) . . . and am eager to

avoid anything like a tomb (*sepulchrum*)', he wrote to Atticus. Under the
stress of his emotions he wants to give Tullia the same honours as those
outstanding human beings – heroes and others – whom the Greeks
believed had at death gone straight to share the glory of the gods. Though
in his letters of this period he does not mention the possibility of a future
life, he clearly hopes that by a kind of apotheosis Tullia's spirit will not
fade away into the vague mass of the Manes, and perhaps that through the
existence of a shrine he might be brought more closely into communion
with the personality whose loss had been such a shattering blow. He also
sought relief by writing a *Consolatio*, which is unfortunately lost, but in
a passage quoted from it in his *Tusculan Disputations* (1.66) he insists on the
spiritual nature of the soul: 'whatever it is that is conscious, that is wise,
that lives, that is active must be heavenly and divine and for that reason
eternal'.[12]

But if some Romans could dream of heaven, did others fear hell?
Lucretius thought so, since his poem was designed to free men from such
baseless fears, and Polybius in the passage quoted above refers to similar
terrors. It is true that one of the festivals for the dead, the Lemuria, suggests elements of fear, that the Etruscans believed in the tortures of the
damned, and that Greek stories of Hades provided material for Latin
poets, but on the whole one does not get the impression of widespread
popular fears or that the Romans of the late Republic, who were certainly
not priest-ridden, were haunted by fears of punishment after death. Unfortunately, however, the voice of the ordinary Roman seldom gets
through to us, and we therefore know more about what he did than what
he thought in his religious life. Most Romans probably entertained the
vague idea that the gods approved of good conduct and that certain crimes,
such as incest, were offensive to them, but Roman religion did not provide
private moral teaching, such as Jews and Christians received from their
faiths. When a Roman noble built a temple to an abstract virtue, such as
Fides or Pietas, he was presumably declaring that such a moral quality was
desirable, but it may not be too cynical to suggest that his own personal
glory and that of his family was an equally strong motive: in general
private morality was divorced from public religion.[13]

7 Holidays: Feriae and Ludi

Feriae in general terms were holidays. The word, though plural in form
(like *Kalendae* and *Nonae*), was applied to a single day, which alternatively
might be called *dies ferialis*. Usage was sometimes loose, since Public

Games (Ludi) were not strictly *feriae*, but the days of their celebration were *dies festi*. *Feriae* fell into two groups: public festivals which were ordained and paid for by the State, and *feriae privatae* which were observed by individuals and families. These family celebrations are referred to as *feriae Claudiae, Aemiliae, Juliae* and the like and were held to mark birthdays or other important days in the life of the members, such as also the ten days of mourning (*denicales*) after a death. These, however, remained private affairs, though under the Empire the birthday of the emperor became a national public holiday.[14]

The *feriae publicae* comprised three groups: *stativae, conceptivae* and *imperativae*. The *feriae stativae* were the annual festivals, such as the Lupercalia, whose date was fixed and recorded in the official calendar. *Feriae conceptivae* were also held annually, but their date was fixed each year by the magistrates or priests; the most famous were the *feriae Latinae*. *Imperativae* on the other hand were irregular holidays, proclaimed by the consuls, praetors or dictators to meet an emergency or celebrate a victory. They might last several days and result from some prodigy such as a rain of stones or an earthquake which seemed to indicate that the gods needed to be appeased; for instance, in 192 BC a period of earth-tremors lasted thirty-eight days and the *dies feriae* were spent in apprehension and fear (*in sollicitudine ac metu*). Thus many of these *feriae imperativae* tended to be less cheerful than other *feriae*.[15]

The essence of *feriae* was that they were days on which religious rites were performed, civil lawsuits and quarrels avoided, and all men, including slaves, could take a period of rest. They were 'days instituted for the sake of the gods' (*dies deorum causa instituti*, Varro, *LL*,6.12, and '*dis dedicati*', Macrob. 1.16.2), while Cicero in his *Laws* says (2.29) that on holidays freemen should rest from lawsuits and controversies, and slaves from labour and toil. Agricultural writers record what work might or might not be done on the land. Thus Cato (*Agr.* 138) says that on *feriae* oxen might be yoked in order to haul firewood, beanstalks and grain for storing, but there was no holiday for mules, horses or donkeys except at family holidays (*nisi si in familia sunt*), and, according to Columella (2.21.2), the pontiffs said that a grain-field should not be fenced nor sheep washed; Columella also lists permitted tasks and indicates that some forbidden jobs could be tackled if a piacular sacrifice of a puppy (*catulus*) was made first. In the city the Rex Sacrorum and the *flamines* were not allowed even to see any work being done: if they went out, they were preceded by heralds who ordered anyone they met to stop working lest the holiness of the day be polluted. Neglect of this warning involved a fine or the offering of a pig, while deliberate disregard was too serious to be expiated according to the pontiff Scaevola but a certain Umbro more liberally declared that a man was not guilty if the work was connected with the gods or sacrifices or was vital to human life: thus if a house threatened to collapse, the inhabitants could take suitable measures without polluting the *feriae*. While priests might argue about how far the rules could be bent to meet the needs of everyday life (as Jewish rabbis considered the claims of the Sabbath), no doubt much work went on as usual just the same. *Feriae* offered the opportunity for rest: the religiously minded would visit the temples and offer prayer and sacrifice, but many would probably only take as much rest from work as they wanted or could afford.[16] Apart from the priests, who had to perform prescribed rites, and individuals who were obliged to honour the claims of any inherited worship or cult peculiar to their clan (*sacra gentilicia*), a Roman citizen, although bound to abstain from certain activities, was not obliged to attend a festival or perform any act of worship. Yet in the countryside the wise farmer would participate in the annual festivals such as the Compitalia, and, if absent, arrange for the normal ceremonies to be maintained on his farms. Thus, according to Cato, the duties of a bailiff (*vilicus*) included observing the feast days (*feriae serventur*), though later the bailiff is told not to perform religious rites (*rem divinam*) except at the Compitalia or at the hearth. Similarly the housekeeper (*vilica*) must not perform religious rites without orders from her master or mistress, though on the *Kalends*, *Nones* and *Ides* and when a holy day (*festus dies*) comes, she must garland the hearth and pray to the household god (*lari familiari*) as opportunity offers. The absentee landlord, living in the city, pleased himself whether he attended any ceremony.[17]

The Ludi, though not strictly *feriae*, were recorded in the calendars, held on *dies festi*, and have a religious origin and ritual, beginning as votive Games vowed in honour of Jupiter Optimus Maximus by a general and celebrated on his return from a successful campaign. However, at least as early as 366 BC they had become annual events held each September and remained unique until Plebeian Games were established *c.*220 BC. Then, during the anxieties of the Hannibalic War, the authorities tried to bolster up public morale by establishing the Ludi Apollinares in 212, the Ludi Megalenses in 204, the Ludi Ceriales in 202, and then finally the Floralia in 173. The duration, as well as the number, of some of the Games was increased to several days: thus in the later Republic no less than 17 days of April were devoted to Games, 7 to the Megalenses, 8 to the Ceriales and 2 to the Floralia. Games were also established to commemorate the victories of Sulla (in 81 BC) and of Julius Caesar (in 46). (Pls 403-8).

Thus, at a time when public interest in some of the older festivals was beginning to flag, new forms of entertainment were provided, and provided free by the State for all citizens who could get in (slaves were not apparently admitted in Republican times). However, as the demand for magnificence increased, the sum allocated by the State often had to be supplemented by the magistrate in charge of the Games, normally an aedile, who, unless he was to damage his chances of election to higher office in the future, had to dig deeply into his own pocket or those of his friends. This often landed a man in debt, if he lacked a large private fortune, as Caesar found to his cost when he was aedile. How a man might pester his friends for help is illustrated by Caelius' importunate letters to Cicero who was in Cilicia, begging him to get a good supply of panthers for his Games. The Games themselves consisted originally of chariot-racing in the Circus Maximus (*circenses*) with later elaboration and animal-hunts (*venationes*) and of theatrical performances (*scaenici*) which varied from plays by Terence and great actors as Aesopus and Roscius to farce and vulgar mime. They did not yet include gladiatorial contests under the Republic: these were staged as private shows (*munera*) more particularly at important funerals, often in the Forum (p. 221). The earliest recorded was in 264 BC; such funerals might also include theatrical performances; thus in 160 Terence's play the *Adelphi* was given at the funeral of Aemilius Paullus. The nature of the Games is described more fully in connection with the Ludi Romani (p. 183ff.).

8 The Roman Calendar

The great majority of festivals and Games had a fixed place in the Roman calendar, which can be reconstructed from literary sources and especially from the numerous, though fragmentary, inscribed copies that survive. The vexed problems of its early history do not concern us here, except to note that the early change-over from a ten-month to a twelve-month year left its mark in the names of the months. The ten-month year started in March: hence the seventh to tenth months were named Quinctilis, Sextilis, September, October, etc. (the first two later being renamed Julius and Augustus in honour of Julius Caesar and Augustus). The twelve-month calendar, as preserved in later copies, lists many festivals written in large letters, but these do not include a feast-day to Jupiter Capitolinus; thus it is older than the dedication of his temple on the Capitol in 509 BC and very probably was introduced under Etruscan rule in the sixth century. It ended in February, but in 153 BC, if not much earlier, for reasons of administrative convenience, the beginning of the civil year was transferred from 1 March to 1 January, when the newly elected magistrates entered office.[18] In this book we shall start our survey of the year in January, but it is well to remember that the Roman farmers would not feel much change at the end of December, since the real break in the agricultural year came in March after a period of comparative rest, as the March festivals show. On the other hand, in the later Republic, the city-dweller would be more conscious that public life was astir from 1 January.

The year normally consisted of only 355 days. March, May, July and October had 31 days, February 28, and the other months 29 each. In consequence adjustments had to be made to keep it in line with the solar year. This was done by a process of intercalating a period of 22 or 23 days, called Mercedonius or Intercalaris. This action was taken by the College of Pontiffs, but in so irregular and negligent a manner that the calendar was often out of line with the solar year, sometimes by as much as two or three months; for instance New Year's day in 46 BC corresponded to 14 October of the old year. This meant that the farmer, for whom in the old days the calendar had been a general guide, could no longer trust it and had to rely on the stars and weather signs. Further, on occasion political reasons may have led to a deliberate 'fiddling' with the process, and inconvenience might be caused by delayed announcement as to whether intercalation would or would not take place. Reform was long overdue and Julius Caesar successfully undertook this in 46 BC, the last 'year of confusion' (*ultimus annus confusionis*). The new Julian calendar, with its readjustment of the number of days in some months and an arrangement for leap year, came into use on 1 January 45 BC and, with minor changes, has continued until the present day.

But if the months remain much the same, the days of the month were reckoned in a very different manner by the Romans, with no system of numbering them serially in sequence. Instead, each month had three fixed points, from which the date was counted retrospectively. These were the *Kalends*, always the first day, the *Nones* (so called because they came nine days before the *Ides*) and the *Ides* which originally corresponded with the full moon of the lunar month. In the long months (March, May, July, October) the *Nones* were the seventh day, the *Ides* the fifteenth, while in the other months they fell on the fifth and thirteenth respectively. Thus all dates were counted as so many days *before* the *Kalends*, *Nones* or *Ides*, the reckoning being inclusive; so e.g., the anniversary of Rome's birth on 21 April was 'ten days before the *Kalends* of May' (*ante diem x Kalendas Maias*).

Each month these three fixed days were marked by special ceremonies. On the *Kalends*, which were sacred to Juno, a minor pontiff watched for the appearance of the new moon, and after he had reported the sighting to the Rex Sacrorum, they offered sacrifice together. The pontiff having called the people (*calata plebe*) to the Curia Calabra on the Capitol hill, announced the date on which the *Nones* fell, whether the fifth or seventh (*calantur Nonae*): 'Juno Covella, I announce thee on the fifth (or seventh) day' (Juno Covella was Juno of the Hollow Moon, i.e. crescent or new). This was done in order that the people might assemble again on the *Nones* to hear about the festivals and what must be done during the month. No festivals (with the single exception of the Poplifugia in July) were held in any month before the *Nones*. Meanwhile the wife of the Rex Sacrorum sacrificed a pig or a lamb to Juno in the Regia. When the *Nones* (originally the first quarter of the moon) arrived, the people assembled in the city from the countryside and the *rex* on the citadel (*arx*) of the Capitoline proclaimed the holidays (*feriae*) of the month. The *Ides* were the days of the full moon; they were sacred to Jupiter, and the *flamen Dialis* led a sheep (*ovis Idulis*) along the Via Sacra to the *arx* and there sacrificed it to Jupiter. The day was said to be called 'the trust of Jupiter' (*Iovis fiducia*) because light did not fail with the setting of the sun but was prolonged by the moon. Thus all three days were linked to phases of the moon and derive from very early times when a lunar calendar was used: they continued to be observed throughout the Republic but meant much less by the time of Varro who apparently witnessed them, though he refers to the ceremony of the *Nones* as a survival (*vestigia*).[19].

Since these ceremonies were regularly performed month by month, they have been described here and need not be repeated as we review each month in turn.

The official calendar, which was drawn up by the pontiffs, contained the dates of the religious festivals, but it was equally important for the early Romans to know the market days when the farmers could sell their produce to the townsfolk who in turn supplied the countryside with some of the wares it needed. Every eighth day was a market day called *nundinae* (the number was reckoned inclusively), and the period between one *nundinae* and the next was called *nundinum*. The calendars were therefore marked with a recurring cycle of the letters A to H, starting on 1 January and running on throughout the year, without any break at the end of a month (e.g. 28, 29 August, 1, 2 September might have the nundinal letters DEFG). Farmers coming into the city might also use the occasion to attend to other business, such as settlements of lawsuits or attending the *comitia*. However in the first century BC *nundinae* had become *dies fasti*; *comitia* and *contiones* (public meetings addressed by magistrates) could not be held, though the courts were still open. This cycle of eight days may have helped the Romans to move towards a seven-day week which had been used in Babylonia and was marked among the Jews by the Sabbath's day of rest; further, in Hellenistic astrology some days received the names of the planets: Saturn, the Sun, the Moon, Mars, Mercury, Jupiter and Venus. The earliest record of the use of a seven-day period at Rome is found in a calendar of the Augustan age from Sabine country (though the days have letters, A–F, and not yet names). The custom grew rapidly in the early Empire, but since it scarcely preceded the Empire, we need not follow its development here.[20]

Finally, the hours, though 24 to each day, differed from the modern hour of 60 minutes. Though each 24 hours was divided into 12 hours of night and of day, Roman hours varied in length (except at an equinox), being measured from dawn to dusk and from dusk to dawn. Thus a daylight hour was not the same length as a night hour, and both varied from month to month, though midnight was always the sixth hour of the night, and noon the sixth hour of the day. This meant, for instance, that an hour in midwinter lasted about 45 minutes, at midsummer 1½ hours.

Each day in the calendars, besides having its nundinal letter, was marked by another letter, which indicated whether it was an ordinary working day or a holiday. The most common of these letters were F, N, NP, EN, C; Q.R.C.F. occurs twice (on 24 March, q.v., and 24 May) and Q.S.D.F. only once (on 15 June, q.v.p.153), these three days being called *dies fissi*; FP, which occurs three times but only in some calendars, defies satisfactory explanation.[21] F stands for *dies fasti*, of which there were only 42 in the year. These were days on which citizens could initiate civil law suits (*legis actiones*) in the court of the urban praetor. Although there were only 42 *dies fasti* in the year, some more days were available for these court proceedings, since *nundinae* were *dies fasti*, and those *dies comitiales* on which the *comitia* did not in fact meet could be used for this purpose. Further, the praetor played only a preliminary part, namely to determine whether or not a point of law was involved, and if it was he appointed a *iudex* or *iudices* or another court (the *centumviri* or *decemviri stlitibus iudicandis*) to deal with the case. Thus the continuing process of the administration of justice was not limited to *dies fasti*, while the standing courts (*quaestiones perpetuae*) of the last century of the Republic handled criminal law offences and were not limited to *dies fasti*.[22] By contrast N stood for *dies nefasti*, 58 days in the pre-Julian calendar, which were the opposite of the *dies fasti*: on them what was allowed on *dies fasti* and *dies comitiales* was banned, i.e. legal proceedings in the praetor's court and meetings of the *comitia*. It has sometimes been argued that on them all activities except those connected with religion were forbidden, but it appears that other courts could function, the Senate could meet, *contiones* and markets be held. The name *nefasti* originally did not imply that they were unlucky or that they had any more religious associations than did *dies fasti*. The letter C stood for *dies comitialis*, of which there were 195. On them Roman citizens could meet in their assemblies, *comitia*, to vote on electoral candidates or on legislation or on the verdict of some kinds of criminal trials (*iudicia publica*). But there were some restrictions on holding *comitia* even on *dies comitiales*; they could not be held on *nundinae* nor if *feriae conceptivae* or *imperativae* had been fixed to be held on the day nor would it be easy to get people to attend during any of the Games.[23]

The letters EN meant *endotercissus* (an archaic form of *intercissus*) and these were eight days which were 'cut' because they were *nefasti* in the morning and evening when sacrifices were prepared and later offered, while in the period in between they were *fasti*. Finally, we come to the 49 puzzling letters NP which originally seem to have been written as a ligature. The great majority, though not all, of the festivals written in the calendars in large letters, together with all the *Ides*, are marked NP. Thus they were *feriae*, public holidays, on which religious ceremonies were held, lawsuits avoided, and general days of rest for all men, including slaves (though whether a free man took the day off largely depended on his own decision). In the light of this a variety of explanations of NP has been offered: perhaps the most attractive is *dies nefasti publici*, sponsored by Wissowa. This view has been developed by Mrs Michels who believes they refer to fixed public *feriae* which were held on behalf of the whole people, as opposed to a subdivision (e.g. *pro pagis* or *curiis*): namely *feriae publicae stativae universi populi communes*.[24].

Some days came to be regarded as unlucky or ill-omened (*dies religiosi* and *atri*), although they were not recorded in the calendars as such. According to Aulus Gellius 'days called *religiosi* are those of bad reputation and are hampered by an evil omen, so that on them one must refrain from religious activities (*res divinas facere*) or beginning any new undertaking whatsoever; they are the days that the ignorant multitude falsely and wrongly call *nefasti*.' He then quotes a letter in which Cicero tells Atticus that the day of the defeat of the Romans by the Gauls at Allia was still *religiosus*. According to Festus *religiosi* were days on which it was considered wrong (*nefas*) to do anything that was not necessary. Thus on one of these days, when a ritual pit, the *mundus*, was open (see p. 180), one did not engage in battle, enlist soldiers, hold *comitia*, start on a voyage, or marry. That some restrictions were taken seriously even in the later Republic is shown by the fact that Cicero appears to have postponed his daughter's engagement because two *dies religiosi* after the Latin Festival interfered.[25] On the other hand Gellius' restriction on religious activities must refer only to private rites, since we know that the public festival of

Matralia was held on a *dies religiosus* (11 June) and some temples were dedicated on similar days (7–15 June, when the temple of Vesta was open). The days so designated were the day of the Roman defeat at the battle of the Allia (*dies Alliensis*: 18 July), the three days (24 August, 5 October and 8 November) when the mysterious *mundus* with its connection with the dead was open, the days (7–15 June) when the inner shrine (*penus*) of Vesta's temple was open, the days (1, 9, 23 March and 19 October) when the Salii moved their sacred shields, and perhaps two days after the Latin Festival. The *dies parentales* (13–21 February) and the Lemuria (9, 11, 13 May, when the temples were closed) are likened to *dies religiosi*.

The Black Days (*dies atri*) were the days which followed the *Kalends*, *Nones* and *Ides* of each month; on these 36 days nothing new must be done, and, unlike the other *dies religiosi*, even the ceremonies of the State cults ought not to be held on them.[26]

In addition to these days, many others were less formally considered unlucky. Not only the days after the *Kalends*, *Nones* and *Ides*, but the fourth days before them were treated by some as ill-omened. Aulus Gellius says that the only reason he could find for this was that Claudius Quadrigarius told how the disaster at Cannae had occurred on the fourth day before the *Nones* of August (216 BC). Other military defeats might also be remembered: Trasimene on 21 or 23 June (217 BC) or Arausio on 6 October (105 BC). The *Kalends*, *Nones* and *Ides* were avoided for marriages, because the following days were unlucky days for brides to start their married lives; it was also thought unlucky to marry in May or in the first half of June. Further, in the last century BC at least, if not earlier, it was considered that the whole year would be unlucky if the *Kalends* of January or the *Nones* of any month coincided with the *nundinae*, and this was thought to be borne out because when it happened in 78 and 52 BC public troubles ensued. But clearly coincidences of *nundinae* with the *Nones* must have occurred often: they could not be avoided, but possibly the superstitious felt slightly uncomfortable. Some private individuals also might like to be reminded of unlucky days: thus Trimalchio had two calendars affixed to the doorposts of his dining-room: one told the household of its master's movements ('our master is out to dinner on 30 and 31 December') the other, painted with the moon and stars, had the lucky and unlucky days marked with distinctive knobs.[27]

Our knowledge of the calendar depends both on references in literary sources and above all on the surviving fragments of ancient calendars. Parts of over forty of these Fasti, inscribed on stone, have been found: the largest is the splendid Fasti Praenestini nearly 2 m high and 5.5 m broad, though some others are comparatively small. All but one date from the time of Augustus or Tiberius. The exception is the Fasti Antiates maiores, which was found in 1915; it is painted in red and black letters on plaster and dates between 84 and 46 BC, thus being the only pre-Julian calendar of the Republic. The rest vary in completeness, one (Fasti Maffeiani) covering nearly all the year, and a complete calendar of the whole year can be constructed from them. Many come from or near Rome, others from Italian towns such as Praeneste, Caere, Amiternum, Allifae and Venafrum. One indeed (the most recently discovered fragment, found in 1962) was discovered at Taormina in Sicily, which shows that copies of the Julian calendar were set up not only in Italy but in the provinces as well. All these Fasti have been given modern names: a list will be found, together with the conventional abbreviations, on p. 258). In addition two calendars in manuscript survive, but they are very late: that of Philocalus AD 354 and the other by Polemius Silvius, AD 448. Lastly reference may be made to two farmers' almanacs (*menologia rustica*) on cubes of bronze which indicate agricultural tasks month by month, together with some astronomical information.[28]

Knowledge of the calendar had originally been the exclusive possession of the priests, who were responsible for maintaining it, but in 304 BC Cn. Flavius is said to have exhibited in the Forum a calendar of court days, together with forms of pleading at law (*legis actiones*), so that all might know when legal business could be handled. Four years later the priestly Colleges of Pontiffs and Augurs were opened to plebeians. Thus access to the calendar would become more widespread. In 189 BC a consul M. Fulvius Nobilior set up a calendar, with accompanying notes, on the walls of the temple of Hercules and the Muses. Later the Augustan scholar Verrius Flaccus drafted a calendar with notes and put it up in the Forum of Praeneste; parts of this survive in the 'Praenestine calendar'.[29]

The arrangement of the material can be seen from the illustration on p. 49. The months are set out in columns, side by side, from left to right. On the left side of each month there are two vertical columns: the first gives the nundinal letters (A–H), the second the *Kalends, Nones* and *Ides*, the appropriate letters (F, N, C, etc.) and abbreviated forms of the names of the festivals. These are written in large letters, but there are also a number of additions, which vary in detail, written in smaller letters; the most numerous are names of deities in the dative case, though some are substantial notes. At the bottom of each column the number of days of the month is given. The Republican Fasti Antiates maiores has a thirteenth column, which contains fragments of the intercalary month.

The material in large letters was interpreted by Mommsen as the original 'calendar of Numa', dating from the pre-Etruscan regal period and remaining unchanged throughout the Republic until the reform by Julius Caesar. This view has been accepted, modified or rejected. Some think that an origin in the Etruscan period at Rome is more likely, others that (since the Cerialia, for instance, can scarcely go back quite so far) more festivals were added to an original list or that the calendar was introduced for the first time a little later in 451/0 BC by the Decemvirs.[30] But we are not really concerned with this vexed problem here, since few would believe in any essential change after the fourth century. It is clear that the festivals in large letters are older than the small-letter additions, and that some, if not all, of these are very old indeed, going back into the archaic period and enshrining some ideas of a primitive population. Some long continued to be celebrated with interest, but others had been almost forgotten and become fossilized in the late Republic, the subject of concern mainly to Roman antiquarians.

In the following pages under each day the large-letter calendar entries are printed in capitals, the small-letter entries in lower-case italics, and additions made from the literary sources in bracketed lower-case italics. The individual calendars are not generally cited here by name in cases where they offer no significant differences among themselves, but the calendar source for each entry will be found in the list of 'Festivals as recorded in the Calendars' on p. 259. Further, the Roman dating of individual days is given according to the Republican calendar and not according to the more usual Julian calendar which in 45 BC introduced ten more days into the year, near the end of each of the seven short (29 day) months, making a difference of either one or two days between the pre-Julian and Julian reckoning: thus for instance 23 September, which under the former was *a.d. VIII Kal. Oct.*, became under the latter *a.d. IX Kal. Oct.* The Julian dates are added in brackets.

Calendar from Antium (Fasti Antiates Maiores)

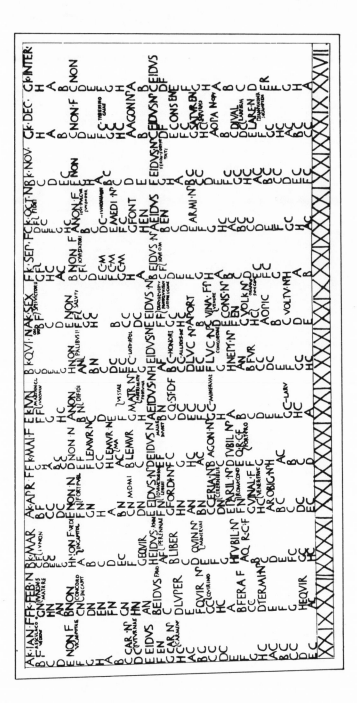

Part Two

THE ROMAN YEAR

January

For the Roman farmer January was a comparatively slack period. Varro, who divided the agricultural year into eight periods, indicates that the eighth (from the solstice until the beginning of the west wind, Favonius, namely 7 February), was rather a time for tidying up and odd jobs than for really strenuous work. Columella says that the more scrupulous (*religiosiores*) husbandmen refrain from work on the soil until 13 January, except that on 1 January they make a beginning of work of every kind to ensure good luck (*auspicandi causa*). He then details the sort of jobs that are appropriate to the second half of the month. The farmers' calendars (*menologia*) for January record:

January
31 days
Nones on the 5th
Daylight: 9¾ hours
Darkness: 14¼ hours
Sun in Capricorn
Protector: Juno
Sharpen stakes
Cut willows and reeds
Sacrifice to the Dei Penates[31]

The relative relaxation enjoyed by farmers in December could thus be extended into January, when two very primitive festivals, the Compitalia and the Sementivae, were held on days decided each year (no doubt in relation to the prevailing weather): neighbouring farmers and 'parishioners' (*pagani*) used to meet to celebrate the end of one agricultural period and the beginning of the next. This practice continued not only in the countryside but also in Rome even long after the average Roman had ceased to have any close connection with the soil.

January also included two of the old festivals marked in the calendars in large letters, the Agonia and Carmentalia. At the former sacrifice was offered in the Regia, apparently to Janus, the god of beginnings, while the latter was concerned with child-birth and family hopes. However, when January became the first month of the official year, it opened with civic as well as religious activities, and to these we must first turn.

1 January   KAL. IAN.   F

[Ann] us no [vus incipit] quia eo die ma [gistratus] ineunt (Note in Praen.)
(Vota Publica)

In early times consuls entered office at various dates, but at least from 153 BC 1 January became the fixed date. Ovid hails the happy day, 'a day worthy to be kept holy by a people the masters of the world'. He briefly describes the ceremonies in poetic phrase:

> In spotless garments the procession wends to the Tarpeian towers [the Capitol]: now the people wear the colour of the festal day; and now new rods of office lead the way, new purple gleams, and a new weight is felt by the far-seen ivory chair. Heifers, unbroken to the yoke, offer their necks to the axe, heifers that cropped the sward on the true Faliscan plains. When from his citadel Jupiter looks abroad on the whole globe, naught but the Roman empire meets his eye.

Ovid again pictures the scene when writing a poem to Sextus Pompeius who entered on his consulship at the beginning of AD 14.[32] (Pl. 409).

The consul's first duty was to observe the auspices: the phrase *'auspicari magistratum'* was the equivalent of entering a magistracy *(inire magistratum)*. A solemn business in early days, this had become a mere formality, if not something of a farce, by the late Republic. The magistrate spent part of the preceding night 'camped out', and then at break of day he offered prayers under the open sky. Even if he himself happened to be a member of the College of Augurs, he apparently normally appointed a helper, who in early times was someone skilled in the art of augury *(peritus)*, but in Cicero's day was anyone the consul wished *(qui libet)*.[33] This compliant agent scanned the skies until he saw, or reported that he had seen, a good omen such as a flash of lightning from the left. With such help the consul would not have to wait long before the approval of Jupiter was given by a favourable sign. The auguries could be observed in any place that was officially designated as a *templum*, but there was an official *auguraculum* on the Capitol (probably near the apse of the present church of S. Maria in Aracoeli); since the consuls were to sacrifice on the Capitol later in the day, they possibly took the auspices there in the early morning: usually auspices for an act were taken at the place where the magistrate intended to perform the act. Alternatively, the auspices could have been taken at home: a famous example of a consul using his own home in order to 'watch the skies' was when Bibulus used this device in a futile attempt to thwart his colleague Julius Caesar in 59 BC.[34]

With the favour of heaven thus secured, the consuls then put on their purple-bordered togas (*pratetexta*) in the privacy of their own homes. In denouncing Flaminius, who had left Rome secretly in 217 and thus avoided all the traditional ceremonies, Livy scornfully proclaims that he had entered office in Ariminum rather than in Rome and 'had assumed the purple-bordered toga in an inn rather than in the presence of his household gods' (*apud penates suos*). Thus arrayed, each consul then received formal visits (*salutatio*) from senators, friends and clients. Thereafter, preceded by his lictors marching in single file, he set out in solemn procession, escorted by his supporters, the senators behind and the Equites in front. The processions of the two consuls then presumably met, perhaps on the Via Sacra in the Forum, and together they began to climb up the Capitoline hill. The people, suitably dressed for the festive day, crowded around. At the Aequimelium, an open space on the lower slopes of the hill above the Vicus Iugarius, where in Cicero's day there was a market for lambs used in household worship, the procession was probably joined by the sacrificial animals. Then in the confined space before the temple of Jupiter Optimus Maximus the consuls took their seats on their official ivory chairs (*sella curulis*), probably placed conspicuously on a tribunal ('*et nova conspicuum pondera sentit ebur*': Ovid). There they received public acclaim. Then each in turn sacrificed to the god a white bull, in payment of vows for the safety of the State made a year before by the previous consuls; new vows (*vota publica*) were then made by the incoming consuls, and the ceremonies had reached their peak.[35]

Thereafter the senior consul summoned a meeting of the Senate on the Capitol and laid before it first religious and then secular matters. He announced the date of the *feriae Latinae* and then moved on to such questions as the distribution of the provinces. With this business completed, the consuls were escorted home by the whole Senate ('*toto comitante senatu*': Ovid), and a solemn but cheerful day ended.[36]

Our picture of the day is slightly blurred because the specific action of each consul is not always made clear. Though they had equal authority, for practical reasons they often divided some of their functions either by agreement (*comparatio*) or by lot (*sortitio*). Generally, however, they acted on the principle of rotation, which assigned the administration and the *fasces* (the lictors' bundles of rods) to each consul for a month at a time. One was called *maior consul*: this probably meant not the elder of the two, but rather the man who had been elected first (in the electing body, as soon as a majority of voting-groups (*centuriae*)had recorded their vote for a candidate, his election was announced, and then the voting continued in order to decide who his colleague would be). Thus the *maior consul* started the year by taking priority in January. How this affected the inaugural ceremonies is uncertain. Each consul may have taken his own auspices and then may have been visited by his own friends; alternatively, one consul may have taken the auspices on behalf of both. No doubt they processed together (if side by side, no problem about the arrangement of the lictors and *fasces* would arise) and then sat together. Each shared in the sacrifice, but possibly only the senior man actually proclaimed the fulfilment of the vows and the undertaking of new promises, and it was he who subsequently summoned the Senate and took the initiative in its business. Both consuls gave their names to the year in which they held office, but in the Fasti, the lists of consuls from the beginning of the Republic, the name of the *maior consul* came first.[37]

Two other actions were required to complete the initiation of the consuls. Within five days of entering office they had to swear to obey the laws[3] (*iurare in leges*) in the presence of the quaestors in the temple of Saturn at the end of the Forum. Within the same period they also had to receive a formal grant of *imperium* by vote of the old Comitia Curiata; but before the end of the Republic this solemn occasion had become a mere formality and the thirty *curiae* (voting-groups of the whole people) were represented in the comitia by thirty lictors. The new consul, who had met the Senate on 1 January, addressed the people soon afterwards in a *contio*, reminding them of the achievements of himself and his ancestors and proclaiming his political views and aims.[38]

> *Aesculapio, Co [.]o, Vediove* (Ant. mai.)
> *Aesculapio, Vediovi in Insula* (Praen.)

'And now for what I have been allowed to learn from the calendar itself. On this day the senate dedicated two temples. The island, which the river hems in with its parted waters, received him whom the nymph Coronis bore to Phoebus. Jupiter has his share of the site. One place found room for both, and the temples of the mighty grandsire and the grandson are joined together.'

So wrote Ovid in his *Fasti*. (1,289ff.). The son whom Coronis bore to Apollo in Greek mythology was Asclepias, or Aesculapius in his latinized form. The cult of this Greek god of healing was centred at Epidaurus where pilgrims went to seek cures, especially by the ritual of incubation, that is by sleeping in the temple in the hope that the god would reveal a cure in a dream. The cult spread widely in the Greek world from about 400 BC onwards and was first received in Rome in 293-291 BC. During a plague the Sibylline Books were consulted and on their instructions envoys were sent to Epidaurus to bring over an image of the god; in fact they brought back a snake which had crawled into their ship and was regarded as embodying the god. In Greek art Asclepias' two chief attributes were a sacred snake and a staff, around which the snake was often coiled. When the ship reached Rome, the snake slid ashore on the island in the Tiber and there a temple was erected to Aesculapius and dedicated on 1 January 291: *venitque salutifer urbi'*. The cult on the Tiber Island, which was modelled on that of Epidaurus, included Aesculapius' child Hygeia (Health), who received the name of the Italic goddess Salus, probably in 180 when Aesculapius, Salus and Apollo were all given gilded statues.[39]

The temple lay at the south end of the island, where the church of S. Bartolomeo now stands, but no traces of it or of other sanctuaries on the island have been found. Varro records that he had seen in the temple a painting of cavalrymen armed with javelins. At some time embankment walls were built in the form of a ship, commemorating the arrival of the snake; surviving parts include the bow which is decorated with the snake of Aesculapius and a bull's head. This travertine embankment dates from the first century BC, when two stone bridges, linking the island to each bank of the Tiber, replaced earlier wooden structures.[40] (Pl. 8).

The introduction into Rome of this widely-known Greek god, with the practice of incubation and presumably Greek priests, was an important step in Rome's religious history. Not only did it mark the renewed acceptance of foreign gods direct from Greece rather than via Magna Graecia, but it would also appeal to the individual Roman in a manner that the older and more formal state religion could not do: it afforded him direct personal contact through dreams with a god and the hope of relief from illness or trouble.

No doubt the cult was very popular at first. Ovid's somewhat brief description in his *Fasti* might suggest that the novelty gradually wore off, but he devoted over a hundred lines of his *Metamorphoses* to the story of its institution, and a number of offerings of Republican date made to Aesculapius have been found in the bed of the Tiber; other inscriptions attest its strength during the Empire. An unpleasant custom grew up when callous masters began to expose their sick and old slaves on the Island in order to avoid the trouble of treating them, until the more humane emperor Claudius proclaimed all such slaves free and decreed that if they recovered they were not to return to the control of their master, while if anyone preferred to kill such a slave rather than abandon him, he was liable to a charge of murder.[41]

Despite this later link with slaves, the cult may long have retained its popularity, and one can well imagine some of the crowd that had flocked to watch the consuls' New Year's Day procession might go on to the celebration on the Tiber Island, grateful for past, or hopeful for future, services from the god of Healing.

Of the two other deities recorded in the Calendars, Co[.]o is mysterious. Consus (p. 163) has been suggested, but there is hardly room for two letters (ns) on the inscribed stone. Degrassi, therefore, prefers Co[r]o(nidi). Coronis was the mother of Aesculapius, and was connected with him in cult in Greece, while examples occur in Rome of mothers being associated with their sons, such as Maia and her son Mercury (see 15 May).[42]

Vediovis (Veovis or Vedius) had festivals on 1 January, 7 March and 21 May and two temples, one on the Tiber Island, the other on the Capitol. The sources are somewhat confused, partly because he was closely connected with Jupiter, but both temples apparently were vowed by L. Furius Purpureo, the island one in 200 BC during a campaign against the Gauls, the Capitoline temple when Purpureo was consul in 196; they were dedicated respectively on 1 January 194 and 7 March 192 (for the latter see also p. 87).[43]

But who was Vediovis? The problem is not perhaps of major importance, but the matter is worth consideration if only as a good example of the difficulties so often inherent in trying to define the nature of some of the lesser deities. Cicero, speaking of strained efforts to explain the etymology of the names of some gods, asks 'What will you make of Veiovis?' (*quid Veiovi facies?*). But although the derivation was apparently unknown to Cicero and his generation, modern scholars have not been deterred from seeking answers, which are naturally more speculative than conclusive, and as a result Vediovis has appeared in a staggering variety of roles. He has been seen as an Etruscan god imported into Rome, with the first two letters of his name considered as the stem of the word rather than the usually accepted prefix (cf. Veii and Veientes). Others would follow Aulus Gellius in seeing Vediovis as Apollo because he is depicted holding arrows and with a goat beside him, but this identification was probably a late suggestion and scarcely explains the god's early nature. The majority of modern scholars connect the name with Jupiter. It appears with the same variations as Iovis with the particle ve– prefixed: Vediovis, Diovis; Vedius, Dius; Veiovis, Iovis. The meaning of ve– is ambiguous because it can be either privative or diminutive. Gellius explains Jupiter as derived from *iuvare* (to help), and so Vediovis is 'the non‑helper', i.e. hostile. Others, rejecting the derivation from *iuvare*, interpret Vediovis as an 'anti‑Jupiter', a chthonic deity and a god of the dead, since he is linked with the *di manes*, the departed spirits, in a prayer cited by Macrobius. Or is he the god who disappoints: thus in the satires of Lucilius *vesanus* means *male sanus* ('of unsound mind'). Others see Vediovis as a 'little Jupiter', accepting the diminutive force of ve‑ and thus following Festus who says that the syllable ve‑ often refers to small things *'unde Vediovem parvum Iovem'*. Ovid also says *'Iupiter est iuvenis'* and records that farmers' wives called stunted corn *vesca*. Or was he originally an old 'Mediterranean' god, going back to pre‑Indo‑European times? Amid such a welter of ideas Vediovis remains a mystery, but his connection with Jupiter seems fairly secure. Possibly his was originally only a second name of Jupiter and later he was separated off as an independent deity whose precise functions are now obscure.[44]

Vediovis, according to Varro, was brought to Rome by the Sabine king Titus Tatius, a statement which certainly should not be contemptuously rejected out of hand as is often done. For even if Vediovis was not a Sabine deity his Italic origin may be very early: under his temple on the Capitol a ritually buried deposit of *ex‑votos* included Advanced and Buccheroid Impasto ware of the seventh century BC. Outside Rome his cult is attested only at Bovillae, where an altar, set up *c.* 100 BC, was dedicated to 'father Vediovis by the gens Iulia in accordance with the laws of Alba'. This reference takes us back to the Iron Age. When Alba Longa was destroyed by Hostilius its cults were preserved at Bovillae, which had been founded by Alba and whose inhabitants were still called Albani Longani Bovillenses as late as the Roman Empire. The Julii had very close links with Bovillae and held private games and festivals there. Thus the cult of Vediovis at Rome may have received some encouragement at the times when the Julii were politically influential, namely in the fifth and first centuries BC.[45]

A cult statue of Vediovis in his temple on the Capitol was made of cypress wood and was seen by Pliny, who died in AD 79. During excavations of this temple in 1939 a marble statue was found: a male figure of Apolline type, with a cloak hanging over the left arm, although the arms and head were missing. This must have replaced the earlier wooden statue which may have been destroyed in the fire of AD 80. Vediovis is said to have carried arrows and been attended by a goat, but these have not survived. According to Aulus Gellius the sacrifice offered to him was a she-goat which was killed *humano ritu*. This phrase might imply that the goat was a surrogate for human sacrifice or was an offering to Vediovis regarded

as a chthonic deity, but more probably it refers to an offering for a
(dead) man in contrast to an offering to the gods. However, the whole
matter may be a mistake: Gellius may have deduced the sacrifice of a goat
from the animal accompanying the statue: an attribute does not necessarily
involve it being an object of sacrifice.[46] (Pl. 9).

Although Vediovis and Aesculapius were close neighbours on the Tiber
Island, no real link between them is known.

c. 3-5 January   C. III NON.IAN – NON.IAN   C

Feriae Conceptivae
(Ludi Compitales)

The Compitalia were moveable feasts, held between the Saturnalia of 17
December and 5 January; the Calendars of Philocalus and Silvius show
that in the later Roman Empire they were traditionally held on 3-5
January, though Macrobius still regarded them as *conceptivae*. In Cicero's
day they fluctuated around the beginning of January and were confined to
one day. Their history spans a thousand years, from primitive agricultural
beginnings, through 'the solemn and sumptuous' celebrations which
Dionysius witnessed in Augustan Rome, and on to the late Empire.[47]

Compita were places where the paths of farms crossed each other or
country cross-roads met. At a point where four small holdings converged,
shrines like towers *(quasi turres)* were built; here the country folk used to
sacrifice at the end of the agricultural year *(finita agricultura)*. The shrine,
which had four small altars around it, was left open in all four directions
and thus provided access for the deities of the farmland (Lares) who protected each farm. The belief that cross-roads are sacred, holy or haunted is
widespread in man's folklore. Further, farmers hung up there a broken
plough, as a sign of work completed, but these *fracta iuga* may well
originally have had some magical purpose. One modern suggestion is that
the *iugum* was not a plough but the cross-beam of a wooden gateway
which was put up as a marker or guide to a bridge in open country where a
traveller might otherwise miss the bridge which was presided over by
Janus. However, little connects Janus with water crossings.[48]

On the night before the sacrifices one woollen doll was hung up for each
free member of the household, and a woollen ball for each slave. One in-
genious explanation of the difference between these woollen symbols is
that the doll must have had some sort of head or *caput*, which also means 'a
legal personality', while the woollen ball, lacking a head, represented a
slave who, not being a person in law, lacked a *caput*. A sinister background
is implied by Macrobius when he says that boys used to be sacrificed to the

goddess Mania ['the Good Lady', not Madness], the mother of the Lares, for the well-being of the household, although he adds that this was changed by Brutus, the first consul, who substituted heads of garlic and poppy. It is very far from certain, though believed by Festus, that these heads or the woollen balls were substitutes for human victims offered in the hope that the Lares would take the surrogates and spare the living. This view would only be acceptable to those who see in the Lares the ghosts of the dead rather than deities of the farm-land. The main emphasis may have been lustration, a plea for purification before the coming year's work or perhaps the purpose was to seek the *numen* of the Lares which could be transmitted to the dolls and then to their donors: since a *numen* was a mysterious power, a lightning-conductor between deities and men might seem desirable. On the human side at any rate the Compitalia provided a time for neighbouring households to get together and relax for a New Year's Day.[49]

When the agricultural villages which formed earliest Rome developed into a town, the *compita* were the crossing-points of *vici*, streets with houses. There *sacella* were erected, as in the countryside, and formed the cult centres for each *vicus*. Thus the state, as so often, developed its urban counterpart of what had originally been a country festival. Since the origin of the Compitalia was assigned by the Romans to Servius Tullius, and its development to Tarquinius Superbus, the city cults were probably organized by the Etruscan kings, who doubtless announced the festival. Later the proclamation was made by a praetor in a formula which is quoted by Aulus Gellius in commenting on an old usage: '*Dienoni populo Romano Quiritibus Compitalia erunt; quando concepta fuerint, nefas*' ('on the ninth day the Roman people, the Quirites, will celebrate the Compitalia; when they have begun business ceases'); the praetor used an old form *dienoni* in place of *die nono*. Fattened pigs were sacrificed according to Propertius, while Dionysius of Halicarnassus says that each family contributed a honey-cake and that the men preparing the sacrifices at the shrines should be slaves from whom all signs of servitude had been removed. The bailiff, *vilicus*, officiated on this the only occasion he was so permitted. As at the Saturnalia, here too slaves were allowed a full part in the festivities, and these were the two occasions when the parsimonious Cato allowed his slaves and household an extra ration of wine. Thus the Compitalia involved not merely a formal religious sacrifice, but, as our New Year's Day follows Christmas, so a short time after the Saturnalia the Romans enjoyed a second period of feasting and goodwill. In the country this centred around neighbouring farms, in the town it spilled out into each group of streets, with jollity, dancing and games.[50]

Writing to Atticus about the beginning of January 59 BC, Cicero tells his friend to 'reserve it for our strolls at the Compitalia (*ambulationibus Compitaliciis reservemus*). Do remember the day before the festival. I will order the bath to be heated, and [my wife] Terentia is going to invite Pomponia [sister of Atticus and wife of Cicero's brother Quintus]. We add your mother to the party'. Some years later in December 50 Cicero tells Atticus that as 2 January was a holiday (*compitalicius dies*) he will not go to Pompey's Alban villa until the 3rd in case he is a nuisance to the household (*ne molestus familiae veniam*). Both these references show that celebration still remained very much a family affair, when slaves might be given greater freedom, but only within the circle of the household. For Cicero to arrive as Pompey's guest in the middle of the festivities would be embarrassing to everyone. A different sort of embarrasment was evolving in the city when the *collegia compitalicia* took on a political flavour. Regarded by the Senate as potentially subversive 'cells', they were abolished in 64 BC, re-established six years later by Clodius, prohibited by Caesar together with the Games (which had apparently become more formal by this time), and ultimately revived by Augustus as an important item in his religious reconstruction of old cults, with the worship of the Lares Compitales now linked to the Genius Augusti.[51]

5 January   NON.IAN.   F

Vicae Potae (Ant.mai.)

The birthday of the shrine of Vica Pota on the Velia, near the family house of the Valerii in early times, is recorded only in the Fasti Antiates. Vica Pota was an old Roman goddess, whose name was thought to be derived from *vincere* and *potiri;* she was therefore identified with Victoria, who later overshadowed the older deity (for the Palatine temple of Victoria, which was dedicated in 294 BC, see 1 August).[52]

9 January   V.ID.IAN.   NP

AGONALIA

The entry AGON (Agonalia, Agonia: various forms are preserved) appears in the calendars also for 17 March, 21 May, and 11 December, but it is difficult to discover any convincing links. Ovid, who offers a great variety of explanations of what he calls this *dies agonalis,* thereby shows that neither he nor his contemporaries knew the true derivation. His alternatives are: *agone* ('Shall I proceed?'), the phrase used by an attendant brandishing his sacrificial knife; the sheep do not come (*non veniant*) but are driven (*agantur*) to the altar; from Agnalia, a festival of lambs (*agnae*); the victim's agony when he sees the flash of the knife mirrored in the water; named after Greek Games (*agones*); *agonia* was an old word for *hostia*, 'victim'. Not much light is thrown on the problem by Festus' somewhat doubtful statement that the Quirinal hill was first called Collis Agonus, with a *porta agonensis*, while Varro mentions a College of Salii Agonenses. Perhaps, in fact, *agonium* was merely the ritual word for a festival or a sacrifice.[53]

On all four *dies agonales* the Rex Sacrorum sacrificed a ram in the Regia: '*dies agonales, per quos rex in Regia arietem immolabat*'. Ovid records that on 9 January, on the Agonal morning, Janus had to be appeased (*Ianus Agonali luce piandus erat*'), and ends his etymological speculations with mentioning the ram: '*ita rex placare sacrorum/numina lanigerae coniuge debet ovis*'. He does not specifically state that this ram was sacrificed to Janus, but he implies this, while we know from the ritual of the Arval Brethren that on occasion a ram was sacrificed to Janus.[54]

When in earliest times (under Etruscan rule?) the Romans added two new months to their ten-month year, the new month was named Januarius after Janus, and the festival on the 9th may originally have been called Januar, though the word does not survive. *Janua* means a door or gate. In primitive times to go out from one's house or settlement meant leaving the safety of the known for the lesser known, and so care must be taken to secure the favour of the spirit who presided over the entrance, namely Janus, the god of the Doorway. Indeed one could not be too careful, and his functions might be particularized.(p. 17) Further, since to go through a door or a city gate involves a new start, Janus gradually became a god of beginnings. He thus heads a list of deities in a formal prayer, coming even before Jupiter: when Decius Mus in 340 BC 'devoted' the enemy and himself to the deities of the lower world, in a desperate attempt to win victory for Rome, he formally invoked Janus, Jupiter, Father Mars, Quirinus, Bellona and others. Janus' power was emphasized in the hymn of the Salii, where he is called 'god of gods' (*divom deus*), while to some in Ovid's time he had become a sky- or cosmic god. Further, the ordinary Roman in the later Republic was often reminded of the god when he looked around at the numerous temples, archways, shrines and altars of Janus in the city, and indeed each time that he looked at his petty cash: the two-facing Janus had pride of place on the *as*, while other deities (though not Jupiter) appeared on the subdivisions of the copper coinage. How such a Roman celebrated 9 January we do not know, apart from the formal sacrifice that had taken place in the Regia for many centuries.[55]

11 January	IID ID. IAN	NP

CARMENTALIA

15 January	XVI (Julian XVIII) KAL.FEB.	NP

CARMENTALIA

The deity Carmentis or Carmenta (both forms are found) had festivals on two days, with a three-day interval. Nearly all festivals were held on days of uneven number, but it is not known why the second celebration was not held on 13 January. Since the cult was very ancient, the two days might represent two originally separate celebrations by two communities, on the Palatine and Quirinal (Romans and Sabines?), which later coalesced. The Fasti Praenestini record that the festival on 15 January was established by a victorious Roman general (Romulus?) to celebrate his capture of Fidenae. Ovid offers a much wilder explanation: when the matrons of Rome were deprived of the right to drive in carriages (*carpenta*, which is wrongly associated with Carmenta), they refused to bear children and procured abortions. The Senate thereupon rescinded the decree and ordered a second festival in honour of Carmentis in order to promote the birthrate. The right to use *carpenta* was in fact granted in historical times when the matrons contributed gold ornaments towards a thank-offering to Delphi after Camillus had captured Veii in 394 BC; this privilege was temporarily withdrawn for some twenty years in 215 BC. Thus in the view of Ovid (probably from Varro) the festival on 15 January would have been a later adoption, but the ridiculous etymology makes the explanation most improbable.[56]

Ovid, however, offers other more hopeful clues: he refers to Carmentis as the 'happy prophetess' (*felix vates*), while Virgil calls her 'the soothsaying prophetess, who first foretold the greatness of Aeneas' sons and the glory of Pallanteum':

> *vatis fatidicae, cecinit quae prima futuros*
> *Aeneadas magnos et nobile Pallanteum.*

Her name probably derives from *carmen*, which meant a spell or prophecy as well as a poem, and her cult was closely connected with women, who are said to have built her shrine or temple near the Porta Carmentalis at the foot of the Capitol and worshipped her there. An archaic altar, found in the Forum Boarium, *may* be hers. Varro records that 'in order to avoid abnormal births when the infant is born feet first, altars were set up in Rome to the two Carmentes, of whom one is called Postverta (Backward) and the other Prorsa (Forward) in reference to the birth of the child in the direct or reverse position'. Since such a subdivision of function was a common early approach to somewhat vague spirits, Carmentis was perhaps a goddess both of child-birth and of prophecy. This would be a natural connection since women might well have consulted her about their prospects in child-birth, which was perhaps the earlier function: the magical power (*carmen*) of an old deity connected with the Palatine was sought by women, while later the prophetic aspect of *carmen* increased. Centuries later Augustine linked the two aspects: 'those goddesses who sing the fate of infants at birth and are called Carmentes'. Whether or not his contemporaries knew anything about them, at least Ovid and Virgil turned Carmentis to poetic advantage. A bridge from the distant past was provided by mythology which made the old Italian deity, who had a link with the Palatine, into the mother of Evander, who came from Arcadia to Italy and established a settlement at the site of Rome on the Collis Palatinus which he so named after his Arcadian mother-city Pallanteum; he later welcomed Aeneas to the site. Carmentis has also been interpreted as a moon goddess or a goddess of beginnings, but these explanations are very improbable. The claim that she was a water- or fountain-nymph has been widely held, but it rests on little more than the fact that Virgil called Carmentis a nymph.[57]

The cult was clearly old: it was inscribed in large letters in the Fasti and Carmentis had a priest (*flamen*) of her own. A reference by Ovid to *sacrum pontificale* may suggest that the pontiffs also were involved. The *flamen*'s duties included sacrifice, but all skins of animals (*scortea*) were excluded from the shrine. Varro records that at some shrines nothing dead might be brought in. He also recalls that the word *scortum* means both 'skin' and 'whore', so it is just possible that the reference to skins may have arisen from some misunderstanding of an obligation for the women worshippers to remain chaste. However, an old taboo on leather is perhaps more probable, since skins of animals killed in sacrifice could create a fear that the women might give birth to dead children, and we know that the *flaminica Dialis*, the wife of the *flamen Dialis*, might not wear shoes made from the skin of an animal that had died a natural death. The shrine of Carmentis lay at the foot of the Capitol, near the Porta Carmentalis which was named after it, and probably within the Forum Holitorium.[58]

The cult in early Republican times is recalled in an anecdote quoted by Cicero who regarded the *cognomen* Laenas, used by the Popillii, as derived from *laena*, a priestly lined-cloak. While Marcus Popillius as consul (probably the consul of 359 BC rather than that of 316) was involved in a public sacrifice, robed in his *laena*, because he was *flamen Carmentalis*, he had to hurry off to allay some trouble between plebeians and patricians.[59]

The month of January may seem a curious time of year for a festival concerned with birth, but many births probably occurred at this time, since
we know that marriages were favoured in April but were less popular in
May or early June.

11 January   III ID.IAN.   **NP**

Iuturnae (Ant.mai.)

Though Carmentis is unlikely to have been a water-nymph, Juturna certainly was, and she shared 11 January as the day of her cult. The spirit who
presided over a spring in the south-west corner of the Forum at the foot of
the Capitol was later identified with Juturna, who in turn was originally
the spirit of the river Numicus (or of a spring nearby), the Rio Torto
which ran between Lavinium and Ardea. The site in the Forum became
known as the Lacus Iuturnae, with a formal pool and shrine. The cult was
accepted early (before 500 BC?), since it was not made under the supervi-
sion of the *duoviri sacris faciundis* and therefore antedates consultation of the
Sibylline Books. In historical times water from this pool was used in official sacrifices in Rome, and thus Juturna played an important role in
Roman cult.[60]

Juturna was linked by legend with Castor and Pollux, whose temple lay
beside her own: the Great Twin Brethren were said to have watered their
horses at her pool after bringing news of the victory at Lake Regillus in
494 BC, and again in more historical times after the victory over Macedon
in 168. The site was excavated early this century, and Juturna's shrine
(*aedicula*) was restored in the 1950s. Badly broken statues of Castor and
Pollux were found in the basin of the pool, while in an adjacent precinct,
which formed the headquarters of the water-department of Rome (*statio
aquarum*) in the fourth century AD, an early statue of Aesculapius was
found: this might suggest that Juturna was regarded as a goddess of healing, as Varro recorded.[61] (Pl. 10).

In addition to the Forum site, Juturna received a temple in the Campus
Martius; Ovid tells us that its cult day was 11 January. It was built in comparatively late times by a Lutatius Catulus, probably the consul of 241
who brought the First Punic War to an end by his victory at the Aegates
Insulae, or possibly the victor over the Cimbri in 101 BC. We do not know
the precise relation between this temple and the centre in the Forum:
perhaps Lutatius dedicated it on 11 January because that may have been the
date of the festival of Juturna in the Forum. At any rate we are told that
the Juturnalia was celebrated by 'those whose business was connected
with water' (*qui artificum aqua exercent*). Besides these worshippers, who

had a professional interest, one wonders if ever literary men attended the festival, since quite a large mythology grew up around Juturna, who received widespread advertisement when Virgil gave her a considerable role in the last book of the *Aeneid* as the sister of Turnus, prince of Ardea.[62]

27 January   IV (Julian VI) KAL.FEB.   C

Castori, Polluci ad Forum (Verul.)

The temple of Castor and Pollux, the Dioscuri, was vowed after they had helped to secure Rome's victory at Lake Regillus. It was dedicated in 484 BC, on 27 January according to the Fasti Praenestini and Ovid, a date on which *Ludi Castores* were celebrated at Ostia during the Roman Empire. Livy, however, named the day as 15 July. Since Tiberius rebuilt and dedicated the temple in AD 6, Livy's date has sometimes been accepted for the original temple, and 27 January for its restoration. At any rate 15 July was the date for the ceremonial parade of the Equites (Transvectio Equitum) which commemorated the battle and the help given by Castor and Pollux. However, Mommsen may well be right in thinking that Livy has confused the date of the battle (15 July) with that of the restoration of the temple, and so the Fasti and Ovid may be correct.[63]

The Dioscuri were identified with the Dei Penates who must have been worshipped in Rome long before the arrival of Castor and Pollux. While each early Roman household had a private cult of its own *penates* (the spirits that presided over the store-cupboard, *penus*), those of the king were especially regarded by the community and later became known as the Penates Publici. These Penates Dei had a temple on the Velia, on the site

A Pompeian painting showing two chapels at the meeting of three roads (a *compitum*)

once occupied by the house of King Tullus Hostilius. When the Dioscuri were introduced into Rome, the two groups were merged, and thus archaic statues of the Dioscuri as the Dei Penates stood in the temple. The immediate source from which the cult reached Rome is debatable, since they were widely worshipped in Italy: in Latium their chief centre was Tusculum. However, an archaic inscription of *c.* 500 BC, found in 1959, at Lavinium, where we know that the Penates were also worshipped, records a dedication to Castor and Pollux, the Kouroi: *Castorei Podlouque qurois.* The Greek title of *qurois* shows that the cult reached Latium via Magna Graecia directly, and not through Etruria, but nevertheless Tusculum rather than Lavinium may have been the more immediate channel by which it came to Rome. The fact that Lake Regillus, where the Dioscuri had helped the Romans in battle, lay in the territory of Tusculum, strengthens this city's claim. At any rate since the *decemviri sacris faciundis* were not involved in introducing the cult, the immediate source was Latin rather than Greek.[64]

The Brothers were often called simply Castores and their temple the *aedes Castoris.* They came to be regarded as 'saviour gods'. As they were often depicted with their horses on which they rode from Regillus to Rome with news of the battle, they became the patrons of the Roman cavalry; they also gave help against the dangers of storms at sea. Their images were often in the hands of ordinary Romans for over half a century, since they were depicted, mounted with couched spears and often with stars above their heads, on the reverse of the early denarii from 211 BC onwards. Their names too were often on the lips of exasperated men and women, since the former used *edepol* as an expletive, while *ecastor* or *mecastor* in early times was reserved for women. (Pl. 40ii)

Their temple was one of the most striking in the Forum, and since it was used for various political as well as religious purposes, it warrants further description. The three surviving columns, with the entablature still in place on top, provide a conspicuous feature of the Forum today, but, like most of the existing remains, they belong to the reconstruction under Augustus, and little, if anything, survives of the earliest temple or of its reconstruction in 117 by L. Caecilius Metellus in a more Hellenistic style. This grand peripteral temple rested on a high podium which rose some twenty-two feet above the pavement of the Forum. In early days a platform (tribunal) seems to have stood in front, but it was later (in 117?) integrated with the front of the podium. Steps led from its top to the front of the temple, but access to it from the Forum some twelve feet below was by means of lateral staircases (central steps from Forum to platform were provided only much later, after the Augustan reconstruction). Its importance

Reconstruction of Temple of Castor and Pollux

was that it served as a second Rostra, speakers' platform, and as such it played an important role in Roman public life. It was used, probably since 304 BC, for the quadrennial review (*census*) of the eighteen centuries of Equites, and thus formed the stage for a colourful ceremony (see p. 164). It also served both as a platform for magistrates who wanted to address the people in an unofficial meeting (*contio*), and as the centre where formal meetings of the people (*comitia*) might record their votes; they probably advanced up one of the lateral staircases, walked along a narrow 'bridge' (*pons*) and then recorded their vote under the eye of the seated magistrate.[65] (Pls 11, 12, 41**38**).

With the decline of the Republic meetings became increasingly disturbed, and the temple and its rostra witnessed many important events in Rome's history. Thus in 62, Cato, when tribune, was involved in a fracas on the platform as he forcibly tried to stop Metellus Nepos from reading a bill to the people. In 59 Caesar here put his first agrarian bill to the vote, but while he was speaking from the lower platform, his political opponent and fellow-consul, Bibulus, with a gang of ruffians forced his way up to the top of the podium, where he tried to speak in opposition to Caesar: however, he was thrust down the steps and his *fasces* were broken. Here Clodius presented his legislation in 58, amid increasing disorders. On one occasion the doors of the temple were removed and the steps torn up as he and his followers apparently tried to barricade themselves against attack. In 57 Sestius, who with Milo was supporting proposals for the return of Cicero from exile, entered the temple to report unfavourable omens to the consul; he was set upon by Clodius' gangsters and left lying on the ground for dead. But in contrast to such popular outbreaks, the temple was also used for more dignified gatherings, since the Senate met often in it.[66]

Thus the temple of Castor and Pollux often formed the centre of stirring events, but how well it was attended by worshippers on each 27 January, we do not know.

Feriae Conceptivae
Sementivae or Paganalia

A Festival of Sowing (Sementivae), held at a moveable date, is described by Ovid under 24-26 January. His account suggests that he regarded it as identical with the Paganalia, though Varro's briefer notice possibly implies two festivals. However, the Sementivae may well have been originally celebrated by the various parishes (*pagi*). Although the main season of sowing was from autumn to early December, spring sowing was normal for some crops (*trimestre*, 'spring wheat', and some millet and legumes). Thus the festival may have sought to secure divine protection for the seed already sown, and for what would soon be sown. It was held on two days, with an interval of seven days between them.[67]

When the early Romans began to think in terms of deities rather than vague spirits, they sacrificed to Mother Earth (Tellus) on the first day, and to Ceres, the goddess of growth, on the second. The offerings consisted of a cake of spelt and a pregnant sow. The oxen, which had been used in the ploughing, were adorned with garlands, and prayers were offered for the protection of the seed against birds, beasts and diseases, while possibly *oscilla* were hung from the trees, as at the Latin Festival (p. 113). The first known temple of Ceres was dedicated on the Aventine in 493 BC after a famine three years before, while Tellus had to wait until his was vowed in 268 and built on the Esquiline, but since his worship was very ancient the temple probably occupied the site of a much earlier cult centre (see 13 December). In fact Varro sets the dramatic scene of his treatise on agriculture in the temple of Tellus, where he and some friends had gone to pass the Sowing Festival 'in the manner of their father, and grandfathers.'[68]

February

February was the last month of the year in the old calendar, as Ovid remarks: *qui sequitur Ianum, veteris fuit ultimus anni.*

The farmers' almanacs (*menologia*) record:

February
28 days
Nones on the 5th
Daylight: 10¾ hours
Darkness: 13¼ hours
Sun in Aquarius
Protector: Neptune
Weed the grain fields
Tend the part of the vines above ground
Burn reeds
Parentalia
Lupercalia
Cara Cognatio
Terminalia

The official beginning of spring fell on 5 February (Varro) and the fields required much attention: the meadows and cornfields were cleansed (*purguntur*: Columella) and tidied up; vineyards tended; trenching and planting were completed; supporting willows and other trees were pruned; some spring corn was sown, and generally the olives and fruit trees were looked after.[69] The early Romans felt that this turning-point in the year, with its promise of new birth after winter sleep, had to be approached with care. Hard work alone was not enough: the farmers must enjoy the favour of those powers that controlled the fertility of the land. Nor must the past be forgotten: the dead ancestors, who like the seed also rested in the earth, must be remembered and propitiated. Thus the whole community, living and dead, must be made ready for a new start; a solemn mood must succeed the jollier festivals of mid-winter.

The name Februarius derived from *februa* (cf. also *februum*), 'the means of purification', or 'expiatory offerings'; according to Varro *februm* was a Sabine word, equivalent to the Latin *purgamentum*. Ovid who says that the early Romans gave the name of *februa* to *piamina* ('instruments of purification'), cites examples of the meaning which survived until his own day.[70] Thus 'the pontiffs ask the king and the *flamen* for woollen cloths (*lanas*) which in the tongue of the ancients had the name *februm*'. Unfortunately nothing more is known about this ceremony, unless it is to be

linked with Varro's statement that when the king proclaimed the monthly festivals on the *Nones* (5th) of February, he called a day *februatus*; but
Varro's remark is made in the context of the Lupercalia, and it is not clear
whether the *dies februatus* refers to this festival or to the day of the announcement. Ovid's second example is that 'when houses are swept out,
the toasted spelt and salt which the officer (*lictor*) gets as a means of cleansing (*purgamina*) are called by the same name'. Here Ovid is probably referring merely to the usual custom of purifying an ordinary house after a
death had occurred and the corpse had been carried out. The house was
then swept with a broom, almost certainly in early days in order to get
rid of the ghost of the deceased, a widespread practice found, for instance,
among the Esqimos and in early Germany. Paulus suggests that the
Sweeper-Out (*everriator*) was the heir himself, but Ovid calls him a *lictor*,
presumably a *lictor* of the *flamen Dialis*.[71] Unless Ovid's account masks
some forgotten annual state ceremony, it would seem that the *flamen*
was responsible for ordering the purification of all private houses after
deaths, while the actual sweeping was delegated to his *lictor* or perhaps
later to the heir. Ovid's third example of the meaning of *februa* is that the
name was given to 'the bough, which, cut from a pure tree, wreaths with
its leaves the holy brows of priests. I myself have seen the *flamen*'s wife
(*flaminica*) asking for the *februa*; at her request a twig of pine was given her'.

Ovid concludes by saying that the month was called after these things
'because the Luperci purify the whole ground with strips of hide which
are their instruments of cleansing'. This famous ceremony of the Lupercalia, which aimed primarily at promoting the fertility of women, was in
part an act of purification. But it, and the other February purificatory
festivals, must be seen in a Roman context. They were not the expression
of repentance by a sin-conscious community, stirred up by some Old
Testament-like prophet. Rather they were intended in a down-to-earth
manner to keep off evil influences, to set right any involuntary acts of
omission or commission that might offend the gods; to avert future
troubles and to induce future well-being. At the turn of the season the
slate must be wiped clean and good relations secured with the spirit world:
then all would be well and the processes of the natural world would take
their course.

1 February   KAL. FEB.   N

Iunoni Sospitae Matri Reginae (Ant. mai.)

Ovid records that 'at the beginning of the month Sospita, the neighbour
of the Phrygian Mother Goddess, is said to have been honoured with new

shrines. If you ask where are now the temples which on those *Kalends* were dedicated to the goddess, they are tumbled down with the long lapse of time' (*F*.2.55–8).

Livy records that in 197 BC during a battle against the Insubrian Gauls C. Cornelius Cethegus vowed a temple to Sospita (*Saviour*) Juno and that in 194 he dedicated a temple to Juno Matuta in the Vegetable Market (Holitorium). The issue is further complicated by Ovid's statement that Juno's temple was near that of the Mother Goddess which was on the Palatine. Perhaps both Livy and Ovid are wrong: Livy could simply have made a slip in referring to Matuta in the second passage, while Ovid may have confused the Mater Magna of the Palatine with Mater Matuta in the Forum Boarium near the Holitorium. Alternatively, we could suppose that Juno Sospita had one temple in the Forum Holitorium and another (about which nothing else is known) on the Palatine. In the Forum Holitorium remains of three temples survive under the church of S. Nicola in Carcere, and the most southerly is often identified with that of Juno Sospita; however, it cannot be the temple mentioned by Ovid, since this had disappeared before the poet's day, but it could be the temple vowed by Cethegus (if that really was in the Forum Holitorium). A temple of Juno Sospita was restored by L. Julius, consul in 90 BC, as a result of a dream of Caecilia, daughter of Metellus Balearicus, who reported to the Senate that she had dreamt that the temple had been defiled.[72] (Pls 13, 14).

Juno Sospita (originally Seispita) was especially worshipped in the Latin town of Lanuvium. When in 338 BC the Romans granted Lanuvium Roman citizenship, they officially adopted the cult of Juno there; it came under the control of the pontiffs, and the Roman consuls had to make an annual sacrifice to her at Lanuvium. She is depicted on many Republican and imperial coins, and on imperial statues and reliefs. She wore a goat-skin, with the head and horns drawn over her head to form a helmet. She carried a spear and shield and wore shoes turned up at the toes. Sometimes a snake stands up in front of her. As her full title of Juno Sospita Mater Regina suggests, her character was complex. Her type may have been influenced by that of Athena Polias, while the upturned shoes suggest that the cult came to Latium via Etruria. How soon it reached Rome we do not know: Juno, of course, had formed one of the Capitoline triad, while Juno Regina received a temple on the Aventine in 392. At Lanuvium each year blindfolded girls entered her sacred grove, bearing gifts of barley cakes for a snake that lived there; if the offerings were accepted, the girls were proved to be virgins and the fertility of the year was assured. Thus Juno here may originally have been a fertility goddess, who later assumed warrior attributes as protectoress of the city.[73] (Pls 4012, 13).

(Helerno)

Ovid says that on 1 February the grove of Helernus was thronged with worshippers and 'the pontiffs still bring sacrifices thither' *(sacra ferunt)*. The god's name is uncertain: some MSS of Ovid give *Avernus*, while Festus (s.v. *furvum*) records that a black ox was sacrificed *A (e)terno*, where perhaps we should read *Elerno*; if so, Elernus may have been a primitive god of the underworld. His grove may have been by the Tiber below the Palatine.[74]

5 February	NON. FEB.	N

Concordiae in Capitolio (Ant. mai.)
Concordiae in Arce (Praen.)

The praetor L. Manlius vowed a temple to Concord after he had crushed a mutiny of his troops in Cisalpine Gaul in 218 BC, and dedicated it two years later. Situated probably on the east side of the Capitol, it overlooked the great temple vowed by Camillus which lay in the Forum below.[75]

We now enter upon two weeks of much activity. Apart from the minor cult of Faunus on the 13th, the Fornacalia, which ended on the 17th, must have started about now; the Parentalia began on the 13th and lasted till the 21st or 22nd. On the 15th came the Lupercalia and on the 17th the Quirinalia. The end of the Parentalia was followed by three more festivals in quick succession: the Terminalia (23rd), Regifugium (24th) and Equirria (27th).

13 February	ID. FEB.	NP

Fauno in Insula

Faunus was essentially a deity of the countryside and of farmers. A winter festival in his honour was held 5 December, and is described below (p. 201). In 196 BC, however, the aediles used money which derived from fines levied on defaulting farmers of public land *(pecuarii)* to build a temple to Faunus on the Tiber Island. It was dedicated two years later, but no trace of it remains. To judge from the absence of evidence, this attempt to urbanize a rural cult was not very successful; it did not 'catch on' in the city and Faunus remained chiefly a wild spirit of the countryside, where his winter festival continued to be celebrated in the *pagi* with dancing and merry-making.[76]

Feriae Conceptivae
(*Fornacalia*) (ended 17 February)

The 'Feast of Ovens' (Fornacalia) was a moveable feast of the *curiae*. These were thirty primitive divisions of the Roman people, originally consisting probably of families who were neighbours; they provided the basis for the early political and military organization. Each *curia* had a leader (*curio*) and its own *flamen*, and the whole group was under the direction of a *curio maximus*; these officers were laymen, not priests, though they performed religious duties. Every *curia* had its own assembly hall where the members met to feast together on holy days. This practice was still followed in the time of Augustus when Dionysius of Halicarnassus records (2.23) that he himself had seen the modest sacrifices and 'meals set before the gods on ancient wooden tables, in baskets and on small earthern plates, consisting of barley-bread, cakes and spelt, with the first-offerings of some fruits . . . simple, economical and lacking all vulgar display'. He was greatly impressed by the retention of this archaic simplicity and that the libation wine was mixed in little earthern cups and jugs, and not in silver or gold vessels. Festus (82L) records that the Feast was established for the purpose of toasting the spelt (*far*), because a sacrifice used to be made at the oven (*fornax*) which was in the bakehouses. Either each household baked its own bread at home and then took it to the common meal that followed or the cakes were baked at the central building of each *curia*; the latter practice, which could have derived from very early times when neighbours shared a common oven, is perhaps more likely. (Pl. 16).

Each year, continuing till Ovid's day (*F.2.527*), the Curio Maximus proclaimed in a set formula of words the time for holding this moveable feast and posted separate notices for each *curia* in the Forum, perhaps marking the place where each should assemble for the final meeting. But anyone who did not know his own *curia* or forgot its meeting, could perform his *sacra* at a general assembly of all thirty *curiae*, which was held on the 17th, the day of the Quirinalia, which became known as the Feast of the Fools (*stultorum feriae*). Although Dionysius (2, 50) tells us that the tables of the *curiae* were dedicated to Juno Curitis, the Fornacalia does not appear to have been held in honour of any of the great deities, since later a Goddess of the Oven (Fornax) was invented; she protected the corn from being burnt. True, at the Umbrian town of Iguvium cakes of *far* were offered to Mars in his capacity as an agricultural deity, but he cannot be linked directly to the Roman Fornacalia which however may well have been an agricultural festival: according to Ovid (*F.2. 525*) the happy farmers (*coloni*) prayed to Fornax.

| 13 February | ID. FEB. | NP   *Dies religiosus* |

[*Parentatio incipit*] (Farn.)
Parentatio tumulorum incipit (Silv.)
Virgo Vestalis parentat (Phil.)

21 February	IX KAL. MART.	F(Ant. mai; Maff.)
		FP (Caer.; Verul.)
		Dies religiosus

FERALIA

| 22 February | VIII KAL. MART | C |

Caristia

These three festivals of Parentalia, Feralia and Caristia are closely linked together. A period for appeasing the dead (*placandis Manibus*) started at the sixth hour of 13 February and lasted either to the 21st (Feralia) or 22nd (Caristia or Cara Cognatio). Until the 21st all temples were closed, no fires burned on the altars, marriages were forbidden, and the magistrates laid aside their insignia. However, only the Feralia on the 21st was a public festival. The days of the Parentalia comprised one of two annual festivals for honouring the dead, and perhaps were not so old as the Lemuria which were held from 9 to 13 May when each day was marked in the calendars with a N, whereas the *dies parentales* were not and the Feralia were partly a *dies festus* (the 21st was marked F in some calendars, FP in others: see p. 44). Others believe in the antiquity of the Parentalia and seek its origins in the private rites of individual families.[77]

Unlike the more frightening laying of ghosts at the Lemuria, the All Souls Days of the Parentalia provided a quieter period of remembrance, in which the living respectfully and lovingly carried out their duties to the friendly dead and thus secured their mutual well-being. The atmosphere was that of a gentle reunion and holiday time. Since the dead were buried outside the city, groups of mourners would go out to visit their family tombs and there perform their *sacra privata*. The offerings were normally simple: 'a tile wreathed with votive garlands, a sprinking of corn, a few grains of salt, bread soaked in wine, and some loose violets, these are offerings enough; set these on a sherd and leave it in the middle of the road', i.e. near the tombs that lined the roads (Ovid, *F*.2. 537ff.). The commemoration was primarily that of the dead kinsfolk and especially of parents rather than that of the dead as a whole. Thus in a letter, which may well be genuine, Cornelia reproached her revolutionary son Gaius Gracchus: 'When I am dead, you will sacrifice (*parentabis*) to me and invoke the parent god. Will you not then be ashamed to ask for the prayers of the gods whom in your lifetime you abandoned and deserted?'[78] While no doubt many Romans might commemorate at home in a simple way the actual anniversary of their parents' deaths (birthdays at any rate were regarded as important), they liked to show their respect in a corporate act at the tombs, and the days of the Parentalia reflect a pleasing facet of Roman life.

On the first day of the Parentalia a Vestal Virgin (presumably the Senior Vestal) performed ceremonies in honour of the dead (*parentat*) as recorded in the calendar of Philocalus. Since Tarpeia, who according to legend had betrayed the Capitol to the Sabines, was said to have been a Vestal and libations were offered annually to her restless spirit at her tomb on the Capitol, this attempt to lay her ghost could have been made at the Parentalia, but this conjecture is far from certain.[79]

The Parentalia culminated in the Feralia on the 21st. According to Varro the name derived from the infernal powers (*inferi*) and from *ferre* 'to carry' since the offerings were carried to the tomb. Festus derives the name either from *ferre* or from *ferire*, 'to strike', because sheep were sacrificed to the dead. In contrast to the family visits to the tombs, Ovid describes the spell which an old hag cast on the day of the Feralia.[80] The gruesome rites belong rather to private sympathetic magic than to the official religion, and it may be doubted if they had much or any real connection with the Feralia, but they may be described here since they well illustrate how witchcraft survived in Ovid's day. They were celebrated, according to the poet, in honour of Tacita (the Silent Goddess), later called Muta (the Mute Goddess) and identified with the Mother of the Lares. An old hag, seated among some girls, 'with three fingers put three lumps of incense under the threshold, where the little mouse has made for himself a secret path. Then she binds enchanted threads together with dark lead, and mumbles seven black beans in her mouth; and she roasts in the fire the head of a small fish which she has sewed up, made fast with pitch and pierced through and through with a bronze needle. She drops wine on it'. She and her companions then drink the wine that is left over, and as she leaves in a drunken state she says, 'we have bound fast hostile tongues and unfriendly mouths'. The purpose of the magic will have been to silence enemies and prevent them cursing the persons on whose behalf the rite was performed.

Very different were the celebrations of the next day, the 22nd, the Caristia or Cara Cognatio (Dear Kindred). After establishing good relations with the dead, it was now the turn of the living members of the family to renew their mutual ties and patch up any quarrels. The day was named from the dear kinsfolk (*cari*). How old the custom was is uncertain. It seems such a natural development of the Parentalia that its antiquity would be reasonable, though some scholars incline to a somewhat later origin. A family meal was held, to which everyone brought his own contribution, and 'a crowd of relatives come to meet the family gods (*socios deos*)', all unkind or guilty members being excluded. Worship was paid to the Lares: 'give incense to the family gods (*dis generis*), ye virtuous ones . . . and offer food that the Lares, in their girt-up robes, may feed at the platter presented to them as a pledge of the homage that they love' (Ovid, *F.*2. 631ff.). In every house stood images of the family or domestic Lares and many representations of them survive. The Lar is usually a youthful male figure, standing or dancing, wearing a short tunic which is girt around his waist: he is shown pouring wine from a drinking-horn into a saucer. Tibullus tells us that in early days the images of the Lares were carved in wood and stood in wooden shrines and that grapes, corn, honeycombs and cakes were offered to them; other offerings included wine, incense, flowers and even pigs. This pleasant family 'love-feast' continued to be celebrated in Christian times and was converted by the Catholic Church into a feast of St Peter (Cathedra Petri) which was still held on 22 February until at least the twelfth century AD.[81] (Pl. 15).

| 15 February | XV KAL. MART. | NP *Dies religiosus* |

LUPERCALIA

Thanks to Mark Antony's offer of a crown to Julius Caesar at the celebration of the Lupercalia in 44 BC and to Shakespeare's account of it, this is one of the best known of Roman festivals. It was also one of the most enduring: it arose in the uncertain spirit-world of prehistory and lasted until its final suppression in AD 494 by Pope Gelasius I who converted it into the Feast of Purification of the Virgin Mary. The outline of its ritual is known, but little certainty about the meaning of its inner significance has been reached despite much research and speculation.

The priesthood comprised two colleges: the Luperci Quinctiales (or Quintilii) and Luperci Fabiani (or Fabii), founded respectively by Romulus and Remus, so it was believed. A third college, the Julii, was established in 45 BC in honour of Julius Caesar, with Antony as its head, but it did not long outlast his death. On 15 February the priests of the two colleges met at the Lupercal at the south-west foot of the Palatine: this was a sacred cave where traditionally the she-wolf had suckled Romulus and Remus under the shade of the Ruminal fig-tree. In the late Republic the cave with its bubbling spring was still preserved, but the surrounding grove of oaks had given place to buildings and the *ficus Ruminalis* had been (magically) moved to the Forum. The ceremony started with the sacrifice of goats and a dog (unusual victims) and the offering of sacred cakes prepared by the Vestal Virgins: the *mola salsa* had been made from the first ears of the previous harvest (two earlier batches had been used at the Vestalia in June and on the *Ides* of September). Some of the Luperci then smeared the foreheads of two young men of good family (the team-leaders?) with the blood-stained sacrifical knife, and others wiped away the blood with wool saturated with milk (note the pastoral background of wool and milk); at this the youths had to laugh. The Luperci next cut up the skins of the goats into strips with which they girdled themselves; they then enjoyed an apparently rowdy feast. After this, naked apart from their goat-skins, the Luperci in two groups ran wildly in a circuit from the Lupercal, striking with the thongs all bystanders, especially women, who approached them. Their route is uncertain: originally they ran around the Palatine, later in Caesar's time perhaps only around part of it and up and down the Via Sacra.

Amid a wealth of speculative hypotheses, the most satisfactory explanation of the ceremony is perhaps that it was a rite of fertility magic combined with purification and the beating of the bounds of the early Palatine settlement. It would be inappropriate here to enter into much detail, because the Romans themselves clearly did not understand its original significance and were even uncertain which god the Luperci served (a god 'Lupercus' was only an invention of Augustan times): this was probably because the rites went back to a pre-anthropomorphic animistic stage of development. According to Ovid the god was Faunus, who presided over woodlands and cattle, but Livy named the god Inuus (if not a pre-Italic word, this might mean the Goer-in, the god of sexual intercourse?); both deities were identified with Pan. Livy and others alleged that the cult had been imported from Arcadia by Evander long before the days of Romulus, but this view rests on a false comparison with the cult of Zeus Lycaeos in Arcadia.

The etymology of the word Lupercus remains uncertain; if the explanation of *luere per caprum*, 'to purify by means of a goat', is dismissed, some connection with *lupus*, wolf, is almost certain. The derivation from *lupus* and *arcere*, 'he who wards off wolves', is attractive as an explanation of a pastoral festival, but the etymology is dubious. A derivation from *lupus-hircus*, 'wolf-goat', might help to explain the two colleges, each originally concerned with one animal (others would explain the duality as a coalescing of two primitive groups, one serving the Palatine, the other the Quirinal). Some have thought *lupercus* merely to be an emphatic form of *lupus* (cf. *noverca*, 'a new mother', i.e. a step-mother). But even if 'wolf' is at the root of the word, the significance remains uncertain: were the Luperci protectors from wolves or wolf-men who took the form of wolves which they could control? It has even been suggested that the dead showed themselves in the form of wolves, against whom the community must be defended (the Lupercalia did, in fact, fall in the middle of the Parentalia when the dead were propitiated). Others again, abandoning wolves, see the ceremony as a fertility rite in which flagellation promoted fertility in women: the he-goat was noted for sexual strength. But most theories run up against some objection or other: e.g. the priests wore goat-, not wolf-skins, while any passer-by, male as well as female, could be struck by the running priests. But whatever the origins, by the time of Caesar the annual ceremony had become a spectacular public sight, with the young men running through the streets playfully and licentiously (*per lusum atque lasciviam*; Livy), and those who bothered to think about its significance may have believed that it helped to purify and protect the city, not least by promoting the fertility of the population. Thus a primitive pastoral rite was adapted to urban use and provided an exciting public occasion at which large crowds gathered. Antony chose an emotionally-charged moment to appeal to the crowd to acclaim Caesar as king.[82]

17 February   XIII KAL. MART.   NP *Dies religiosus*

QUIRINALIA
Quirino in Colle (Caer.)

In addition to the Lupercalia, a second festival, the Quirinalia, was celebrated during the period of the Parentalia, and because it was held on the last day of the Fornacalia, it was also known as the Stultorum Feriae (see above p. 73). Quirinus was the god of the primitive Sabine settlement on the Quirinal hill before it merged with the village on the Palatine to form Rome. Later he was identified with Romulus when the latter underwent apotheosis, thus linking the two hill communities. The meaning of the name Quirinus is uncertain, but most probably derives from *co-viri-no*, 'the god of the assembly of men', which connects it with Quirites, a name which designated the Roman people in their civil capacity.[83] Some writers (e.g. Dion. Hal. 2., 48, 2) regarded Quirinus as a god of war (whether or not to be identified with Mars) and he had his Salii Collini corresponding to the Salii Palatini (armed priests) of Mars.

However, the facts that he and Mars had separate individual *flamines* and that he was later closely linked in name to Roman civilians throw some doubt on this view. Yet it could be that he was the war-god of the Sabine settlement (though some even deny his original Sabine connection) and that when the Quirinal and Palatine villages joined hands, he came to be regarded as guardian of the whole settlement when at peace.[84] His cult-partner was Hora, who was regarded as his wife, but originally may have been one of his own qualities, perhaps meaning power (cf. Virites Quirini). He was closely connected with other gods: in early cult he was grouped with Jupiter and Mars and he was invoked in prayers alongside them and Janus: 'Jane, Iupiter, Mars pater, Quirine'. The *flamen Quirinalis* ranked third among the three *flamines maiores* (after *Dialis* and *Martialis*), but served other deities as well as Quirinus, such as Consus and Robigo at their annual festivals. (Pl. 4015).

Quirinus had an archaic shrine on the Quirinal, but his temple was not vowed until 325 and not dedicated until 293; it was built perhaps near, rather than on, the site of the shrine.[85] In front of the temple two myrtles grew, one called patrician, the other plebeian; after the Social War of 90-89 BC, the former was said to have withered, the latter to have flourished.[86] Little is known about the ritual of the Quirinalia, but the festival may have still been well patronized in the late Republic: most Roman citizens must have known that they were Quirites and presumably under Quirinus' protection, since by scornfully calling his soldiers Quirites ('civilians') Julius Caesar nipped a mutiny in the bud, while in 45 the Senate erected a statue to Caesar and 'the unconquered god' in the temple of Quirinus, which four years earlier had been damaged by lightning.

21 February   (see above p. 74)

22 February   (see above p. 74)

23 February   VII KAL. MART.   NP

TERMINALIA

The worship of Terminus, the god of boundaries, was traditionally established by Numa, in whose time a public festival may well have been founded to correspond with farmers' primitive private worship of the spirit (*numen?*) which inhabited their boundary stones. Terminus had a rough stone shrine on the Capitol and the story was told that when Tarquin was building the new temple to Jupiter, the gods of the other

shrines there willingly left the ground free for the new temple but
Terminus refused to move; his shrine was therefore allowed to survive in
the *cella* of Jupiter under an opening in the roof since Terminus had to
receive sacrifices under the open sky. Thus Terminus came to be associated
with Jupiter, while an early law, ascribed to Numa, forbade the removal of
boundary stones (*qui terminum exarasset, et ipsum et boves sacros esse*) (Festus
505 L; cf. the inscription under the Lapis Niger); the remover of such
stones became accursed (*sacer*). We do not know what precise boundary
was marked by the stone on the Capitol: a demarcation between the
primitive Palatine and Quirinal settlements would perhaps not have run
along the top of a hill, as Wissowa observed.[87]

The gromatic writer Siculus Flaccus describes the ritual by which
boundary stones were first planted:[88] the blood and ashes of a sacrificial
victim, together with fruits of the earth, honey and wine, were placed in a
hole by the owners of converging fields and covered with a stone or stump
of wood. This original ceremony was reflected in the annual ritual of the
Terminalia on 23 February, of which Ovid gives a pleasant picture. Each
landowner garlanded his side of the stone and they built an altar; while the
farmer's wife brings fire from the hearth, the old man chops wood and
prepares the bonfire. A young son three times throws corn from a basket
into the fire and a little daughter presents honey-combs; others offer wine.
The rest of the company, dressed in white, look on in silence (*linguis
candida turba favet*). The stone is then sprinkled with the blood of a lamb or
sucking pig (though Plutarch says (wrongly?) that the sacrifice was
originally bloodless).[89] A feast follows and songs are sung in praise of holy
(*sanctus*) Terminus.

Such sacrifices at chosen stones (*termini sacrificiales*) clearly go back to
very primitive times of animistic beliefs when stones were regarded as the
dwelling-places of vague spirits (*numina*?); they continued into historical
times and doubtless helped to promote neighbourliness and to keep in
check those strong feelings for 'territory' which man has inherited from
his animal past. But beside these primitive country customs at least one
public celebration was held: Ovid refers to the annual sacrifice of a sheep at
the sixth milestone from Rome along the Via Laurentina which had
marked the boundary between the early Romans and the Laurentes. Such
spots were apparently not forgotten: Trajan replaced with stone some
decayed wooden stumps on the road to Ostia, as did Hadrian in Campania, inscribing them as Terminus primus, Terminus secundus, and so
on.[90]

REGIFUGIUM

Cum Tarquinius Superbus fertur ab urbe expulsus (Silv.)

The old Roman year ended on 23 February after which a period of inter-calation might follow. The discovery of the Fasti Antiates maiores in 1921 showed that in such circumstances the Regifugium was held not on 24 February, but on its proper date of the sixth day before the *Kalends* of March, i.e. *during* the intercalary month.[91]

As indicated by Ovid and centuries later by the calendar of Silvius, Romans of the Republic regarded the Regifugium as a kind of Independence Day, celebrating the expulsion of the tyrant Tarquin and the establishment of the Republic. However, this was certainly not its origin. Confusion arose from an entry of the letters Q.R.C.F. in the calendars under 24 March and 24 May, which indicated *'Quando Rex Comitiavit Fas.'* and meant that on those days after the Rex Sacrorum had performed some ceremony in the *comitium*, legal business could then be transacted in the city *(Fas)*. But a note in the Praenestine calendar recorded that the letters were often, but wrongly, interpreted as *'Quod Rex Comitio Fugerit'* (that the king fled from the *comitium* '); the error was also apparently corrected in a mutilated passage of Festus.[92]

Little agreement, however, has been reached about the true meaning of the ceremony. The 'flight of the king' is probably to be connected with the Poplifugia, the 'flight of the people', a purificatory ceremony held on 5 July (q.v.) when the crowd appears to have recoiled from something accursed *(sacer)*. Plutarch records that the Rex Sacrorum offered a sacrifice at the *comitium* and then fled from the Forum as fast as he could; this was seemingly at the Regifugium. A not dissimilar festival was held at Athens, the Bouphonia, when an ox was sacrificed to Zeus (the word *phonos* could be used of killing a man, murder); the priest, named the Bull-slayer, then threw down the pole-axe and fled, and the guilty axe itself was actually 'tried' in a lawcourt.[93] The sacrifice at the Regifugium was likewise accompanied by a feeling of guilt, but its precise nature remains a happy hunting-ground for anthropologists. There does not seem to be much evidence to support the idea that the victim was a polluted scapegoat which must be quickly put at a distance; rather perhaps the victim was somehow regarded as sacred and its slaughter therefore a kind of murder. Sir James Frazer suggested that as the Regifugium on 24 February was followed by the intercalary month, the *rex* concerned was a temporary king for this intermediate period, when the real king's power was in temporary abeyance (i.e. something like the mock king of the Saturnalia).[94]

However that may be, since Festus mentions that the Salii took part in the sacrifice with the *rex*, the ceremony has also been connected with war. But in fact its real significance escapes us, though the later Romans who celebrated it were doubtless thinking of their *Res publica*. It would be interesting to know whether Brutus and Cassius gave a thought to the festival on 24 February 44 BC, so soon after the events of the Lupercalia.

27 February	III KAL. MART.	NP

EQUIRRIA

This was a festival of horse-racing, traditionally instituted by Romulus and held in honour of Mars in the Campus Martius, or, if this was flooded, on open ground on the Caelian hill. It is uncertain whether chariots were involved. The site in the Campus Martius may be the Trigarium on its west side.[95] Another day of racing was celebrated on 14 March, but we do not know why these two Equirria fell so close together. At any rate Mars was honoured twice, once before his own month began, and the spring was the time to prepare for the campaigning season and to exercise the horses after the winter rest.

Feriae Conceptivae
(Amburbium)

February was, as we have seen, a month of purification, and so a ceremony to purify the city as a whole might be expected. This was the Amburbium which was a moveable feast, but seems to have been held sometime in February: at any rate that is where it was placed by Macrobius (1.13.3) who says that King Numa ordered the city to be lustrated in February and sacrifice offered to the Di Manes. The rites were probably similar to those of 'the beating of the bounds' of the fields at the Ambarvalia in May, which are better known (see p. 124). Servius (*ad Ecl.* 3.77) merely says that the rite was so called because the victim went round the city (*urbem circuit at ambit victima*). Probably a pig, a sheep and an ox were led in procession around the boundaries of the city (*pomerium?*) and were then offered in sacrifice with prayers to purify and bless all that lay within the hallowed circle. Since we hear little about the ceremony, its celebration may have become somewhat irregular (though the Romans did not lightly abandon any of their traditional practices): at any rate the two occasions of its celebration mentioned in the sources refer to periods of crisis. When Caesar was marching against the city in 49 BC, the senatorial government in Rome, according to the poet Lucan (5. 584 ff.), sent for an Etruscan soothsayer who advised that 'the frightened citizens should march around the city (*urbem ambiri*), and the pontiffs, who had the authority to perform the ceremony, should purify the walls with solemn lustration, and circle round the outer limit of the long *pomerium*'. They were to be followed by a procession of lesser priests dressed in the Gabinian style (that is with the toga arranged to allow the arms free, a form of dressing used on certain religious occasions, as originally at Gabii), the Vestal Virgins, the College of Fifteen (Quindecimviri), the augurs and others, with the Salii and a *flamen* bringing up the rear. An ox was sacrificed, but its entrails, when examined, foretold disaster and civil war. Lucan is clearly describing some kind of *amburbium*, whether a special one that was held in 49 or merely a figment of his poetic imagination. The ceremony was still observed as late as AD 271 when, according to the *Scriptores Historiae Augustae* (*Aurel.* 20.3), at a time of national danger the Books of Fate (the Sibylline oracles) were consulted on 11 January: the city was to be purified, hymns chanted, the Amburbium celebrated and the Ambarvalia proclaimed (*lustrata urbs, cantata carmina, Amburbium celebratum, Ambarvalia promissa*).

Amburbium at Iguvium

Much light is shed on the spirit, if not on the detail, of the Amburbium at Rome in its early days by the surviving account of the purification of the Umbrian city of Iguvium (modern Gubbio).[96] The famous Iguvine bronze Tablets record in much detail the procedures to be followed by the local priesthood, a body of twelve Fratres Atiedii. Some points may be quoted from this liturgy. A procession made its way through the town; at each of the gates 'the officer with the herald's staff' three times orders members of four potentially hostile tribes (one of which being the Etruscans) to depart; if they do not go and are caught 'they are to be carried where they ought to be carried, and suffer what they ought to suffer' (their precise fate, doubtless gruesome, is not mentioned). At each gate sacrifices followed the observing of auspices: thus 'commence the ceremony by observing the birds, those in front and those behind. Present grain offerings, place the ribs on a tray, sacrifice either with wine or with mead, for the Frisian Mount, for the State of Iguvium. Pray over each (portion) in a murmur with (offerings) of fat and grain'. Other sacrifices of various kinds were made at the other gates. When the people were to be lustrated, they were ordered to 'arrange themselves in priestly ranks and in military ranks'; they then made the circuit three times. Prayers were said and even longer curses were invoked against the enemies of the State. Two curious features deserve mention. Three heifers were chased through the town;

when caught, they were sacrificed to Tursa Jovia. Then in the procession itself a sheep was carried on a sort of stretcher; at the place of sacrifice a framework of two storeys was somehow erected around the cage, fastened with bronze nails or clamps. This contraption is particularly interesting because in modern times on 15 May a ceremony called The Elevation of the Ceri is held in Gubbio, in which three teams run round the town, carrying *ceri*. A *cero* is a wooden construction twelve feet high, with a marked 'waist', and the figure of a saint on the top. It bears a suspicious resemblance to what the elaborated sheep-cage may have looked like. The ceremony is secular, but is patronized by the Bishop of the Diocese. Whatever may be thought of the possibility of a direct link, at any rate the tireless energy and enthusiasm of the *ceri*-bearers may reflect the devotion of the ancient Iguvines whose rites ended in a banquet and 'jumpings'.

March

March, which until perhaps about 153 BC was the first month of the Roman year and one of the few to be named after a god, marked the reawakening of nature after its winter sleep, a renewal of energy and fertility for vegetation, animal and man. Mars, the chief Roman god next to Jupiter, was a war-god, but also much else. Thus one of the prayers for use by farmers which the elder Cato gives in his book on agriculture (142) is addressed to Mars: 'Father Mars, I pray and beseech thee that thou mayest be propitious and well disposed to me, our home and household, for which cause I have ordered the offering of pig, sheep and ox to be led round my field, my land, and my farm, that thou might prevent, ward off and avert diseases, visible and invisible, barrenness and waste, accident and bad water, that thou wouldest permit the crop and fruit of the earth, the vines and shrubs to wax great and prosper, that thou wouldest preserve the shepherds and their flocks in safety and give prosperity and health to me and our house and household.' Thus Mars was regarded as a protector of land and crops. How this came about we do not know. He could have been a war-god whose functions were extended to guarding the land of his worshippers from spiritual as well as human forces, or a protector of fields who enlarged his scope to help against physical attack, or indeed a somewhat vague but powerful god who looked after a people whose main pursuits were agriculture and war. Whatever his origins, in later times Mars was clearly much more than a god of war, and he was appropriately worshipped in the month of the renewal of nature when Roman farmers had to think of farming their lands and also often of protecting them in war.[97] The rustic calendar for March told the farmer that the month had '31 days, with the *Nones* on the 7th; 12 hours of day and 12 of night, with the equinox on the 25th and the Sun in Pisces. Minerva is the protector. Prop up vines in prepared ground, and prune. Sow spring wheat (*trimestre*). A sacred rite to Mamurius. Liberalia. Quinquatrus'.

| **1 March** | KAL. MART. | NP *Dies religiosus* |

Feriae Marti
Iunoni Lucinae Exquiliis quod eo die aedis ei dedicata
est per matronas quam voverat Albin [i filia] vel uxor (Praen.)

This old New Year's Day was marked by a festival to Mars, while women's interests were catered for in the cult of Juno Lucina and the so-called Matronalia. It was a day of renewal when the sacred fire on the hearth of Vesta's temple was tended, and fresh laurels were affixed to the Regia, to the houses of the *flamines* and to the Curiae Veteres (the old centre of the *curiae*, which was probably situated north-west of the Palatine, near the later Arch of Constantine). This practice probably goes back to Rome's earliest days when the *rex*, with *flamines* and Vestals (his titular sons and daughters), performed this religious duty at the buildings named.[98] It also had a link with Mars, to whom the laurel was sacred: two laurels grew in the courtyard of the Regia which contained his shrine (*sacrarium*). (Pls 17, 18).

The most spectacular public tribute to Mars was the dance of his priests, the Salii (the Dancers or Leapers) who formed one of the lesser priesthoods (*sodales*). They comprised two groups, each of twelve men, the Palatini and the Agonenses or Collini; the former were especially devoted to Mars Gradivus (the ancient derivation from *gradus*, a step, and so the Marching God, is not accepted by many modern etymologists), while the latter originally belonged to Quirinus. They had to be of patrician birth, with both parents still living when they were chosen (*patrimi* and *matrimi*). Their dress was military: a bronze-girdled *tunica picta* with a rectangular breastplate covered by the short military cloak with scarlet stripes and purple border (*trabea*), and a conical helmet (*apex*); they also wore swords. In their right hands they carried a spear or staff, while on their left arms they bore a sacred figure-of-eight shield (*ancile*).[99] All but one of these shields, which were kept in the Regia, were copies of the original shield which according to legend had fallen from heaven as a gift from Jupiter to Numa; the king feared that it might be stolen and so had other identical shields made by the smith Mamurius (?Mars, but an Etruscan name) in order to confuse pontential thieves. On 1 March the Salii set out (*arma ancilia moventur*) on the first of their processions through the city in a kind of ritual war-dance, beating their shields with their swords and halting at certain places to perform elaborate dances to the tune of a flute and singing their ancient Carmen Saliare. Since this hymn was already unintelligible to the priests themselves by the late Republic, the fragments that survive can mean little to us, but they do show that Mars was not the only deity to be addressed. In the evening the Salii rested at a *mansio Saliorum* where they hung up their arms and enjoyed a feast; a good one too, since Horace (*Od.* 1.37.2) refers to a banquet fit for the Salii (*Saliaribus dapibus*) and the emperor Claudius once deserted a dinner party to join the Salii because their food and drink looked better. The festival lasted until the 24th or possibly until the end of the month, but processions were held perhaps only on the 1st, 9th and 23rd. (Pls 19, 402, 16).

The primitive armour (reflecting late Bronze Age shields), the antique language and the grouping according to the early villages on the two hills show that the ritual was very ancient. It looks much like a preparation for war and the campaigning season, but Sir James Frazer thought that it was not essentially a war-dance, but rather that the beating of arms represented an attempt to expel evil spirits of all kinds: its purpose was to concentrate the demons in preparation for transferring them to a human scapegoat (see below under 14 March) and secondly the dancing and leaping was to promote the growth of corn by sympathetic magic.[100] Thus since Mars certainly had an agricultural as well as a military aspect, a very primitive apotropaic magical ceremony may have been converted to military purposes, and some idea of the early dances may be gleaned from the figures on an eighth-century bronze urn from Bizensio on Lake Bolsena (the Salii in fact are found in many other towns in Latium beside Rome itself). In historical times their procession in Rome must have been a colourful feature of March, with members of the nobility dancing through the streets. But it was nevertheless a religious ceremony, which could be taken very seriously. Thus in 190 BC when a Roman army was about to cross the Hellespont to face Antiochus the Great, Scipio Africanus refused to move for a month because he was a Salian priest and during the holy days (*dies religiosi*) when the *ancilia* were carried in procession in Rome any Salian who was absent had to remain where he happened to be. (Pl. 20).

The 1st of March was also the birthday (*dies natalis*) of the temple of Juno Lucina on the Esquiline (near the church of S. Prassede on the Cispius), but though the building was not older than 375 BC, it lay in a grove (*lucus*) that had long been consecrated to the goddess. Her title Lucina, however, is probably not derived from *lucus* nor from *luna* (the moon), but from *lux* (light) since she was especially the goddess of women and childbirth and presided over the arrival of the baby into the light. Women who took part in her worship had to unbind their hair and untie any knot in their dress: nothing must, even symbolically, be allowed to hamper safe delivery. Further, Servius Tullius is said to have ordered that for every birth a coin should be deposited in her temple in order to record the growth of the population. The grove was famous for two lotus trees of great antiquity: on the older (called *capillata*) the Vestal Virgins used to hang offerings of their hair. A late legend told how Juno became the mother of Mars and that the child was born on 1 March: in fact the late calendar of Philocalus marks this day as *N. Martis*, the birthday of Mars.[101]

The first day (*Kalends*) of each month was sacred to Juno, and especially the *Kalends* of March when it was customary for husbands to pray for the health of their wives and to give them presents, while the wives entertained their slaves and served their food; the day was unofficially called the Matronalia. The giving of presents seems in fact to have been widespread and is mentioned frequently in Latin literature. Thus Plautus refers to a husband who is woken up before cockcrow by his wife who asked him for money for a present for her mother 'on the *Kalends*'. Much later Tibullus describes how on this day the streets and houses of Rome were busy with people delivering presents and how ladies dressed for the occasion: 'Great Mars, it is thy Kalends, and Sulpicia is dressed for thee' (*Sulpicia est tibi culta tuis, Mars magne, kalendis*). Even two hundred years later Tertullian complained that Christians observed both Matronalia and Saturnalia, when presents were sent and all was gambling, feasting and noise.[102]

Thus all in all 1 March must have been a lively day in Rome: dancing processions, a celebration perhaps at the ancient altar of Mars in the Campus Martius, women going to a women's festival at the temple of Juno Lucina or else staying at home, dressed up to receive presents, and perhaps a general feeling of jollity.

7 March　　　　　　　NON. MART.　　　　　　　F

[Vedi]ovi Artis, Vediovis inter duos lucos (Praen.)
Vedi [ove] in Capitol [io] (Ant. Mai.)

The letters ARTIS remain obscure (? = AEDIS).

The importance of Vediovis has been discussed above under 1 January (p. 56). His temple on the Capitol, dedicated probably in 192 BC, lay '*inter duos lucos*', that is between the two summits of the Capitoline. Ovid associates this temple with the very old enclosure which Romulus is said to have set aside *inter duos lucos* as a place of refuge (*asylum*). Dionysius of

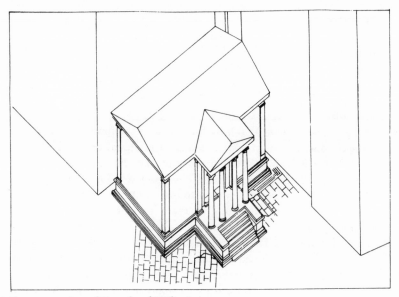

Reconstruction of Temple of Vediovis

Halicarnassus adds that Romulus had also built a temple there, but he himself does not know to which deity it was dedicated. However, Ovid's association of this early site with Vediovis seems not improbable, though some scholars believe the poet's idea to be merely a piece of antiquarianism. Substantial remains of the temple were found in 1939 behind the Tabularium (Record Office) under a corner of the Palazzo Senatorio, together with the marble statue mentioned above (p. 57). Below the remains of this temple, which belongs to the same period of construction as that of the Tabularium in 78 BC, were found traces of a mid-second-century temple and of the still earlier temple vowed by Purpureo, and also the much earlier seventh-century pottery mentioned above (p. 57).[103]

| **9 March** | VII ID. MART. | C *Dies religiosus* |

Arma ancilia moventur (Phil.)

The sacred shields were carried round the city by the Salii for the second time (cf. above p. 85).

14 March   PRID. ID. MART   NP

EQUIRRIA
Feriae Marti (Vat.)
Mamuralia(Phil.)
Sacrum Mamurio (Rustic calendars).

Another horse-racing festival on 14 March quickly followed that of 27
February, again linked with preparations for the campaigning season.
Since the date would contradict the custom that festivals were held on odd
days of a month, it has been suggested that the March Equirria originally
fell on the *Ides* (15th) and was later put back a day in order not to clash
with the festivals to Jupiter and Anna Perenna on the 15th, but this is
improbable.[104]

Greater problems arise from the references to Mamurius Veturius, the
legendary maker of the *ancilia*; these occur in the late calendar of Philocalus
and the Menologia but not in the earlier calendars. Was there a separate
ceremony for Mamurius or is Mamuralia a late name for the Equirria? Is
Mamurius to be equated with Mars or was it an Etruscan word? Was his
story developed at a relatively late date, his name being found in the Salian
Hymn, or are there traces of the survival of an old separate cult? The latter
view derives some support from a statement by Lydus (sixth century AD)
that on the *Ides* of March (an error for 14th?) a man, dressed in skins, was
beaten with rods and driven out of the city, with shouts of 'Mamurius':
this commemorated the story that the smith Mamurius was driven from
the city because misfortune befell the Romans when they changed the use
of the shields (Lydus is somewhat confused about this, since he refers to
the disuse of ancient shields, whereas only one had fallen from heaven).
Further, Servius records that on a day consecrated to Mamurius the Salii
'pellem virgis caedunt ad artis similitudinem', i.e. they beat a skin like a smith
beats metal, while according to Minucius Felix they carried around the
shields and *'pelles caedunt'*. Does this mean that they beat a man dressed in
skins, and if so was Mamurius Veturius the personification of the old year
(the old Mars?) in whom all the sins of the community were concentrated
(or perhaps the withered vegetation of the old year), in other words a
scapegoat? But if this was an annual ritual during the Republic, it is
suprising that no writer mentions it, unless there be a reference in
Propertius which may imply that Mamurius is expelled to hostile Oscan
territory. But amid much speculation Mamurius remains a mystery.[105]

15 March   ID. MART.   NP

Feriae Iovi
Feriae Annae Perennae via Flaminia ad lapidem primum

There was apparently no objection to holding two festivals on the same day, in this case to Jupiter and to Anna Perenna. Anna was clearly a female personification of the year (*annus*), while Perenna may signify her care for the continual succession of years rather than only for the beginning and end of the current year, since Macrobius says that offerings were made to her '*ut annare perennareque commode liceat*'. Her festival was held on the first full moon of the new year, and she was represented as an old woman. Mythology identified her with Dido's sister, Anna, who came to Italy where she finally fell a victim to the plotting of Aeneas' wife Lavinia, but this legend, which Ovid told at length and perhaps had invented, rests merely on the identity of name, while the story that she perished in the river Numicus near Rome has been responsible for the wild suggestion that she was in fact a water-nymph!

Macrobius says that in March people went to sacrifice to her both publicly and privately. Her festival was held in a grove near the Tiber at the first milestone on the Flaminian Way (near the modern Porta del Popolo). Ovid gives a vivid picture of what he himself saw there: the people were scattered about on the grass, men and women in couples, some in tents or home-made huts, revelling, and drinking as many cups of wine as the number of years they prayed to live. They sang popular songs which they had picked up in the theatres (*quicquid didicere theatris*) and staggered about in dances. On his way home Ovid noted a drunken old woman lugging along a drunken old man. Whether Martial's obscure observation that Anna's grove 'delights in virgin blood' refers to the sexual licence of the occasion is uncertain, as also is the precise relation of this general spree to the formal sacrifice and the public prayers which Lydus says were offered to secure a healthy year. The popular side of this New Year's Day festival clearly outweighed the more formal: its dim origins may have been linked with fertility rites, but it had become an uninhibited 'day-out in the country' for an urban population.[106]

16-17 March   XVII-XVI KAL. APR.   *Dies religiosus*

(Itur ad Argeos) (Ovid, *F*.3.791)

A procession 'went to (the shrines of) the Argei': these were twenty-seven *sacraria* at various points within the four 'Servian' regions of Rome. The ceremony goes back to a very early stage in Rome's growth when the city did not yet include the Capitol or the Aventine. Since puppets, called Argei, were thrown into the Tiber on 14 May, discussion of the festival is better postponed until we reach that date.

17 March   XVI KAL. APR.   NP

LIBERALIA
AGONALIA

The calendars vary. Two (Ant. mai. and Maff.) give Liberalia only, a third (Farn.) adds 'Libero in Capitolio'; two (Ver. and Vat.) give both Liberalia and Agonalia, while one (Caer.) gives both and adds 'Libero Liberae'.

A Roman going out to the streets on 17 March was likely to see not only the procession of the Argei but also some old women, acting as priestesses of Liber Pater, crowned with ivy and sitting here and there in the city; they displayed cakes (*liba*) made of oil and honey, and had small altars on which they offered sacrifice on behalf of any customer. Liber was an old Italian god of fertility and especially (though perhaps not originally) of the vine. Thus when the Greek god of wine, Dionysus, became known in Italy, the Romans connected him with Liber Pater; they also linked Liber on occasion to Jupiter as Jupiter Liber (possible a translation into Latin of Zeus Eleutherios). He is not known to have had a temple in Rome in Republican times, and his festival appears to have been largely rustic. The Calendar of Caere tells us that the Liberalia was held in honour of both Liber and his female counterpart Libera, while Augustine, following Varro, records that Liber presided over the seed of men (*virorum seminibus*) and Libera over that of women, and that to the accompaniment of crude songs a phallos was carried around the countryside on a cart and then escorted into the town (at Lavinium, where Liber was worshipped for a whole month, after the phallos had been brought into the market-place, 'a virtuous matron was obliged to lay a wreath on the obscene image'). Augustine adds that this was done for the sake of the crops and to repel witchcraft (*fascinatio*) from the fields. In later times comparison with Dionysus led to the hellenization of Liber. Liber and Libera were also worshipped alongside Ceres in the most famous of her cult centres in Rome, the temple on the Aventine, founded in 493 BC; the three deities corresponded to Demeter, Kore and Iacchos in the great cult at Eleusis (Iacchos was confused with Bacchus = Dionysus = Liber).[107] (Pl. 4017, 18).

Ovid says that in his day Liber shared Ceres' Games (the Cerialia) on 19 April; he implies that there were no Games at the Liberalia on 17 March, but that in earlier times Liber had his own Games, presumably on 17 March, and this view gains some support from a line of the poet Naevius, preserved by Festus, '*Libera lingua loquimur ludis Liberalibus*'. According to the late calendars of Philocalus and Silvius and the evidence of Ausonius, Games were held in the Campus Martius on 17 March: was there then a reversion in the fourth century AD to honouring Liber in the earlier month?[108]

On 17 March, as on three other days of the year, the entry 'Agonalia' occurs in the calendars. As we have seen (under 9 January, p. 60), this probably meant a sacrifice or festival, when the Rex Sacrorum sacrificed a ram in the Regia. Although we know from Macrobius that the day of the Liberalia was named by the priests *agonium Martiale*, and from Varro that in the books of the Salii Agonenses the day of the Liberalia was called Agonia, it is far from certain that Mars had a share in the festival of Liber; a separate sacrifice (*agonium*) may have been made to Mars on this day.[109]

A more domestic feature of 17 March was that it was the normal day on which boys 'came of age' (though in the late Republic and Empire some other days were used as well). Thus Cicero, writing to Atticus, says 'I intend to give Quintus his *toga pura* at the Liberalia'; Quintus was sixteen years old, but the age could be any time after puberty. In this simple ceremony the boy put aside the purple-edged toga (*praetexta*) and the golden ornament (*bulla*) of boyhood in the presence of the images of the domestic gods (Lares) to whom he sacrificed and put on a new toga which was known as *virilis* (of manhood), or *pura* (pure) because it lacked the purple-edge of the *praetexta*, or *libera* (of liberty; whether there was a connection with Libera as a god who frees is uncertain). He was then escorted by his family and friends to the Tabularium in the Forum (*deductio in forum*) where he was registered as a full citizen and enrolled in a tribe. He then made another sacrifice, this time on the Capitol to Liber or Iuventus or both. Wealthy families would celebrate the occasion by entertaining their clients and holding a grand family dinner. The boy was now ready for preparation for public life (*tirocinium fori*), the details of which were gradually explained to him by his father or some eminent friend; thereafter he was ready to start his preliminary military service (*tirocinium militiae*).[110]

19 March   XIV KAL. APR.   NP

QUINQUATRUS
Minervae (Ant. mai.)
Feriae Marti (Vat.)

This day was called Quinquatrus because it was (by Roman inclusive reckoning) the fifth day after the Ides,[111] but it came popularly to be regarded as a period of five days, namely 19 March and the next four days.

Among other beneficiaries of this misunderstanding were schoolboys who thus received a five-day holiday. Quinquatrus (later Quinquatria) was a festival of Mars, as the Fasti Vaticani clearly state. A note to the Fasti Praenestini, which records that '[Sali] faciunt in comitio saltus [adstantibus po]ntificibus et trib [unis] celer[um]' ('the Salii dance in the comitium in the presence of pontiffs and tribuni celerum'), is confirmed by Varro's statement that in their annual ceremonies the Salii had to perform a dance in the comitium. The grammarian Charisius, who (wrongly) derives Quinquatrus from a word quinquare, 'to purify' (a quinquando, id est lustrando) adds that on that day the arma ancilia were purified.[112] Thus the ceremony was at very least an annual purification of the sacred ancilia, but the presence of the tribuni celerum suggests a wider basis. These were officers of the mysterious Celeres who were the cavalry of the earliest Roman army, or less probably a royal bodyguard. This organization very soon disappeared from the military scene, but the tribuni survived to perform certain religious rites.[113] Their continued presence at the dance of the Salii in the comitium may suggest that they represented the army and that the ceremony was designed to purify the weapons not only of the Salii but of the whole army. It would thus, like the Equirria, be a ritual preparation for the new campaigning season.

Quinquatrus, 19 March, although sacred to Mars, came also to be considered as a feast day for Minerva, despite the lack of any clear link between the two deities.[114] The reason probably was that Minerva's temple on the Aventine was dedicated on that day. This goddess of handicrafts makes her first appearance in Rome as a member with Jupiter and Juno of the triad worshipped in the Capitoline temple built during the regal period, but she is probably an old native Italian goddess rather than an adoption of the Greek goddess Athene via the Etruscans. The date of her Aventine temple outside the pomerium is not known; it is first mentioned during the Second Punic War when it became a centre for a guild of writers and actors and perhaps also of skilled craftsmen, since Minerva was a patroness of the crafts as well as of the arts. Ovid (F.3.815ff) poetically appeals to a wide variety of people to pray to her; boys and girls to become learned; girls to gain skill in spinning and weaving; fullers, dyers and cobblers to ply their craft (the comic poet Novius refers to a fuller celebrating the Quinquatrus, and Pliny tells of a picture by an artist named Simus which showed a fuller's shop celebrating the festival). Ovid also urged doctors, schoolmasters, sculptors and painters to sacrifice to her. Her patronage of doctors is shown by her epithet Medica, and as such she had a temple on the Esquiline which appears to date from the Republic (hundreds of later votive offerings found near the Via Merula may mark its site).Schoolmasters will gain new pupils if they worship her. Tertullian refers to one who at the Quinquatrus dedicated to Minerva his first fee (*stips*) from a new pupil, while Juvenal speaks of a boy who worshipped Minerva with a penny (an *as*).[115] Thus if Ovid's exhortations were heeded, Minerva's temples on the Aventine and Esquiline must have been busy on the Quinquatrus, and also a shrine to Minerva Capta on the northern part of the Caelian (probably near the church of SS. Quattro Coronato) which had been built when a statue of the goddess was brought from Falerii after this city had been destroyed by the Romans in 241 BC. [116] Though the 19th itself seems to have been free from bloodshed, Ovid implies that at least in his day there were gladiatorial contests on the next four days. (Pl. 21).

23 March   X KAL. APR.   NP *Dies religiosus*

TUBILUSTRIUM

The ceremony of the Purification of the Trumpets, held on 23 March, was repeated on 23 May and in both months the following day was marked in the Calendars as Q.R.C.F. (*Quando Rex Comitiavit Fas*). A note in the Praenestine calendar records that 23 March was called Tubilustrium because during it 'the trumpets used in the sacred rites are purified in the Hall of the Shoemakers' (*in atrio sutorio tubi lustrantur, quibus in sacris utuntur*); a ewe lamb was sacrificed. The site of the Hall is not known. The note further describes the Tubilustrium as a festival of Mars, though Ovid attributes it *forti deae*, namely Minerva. John Lydus, who mentions the purification of the trumpets and 'a moving of the arms', i.e. a dance of the Salian priests, says that the worship was paid to Mars and a goddess called in the Sabine tongue Nerine; she will be Nerio, the alleged wife of Mars (see n. 114).[117] Thus the Tubilustrium developed in the same way as the Quinquatrus.

The nature of the trumpets (*tubi*) is not quite clear. They are generally taken to have been ritual instruments (like the sacred *ancilia*) for use in summoning the assembly on the following day, but presumably the ceremony also involved a symbolic purification of the trumpets of the whole army. Whether any actual military instruments were used or representatives of the army (as the *tribuni* at the Quinquatrus) were present, we do not know. Another suggestion is that ordinary trumpets were used which then became purified, that is when Ovid says '*lustrantur purae . . . tubae*', the *purae* is proleptic.[118] In any case the ceremony was designed to help to make the army fit for war, and many Romans who did not attend it would be reminded of the occasion by seeing the Salii dancing through the streets of the city.

24 March   IX KAL. APR.   F

Q[uando] R(ex) C[omitiavit] F[as]

This day, together with 24 May, were days when in early times the Comitia Calata met to sanction wills; court proceedings could start only after the *rex* had dismissed the *comitia* (Q.R.C.F.). A note in the Praenestine Fasti, which gives this interpretation of the abbreviations, at the same time rejects a view that they meant the day on which the king, namely Tarquin, fled from the *comitium* (*ex comitio fugerit*), because Tarquin did not in fact leave the *comitium* when he fled the city (this view involves confusion with the Regifugium on 24 February: see   p. 81 above). The Comitia Calata was in early times a special meeting of the Comitia Curiata summoned to witness (or perhaps to ratify by their votes) the will that a testator proposed to make. However this early form of will had become obsolete at some time before the first century BC (it was succeeded by the private mancipatory will which required only five Roman citizens as witnesses).

31 March   PR. KAL. APR.   C

Lunae in Aventino (Praen.)

The temple of the Moon on the Aventine was attributed to Servius Tullius; it is first mentioned as damaged by storm in 182. Mummius dedicated in it some of the spoils from Corinth, Gaius Gracchus hurt himself in jumping down from it when fleeing from his enemies, and its damage by lightning led to the postponement of the consular elections in 84. It probably lay at the northern end of the Aventine near the Porta Trigemina. Luna also had a shrine on the Palatine which was illuminated at night. The introduction of the worship of the Moon (and Sun) into Rome, attributed by Varro and Dionysius of Halicarnassus to Titus Tatius, is likely to have been early rather than a late importation from Greece, since Varro, when invoking twelve gods, appeals not to those who have gilded images in the Forum, but to those who are 'guides of husbandmen': this list starts with Jupiter and Earth (Tellus), then come the Sun and Moon 'whose seasons are observed at sowing and harvesting'. Thus Luna may have been an old rural deity, whose cult would have less appeal in the city.[119]

April

In Roman times a widely accepted explanation of the word *Aprilis*, given
by Cincius and Varro, was its derivation from *aperire*, 'to open', and the
Praenestine calendar adds the reason: 'because fruits and flowers and
animals and seas and lands do open'. Cincius and Varro reject the derivation from Aphrodite (= Venus), which was supported by some other
antiquarians and by Ovid.[120] If the worship of Venus in Rome arose somewhat later, an earlier derivation from *aperire* appears probable. Although
the Etruscans themselves called this month Cabreas, Etruscan influence is
possible: a word *apru* might have been formed from Etruscan *aprodita*. At
any rate April was under the protection (*tutela*) of Venus, as the rustic
Menologia indicate. They also say that sheep must be purified, while
Varro (*Rust*.1.30) mentions other duties: crops must be weeded, oxen
must break the ground, willows be cut, meadows fenced, olives planted
and pruned. Such agricultural needs are reflected in many of the festivals of
this month, such as the Fordicidia, Cerialia, Parilia, Vinalia and Robigalia,
while Venus probably originally presided over gardens.

1 April   KAL. APR.   F

Veneralia (Phil.)

A note on the Praenestine calendar (probably by Verrius) records that at
the festival of Venus (Veneralia) 'women in crowds supplicate Fortuna
Virilis, and women of humbler rank (*humiliores*) do this even in the baths,
because in them men exposed that part of the body by which the favour of
women is sought.' Lydus (4.45), who does not mention Fortuna Virilis,
however says that women of rank worshipped Aphrodite in order to
achieve concord and a modest life, while humbler women bathed in the
men's baths, wearing myrtle wreaths. In order to harmonize these two
references Mommsen suggested that the stone-mason had carelessly
omitted three words, and he would read '*Frequenter mulieres supplicant,
[honestiores Veneri Verticordiae], Fortunae Virili humiliores*', i.e. the richer
women worshiped Venus, the poorer Fortuna. Whether or not this be
accepted, it does look as if two originally separate cults (of Venus and of
Fortuna) somehow became confused. (Pl. 4019).

Ovid (*F*.4.133ff.) who poetically summons to the worship prostitutes as
well as mothers and brides, bids them take off the ornaments from the
statue of Fortuna Virilis, wash it and then restore the jewels and offer
flowers. He then explains that women offer incense to Fortuna Virilis
when they enter the baths in order that the goddess, seeing any physical

blemishes exposed, may conceal these from men. Little is known about this goddess: she apparently had a shrine near an altar of Venus, and a temple dedicated by Servius Tullius. The other goddess, worshiped on 1 April, appears to have been a specialized aspect of Venus, namely Venus Verticordia, as shown by Ovid (hence Mommsen's supplement). This Venus, the Changer of Hearts, received a statue in response to the bidding of the Sibylline Books; the *simulacrum* was dedicated by Sulpicia, wife of Q. Fulvius Flaccus (consul IV in 209), as the most chaste woman in Rome. A temple was dedicated to Verticordia on 1 April 114 BC to atone for a case of incest among the Vestal Virgins; its site is unknown, but may have been close to a shrine of Venus Murcia near the Circus Maximus, which Servius (*ad Aen*.8. 635) confuses with Venus Verticordia (confusion is increased by the existence of another temple of Venus near the Circus, begun by Q. Fabius Gurges in 295 BC, but this was to Venus Obsequens).

A 'spring-cleaning' of statues, though not attested in early Rome, is not unparalleled in the classical world. Its practical hygienic use is more obvious than its religious significance; possibly it was an annual cleansing of the deity from the (previous year's?) sins of her worshippers. However, the bathing of the women in men's baths must have been a fairly late development, since public baths are not found at Rome before the second century. Although the reference to *honestiores* and *humiliores* smacks of the later Roman empire, a social distinction between two groups of worshippers is quite likely, at least for the late Republic, since, as we shall see, on 4 and 12 April the two classes had separate days for entertaining their friends to dinner. But the earlier growth of the cult and the confusion between the two deities (it does not appear justifiable to suppose that they are one and the same) must remain obscure. However it may have been common knowledge at least by late Republican times that on 1 April women, both chaste and wanton, sought divine support for their sexual lives.[121]

4 April   PRID. NON. APR.   C

Ludi Matri deum Magnae Idaeae (Praen.)
Ludi Megalesiaci (Phil.)

Under the continuing strain of the Hannibalic War the Romans in 204 BC introduced the cult of the Great Mother Goddess (Mater Magna, Cybele) from Phrygia: the sacred black stone of the goddess was brought from Asia Minor and arrived in Rome on 4 April.

After temporary lodgement it was placed in a temple on the Palatine, which was dedicated to the goddess on 10 April 191. An annual festival, the Megalesia or Megalensia (or later the Megalesiaca), was established and these Games included theatrical performances and (possibly not from the beginning) spectacles in the Circus.[122] The ceremony was opened by an offering at the temple which included a dish of herbs (*moretum*); this was made by a praetor in the time of Augustine, but possibly by the aedile, who was responsible for the Games, in Republican days. Cicero says that 'our ancestors had decreed that the Games be held on the Palatine in front of the temple in the very sight (*in ipso conspectu*) of Mater Magna herself'.[123] The area by the temple was too restricted for Circus games, which must therefore have been held in the Circus Maximus in the valley below, on which the goddess could have looked from her temple above. But the podium of the temple, which as rebuilt by Augustus still stands today, is approached by a flight of stairs that might have afforded seating accommodation for a limited number of spectators, while some constructions nearby have been interpreted as possibly part of a theatre.[124] Rome, however, had no permanent stone theatre until 55 BC and earlier performances were held in temporary wooden constructions. The plays staged at the Megalesia included four by Terence (between 166 and 161) and at least one by Plautus, but such intellectual fare was not to everyone's taste, and we know that much of the audience, no doubt generally a boisterous crowd, deserted Terence's *Hecyra* for the counter-attractions of a rope-dancer, perhaps to the disgust of the senators who sat in the front row in reserved seats. The literary standard of production gradually declined and the mime, whether merely licentious or with some political satire, became increasingly popular. But whatever the production, it normally had little connection with Mater Magna, though we get one hint of the possibility of a drama enacting her story: Ovid has a stray remark about Claudia, who with miraculous powers had helped in the final stage of bringing the sacred stone from Ostia to Rome, and he adds 'the story is a strange one, but is attested by the stage (*at scaena testificatur*', F.4.326). At the Megalensia of 55 BC there was an outbreak of mob-violence of which Cicero gives a vivid picture.[125] Clodius, who as aedile was responsible for the Games, desecrated them by letting loose hoards of his followers and slaves who swarmed everywhere like bees 'upon the stage or into the auditorium (*in scaenam caveamve*) . . . any person who came as spectators or even out of piety (*religionis causa*: note the motives of those attending) was manhandled, and no matron dared approach, for fear of violence from the throng of slaves'. To heighten the enormity of Clodius' sacrilege Cicero refers to the Megalesia as 'by tradition and usage pious solemn and venerable above all others' (*maxime casti, solemnes, religiosi*). (Pl. 22).

The respectability of the Megalesia is in strong contrast to the worship of Mater Magna in her own cult. The Romans probably did not fully realize its real nature when they admitted it to the city in the hope perhaps of gaining additional divine help against Hannibal, as well as stressing their own supposed Trojan origin. Although the goddess remained a foreign deity outside the *ius divinum*, and her worship was confined to her Palatine temple, her Oriental eunuch priests (Galli) were allowed to carry her image in procession through the streets of Rome. These effeminate fanatics, stained with the blood of self-inflicted wounds, sang hymns in Greek, to the sound of drums and clashing cymbals, and sought alms from passers-by. The statue, which was carried on a litter, showed Cybele riding in a chariot drawn by a pair of lions. The poet Lucretius gives a classic description, based on some Greek poets, but doubtless reflecting many of the features of the annual processions in Rome in his own day: 'her head they wreathed with a battlemented crown . . . she was escorted by her mutilated priests; taut tymbrels thunder under their hands and hollow cymbals sound all around, and horns threaten with harsh-sounding blare, and hollow flutes inflame their minds with Phrygian cadences; they carry weapons in front, symbols of their violent frenzy . . . they strew all the path of her progress with bronze and silver . . . and snow down rose-blossom over her. Then comes an armed band . . . who join in mock conflict and leap in rhythmic movement, rejoicing in the sight of blood and shaking their terrifying crests as they move their heads'. Though such estatic processions must have offended many old-fashioned Romans, it is curious that Cicero, who bans collections by mendicants in his ideal city, makes an exception for the priests of Mater Magna on the appointed days.[126]

However, the Romans had made some efforts to limit the spread and to curb the excesses of the cult, as Dionysius of Halicarnassus emphasizes in his description of the procession: no Roman citizen could walk in it, or take any part in the cult and still less become a priest 'so great is the aversion of the Romans to all undue display that is lacking in decorum'. We are not here concerned with the later developments of the cult under the Empire when a whole week in March was given over to its celebration, with the more orgiastic aspects of the blood-bath of the *taurobolium* and the mysteries. Much earlier than this the Megalesia in April had lasted from the 4th to the 10th, at least by Ovid's day, but whether it had always been a seven-day festival remains uncertain. At any rate it was in the evening of the 4th that patrician families invited each other to banquets (*mutitationes*), though by a decree of the Senate in 161 BC they had to swear before the consuls that they would not spend on each dinner more than 120 *asses* in addition to vegetables, bread and wine, nor serve foreign wines, nor display more than 120 lbs of silverware. These dinners were presumably linked to the clubs (*sodalitates*) which were established in honour of Cybele in 204 when the cult was first introduced; such aristocratic clubs may have afforded additional means of controlling the cult.[127]

Thus 4 April was a very lively day in Rome, with plays to suit all tastes, horse-racing, an exotic procession through the streets, and dinners, albeit not too extravagant, for the patricians in the evening.

4-10 April   PRID. NON. – IV ID. APR.

Ludi (Megalesia)

At least as early as Ovid's day these Games lasted until 10 April (q.v.) when they culminated in Games in the Circus.

5 April   NON. APR.   N

Fortunae Publicae Citeriori in Colle (Praen.)

'On this day of old the temple of Fortuna Publica was dedicated on the hill of Quirinus' (Ovid,*F*.4.375). There were three temples of Fortuna in this area which was known as the Three Fortunes; one of them was near the Colline Gate (Vitr.3.2.2.). One, which was dedicated on 25 May, was to Fortuna Publica Populi Romani Quiritium in Colle Quirinale (Caeretan calendar) or Fortuna Primigenia in Colle (Venusine calendar). All three were probably dedicated to Fortuna Publica, two being differentiated as Citerior (nearer the city) and Primigenia (unless the Venusine calendar is wrong in naming Primigenia). Little is known about them or their sites.

Fors Fortuna was an Italian goddess, probably the 'Bringer' (from *ferre*) of increase. She was later identified with the Greek Tyche (Luck) and worshipped under various titles. One great centre of her worship was her temple at Praeneste, one of the largest in Italy; its imposing remains still dominate the hillside. Here was an oracular shrine which was widely consulted; inscribed tablets of oak were drawn from a chest at random, and the enquirer had to interpret the message for himself. An archaic dedication to *Diouo filea primocenia* (i.e. the First-born daughter of Jupiter) was made *nationus cratia*, 'for offspring'. This oracle was very 'popular'; Cicero, when deprecating sortition, says that no magistrate or man of reputation (*vir illustris*) would consult it. Inscriptions show that many of the worshippers were local tradesmen. It was to this Praenestine Fortuna that one of the temples on the Quirinal was dedicated, probably on 25 May 194 BC.[128] (PL. 4124).

10 April   IV. ID. APR.   N

Matri deum Magnae Idaeae in Palatio

The Praenestine calendar adds 'because on that day the temple was
dedicated to her'. It was the culmination of the Megalesia: the earlier days
had been given to theatrical performances and lesser sports, while on the
tenth came the great Games in the Circus *(ludi in Circo)* as recorded by the
calendars and by Ovid *(F.*4 391). In another poem *(Amor.*3.2.43ff.) Ovid
describes the 'golden' procession of the statues of the gods which paraded
around the Circus Maximus before the praetor signalled the start of the
chariot races: first came winged Victory, to be followed by Neptune,
Mars, Apollo, Minerva, Ceres, Bacchus, Pollux and Castor, and Venus.
This procession had started from the Capitol and wound its way down
through the Forum and the Velabrum to the Forum Boarium and so
·entered the Circus Maximus. More will be said about these splendid
processions at the public Games, when we consider the Ludi Romani
which were held in September.

12–19 April   III ID. APR. – XIII KAL. MAI.

Ludi Cereri

Hardly was the Megalesia finished when the Cerialia began. Both
culminated on the final day, which for both was marked in the calendars
with *'ludi in Circo'*. On the preceding days lesser entertainments were
presumably available, and in the middle of the Cerialia the Fordicidia was
held on the 15th. The foundation date of the Ceralia is not known, but the
festival was certainly established before 202 BC. (Pl. 4014).

The Games were held in the Circus Maximus, not the Circus Flaminius.
It may be noted here that by the late Republic all the major Ludi Circenses
were probably held in the Maximus. Indeed it has been shown that the
Circus Flaminius was probably not a long narrow race-track like the Circus Maximus, but an open space (originally fields) surrounded by buildings
where the only horse-racing that continued to Varro's day was the quinquennial Ludi Taurei (p. 156).[129]

13 April   ID. APR.   NP

Iovi Victori, Iovi Libertati (Ant. mai.)

A temple to Jupiter Victor on the Palatine was vowed by Fabius Rullianus
at the battle of Sentinum in 295 BC. (In the following year L. Postumius
dedicated a temple to Victoria, where later the stone of Mater Magna was

temporarily lodged). The temple of Jupiter Libertas was on the Aventine (perhaps near the church of S. Sabina) and probably predates a temple dedicated to Libertas by Ti. Gracchus *c*.238 BC. The *Ides* of each month were sacred to Jupiter and were *feriae publicae*. A white sheep (*ovis idulis*) was led along the Sacred Way through the Forum and up to the temple of Jupiter Capitolinus where it was sacrified by Jupiter's own priest, the *flamen Dialis*. Other temples of Jupiter must have received special attention on the days of their anniversaries.[130]

| 15 April | XVI (Julian XVII) KAL. MAI | NP |

FORDICIDIA

This festival of a 'killing of a cow in calf (*forda*)' takes us back to the earliest days of Rome; it was designed to promote the fertility of the land and flocks. Ovid gives a clear account of the ritual. Pregnant cows (*fordae* or *hordae*) were offered to the Earth (Tellus, or later Terra Mater), who in early days was probably regarded as the spirit inhabiting a farmer's fields, but later might be thought of more as an Earth-Mother like the Greek Demeter.[131] One cow was sacrificed on the Capitol by the pontiffs, and one in each of the thirty *curiae*. With the Fornacalia, this was the only festival to be organized on the basis of the *curiae*. Attendants of the senior Vestal Virgin tore the unborn calves from their mothers' wombs and burnt them; the Vestals kept the ashes to use at the Parilia on 21 April (q.v.). By a process of sympathetic magic the fertility of the cows was to be encouraged to pass into the corn growing in the womb of the earth. If the unfortunate cattle were dispersed to the various *curiae* from some central point, their passage through the streets of Rome and their bloody end must have been noted by many an urban dweller whose interest in propitiating the goddess Earth may have been somewhat slender.

| 19 April | XII (Julian XIII) KAL. MAI. | NP |

CERIALIA *Cereri, Libero, Liberae* (Ant. mai.)

Though the Games (Ludi) in honour of Ceres are not attested before 202 BC, she was worshipped in very early times. She was an ancient Italian corn-goddess (growth; cf.*creare*) who had her own priest (*flamen Cerialis*), a mark of antiquity. She was sometimes associated in cult with Tellus. Her most famous temple in Rome was dedicated in 493 BC on the Aventine where she was worshipped with Liber and Libera, thus corresponding to the Eleusinian deities, Demeter, Kore and Iacchus; this was a Greek cult and was introduced into Rome perhaps from Campania or Sicily. The temple, which was built at a time of great tension between patricians and plebeians, became a centre of plebeian interests; it was the headquarters of the plebeian aediles and contained their archives as well as copies of *senatus consulta*. It was decorated by Greek artists and was described by Cicero (*Verr.* 4.108) as extremely beautiful and magnificent (*pulcherrimum et magnificentissimum*). It is probably to be identified with the remains of the podium of a temple under the church of S. Maria in Cosmedin in the Forum Boarium, adjacent to the later Statio Annonae, the centre of Rome's corn supply; it was thus near the Circus Maximus at the starting point of the chariot races. The establishment of this cult marked an impor-tant stage in the religious and political history of Rome.

Ovid tells farmers that Ceres delights in peace and in offerings of spelt and salt (perhaps made up into sacrificial cakes, *mola salsa*) and of incense on old hearths (*in veteres focos*). This celebration of Ceres by country folk, presumably on 19 April, may also be that referred to by Virgil 'when the clear spring has come (*vere sereno*). . . then let all your country folk wor-ship Ceres' and offer milk, honey and wine, and for good luck carry the luck-bringing sacrificial victim three times round the young crops. We know nothing of the ceremonies in her temple, but at the Games white robes must be worn. Here the most striking cult act was performed: foxes, with burning brands tied to their tails, were let loose in the Circus Max-imus. The original purpose of this rite must remain obscure, despite much speculation (e.g. that a red fox would avert mildew, *robigo*, from the crops, or that the fox was a corn spirit or his tail a phallic symbol!). The story (*Judges*, 15.4-6) of Samson burning the corn of the Philistines does not really help. It is puzzling, since the fox plays little part in Italian legend. Ovid's explanation is complicated by a textual corruption, but he suggests that at Carseoli a fox was ritually burnt, perhaps as a warning to other vermin to keep away. At any rate the cruel streak in the Roman character was catered for in the Circus Maximus on 19 April, while in the evening plebeian families could exchange hospitality and dine together as the patricians had done at the end of the Megalesia. The links between the plebeians and Ceres were of long-standing.[132]

| 21 April | x (Julian XI) KAL. MAI. | NP |

PARILIA *Roma condita* (Ant. mai.)

Two other calendar entries need brief mention, namely *Circenses* (Phil.) and *Feriae coronatis omnibus* (Caer. and Esq.). In order to honour Caesar's victory at Munda in 45 BC, special Games were decreed to be held on the day of the Parilia, but they soon lapsed, though other Games were later established by Hadrian. The Games in 44, however, are mentioned by Cicero in two letters to Atticus, written a month or so after Caesar's murder; he complains that his nephew Quintus wore a crown at the Parilia (*coronatus Quintus noster Parilibus*): when reproved (on political grounds) by his father, Quintus had replied that he had worn the garland in honour of Caesar whom he loved even after his death. Thus crowns were worn at the Parilia of 44 not because it was the Parilia but because of Caesar's victory, and the custom continued: the reference in the calendars therefore appears not to apply to earlier celebrations of the Parilia under the Republic.[133]

The Parilia was an ancient agricultural festival designed to purify and protect the flocks; it remained popular not least because it fell on the day that had come to be regarded as the day of Rome's foundation, her birthday. It was held in honour of Pales, a mysterious deity or deities. The Antiate calendar for 7 July even refers to two Pales (*Palibus duobus*) while later Romans were uncertain whether Pales was masculine or feminine. When vague spirits began to be regarded anthropomorphically, there could be doubt about their sex, and offerings could be made '*sive deo sive deae*'. Further, Palilia would have been a more likely name for a feast of Pales (the form is found, and so some scholars dissociate Pales from Parilia), while there was also a goddess called Diva Palatua who had a *flamen Palatualis* who offered sacrifice on the Palatine at the Septimontium on 11 December. Thus many problems arise, but they need not be pursued here: suffice it to say that in the later Republic, although the sex of Pales was uncertain a temple had been dedicated to Pales or perhaps two Pales by M. Atilius Regulus in 267 BC (probably on the Palatine and on 7 July), and Pales was well known as a deity of shepherds.

More important than Pales' obscure origin is the nature of his (or her) worship about which we are well informed, partly because the cult, though agricultural, was maintained in Rome until the time of the Empire, partly because Ovid took part in it, including jumping through bonfires, and has left a fairly full description (F.4.735ff.) of how farmers celebrated the day. The sheep-fold was decorated with leafy branches and its entrance with a wreath. At earliest dawn the fold had to be cleansed with water and swept, and the sheep fumigated with sulphur; then a fire of olive and pine wood was kindled and the crackling of laurel branches thrown into it gave good omen; offerings of cakes of millet, food and pails of milk were brought. The shepherd then prayed to Pales, seeking for protection for himself and his flocks and for forgiveness if he or they had strayed unwittingly into holy ground where his sheep had grazed, or if he had cut wood or sullied sacred waters; Pales is then asked to ward off disease and wolves and to grant prosperity. Four times the shepherd offered this prayer, facing the east, and then washed his hand in dew. Then after drinking milk and heated wine from a bowl, he leapt through the burning bonfire. Ovid here ends his description of the festival, but a little later on (805) he implies that the sheep, as well as the shepherd, had to pass through the fires. Propertius (4.4.75ff.) and Tibullus (2.5.89f.), who mention the shepherd's leap through the fire, do not refer to that of his flocks. However, there is no shortage of evidence for such action by flocks and herds in Europe and the rest of the world, particularly on feast days such as Easter, May Day and Midsummer Day, so it may well have been an ancient Italian custom, which was perhaps practised only in the countryside celebrations and not in the city.

One striking feature of the ceremony remains to be described. Ovid introduces his account of the Parilia by personal recollection: 'truly I myself have often brought with full hands the ashes of the calf and the bean-straws, pure means of expiation (*februa casta*), truly I have leapt over the fires, placed three in a row, and the moist laurel has sprinkled water over me'. He is referring to the fact that the ashes of the unborn calves which had been preserved from the Fordicidia, and the blood of the horse which had been sacrificed in the previous year (see 15 October) were mixed together and thrown on the burning bean-straws; the worshippers then leapt through the flames. The blood and the ashes, which were agents of purification, had been preserved by the Vestal Virgins. Since the supply of this gruesome mixture must have been limited, what Ovid is describing is not very clear. The Parilia was both private and public (*tam privata quam publica:* Varro), and rural and urban. Ovid's longer description clearly applies to the early country cult, but what happened in Rome? We know nothing about the official cult except that it was conducted by the Rex Sacrorum, and it was here presumably that the main offering of the sacred relics was made. However, private celebrations apparently went on throughout the city; bean-straw for the fires could have been distributed freely, but not everyone is likely to have received even a tiny portion of the relics, though Ovid appears to have handled some.

The day must have ended in general festive mood; at any rate Propertius (4.4.75f.) refers to the merry-making (*lusus in urbe*) and the drunken crowd (*ebria turba*) who jumped over the heaps of burning hay. And there was a further reason for public rejoicing: 21 April was Rome's birthday, the anniversary of her foundation in 753 BC.[134]

23 April   VIII(Julian IX) KAL. MAI.   F (Ant. mai.)

VINALIA *Veneri Erucinae* (Ant. mai.)

Rome celebrated two Festivals of Wine, the first (Vinalia Priora) on 23 April, the second (Vinalia Rustica) on 19 August. These were held originally in honour of Jupiter, but later Venus was associated with them. On the priority of Jupiter Varro (*LL*.6.16) is quite definite, '*Vinalia a vino. Hic dies Iovis, non Veneris*'. On 23 April wine of the previous year was drawn from a jar or skin and offered in libation to Jupiter; only thereafter could this new wine (called *calpar*) be tasted by men: '*Vinalia priora . . . degustandis vinis instituta*' (Pliny, *NH*. 18. 287). The Athenians had a similiar festival called Pithoigia, the Opening of the Jars, in honour of Dionysus when the new wine was offered and tasted. What social or commercial meetings this wine-tasting in Rome may have stimulated we do not know.

Verrius Flaccus, if correctly recorded by Paulus, said that 19 August was the day on which the wine might be brought into Rome, and Varro says that he saw a notice on the gates of Tusculum which forbade the bringing of new wine into the city until the Vinalia had been proclaimed on the *Nones*.[135] But the vintage did not normally begin until the end of September, although, of course, the exact date varied in different parts of Italy and according to the weather; thus 19 August is too early for the new wine of the current year. It is, therefore, probable that Paulus has confused the two Vinalia and that 23 April was the day when the wine of the previous year's harvest could first be brought into Rome. What then happened on 19 August? Pliny (*NH*.18. 284) seems to provide the answer when he says that there were three seasons when men had to fear for their crops and therefore established the holidays and festivals of Robigalia, Floralia and Vinalia. He continues, 'the Vinalia Priora, established on 23 April for the tasting of the wines has no reference to the fruits of the earth'. This seems to imply that the Vinalia Rustica had, and he later calls it a holiday established for propitiating the weather (*festum tempestatibus leniendis institutum*). Thus it was a ceremony designed to protect the growing vines against natural or supernatural harm, especially storms, and was perhaps observed even more keenly in the countryside than in the city, as the title Rustica suggests. Finally, Varro (*LL*.6.16) in describing the Vinalia says that the *flamen Dialis* '*auspicatur vindemiam*', that is made an official commencement of the vintage and when he had given orders to gather the grapes, he sacrificed a lamb to Jupiter, and between the cutting out of the victim's entrails and the offering of them to the god he himself first plucked a bunch of grapes. However, as we have seen, 19 August is really too early for starting the vintage, so this may have been a ceremony held slightly later in the year than the Vinalia Rustica.

Varro, who said categorically that the Vinalia was in honour of Jupiter and not of Venus, in another work, the *Res Rustica* (1.1.6), blandly refers to Venus, the protectress of gardens (*procuratio hortorum*), 'in whose honour the Rustica Vinalia was established.' For Ovid also this was primarily a festival of Venus, (F.4.863ff.), as it is in the calendars, of which the fullest entry (Esq.) gives '*Veneri Erucinae extra portam Collinam*'. Some scholars therefore maintain that Venus had a part in the festival from its origin, but this is improbable since her cult in Rome does not appear to be primitive: Varro (*LL*.6. 35) says that he could not find her mentioned in any ancient document. At some unknown date she became identified with Greek Aphrodite, and her first known temple in Rome, that of Venus Obsequens, was built in 295 in the Circus Maximus by Q. Fabius Gurges, whose grandson, Q. Fabius Maximus, dedicated a temple to Venus Erucina on the Capitol in 215. This was based on the cult of Aphrodite (originally the Punic Astarte) at Eryx in Sicily where sacred prostitution was practised. Another temple outside the Colline Gate was dedicated to Venus Erucina in 181 on 23 April, the day of the Vinalia, with which she then became identified, and on this day prostitutes sacrificed to her. Whether the Italian cult of Venus as guardian of gardens could have reached Rome much earlier and have been extended to include vineyards and then linked to 23 April, we simply do not know. At any rate the word *vinalia* is almost certainly derived from *vinum* (wine) rather than from *Venus*, and Plutarch (*Qu.Rom*.45) says that at the Vinalia (which he misnames the Veneralia!) a great quantity of wine flowed from the temple of Venus; presumably he refers to the Vinaria Priora. (Pl. 4121).

Ovid and others (including a brief note in the Praenestine calendar) tell the legendary story of the origin of the Vinalia. When Aeneas was at war with Turnus, the king of the Rutuli, the Etruscan king Mezentius offered to support Turnus in return for what he usually gave to the gods, namely (our sources vary) either the wine of the next Latin vintage, or wine every year, or all first-fruits (which would include wine). The Latins then vowed to give these to Jupiter if he granted victory. And so it fell out: Mezentius was killed in battle and Jupiter received his annual tribute of wine. 'Hence the day is called the Vinalia; Jupiter claims it for his own and rejoices to be present at his own feast': so concludes Ovid who had earlier attributed the feast to Venus.

Thus on 23 April a formal of offering of wine was made to Jupiter, which may well have been followed by general feasting and drinking while the farmers arranged sales for the new wine which they were bring-

ing to market in the city. At the same time, whatever the precise involve-
ment of Venus (and perhaps she was more concerned in the Vinalia
Rustica on 19 August and with prayer for the protection of vines from
disease), she was receiving offerings from the prostitutes of Rome, who
apparently continued to make their gifts on the 24th also, since the
Praenestine calendar notes that the 25th was a holiday for bawds *(festus
puerorum lenoniorium)* because the preceding day (24) was a holiday for
meretrices.

25 April   VI (Julian VII) KAL. MAI.   NP

ROBIGALIA

Feriae Robigo Via Claudia ad milliarium V ne robigo frumentis noceat.
Sacrificum et ludi cursoribus maioribus minoribusque fiunt (Note in Praen.)

The festival of Robigalia was celebrated in honour of Robigus or Robigo
(the Romans were uncertain of the sex), the spirit of *robigo,* namely blight,
red rust or mildew, at the fifth milestone on the Via Claudia lest mildew
should harm the corn. It was an ancient agricultural festival, going back
perhaps to a time when the fifth milestone marked the end of Roman territory, which the disease must be prevented from entering. Its institution
was attributed by Pliny to Numa, who according to Tertullian '*Marti at
Robigini ludos instituit*'. This observation does not mean joint Games nor is
it necessary to accept the view that Robigus was a rural form of Mars. The
cult of Robigus was attended by the priest of Quirinus *(flamen Quirinalis),*
but the reason is unknown. We learn most about the festival from
Ovid.[136] He tells how when he was returning one day to Rome from
Nomentum, he met a white-robed crowd: a *flamen Quirinalis* was on his
way to the grove of old Robigus to throw into the sacrificial flames the entrails of a dog and of a sheep (according to Columella, *RR.* 10. 342, the
dog sacrificed to malignant Robigus was a sucking puppy, *lacteus catulus).*
Ovid must then have joined the procession, since he says that he himself
saw the priest, who had a napkin in his right hand, cast wine, incense and
the entrails on to the fire and heard the prayers to Robigus to protect the
crops. When he asked the meaning of the rites, the priest told him that the
Dogstar, Sirius, was in the ascendant. In fact on 25 April this star disappeared at sunset and rose on 2 August, so Ovid, the priest or some earlier
source may have confused the rising with the setting of the star. Its appearance coincided with the great heat of summer, of which it was
sometimes regarded as the cause, and heat did scorch vines, as Pliny
records, but he also attributes *robigo,* which attacks vines and crops, to
damp in windless valleys (Plin. *NH.*19. 272, 154).

The connection between the sacrifice of the dog and the Dogstar, which the priest asserted, is very doubtful, and an explanation may lie in another sacrifice: Pliny (18.15) preserves a sentence from the Commentarii Pontificum, 'Let a day be fixed for taking augury by the sacrifice of a dog before the corn comes out of the sheath and before it penetrates through into the sheath' (*augurio canario agendo dies instituatur*). Further, Festus (39L) says that red (*rufae*) dogs were sacrificed near the Porta Catularia in order to appease the Dogstar and in order that 'the goldening corn (*fruges flavescentes*) might come to maturity; presumably the rough similarity between the reddish dogs and the reddish-golden corn was designed as an act of sympathetic magic or else the reference was to the red mildew. This sacrifice was not made on a fixed day, but since it was offered during the period of the Dogstar, it possibly could have been made on the 25th to coincide with the similar Robigalia.

A small topographical difficulty arises about the site of the grove of Robigus. The Praenestine calendar placed the festival (*feriae*) at the fifth milestone on the Via Claudia, which led north from Rome and diverged from the Via Flaminia near the Milvian Bridge at the third milestone: however Ovid met the procession on his way back from Nomentum which lay some fifteen miles to the *east* of Rome. The suggestion has been made that he returned to his own gardens near the Milvian Bridge and then met the procession on the Via Claudia nearby, but why then did he say that he met it when he was returning from Nomentum, which implies that the grove was on the Via Nomentana? A not very probable conjecture would be to suppose that a sacrifice was made at the grove on the way to Nomentum, but that the festival and Games were held on the Via Claudia.[137] In any case this was for long presumably a simple agricultural festival and we do not know when the more elaborate Games were added, which catered for runners (*cursoribus maioribus minoribusque*: meaning men's and boys' events?). That these were held in late Roman times on the Via Claudia is confirmed by the fact that later the Roman Church honoured St Mark with a procession on 25 April from S. Lorenzo in the Corso along the Flaminian Way to the Milvian Bridge, whence it returned to S. Maria Maggiore, while the Church still prays for the crops on this same day.

Other deities, who were not sufficiently important or old enough to win a place in the calendar, might be honoured and invoked to guard both crops and beasts. Thus Verminus, who protected cattle against worm disease (*verminatio*), received an altar just outside the Porta Viminalis which was erected in the first century BC by A. Postumius Albinus in accordance with a *lex Plaetoria*. It was probably the work of the consul of 180 in an attempt to counter a pestilence in 175-74 (Livy, 41.21). The altar was discovered in 1876 in a tower of the Servian rampart. (Pl. 23)

27 April (Julian 28)   IV KAL. MAI.   C

Ludi Florae

'*Eodem die aedes Florae, quae rebus florescendis praeest, dedicata est propter strilitatem frugum*' (Note in Praen.)

Flora was an ancient Italian goddess of flowers and of vegetation in general. She had her own priest (*flamen Florialis*) and, along with old Roman deities as Janus, Jupiter, Juno and Vesta, she received sacrifices from the ancient brotherhood of the Arval Brethren in their sacred grove; an altar was said to have been erected to her in Rome by King Tatius. Thus her cult in Rome was ancient, but she apparently did not receive a temple until a drought in 241 or 238 BC led the Romans to consult the Sibylline Books which prescribed the building of a temple, and Games were celebrated in her honour; the plebeian aediles were responsible and they provided the money from fines exacted from encroachments on the public land. At first the Games were not held every year, but later frequent damage to crops led in 173 to their annual performance.[138] The temple which was dedicated on 28 April was on the lower slopes of the Aventine near the Circus Maximus (she received, as Flora Rustica, another temple on the Quirinal, perhaps where the primitive altar had been). Under the Empire the Games lasted for six days, starting with theatrical performances and ending with circus Games and a sacrifice to Flora. They may have been extended beyond one day as early as Caesar's time, if not earlier, since, when he reformed the calendar in 45 BC, he added extra days in such a way as not to upset the incidence of the festivals, and in April he added an extra day before the Floralia on what we call 26 April (VI. Kal. Mai.) rather than at the end of the month on the 29th which followed the first day of the Floralia (Macrobius, 1.14.9).

The worship of a goddess of fertility not unnaturally led increasingly to much licence and indecency. In early days this would be of a primitive rustic nature but with the establishment of regular Games it became more widespread and sophisticated. Prostitutes claimed the Floralia as well as the Vinalia of the 23rd as their feast (later indeed a tradition recorded that Flora herself was a harlot), and according to Juvenal they performed naked and even fought in gladiatorial contests. The younger Cato was so shocked by a strip-tease act in one of the theatrical performances that he left the theatre in disgust. Cicero, however, who as aedile in 69 BC was responsible for the Games, refers to the goddess most respectfully as Our Lady

Flora (Flora Mater) whose favour to the people and plebs of Rome he was to secure by holding the festival. In the Circus the normal sports were no doubt staged, but the Floralia had two special items. Hares and goats were let loose: according to Ovid (5.373f) Venus supplied as a reason for this custom the fact that she was the patroness of gardens and fields and not of woods and wild animals. To this may be added that both hares and goats were thought to be both salacious and fertile. Secondly, Persius says that vetches, beans and lupins were scattered among the crowd, again perhaps partly as fertility symbols at the spring festival. Ovid also mentions (5.355ff.) two other aspects of the Floralia: multi-coloured garments were worn instead of the white that was customary at the Cerialia; the women were thus displaying their spring fashions. Secondly, the festival was well lighted. This may refer to night-shows in the theatres, while an anecdote told how the emperor Tiberius' baldness was mocked by a praetor, L. Caesianus, who sent 5,000 boys with shaven heads to light up the way for the spectators returning from the theatre at the Floralia. Tiberius took it in good part, but henceforth all bald persons were called Caesiani.[139]

Feriae Conceptivae
(Feriae Latinae)

The Latin Festival was one of the moveable feasts (conceptivae). Its date, as we have seen, was fixed at the beginning of each year by the incoming consuls; it was normally held before the consuls went off on the campaigning season in the spring, sometimes a little later and so it may conveniently be described at this point. Although the main celebration did not take place at Rome itself, it nevertheless played a very important part in Roman public life from the very earliest times until the end of the fourth century AD when it was celebrated by a champion of the old Roman culture, the pagan Nicomachus Flavianus, who as consul in 394 sought Jupiter's aid against Theodosius. However Theodosius was victorious and probably suppressed the festival.[140]

The feriae Latinae was originally held by a group of Latin cities, led perhaps by Alba Longa, who sent delegates (presumably their local magistrates) to the towering summit of the Alban Mount, some thirteen miles south-east of Rome, to worship Jupiter Latiaris together. During this celebration any warfare ceased among these Latins, so that all might be able to gather to worship the god of their League, which was one of several early groupings among the Latin cities. At first the Romans may not even have been members, but when their king Tullus Hostilius destroyed Alba Longa, traditionally in the seventh century BC (a date

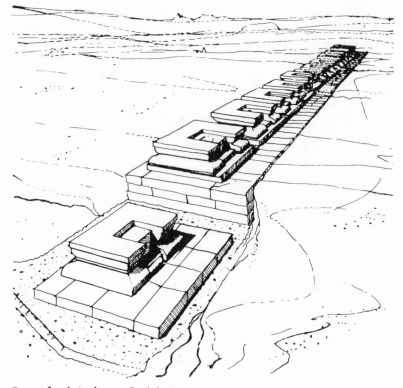

Row of archaic altars at Lavinium

which is supported by archaeological evidence) they succeeded to its position. In the next century Rome's Etruscan rulers may have reorganized the League, and as Roman power gradually spread throughout Latium, Rome ultimately dominated the League which was formally dissolved in 338 BC and then rearranged under Roman control. By this time many of the very small early settlements had gradually disappeared, but Rome kept up their memory by supplying priests to represent them, such as the *sacerdotes Cabenses* who acted for the vanished people of Cabe or Cabum.[141]

The cult was so old that at first Jupiter may have been worshipped at a primitive altar, but later, probably in the sixth century, he received a temple and statue. No remains of the temple exist, but later traces of the Via Triumphalis leading to it have been found. Unfortunately nothing like the impressive thirteen stone altars of the neighbouring federal meeting place at Lavinium has been discovered at the Alban federal sanctuary.

The central act was a sacrifice to the god which may have been made by the Latins in rotation until the Romans gained control and it became the task of the Roman consuls. The leader offered a libation of milk (not wine) and the rest of the cities brought other agricultural produce such as sheep or cheese. The victim of the main sacrifice, which was made on behalf of the whole League, was a pure white heifer that had never known the yoke. After it had been killed, its flesh was divided among all the delegates who zealously claimed their portions of the sacrificial meat (*carnem petere*) in order to share in a common meal. In early days this must have been a very solemn occasion, a sacrament in which the members pledged their loyalty to the god and one another: it was an annual recognition of the kinship of the Latin peoples, and the offerings reflect the gifts of an agricultural or even pastoral community. In later historical times the ceremony recalled the part the Latins had played in helping Rome to her predominant position in Italy. True, Jupiter Latiaris yielded pride of place to Jupiter Capitolinus in Rome as the chief deity of imperial Rome, but his early importance was recalled when Roman generals, to whom the Senate had denied an official triumph on the Capitol, celebrated a less official one on the Alban Mount, turning to Jupiter Latiaris rather than Jupiter Capitolinus (p. 217).[142]

One puzzling feature of the celebrations was that little puppets fashion- ed like human beings (*oscilla*) were said to have been hung up in the trees, as was also done at the festival of Paganalia (p. 68). Many ancient writers regarded these figures as substitutions in a later age for human sacrifices in more primitive times. But despite accusations made much later by some Christian writers, such as Tertullian, Minucius Felix and Tatian, the early

Oscillum hanging from tree

Romans do not seem to have liked human sacrifice, which Livy describes as *'minime Romanum sacrum'* ('in no way a Roman rite') and which official imperial policy opposed among the Druids. The idea behind the *oscilla* may have been less precise, namely the hope that Jupiter would spare the living and accept the puppets instead, or in a more general way they may have been no more than charms against evil influences.[143]

The increasing importance of the festival to Rome in later times is demonstrated by the fact that the consuls were accompanied to the Alban Mount by all the other senior Roman magistrates and, though the Senate remained in Rome, a prefect *(praefectus urbi feriarum Latinarum causa)* was appointed to look after the city during their absence. In the late Republic the consuls still regarded this duty to be of outstanding importance. Thus Cicero, writing to Caelius in February 50 BC, sarcastically refers to the remarkable activity of the consuls who, so far, had put only one resolution to the Senate, that about the date of the Latin Festival. A year later Caesar, who had rushed back from Spain to Rome and was desperately eager to push on to Greece to face Pompey, grudgingly delayed in Rome for eleven days, one at least of which he devoted to holding the Latin Festival. Augustus, who revived many old Roman religious practices, set up on the Alban Mount a list of all the Roman magistrates who had celebrated the festival, and these Fasti were continued into imperial times. Some surviving fragments show that Augustus himself, when consul, wished to carry out this duty: they record that he was prevented twice by illness (27 and 24 BC) and twice by absence in Spain (26 and 25), but in 23 he attended: *'imperator Caesar in monte fuit'*.[144]

The essential part of the festival lasted only one day, but if any flaw was detected in the proceedings, the whole rite had to be gone through again, in accord with the usual Roman practice. Thus in 176 BC at the sacrifice of a victim the magistrate from Lanuvium forgot to pray for the Roman People, the Quirites. This was reported to the Roman Senate, who referred it to the pontiffs; they in turn decided that the festival must be repeated and Lanuvium should provide the victim. Since the festival was not held again until 11 August, the consuls could not go off to their provinces until after that late date. In 199 the festival had to be repeated because the delegates from Ardea had complained that they had not received their customary share of the meat.[145]

The jollification enjoyed by the mass of the people that attended was later canalized by the holding of more regular Games (Ludi) which lasted for at least two days. Though some scholars believe that these events led up to the main day, Cicero writing to his brother Quintus in March 56 BC says that the two days *after* the Latin Festival were *religiosi* (holidays), but otherwise the festival of Jupiter Latiaris had come to an end; this would suggest that the solemn day was followed by the relaxations. Elsewhere Cicero records, or imagines, how Scipio Aemilianus spent the Latin holidays in his country house (*in hortis*) and entertained many friends and relations. But while Roman nobles not involved in the ceremony might relax in the country, what of those Romans and Latins who could not leave their towns to attend at the Alban Mount? Pliny records that a chariot-race was held on the Capitol in Rome on the main day of the festival. In view of the lack of room on the Capitol and its physical un-suitability Pliny's account is often rejected, but he may have got only the place or details wrong (e.g. a chariot-race which ended in the victor pro-cessing up to Jupiter on the Capitol?) and some form of public entertain-ment may well have been provided for the bulk of the population in Rome. And if in Rome, why not also in some of the individual Latin cities? However, when all was completed on the Alban Mount a fire-signal from its summit blazed forth the news to Latium: '*vidit flammifera confectas nocte Latinas*' wrote Lucan.[146] (Jupiter Latiaris 'witnessed the bon-fire at night that ends the Latin festival').

It is not difficult to believe that a festival that lasted over one thousand years played a significant role in Roman public and private life when its celebration came round each year.

May

English poets, from Chaucer onwards, have regarded the month of May as a season of merriment. The Romans, however, might have been more in-clined to listen to James Russell Lowell who was less enthusiastic about the American climate: 'May is a pious fraud of the almanac'. They con-sidered it an unlucky month in which to be married and although the license of the Floralia may have enlivened the first day or so, on the whole the festivals of the month were not very cheerful, while the Lemuria, when ghosts walked abroad, was positively chilling, and further cere-monies of purification were required. There was much work to be done in the fields; as the rustic calendars prescribed, crops must be weeded, sheep sheared, wool washed, young bullocks broken in, vetches cut, and corn-fields lustrated; sacrifices to be made to Mercury and Flora, while Apollo was the protector of the month. On the other hand May was a period of growth and early Roman farmers may have felt that it would be pro-vocative to be too merry and that a more cautious attitude to the spirit world would be a better way to secure a good harvest.

The derivation of the word *Maius* was much debated by Roman scholars whose conclusions are set out by Macrobius, while Ovid, who offered three explanations (namely from *maiestas*, *maius* or the goddess Maia), is embarrassed by the variety of choice (*copiaque ipsa nocet*) and asks in despair what he is to do (*quid faciam?*). The simplest, and perhaps the most likely, explanation is the Roman goddess Maia, whose name derives from the root *mag* and indicates growth or increase. On 1 May, at a time when the crops were growing, she received a sacrifice offered by the *flamen Volcanalis,* and Aulus Gellius says that the books of the priests of the Roman people and many early books of prayers included 'Maia of Vulcan' among the deities to whom prayers were offered, but this connection with the fire-god Vulcan remains quite obscure.[147] Maia was also worshipped on 15 May along with Mercury, but this can be explained as a late development when she was confused with a Greek Maia who was the mother of Hermes (Mercury) in Greek legend.

| 1 May | KAL. MAI | F |

Maia

On May Day Maia received a sacrifice from the *flamen Volcanalis*, as already noted. The victim was a pregnant sow, which was a proper sacrifice for the earth-goddess Terra. Consequently some writers, including the antiqarian Cornelius Labeo, identified Maia with Terra.[148]

(Bona Dea ad saxum)

The first of May was the dedication day of the temple of Bona Dea on the slope of the Aventine, below a large rock. It was dedicated by Claudia, a Vestal Vergin, according to Ovid, but he may have confused her with another Vestal, Licinia, who in 123 BC wanted to dedicate an altar and chapel nearby but was forbidden by the pontiffs. Bona Dea may well have been an earth-goddess; she was so regarded by Cornelius Labeo who identified her with Maia, as well as with other deities as Fauna, Ops and Fatua (Macrob.1.12.21f.). If her name was merely a translation of Agathe Theos, a Greek goddess related to Hygieia (Health), she will have been introduced into Rome only in the third century BC, but she may have been an older deity who was later identified with her Greek counterpart. We know something of her ritual, thanks to Macrobius. Her cult was celebrated by women only: men were rigorously excluded. Wine taken into her temple had to be called milk (*lac*) and carried in a vessel called a honey-pot (*mellarium*); this may suggest an early agricultural origin. The head of the goddess had to be covered with vine-leaves. Many kinds of healing herbs were kept in her temple, as were snakes, which were closely associated with the arts of medicine. Myrtle was not allowed in the temple, according to a myth because Faunus had beaten his daughter Fauna (= Bona Dea) with a myrtle-rod. This reference to beating suggests the possibility of some rite of flagellation, and myrtle may have been normally excluded because it was so holy (taboo) and only to be used on special occasions. However that may be, the sacrifice offered to Bona Dea was a sow (*porca*). We are also told by Festus that the victim was called Damium, the priestess Damiatrix and the goddess herself Damia. There was a Greek deity named Damia, akin to Demeter, whose cult was found at Tarentum, whence it may have spread northwards to Rome.[149]

In general Bona Dea may well have been an earth-goddess who promoted the fertility of women and whose cult received accretions from other sources. She is best known in history from the scandalous attempt by P. Clodius who, dressed as a woman, penetrated into the celebrations; these, however, were not the rites of 1 May, but a ceremony held in the house of a magistrate in December (p. 199ff.).

Laribus (Ven. Esq.)

The Lares were guardian spirits of an individual household, of cross-roads (when they were celebrated at the Compitalia early in January: see above p. 58), and of the State when they bore the title of Lares Praestites and it was as such that they were worshipped on 1 May. These Guardian Lares had an altar (attributed to King Titus Tatius) which is probably the same as a *sacellum Larum* which Tacitus describes as one of the original corners of the *pomerium* at the north-west bend of the Palatine. Another monument was their temple at the top of the Via Sacra (see 27 June, p. 156). Ovid says that at the altar there were small images of the gods which were worn away with age, while a dog which used to stand at their feet had disappeared altogether in his time. He explains the dog as a watchful guardian, like the Lares Praestites: *pervigilantque Lares pervigilantque canes*. According to Plutarch the Lares were clothed in dog-skins, but on a denarius of 112/111 BC they are depicted as two young men, seated and with spears: they are naked to the waist and have garments (not much like dog-skins) draped over their legs; a dog sits between them; they recall two other protectors of Rome, Castor and Pollux.[150] Plutarch adds that some Romans interpreted the Lares as spirits of punishment like the Furies, helped by the dog to track down evil-doers. The connection between the Lares Praestites and dogs is not known; that the animals were sacrificed to the

Lares is possible but not very probable. From Ovid's general description
interest in the Lares Praestites seems to have declined, partly perhaps
because of Augustus' promotion of the Lares Compitales. (Pl. 4122).

3 May   V NON. MAI.   C

Florae (Ven.)

This entry, found only in the Venusine calendar, might refer to the last
day (consisting of Games) of the Floralia which had started on 27 April and
were linked with Flora's temple near the Circus Maximus, but more probably perhaps it was a ceremony at her other temple on the slope of the
Quirinal, of which the foundation date and history are not known (cf.
Degrassi, *In. It.* p. 454).

9, 11, 13 May   VII, V, III ID. MAI.   N *Dies religiosi*

LEMURIA

This festival of the dead was held on three non-successive days (even days
were considered unlucky, and all but two of the forty-five festivals marked
in large letters in the calendars were held on odd days). The calendar-
entries show that the Lemuria was a public cult, but the nature of the
sacrifice offered at it is unknown; nearly all we know, deriving from Ovid,
applies to private and domestic rites.[151]

The dead were celebrated in two periods. The ceremonies in February,
the Parentalia, Feralia and Caristia, as we have seen, were quiet gentle
occasions, but the Lemuria, which Ovid considered to be older than the
Feralia, was a much more fearsome affair when ghosts walked and had to be
propitiated. The *lemures* were wandering spirits of the dead who returned
to visit and perhaps threaten their kinsfolk: indeed Ovid records an
unacceptable derivation of the word from *Remus*, whose violent death was
atoned for by establishing the festival. They are defined by Porphyrion as
'wandering and terrifying shades of men who died untimely deaths'
(*umbras vagantes*), and by Nonius Marcellinus as 'nocturnal apparitions
(*larvae*) and terrors of ghosts and beasts'.[152]

In the domestic rite, described by Ovid, the head of the family gets up at
midnight, his feet bare (knots or impediments of any kind must be
avoided). He then makes an apotropaic gesture with his thumb held
between his closed fingers, washes his hands in pure water, and walks
through the house, spitting out black beans from his mouth, with head
averted, saying, 'with these beans I redeem me and mine'. This he repeats
nine times without looking back, while the ghosts come behind and pick

up the beans unseen. He then washes again, clashes some bronze vessels and repeats nine times the word 'Ghosts of my fathers, be gone' (*manes exite paternae*: words which some scholars regard as an error by Ovid.). He then looks back, and all should be well. The significance of the beans is uncertain. They were sometimes regarded as taboo; thus they could not be touched or even mentioned by the *flamen Dialis*. Possibly they were symbols of fertility, to give strength and new life, or possibly they were surrogates for living members of the family, whom the ghosts might wish to snatch away. But did the Romans of the late Republic take such beliefs at all seriously? R. M. Ogilvie thinks that they did: 'At first sight it is difficult to imagine Livy or Horace or Agrippa solemnly getting out of bed and going through this ritual. And yet they probably did – at least in a modified form.'[153] There was a strong streak of superstition even in many educated Romans.

11 May   V ID. MAI.   N *Dies religiosus*

Ma[niae]. (Ant. mai.)

A sacrifice was made probably to Mania rather than to Mars or Mater Matuta. Mania was the mother of the Lares (Mater Larum); her name probably means 'the good one' and may be a euphemistic way of referring to the death-goddess. Thus the Lemuria would be a suitable time for her to receive sacrifice; we have already seen (p. 59) how she was worshipped at the Compitalia. When danger threatened a family, an effigy of Mania might be hung on the door of the house. We also hear that ugly human figures made from flour were called Maniae or Maniolae, but these may be different from the figures of the goddess herself. Further, nurses used the word for bogeymen with which to frighten small children.[154]

14 May   PR ID   C

Marti Invicto (Ven.)

The temple of Mars Invictus was founded in the Circus Flaminius by D. Junius Brutus Callaicus, consul in 135 BC. Designed by a Greek architect and decorated with verses of the poet Accius, it contained a colossal statue of Mars by Scopas. This is probably the cult indicated in the Venusine calendar reference. An entry, '[. . .]*Invicto*', in the Fasti Antiates maiores for 15 May does not necessarily refer to Mars, and therefore the Venusine calendar need not be assumed wrongly to have anticipated the ceremony by one day.[155]

(*Argeis*)

A procession of the Argei took place, as we have seen on 16–17 March, but we do not know what happened at their *sacella*. However, more is known about the activities on 14 May. Dionysius of Halicarnassus, who witnessed the ceremonies, says that after offering the prescribed preliminary sacrifice, the pontiffs, the Vestal Virgins and the praetors, together with those other citizens that might lawfully attend the rites, threw from the sacred bridge into the Tiber 30 effigies made like men, which were called Argei; this, according to Dionysius, was a later substitution for a human sacrifice to Saturn in primitive times. Other sources add a little more detail: the wife of the *flamen Dialis*, the *flaminica*, who accompanied the procession, was forbidden to comb or dress her hair, that is she must display signs of mourning in place of the wedding dress that she usually wore (Aulus Gellius); the Argei, which were thrown from the Sublician bridge, numbered 27 and were made of rushes (Varro); they were thrown into the river by the Vestals (Festus); according to an ancient tradition old men over sixty were once thrown from the bridge (Ovid) and *sexagenarios de ponte* was a well-known proverb in Cicero's day (Cicero), which Ovid explains away as younger men driving older men from the voting gangways (*pontes*) in order to control the elections. Finally, Plutarch calls the whole ceremony 'the greatest of purifications'.[156]

The ceremony is dated by Ovid to the 14 May and this is probably to be preferred to Dionysius' date of 15 May. Another discrepancy arises about the number of the Argei, namely the puppets and the chapels since the same name covers both. Dionysius puts it at 30, but Varro gives 27 or 24. The reading of Varro's text is slightly uncertain, but 27 is more likely (if 24 be accepted, it might apply to 6 chapels in each of the 4 Servian regions of Rome). The number 27 (3 x 9) had a mystical significance in Greece and Rome: thus in times of stress, e.g. in 207 and 200 BC, processions of 27 virgins marched through the streets of Rome signing hymns to Juno, and at the Secular Games of Augustus in 17 BC choirs of 27 boys and 27 girls sang in the temple of Apollo the ode which Horace had composed. If Dionysius' number, 30, be accepted (and after all he saw the puppets actually being thrown into the river, but of course he might have miscounted or rounded off the number), the 30 chapels probably corresponded with the 30 wards (*curiae*) of the city, one in each. One further reasonable suggestion may be added, namely that the puppets had been placed in the chapels by the procession on 17 March and were collected on 14 May by the procession which then wended its way through the city until it reached the Sublician bridge, where the Vestals finally disposed of them. Lastly there is the question, which the Romans themselves could not answer, as to what deity was honoured or appeased by the rite: Ovid and Dionysius believed it to be Saturn, Verrius Flaccus thought of Dis Pater, and some scholars believe it to be the river Tiber, but the truth escapes us. However it is now generally agreed that it was a very ancient ceremony and that Wissowa was wrong in supposing that puppets were substituted for human victims as late as the third century BC.[157]

Thus we can get quite a good idea of what was to be seen on the streets of Rome on 14 May, but the original purpose of the ceremony remained unknown even to the Romans who witnessed it and thus an immense volume of modern speculation has accumulated, illustrated by numerous parallels from very varied parts of the world. Here it will suffice merely to mention some of the theories. A substitute for human sacrifice? If so, was there a time when the elders of the tribe were periodically killed off or alternatively was some other human sacrifice made to some unseeen power (e.g. the spirit of the Tiber), or had puppets always been used symbolically for men? The Romans, however, had no tradition of human sacrifice, which they practised only rarely and in very exceptional circumstances. Did the puppets represent the dying Spirit of Vegetation, immersed in order to revivify him for the next season? But the date is not very suitable. Was there significance in the fact that the pontiffs had the care of Rome's oldest bridge, the wooden Sublician (whatever may be thought of the derivation of *pontifices* from *pons* and *facere*, 'bridge-makers'), and had therefore the river Tiber to be appeased, since his dignity had been affronted by the building of this early wooden bridge over which his possible victims could cross in safety? Did the presence of the Vestal Virgins suggest any connection with protecting the ripening crops? Was the rite semi-dramatic rather than primarily sacrificial? Did the immersion in water suggest a rain-spell? Had the Argei anything to do with the Greek Argives? And so the guesses go on. Perhaps it is safest to stick to Plutarch's belief that it was a great act of purification, whether or not we tack on the idea that it was a purification from all evils which had accumulated during the past year and which were personified in the Argei as demons, and thus it followed naturally just after the more private and domestic expulsion of ghosts at the Lemuria.

15 May   ID. MAI.   NP

Feriae Iovi (Ven.)

The *Ides* of each month were sacred to Jupiter

[Mercurio], Maiae, [. . .] Invicto (Ant. mai.)
Mercurio, Maiae ad Circum Maximum (Caer.)
Natalis Mercurii (Phil.)
Sacrum Mercurio (Menol.)

The cult of Maia on 15 May was due, as we have seen (p. 116), to her being identified with the Greek Maia, the mother of Hermes = Mercury who was worshipped on this day, which was recognized as Mercury's birthday. His temple was outside the *pomerium* on the Aventine, above the Circus Maximus, and was traditionally dedicated in 495 BC; it seems to have been shared with his 'mother' Maia. Thus the *Ides* of May became a festival for traders (*mercatores*) and Mercury's temple the centre of their guild (*collegium*). Ovid (F.5.673ff.) refers to an *aqua Mercurii* (a spring or fountain) near the Capena Gate, from which a merchant would draw water in fumigated jars; with this water he wetted a laurel bough and then with this he sprinkled the goods he had on sale as well as his own hair. Even Sir James Frazer, with his vast range of knowledge of customs, provides no parallel to this curious procedure. Ovid then cynically makes the merchant pray to Mercury for forgiveness for his past and future perjuries, and for profit and the continued ability to cheat his customers. Mercury, whose name derived from *merx, merces*, 'merchandise', had himself in legend been a thief. It would be reasonable to suppose, despite the lack of any direct evidence, that the guilds of merchants spent the evening of the *Ides* dining and feasting together.[158]

The identity of the Unconquered god (Invicto) must remain a mystery, unless the Venusine calendar has misdated by one day the festival of Mars Invictus, which is not probable (p. 119).

21 May   XII KAL. IUN.   NP

AGONALIA
Vediovi (Ven.)

Since all but one of the calendars name only Agonalia, it is uncertain what deity was worshipped: possibly Vediovis, but not certainly since in the parallel case of 11 January we find Carmentalia on many calendars and *Iuturnae* in Ant. Mai., with the latter not being worshipped in the former ceremony (see above p. 64). For Vediovis see p. 56; for Agonalia, p. 60.

23 May   X KAL. IUN.   NP

TUBILUSTRIUM
Feriae Volcano (Ven. and Amit.)

This was a repetition of the Tubilustrium held on 23 March (see p. 94); if the ceremony was designed merely to purify the trumpets used in summoning the assembly on the next day, the cause of its repetition is obvious. But this is less clear if the purification of the army was in some way involved. In that case it possibly goes back to early days when Rome was struggling against her immediate neighbours and each side wanted to fight during the period when it could spare men from the cultivation of the fields and to deliver a knock-out blow (e.g. the destruction of the enemy's crops) between the sowing and harvesting of its own corn: campaigns therefore tended to be brief, although 23 May does seem very early for the lustration of the trumpets of a *returning* army.[159] What the ceremony meant later, when campaigns lasted months longer, cannot be guessed.

The festival of Vulcan was unconnected with the Tubilustrium, but the Romans invented a link: since he was a smith as well as a fire-god, he was regarded (e.g. by Ovid, *F*.5.725f.) as the smith who made the trumpets of the Tubilustrium. Vulcan had some connection with Maia, as we have seen (p. 116), and his main festival was on 23 August. (Pl. 4123).

24 May   IX KAL. IUN.   F

Q.R.C.F.

As in March, the Tubilustrium was followed by the formal dimissal of the Comitia by the *Rex Sacrorum*: after this, legal business could be transacted (p. 94).

25 May   VIII KAL. IUN.   C

Fortunae Publicae Populi Romani Quiritium in Colle Quirinale (Caer.)
Fortunae Primigeniae in Colle (Ven.)

As we have seen (under 5 April, p. 100), the three temples of Fortuna were probably dedicated to the same Fortuna, namely (in full) Fortuna Populi Romani Quiritium Primigenia. The temple on the Quirinal which Livy (29.36.8) names as Fortuna Primigenia was vowed by P. Sempronius Tuditanus in 204 BC and dedicated ten years later. Unless the Venusine calendar is wrong, another temple of Fortuna Primigenia stood on the Capitol (see under 13 November). (Pl. 4124).

Feriae Conceptivae

(*Ambarvalia*)

This festival was a 'beating of the bounds', a purification of the fields from evil influences, in which sacrificial victims were led around the boundaries of the area involved, and then offered to the appropriate spirits or deities. Within this magic circle the land was thus freed from harm ('lustration' comes from *luere*, to 'free'). The Ambarvalia was both public and private, and concerned the boundaries both of primitive Rome and of individual farmers. It was a movable feast (*conceptivae*) and so was not recorded in the calendars, but it seems to have been held in May when the rustic *Menologia* say '*segetes lustrantur*', and 29 May possibly came to be regarded as a customary date. A similar agricultural festival in honour of Dea Dia was held in May by the Arval Brethren in their sacred grove outside Rome (see p. 30). If it was identical with the Ambarvalia is unsure, though a sentence of Paulus (5L), as emended, may suggest it: *Ambarvales hostiae dicebantur quae pro arvis a duodecim* (MSS *duobus*) *fratribus sacrificantur* ('the victims that were sacrificed on behalf of the fields by the twelve Brethren were called the Ambarvales victims'). What we know about the Arvales reveals little more about the Ambarvalia.

More is known about the private than the public celebration, since Cato records the farmer's prayer and both Virgil and Tibullus give poetic descriptions of the feasts. Cato (*Agr.* 141) tells how the land must be purified. A *suovetaurilia*, a procession of a pig, sheep and ox, must be led around it, and the following words used: 'That with the good help of the gods, success may crown our work, I bid thee, Manius [a bailiff, soothsayer or perhaps a 'John Doe'?], to take care to purify my farm, my land, my ground with this *suovetaurilia*, in whatever part thou thinkest best for them to be driven or carried around. Make a prayer with wine to Janus and Jupiter, and say 'Father Mars I pray and beseech thee . . . ' The first part of this prayer has already been quoted on p. 84. It continues, 'to this intent, to the intent of purifying (*lustrandi*) my farm, my land, my ground, and of making an expiation (*lustri faciendi*), deign to accept the offering of these suckling victims (*suovetaurilibus lactentibus*)'. Also 'heap the cakes with the knife and see that the oblation cake (*fertum*) be near, then present the victims'. Then the pig, the lamb, and the calf are sacrificed, but if favourable omens are not obtained, an atonement must be made by a further offering, or if any particular animal does not satisfy Mars, then 'in as much as thou wast not pleased by the offering of that pig, I make atonement with this pig'.

While Cato takes us to the central act of the ceremony, the poets give more of the background of the country festivals of lustration, where beside

Mars, the god of strength, Ceres, the goddess of growth, might be worshipped. Tibullus (2.1) calls on Bacchus and Ceres and warns that no ill-omened words must be uttered as 'we purify the crops and fields in the fashion handed down from our ancestors of old'. On this holy day man and beast must rest: the ploughman hangs up his share, garlanded oxen stand by their well-filled mangers, the women put aside their spinning; all celebrations must be ritually clean, with hands washed ceremonially, and free from taint of sexual intercourse during the previous night. Then 'to the shining altar goes the sacred lamb, and behind a procession clad in white and with olive leaves in their hair'. Then came prayer, the killing of the victims, and the examination of their entrails, and if all was well portions were prepared on the altar-fire, and the celebrants could settle down to feast and drink. Virgil too describes (Geor.1.345) how the victim was led three times round the young crops, followed by a singing, dancing crowd who, wreathed with oak, bade Ceres come to their homes.

Such celebrations of the Ambarvalia were still held by individual farmers throughout the Republic, but it also became an offical feast. When Rome was a group of Iron Age villages, victims could easily be driven round the bounds of each settlement and later around the united town. But as Rome grew, it would become physically impossible to follow her expanding boundaries beyond a few miles: instead sacrifices were apparently made at certain fixed points. Thus Strabo (5.3.2) recalls that in his day during the reign of Augustus, priests held a festival called Ambarvia both at a spot called Festi, between the fifth and sixth milestones from Rome, and also on the same day at several other places which were regarded as boundaries. This must refer to the Ambarvalia, whether or not the priests are to be identified with the Arval Brethren.

Later parallels (or survivals) lie to hand. The ceremonies of the Christian Church on Rogation Days have much in common with Roman Robigalia (the *maior Rogatio* fell on 25 April, as did the Robigalia), but they also reflect one feature at least of the Ambarvalia, namely the circum-ambulation of the fields. Thus in the ritual of the *Litania maior* prayers are said for the harvest and an Italian priest leads his flock around the fields. At the ceremony of the beating of the bounds of the English parish, common in medieval times, on one of the three days before Ascension Day the minister, churchwardens, and parishioners used to process round the boundaries, praying for the prosperity of the fields and the preservation of the rights of the parish. The bounds were beaten with willow rods and sometimes boys of the parish were also beaten or bumped on the ground. The ceremony would help to fix the parish limits on the minds of the coming generation in an age when maps were rare.

June

The derivation of the name of the month June was debated by the Romans, and Ovid gave the discussion a mythological form by picturing three rival deities claiming the honour: Juno argued that her own name was the origin, while Juventas, the goddess of Youth, submitted that the name derived from *junior*, and then Concordia pointed out that she had reconciled and joined together the Romans and Sabines (*his iunctis*, from *jungo*). The poet tactfully declined to choose. However, *Juno* itself may well derive from *iuvenis*, ('young woman' or 'bride') rather than the same root as that of Jupiter, and, if it is accepted, Ovid's two claims could be reconciled as essentially one. However, the Romans remained uncertain, as shown by the improbable tradition that the name of the month was connected with M. Iunius Brutus, the first consul who performed a sacrifice on the Caelian hill (not to Juno but to a goddess named Carna) on 1 June when Tarquin had been expelled.[160]

If the month was named after Juno (perhaps via Etruscan Uni), her links with it are not outstanding. True, the *Kalends* were sacred to her (see p. 42), but so were the *Kalends* of every month: this was probably because she was thought to help women and their monthly periods and so she became associated with the moon. In very early times, when the Romans were using a true lunar calendar, each month after sighting the new moon a minor pontiff and the Rex Sacrorum sacrificed to Juno and announced the date of the *Nones* (see p. 43), while the wife of the *rex* also sacrificed to her in the Regia.[161] Another link between Juno and the month of June was that on the *Kalends* Juno Regina was worshipped in her temple on the Capitol, which had been dedicated on that day in 344 BC (see below); Juno of course also received worship on the Capitol in September in the temple which she shared with Jupiter Optimus Maximus and Minerva. In all, her connections with the month of June were not at all remarkable.

The first half of June, like all May, was not regarded as an auspicious time to marry. In fact Ovid says (*F*.6.219ff), perhaps with poetic licence, that he consulted the wife of the *flamen Dialis* about the marriage of his own daughter and was advised to wait until after 15 June, that is until after the annual rubbish from the temple of Vesta had been swept into the Tiber. Also many, if not all, of the days between 7 and 15 were *religiosi* when no public or private business should be done or journeys undertaken, not so much because it was technically unlawful but rather ill-omened. According to the rustic calendars the month was under the protection of Mercury and sacred to Hercules and Fons Fortuna, and farmers were told to cut the hay and to fork the soil around the vines.

1 June KAL. IUN N

Iunoni Monetae (Ven.)
Iunoni in Arce (Ant. mai.)

The temple of Juno Moneta, vowed by M. Furius Camillus in 345 BC, was dedicated on 1 June 344; it probably replaced an earlier cult centre of the goddess. The church of S. Maria in Aracoeli on the Capitol later occupied its site. The title Moneta was given to Juno in gratitude for a timely warning (*monere*), either because her sacred geese had saved the Capitol from the attack by the Gauls in 390 when their hissing had awakened Manlius to the danger in the nick of time, or according to Cicero because during an earthquake a voice from Juno's temple warned the people to offer an expiatory sacrifice (*procuratio*) of a pregnant sow.[162] Later, when the Romans started to use money during the Pyrrhic War, a mint was set up in or adjacent to her temple, and so *moneta* came to mean 'mint' and thus by a round-about route our word 'money' derives from Juno Moneta, 'the Warner'. (Pls 24, 4125, 26).

Marti in Clivo (Ant. mai.)

The temple of Mars lay outside the Capena Gate on the Slope of Mars between the first and second milestones on the left-hand side of the Appian Way; this stretch of road was repaired in 189 BC when it was provided with a portico; it became known as the Covered Way (Via Tecta) and the district around as *ad Martis*. The temple contained a statue of Mars and of some wolves. It was dedicated on 1 June, probably in 388. Soldiers when setting off for war assembled here, at least on occasion, and here began the *transvectio equitum*, which was a spectacular commemorative victory march by the Roman cavalry, held on 15 July (see p. 164).

(Tempestatibus)

L. Cornelius Scipio, consul in 259 BC, dedicated a temple to the Tempests after his survival from a great storm off Corsica in the First Punic War. This was recorded in Saturnian verse in his epitaph in the tomb of the Scipios outside the Capena Gate; the temple was nearby. Cicero, in asking whether natural phenomena, such as rainbows and clouds, should be regarded as deities, remarks that the *tempestates* had been consecrated according to the rites of the Roman people. The date of the celebration, however, was doubtful: Ovid assigns it to 1 June, but one calendar (Ant. mai.) gives 23 December. Ovid may, of course, be wrong, but there could have been two temples to the Tempestates or a restoration of the one.[164]

(Carnae)

Carna was a very old goddess, who had a temple on the Caelian hill and was worshipped on 1 June.[165] Ovid clouds the issue by identifying her with the 'goddess of hinges' (Cardea?) who 'by her divine power opens what is closed, and closes what is open'. This may merely have been to allow him to introduce the story of the seduction of Cardea by Janus, who as recompense gave her a white thorn with which she could ward off attacks by vampires *(striges)*. Ovid gives a horrific description of these ghastly screech-owls; their attacks could be thwarted by thrice touching the doorposts with arbutus leaves, and thrice so marking the threshold; after sprinkling the entrance with special water, the raw intestines of a two-month-old sow were offered. Then came the prayer, 'Ye birds of night, spare the child's inner organs: a small victim falls for a small child. Take, I pray ye, a heart for a heart, entrails for entrails. This life we give you for a better life.' After the sacrifice the entrails were exposed in the open air and those present at the sacrifice were forbidden to look back. This example of vicarious sacrifice has been quoted fully, partly to illustrate an interesting piece of magical belief, partly because although Ovid has wrongly identified Carna with Cardea, the ritual may perhaps apply to the former since Macrobius says of Carna 'that this goddess presides over man's vital organs' *(humanis visceribus)*.

Whether or not Carna could help drive off vampires, Macrobius says that prayers were offered to her for the preservation of the liver, heart and other internal organs. As sacrifices bean-meal and lard *(pulte fabacia et larido)* were offered because this was the best food for strengthening the body: 'for the *Kalends* of June are also popularly called *Kalendae Fabariae*, because in this month mature beans are offered in the sacrifice'. Ovid asks why fat bacon is eaten on the *Kalends*, and why beans are mixed with hot spelt; he replies that these plain foods do not hurt the bowels, and implies that such an offering to Carna will guarantee good digestion for the coming year. Varro adds that on this day bean porridge was offered to the gods both publicly and privately. Though this custom long survived (a late inscription refers to the festival as Carneria), Carna herself seems increasingly to have sunk into obscurity. At the Lemuria, as we have seen (p. 118), beans were used to eject ghosts from a house, but this does not necessarily imply that Carna was a goddess of the underworld (as Wissowa suggested), nor need she be turned into a moon goddess (with Pettazzoni). Her function seems to have been to promote a healthy body, even if her name does not, in fact, derive from *caro, carnis* 'flesh'.[166]

1 Sacrificial procession of ox, sheep and pig (*suovetaurilia*). From the Altar of Cn.Domitius Ahenobarbus

2 Sacrifice of bull in front of altar. The victim's head (bottom right) is held to the ground for the blow

3 Marble relief of Vestal Virgins
feasting. From the Altar of Pietas
Augusta
4 Flamen and pontifex. Detail from
the Ara Pacis

5 Bronze liver from Piacenza, used for
hepatoscopy
6 Sacred chickens feeding (*signa ex tripudiis*).
Depicted on *aes signatum*, an early form of
bronze money
7 Haruspex examining entrails after sacrifice

8 The Tiber Island, on which lay many temples, e.g. of Vediovis and Aesculapius
9 Cult statue of Vediovis from his temple behind the Tabularium
10 Restored *aedicula* of Juturna in the Roman Forum

11 Temple of Castor and Pollux after excavation in 1871, showing main stairway and steps on the east side
12 General view of Temple of Castor and Pollux from the Palatine

13 Church of S.Nicola in Carcere built over (and partly incorporating) three temples in the Forum Holitorium. One is ascribed to Juno Sospita, a second to Spes

14 Statue of Juno Sospita, wearing goat-skin and advancing to battle. From Lanuvium

15 Bronze statuette of a Lar

16 Tomb of the baker Eurysaces near the Porta Maggiore in Rome. The Feast of Ovens (Fornacalia) was held in February

17 Air photograph of the Regia in the Forum
18 The Sacra Via, between the Temple of Vesta (r.) and the Regia (l.)

19 Intaglio, showing the moving of the sacred shields (*ancilia*) by two Salian priests
20 Biconical bronze urn, with armed dancers. Early 7th century BC, from Bisenzio
21 Head of terracotta statue of Minerva, found near S.Omobono in the Forum Boarium. Late 6th century BC

22 Front of Temple of Magna Mater on the Palatine, with altar in foreground

23 Altar of Vermina, who protected cattle from worm disease (*verminatio*). Dedicated by A.Postumius Albinus, probably the consul of 180 BC. Found in the Servian Agger in Rome

24 Reconstruction of Temple of Juno Moneta from a relief in Ostia, showing the geese which traditionally saved the Capitol
25 Seated goddess with child
26 Sacred area of S.Omobono. One temple lies on left in front of church, another under the church. One was that of Mater Matuta

27 Temple of Jupiter Stator from the north
28 Part of the Severan marble plan of Rome, showing the Temple
(*aedes*) of Hercules Musarum

29 The earliest temple of Apollo in Rome, in the Campus Martius. The surviving remains belong to a reconstruction by C.Sosius *c*.33 BC
30 Republican temples C, B and A in the Largo Argentina, from the south. Identifications are very uncertain: C has been claimed for Feronia, B for Fortuna Huiusque Diei and A for Juno Curitis

31 Statue of Hercules Victor,
excavated near S.Maria in
Cosmedin
32 Girls sacrificing to Diana. A
fresco in the Vatican
33 Archaic altar in the Roman
Forum, traditionally identified
with the Volcanal

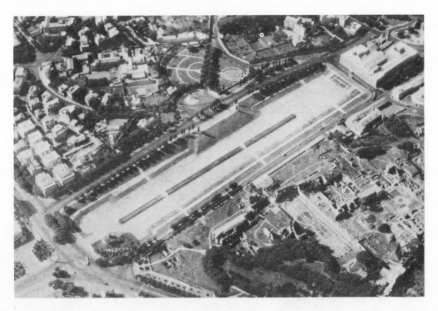

35 Air view of the Circus Maximus between the Aventine and Palatine hills
36 Chariot-race in the Circus Maximus, depicted on a sarcophagus

< 34 Two surviving temples in the Forum Boarium near the Tiber, the one called
the Temple of Fortuna, the round one being assigned to Mater Matuta or Vesta. One in
fact may have been dedicated to the harbour god Portunus

37 Temple of Saturn, where the State Treasury (Aerarium) was housed. Traditionally founded in 498 BC, the existing podium belongs to a rebuilding in 42 BC

38 Remains of the Republican Rostra, during excavations in 1956. To right lies the Lapis Niger and probably the true Volcanal
39 Funeral scene. From Amiternum

41 For caption see page 145

All coins illustrated are Roman denarii, unless otherwise stated. The name of the moneyer and the date of issue is usually given. The illustrations are slightly enlarged (except nos 32 and 35, which are reduced).

40

1 King Numa holding a *lituus*; lighted altar; *victimarius* leading a goat. L.Pomponius Milo. *c*.97 BC (p. 24)

2 Flamen's *apex* between two Salian shields. L.Licinius Stolo. 17 BC (p. 86)

3–8 Five types of coins were issued in 78 BC by M.Volteius, referring (through the deities portrayed) to the Ludi Romani, Plebeii, Ceriales, Megalenses and Apollinares:

3 Laureate head of Jupiter (p. 101)

4 The Capitoline temple

5 Head of Liber, wearing ivy-wreath

6 Ceres in a biga of snakes, holding torches

7 Cybele in a biga of lions

8 Apollo's tripod, with snakes coiled around

9 Genius Populi Romani (?) seated on a curule chair, holding a sceptre and with foot on globe. P.Lentulus. 74 BC (p. 52)

10 Jugate heads of the Dioscuri. M'.Cordius Rufus. 46 BC (p. 66)

11 The Dioscuri on horseback. Common reverse type on denarii after first issue in 211 BC (p. 66)

12 Head of Juno Sospita. L.Roscius Fabatus. 64 BC (p. 71)

13 Obv. of 12. Girl and snake facing each other (p. 71)

14 Ceres seated, with corn-ears and snake. The inscription (C.

MEMMIUS AED. CERIALIA PREIMUS FECIT) alludes to the first celebration of the Cerialia in or before 211 BC. C.Memmius, 56 BC (p. 101)

15 Q.Fabius Pictor, *flamen Quirinalis*, seated and holding a *flamen's apex* and wearing a praetor's armour, namely the praetor of 189 BC. N.Fabius Pictor. 126 BC (p. 79)

16 Helmeted head of bearded Mars. Anonymous didrachm. 280–276 BC (p. 86)

17 Head of Liber, wearing ivy-wreath. L.Cassius. 78 BC (p. 91)

18 Rev. of 17. Head of Libera, wearing vine-wreath (p. 91)

19 Head of Venus. Julius Caesar. 47–46 BC (p. 96)

41

20 Half-length figure of a boy, holding a tablet inscribed SORS. M. Plaetorius. 69 BC (p. 100)

21 Temple of Venus Erucina on Mt Eryx in Sicily. C.Considius Nonianus. 57 BC (p. 107)

22 Lares Praestites seated, with dog between. Bust of Vulcan, with tongs, above. L.Caesius. 112 or 111 BC (p. 118)

23 Bust of Vulcan, with tongs over shoulder. L.Cotta. 105 BC (pp. 123,179)

24 Head of Fortuna Populi Romani. Q.Sicinius. 49 BC. (P. 123)

25 Head of Juno Moneta. T.Carisius. 46 BC (p. 127)

26 Rev. of 25. Anvil and punch dies, with tongs and hammer (p. 127)

27 Head of Vesta. Q.Cassius.

55 BC (p. 149)

28 Rev. of 27. Temple of Vesta. Within, curule chair. urn, and tablet inscribed A C (*absolvo, condemno*) (p. 149)

29 Hercules playing lyre. Inscribed HERCULES MUSA-RUM. Q.Pomponius Musa. 66 BC (p. 171)

30 Jugate heads of Honos and Virtus. Fufius Kalenus. 70 BC (p. 165)

31 Victoria in biga. T.Cloelius. 128 BC (p. 166)

32 Sestertius of the emperor Tiberius, showing the Temple of Concord. In the central shrine is a statue of Concordia, flanked by Mercury (l.) and Hercules (r.); above the pediment are statues of other deities. AD 35–36 (p. 167)

33 Radiate head of Sol. M.Antonius. 42 BC (p. 171)

34 Head of Diana. A.Postu-

mius Albinus. 81 BC (p. 174)

35 Head of Janus on a bronze libral *as*. 225–217 BC (p. 176)

36 Sulla, crowned by Victory, in quadriga, celebrating his triumph. L.Sulla. 82 BC (pp. 196,215)

37 Rome, seated on a pile of armour and crowned by Victory. Records the first celebration of Sulla's Ludi Victoriae; *Sex. Nonius praetor ludos Victoriae primus fecit*. M.Nonius Sufenas. 59 BC (p. 196)

38 Voting scene. One voter receives ballot from attendant below the *pons*; another places his in the box (*cista*). P.Nerva. 113 or 112 BC (p. 229)

39 Voting scene. Voter dropping tablet marked V into *cista*. L.Cassius Longinus. 63 BC (p. 229)

3 June   III NON. IUN.   C

Bellonae in Circo Flaminio (Ven.)

A temple to Bellona, the war-goddess, was vowed by Appius Claudius
Caecus in 296 BC during a war against Etruscans and Samnites, and
dedicated a few years later in the Campus Martius near the later Circus of
Flaminius. Fragments of the Severan marble plan of Rome now show that
it can no longer be identified with the Republican temple discovered in
1937. It was just outside the walls of Rome and so it could conveniently be
used as a meeting-place for the Senate for receiving those foreign
ambassadors who were not to be admitted into the city or for welcoming
returning Roman generals who were reporting to the Senate or asking for
a triumph, since as long as they held *imperium* they could not enter within
the walls. In front of the temple stood a little pillar (*columella*) over which a
fetial priest, in declaring war on an overseas enemy, hurled a spear into
'enemy territory' (see p. 30).

Bellona was sometimes identified with the shadowy Nerio, the cult-
partner of Mars (see n. 114), and with the Greek war-goddess, Enyo (some
even think her origin may have been Greek, since she cannot be traced
back earlier than 296 BC).[167]

4 June   PR. NON. IUN.   C

Herculi Magno Custodi (Ven.)
Ludi in Minicia (Phil.)

Ovid (*F*.6.209ff.) says that the temple of Custodian Hercules was near the
Circus Flaminius and refers to an inscription of Sulla, who may have
restored rather than first dedicated the temple. It probably was the temple
of Hercules, built on the ordering of the Sibylline Books, at which
supplicationes were offered in 218 BC after Hannibal's initial victories. The
Porticus Minucia was built in the Circus Flaminius in 110, and the Games
held there may have been linked to the neighbouring cult of Hercules.

5 June   NON. IUN.   N

Dio Fidio in Colle (Ven.)

Dius Fidius appears to mean 'Divine Good Faith (*fides*). There has been
much discussion whether this spirit was originally the same as or different

from Semo Sancus: at any rate they ultimately came to be unified.[168] The Semones were probably vague spirits and are to be identified with the *semunes* in the hymn of the Arval Brethren (though whether these had something to do with 'sowing' is uncertain). One of them became personalized as Sancus, which seems to have been a Sabine name (Sancus was sometimes corrupted into Sanctus, as in Propertius 4.9.74, where he is identified with Hercules). In historical times he was linked with oaths and treaties, and an everyday oath was *medius fidius* or *me dius fidius* (or indeed *me hercule*). These oaths curiously had to be taken in the open air: thus one of Plutarch's *Roman Questions* (28) was 'Why are boys made to go out of the house when they want to swear?'. The correct answer presumably was in order that the oath-taker might not hide from the god of the sky. In fact Dius Fidius may be merely a specialized form of the sky-god Jupiter, an example of the common practice whereby specialized functions of major gods were channelled off into a new minor deities. The roof of the temple of Dius Fidius had to be open to the sky. He may also perhaps be related to Fisius Sansios or Fisouios Sansios of the Iguvine Tablets (see p. 83).

The temple of Semo Sancus Dius Fidius (to give him his full title) was on the Quirinal, between the Vie Nazionale and Quirinale near the gardens of S. Silvestro degli Arcioni. Allegedly founded by Tarquinius Superbus, it was not dedicated until 466 BC. It contained a statue of Gaia Caecilia or Tanaquil, wife of Tanquinius Priscus; on the girdle were amulets called *praestia* from which worshippers used to take scrapings as protective talismans. It also housed the early treaty between Rome and Gabii, inscribed on an ox-hide. In a shrine was a deposit of bronze rings (*aenei orbes*) which had been made from the confiscated goods of a traitor Vitruvius in 329; these could be parallel to the *urfeta* (= *orbita*), the ring or disk held by the officiating priest at Iguvium. A dedication to Semo, found on the Quirinal, was made by a company of Bidental priests (*decuria sacerdotum bidentalium*); another from the Tiber Island indicates a cult there also. A *bidental* was a place struck by lightning, where an expiatory sacrifice of two-year-old sheep (*bidentes*) had been offered. The priests presumably made such offerings to Semo Sancus. The inscription from the Tiber Island was seen by, or known to, the Christian writers, Justin Martyr and Tertullian, who also mention a statue, and misinterpreted it as referring to Simon Magus, the magician. Near the Quirinal temple was a gate called Porta Sanqualis which embodied the name of Sancus. The cult of Semo, who guaranteed oaths, thus long continued in Rome and may have been more prominent in public life than its minor character suggests.[169]

7 June   VII ID. IUN   N *Dies religiosus*

(Vesta aperitur)

The worship of Vesta culminated in the Vestalia on 9 June, but some days both before and after were consecrated to her and declared *dies religiosi* as well as *nefasti*. On the 7th the storehouse (*penus*), the inner sanctum, of the temple of Vesta was opened, but only for women, since men were forbidden to enter the temple; it was closed again on the 15th. The cult will be discussed in connection with the festival on 9 June.

(Piscatorii Ludi)

Ovid recalls seeing Games held on the Campus Martius, named after the river Tiber, which were celebrated by fishermen. Festus, however, places them on the other side of the river. The calendar from Amiternum assigns 8 December to 'Tiberino in Insula'. Thus, as the god controlled the centre of the river, perhaps the celebrations were held on both banks. Festus records that these Games were celebrated by the praetor urbanus on behalf of the fishermen of the Tiber 'whose catch is not taken to the market but to the Area of Vulcan, because that sort of live fish is given to that god as a substitute for human souls'. Varro adds that at the Volcanalia on 23 August (see p. 179) people threw animals into the fire as substitutes for themselves (*pro se*). This curious procedure can be explained as offering to the fire-god creatures that, when alive, were usually safe from him, in order that he might spare objects that might easily catch fire in the heat of June.[170] Vulcan's shrine (Volcanal) was in the Roman Forum at the foot of the Capitol in the Area Volcani which contained no temple. Little is known about the worship of Tiber (Tiberinus), which was very old. Its institution was attributed to Romulus and appeared in the litany of the pontiffs and in the prayers of the augurs.[171]

8 June   VI. ID. IUN.   N *Dies religiosus*

Menti in Capitolio

In accordance with a Sibylline oracle a temple was vowed to Mens (Mind or Right Thinking) by the praetor T. Otacilius in 217 BC after the battle of Trasimene, and dedicated two years later. It was also attributed to M. Aemilius Scaurus in 115, who probably restored it. Thus an abstract idea was deified and personified, possibly in the sense of Reminder, to encourage the Romans at a time of crisis to remember their religious duties, or possibly to provide an avenue of escape for the lack of mind which it was alleged led C. Flaminius into disaster at Trasimene. The goddess was often referred to as Mens Bona.[172]

9 June   V. ID. IUN.   N *Dies religiosus*

VESTALIA

The private cult of Vesta, the guardian of the hearth, goes back to very primitive times when each family in its hut had to propitiate the spirit that watched over its hearth. When the shepherds' villages began to coalesce into a community, a need was felt for a common centre, and this was established in the valley of the Forum which was not within the earliest inhabited areas. Thus a public cult of Vesta was established and her fire was continually attended by Vestal Virgins, who were perhaps the successors of the king's daughters who once had tended the hearth in the palace. The cult was centred on a round building which in fact was technically a 'house' (*aedes*) and not a *templum*; its unusual shape retained the form of the early huts. (No part of the surviving building pre-dates the Augustan age). It contained no statue of Vesta, but a fire which must never be allowed to go out: this was ritually rekindled every 1 March by the primitive method of rubbing two sticks together, and the lighted tinder was carried to the hearth in a bronze sieve. A similar method was used if the fire ever did go out: the Vestals were whipped, as well as having to undertake this laborious task. An inner sanctuary, the *penus*, was curtained off. Its contents are not well known, since it could be entered only by the Vestal Virgins and the Pontifex Maximus; although the temple was open to worshipping women for eight days from 7 June, they were probably excluded from this inmost sanctum. Here were kept the sacred elements used in various rituals (e.g. the ashes for the Parilia: see p. 105), and, it was believed, a statue of Pallas Athene, the Palladium, which was said to have been rescued by Aeneas from the fires of Troy and assured the safety of Rome, together with two small statuettes of the Penates (the gods of the *penus*, the storehouse) of the Roman People. (Pls 4127, 28).

Besides tending the sacred fire, the Vestals made the 'holy' (*casta*) cake, the *mola salsa*, for use at the Vestalia. First they had to fetch water from a sacred spring; this was a normal task since no water was 'laid on' to the temple or the adjoining buildings where they lived. Originally they had to go to the spring of Egeria outside the Capena Gate, but later they were probably allowed to use the spring of Juturna near their temple (in imperial times Egeria's spring had fallen into neglect). The water must not be set down on the way, since contact with the earth might destroy its virtue: it was therefore carried in narrow-based vessels which could not be put down without spilling. The salt also had to be specially prepared: brine was brought from a salt pan and then pounded in a mortar and baked in a jar; the resultant lump was cut up with an iron saw as required. With this the Vestals salted the grain or flour, using the ears of spelt that they had gathered on 7,9 and 11 May, and had threshed and ground. They then made this into the *mola salsa*, though not necessarily by baking it, and they then presumably offered it to Vesta. They also had to sweep the *penus* clean on 15 June (see below).[173]

The day became a holiday for bakers and millers, and Ovid says that both the millstones and the asses that turned them were garlanded with violets and hung with small loaves. A wall-painting at Pompeii depicts such a scene.[174]

Ovid also records that as he was walking (in fact or imagination) to the Forum at the time of the Vestalia, he met a bare-footed matron. This sug-gests that women who were allowed to visit the temple had to take off their shoes before entering it, and they also seem to have brought simple offerings of food: 'a clean platter contains the food offered to Vesta' (*F*.6.310). But in fact very little is known about the public aspect of the festival.

11 June   III ID. IUN.   NP(?) *Dies religiosus*

MATRALIA *Matri Matutae* (Ant. mai.)

The festival of Mothers, Matralia, was held in honour of Mater Matuta, who was an old Italian goddess, worshipped in many places in central Italy. The Romans generally derived her name from *mane*, 'morning', and thus regarded her as a goddess of light: so in Lucretius she is dawn: 'Matuta diffuses the rosy dawn through the regions of ether and spreads out her light' (*roseam Matuta per oras/aetheris auroram differt et lumina pandit*). This view, however, is now generally rejected. Varro's explana-tion is that she looked after ripening corn (*frumentis maturescentibus*), but there is little to suggest that she was in any way an earth-goddess or linked to the fields. Perhaps Varro's 'ripening' could be extended to human child-birth since there is evidence to connect her with women and children. Ovid erroneously identified her with the Greek Leucothea, a sea-goddess, who in turn had been equated with Ino; this provides the poet with good mythological material, but need not concern us here.[175]

Mater Matuta had a temple in the Forum Boarium, which was closely associated with that of Fortuna: both were established by King Servius Tullius, dedicated on the same day, 11 June, and both destroyed by fire in 213 BC and rebuilt the next year. The site of these two adjacent temples has been excavated in recent years near (one partly under) the church of S. Omobono. The long history of the buildings cannot be described here, but they go back to the regal period in the sixth century and show a rich variety of bright terracotta decoration; the site also contains numerous Greek and Etruscan vases of the sixth century. Mater Matuta also had a famous temple at Satricum which the Romans spared when they destroyed the city in 346. Here great numbers of votive terracotta offerings were found dedicated to her: they included models of the inner organs of the human body, swaddled babies and groups of curotrophic statuettes ('mother and child'). These emphasize the goddess' concern for childbirth and the tending of children.[176] (Pls 25, 26).

Her cult involved a number of curious practices. Her statue could be decorated only by the wife of a first marriage (*univira*). Female slaves were excluded from the temple, except that, apparently annually, a slave girl was taken in and then slapped on her head and beaten (merely as a warning to others or the survival of a fertility rite?). Plutarch, who records this, relates that in his native city of Chaeronea a temple guardian, whip in hand, stood in front of the precinct of Leucothea and proclaimed, 'Let no slave enter, nor any Aetolian, man or woman', but he does not specifically refer to whipping a slave girl as at Rome. Sacred cakes (*testuacia*), offered to the goddess, were cooked in old-fashioned earthenware pots (*testu*); Ovid calls them *liba tosta*. Finally, women prayed to the goddess in the first place not for their own children but for their nephews and nieces. This has seemed so improbable to some that the suggestion has been made that the object of their supplications may have been their *pueri sororii* in the sense of adolescent children, *sororii* being taken not as an adjective from *soror* but from *sororiare* which Festus explains as 'the growth of the female breasts'. However, since Ovid and Plutarch seem to believe that the prayer was made for nephews and nieces, this may have been done in their day though arising from a misunderstanding of an earlier practice which involved adolescents. On the other hand, another view is that the rite originated by chance: once in unusual circumstances a woman had to pray for her sister's children and this then became part of the festival: ritual was sometimes influenced by accident. At any rate the Matralia, which was concerned with the birth and care of children, was accompanied by some strange rites.[177]

Fortunae (Ant. mai.)

The history of the temple of Fortuna in the Forum Boarium was very close, as we have seen, to that of Mater Matuta, but there was probably no connection between the cults, especially as this Fortuna was called Virgo, and girls dedicated their robes to her at marriage. The temple contained a mysterious statue, which was thought by some, such as Ovid, to represent Servius Tullius who had dedicated the temple; it was covered with 'wavy robes' (*undulatae togae*), such as had been worn by the kings of Rome. Pliny and Varro, however, thought the statue depicted Fortuna, though the robes had belonged to Servius and had been made by Tanaquil; Pliny believed they had survived until the death of Sejanus in AD 31 (curiously Sejanus had a statue of Fortuna which had allegedly belonged to Servius, whether or not stolen from the temple). Anyway it was there a few years before, since Dionysius apparently saw it: he says that it represented Servius and was made of wood and that it had survived the fire at 213, whereas the temple and all its other contents were replacements; it was still revered by the Romans in his day. Another suggestion was that the statue showed Chastity (*Pudicitia*).[178]

13 June   ID. IUN.   NP *Dies religiosus*

Feriae Iovi (Ven.)

All *Ides* were sacred to Jupiter. Ovid alone mentions the dedication of a temple of Jupiter Invictus on this date; he had already referred to a dedication to Jupiter Victor on the *Ides* (13) of April. Possibly the two birthdays refer to the same temple (a temple replacing an earlier shrine?).[179]

(Quinquatrus minusculae)

The Greater Quinquatrus was celebrated, as we have seen (p. 92), on 19–23 March, the Lesser on 13–15 June. The latter was a festival of the guild of flute-players (*tibicines*) who took an important part in religious ceremonies, if only on occasion to drown any ill-omened noise; they also attended funerals and enlivened feasts. Livy tells how in 311 BC, after they had been forbidden by the censors to hold their traditional banquet in the temple of Jupiter, they had withdrawn to Tibur until the Senate persuaded the Tiburtines to return them; this was achieved by a ruse. After their return they were allowed 'for three days each year to roam through the city in festive robes (*ornati*), making music and enjoying the licence that is now customary, and to those who played at religious ceremonies the right of dining in the temple was restored'. On the other hand Varro said that the *tibicines* wandered through the city and met at the temple of Minerva, and Festus adds that the day was the festival of Minerva whom the *tibicines* worshipped and that she was worshipped at the Quinquatrus in March. Apparently, therefore, they met at the temple of Minerva on the Aventine and dined in that of Jupiter. Their roaming of the streets of the city for three days, wearing masks and long robes (*stolae longae*, which were women's clothes) must have livened Rome up, especially if they played 'in the midst of serious business, both public and private,' as Valerius Maximus asserted.[180]

15 June   XVI (Julian XVII) KAL. QUINCT Q.ST.D.F. *Dies religiosus*

Vesta clauditur (Phil.)

The day was given the title '*Quando stercum delatum fas*' because the dirt was swept from the temple of Vesta, which was then closed, and it became lawful to transact public business. The dirt was moved to an alley half-way up the Capitoline Slope at a *porta stercoria*, and (then) according to Ovid it was carried down to the Tiber. Thus the period centred on the Vestalia was over and the Virgins could return to their normal routine.[181]

19 June   XII (Julian XIII) KAL. QUINCT   C

Minervae in Aventino

This temple had been dedicated on 19 March. Thus this entry for 19 June may refer either to a restoration of the temple by Augustus (*Res Gest.* 6) or to its *constitutio* as opposed to its earlier *dedicatio*.

20 June   XI (Julian XII) KAL. QUINCT   C

Summano ad Circum Maximum

Reddita, quisque is est, Summano templa feruntur
Tum cum Romanis, Pyrrhe, timendus eras (Ovid)

'The temple is said to have been dedicated to Summanus, whoever he may be, at a time when thou, Pyrrhus, wast a terror to the Romans'.

This temple, which was near the Circus Maximus, probably on the west side towards the Aventine, was founded *c*.278 BC after a terracotta statue of Summanus, which stood on the roof of the Capitoline temple of Jupiter Optimus Maximus, had been struck by lightning, probably at night. When the head could not be found, the soothsayers (*haruspices*) said that it had been hurled into the Tiber, but it was soon recovered at the exact spot they had indicated. A temple was then built for Summanus, which ironically was itself struck by lightning in 197 BC. Livy, however, unlike Cicero, says that a statue of Jupiter himself had been struck; it has, therefore, been suggested that Summanus had hitherto been merely an epithet of Jupiter and only became a separate deity c.278. On the other hand the *annales*, according to Varro, recorded that King Tatius had dedicated altars to Summanus and some other deities whose names had a Sabine sound. If this is true, Summanus was a pre-Etruscan Latin deity, whose primitive altar was replaced with a temple in 278 BC.[182]

Who was Summanus? Ovid apparently did not know (*'quisque is est'*). St Augustine records that Summanus was responsible for lightning at night (*nocturna fulmina*) and that at first his worship was more popular than that of Jupiter, but after the building of the splendid Capitoline temple to Jupiter by the Tarquins, his worship quickly declined. He was thus the counterpart of Jupiter who wielded thunderbolts by day. 'According to Etruscan writers', wrote Pliny, 'there are nine gods who hurl thunderbolts, of which there are eleven kinds because Jupiter hurls three sorts. Only two of these deities have been retained by the Romans who attribute thunderbolts in the day to Jupiter and those in the night to Summanus, the latter being naturally rare because the sky at night is colder'. Thus unlike the Etruscans, who divided the sky into many regions in which lightning might appear with its varied implications, the Romans observed it in a looser manner, either by day or by night. Later inscriptions show that the term *fulgur summanium* continued in use.[183]

The meaning of Summanus remains doubtful. Various explanations have been advanced. Warde Fowler thought that 'Summanus' = *sub* + *mane*, the god who sends thunderbolts 'before the dawn'. But even apart from etymological difficulty, this would be a curious way to express 'in the night'. Latte believed that the statue was Jupiter and was called Jupiter Summanus because of its height on the roof; when it was struck c.278 (and Jupiter destroyed his own statue!) Summanus was made responsible for night thunderbolts and given a separate temple. H.J. Rose argued that Summanus was an epithet of Jupiter as 'dweller in the most high places', i.e. the sky, but distinguished from him as the god who hurls nocturnal thunderbolts. S. Weinstock believed that the word was of Etruscan, not Latin, origin. When first introduced into Rome, this foreign god found a home in the temple of the great god of lightning, namely Jupiter: hence Jupiter Summanus. Yet he retained his own independence and later was given his own temple, where he received offerings of black wethers (whereas Jupiter never receives black animals). But this view involves re-jecting the evidence of the altar made by Tatius. Thus it may be suggested that Summanus was an early Latin deity 'on high'; then under Etruscan anthropomorphic influence, he was associated with Capitoline Jupiter in his Etruscan-built temple; later he received his own temple and his own

nocturnal sphere of activity. Gradually, however, he lapsed into comparative obscurity, though he does appear in a list of gods to whom an appeal is made by a character in Plautus' play *Bacchides* (*c.*200 BC), while in
the *Curculio* his name is used for a play upon words. Lucretius later speaks
of '*caeli. . . summania templa*' (the night-thundering regions of the sky).[184]

Only two aspects of his cult are known. In the Acts of the Arval
Brethren two black wethers (*verbices atri*) are named as offerings to Summanus Pater. Secondly, cakes shaped like wheels were also offered to him.
It is safer not to follow those who would seek a solar cult in their shape, if
only because Summanus was active at night. Cakes were, of course, common in many cults, as the Parilia, Liberalia and others at Rome, and widely in other religions. Thus the Roman practice survived in the Christian
Church and cakes marked with sacred symbols still have an attenuated existence as hot cross buns and Simnel cakes.[185]

Though concern for the cult seems largely to have evaporated in the
later Republic, perhaps on 20 June anyone who had suffered from
thunderstorms at night or feared such mischance, might still have considered the modest offering of cakes, if not of a wether, worthwhile as an
insurance policy for the future.

24 June   VII (Julian VIII) KAL.QUINCT.   C

Forti Fortunae trans Tiberim ad milliarium I et VI

Fors Fortuna (Fortune) had two temples across the Tiber, both founded
by King Servius Tullius and dedicated on 24 June. In 293 BC Sp. Carvilius
celebrated a victory over the Etruscans and Samnites by using part of the
spoils to build a temple to Fors Fortuna 'near the temple of the goddess
dedicated by King Servius Tullius'. Unless in fact Servius founded only
one temple, that of Carvilius must have been a new one either at the first
or sixth milestone. Several inscriptions to Fors Fortuna have been
discovered about five miles outside the Harbour Gate (Porta Portuensis)
and near the grove of the Arval Brethren. Thus the goddess had three
temples across the Tiber; in the early Empire she was given a fourth,
which does not concern us here.[186]

The festival of Fors Fortuna seems to have been a rowdy affair. At any
rate Ovid describes how while some people went on foot, flower-
bedecked boats on the river carried youthful revellers or indeed tipplers to
the festival. A reference by Cicero suggests a little more restraint, when he
asks, 'Who ever experienced so much delight (*gaudium*) from sailing
down the Tiber on the day of the festival (i.e. of Fors Fortuna) as L. Paullus
felt when he sailed up the river bringing King Perseus captive.' Columella

tells gardeners to bring their vegetables and flowers to market, and when they were all sold, to sing solemn praises (*celebres laudes*) to Fors Fortuna. The inscriptions mentioned above record dedications by sellers of violets, roses and garlands, as well as wool-dealers and bronze-smiths, while Ovid records that the goddess was especially popular with the common people and slaves: this, he says, was because of the humble origin of Servius, allegedly the son of a slave woman. The day of the festival happened to be Midsummer's Day, the summer solstice, but attempts to find a connection in the ritual are not convincing.[187]

25–26 June   VI (Julian VII) – V (Julian VI) KAL. QUINCT.   C

(Ludi Taurei quinquennales)

These quinquennial Games were established, according to Festus, in honour of the gods of the underworld, *di inferi*, in accordance with the ruling of the Books of Fate in the reign of Tarquinius Superbus because pregnant women had been stricken with a plague caused by the piecemeal sale of some beef to the people (*ex carne . . . taurorum*: possibly meat that had been offered in sacrifice). They were probably the only Circus Games to be held in the Circus Flaminius (p. 101) and included horse-racing around the turning-post (*circum metam*). The suggestion, made by F. Altheim, that they included not merely the sacrifice of bulls but also the ritual hunting of bulls in the Circus, is not very convincing. They were presumably of Etruscan origin and the only recorded celebration in Republican times was in 186 BC '*religionis causa*'. We might here note how public spectacles could mount up: the Taurian Games in 186 were followed by ten days of Games, given by M. Fulvius Nobilior; these included actors, athletes, and lion and panther hunts. Then came a nine-day feast (*sacrum*) because in Picenum for three days showers of stones and flames from the sky had set fire to the clothing of some people. The pontiffs then decreed a one-day period of prayer (*supplicatio*) because the temple of Ops on the Capitol had been struck by lightning; the consuls atoned for this with full-grown victims and purified the city. Thus the Romans were entertained for twenty consecutive days in 186 BC.[188]

27 June   IV (Julian V) KAL. QUINCT.   C

Laribus V [. . .] (Ant. mai.)

K. Latte proposed to read '*Laribus Vialibus*', but this is rejected by S. Weinstock partly because the Lares Viales, the guardians of roads and travellers, had their altars on the roads outside Rome and not in the city itself. There was a temple of the Lares at the top of the Via Sacra near the later Arch of Titus, which is mentioned in 106 BC and was restored by Augustus.[189] These 'Lares V. . . ' are to be distinguished from the Lares Praestites whose festival was on 1 May (p. 117).

(Iovi Statori in Palatio)

Romulus was said to have vowed a temple to Jupiter Stator, the Stayer, if he would halt the Romans who were retreating in the Forum valley from the Sabines after the rape of the women. The temple was not built, however, until soon after 294 BC when M. Atilius Regulus made a similar vow and erected it at the place (fanum) which Romulus had set aside. It was near the Arch of Titus, and is probably to be identified with the foundations which came to light when the Turris Chartularia was demolished in 1829. In this temple the twenty-seven maidens 'learnt the hymn', composed by Livius Andronicus which they were to sing as they processed through the city in 207 BC – though the hymn was to Juno, not Jupiter. The Senate on occasion met in this temple, most notably on 8 November 63 BC when Cicero denounced Catiline.[190] (Pl. 27).

29 June (= 30 Julian)   PR. KAL QUINCT   C

(Herculi Musarum in Circo Flaminio)

The temple of 'Hercules of the Muses' or 'Hercules and the Muses' was erected soon after the triumph of M. Fulvius Nobilior over the Ambracians, or a little later if Eumenius is right in saying that Fulvius paid for it from the fines he exacted when censor in 179. Eumenius alleges that Fulvius was actuated by his own literary interests and friendship with Ennius and also because while in Greece he had heard that Hercules was Musagetes, the leader of the Muses. In the temple he set up a copy of his Fasti, a work on the calendars, together with many statues. These included the nine Muses, and Hercules playing a lyre, which he had brought from Ambracia, and an old bronze shrine of the Muses, transferred from the temple of Honos and Virtus. The statues of the Muses are depicted on a series of denarii of Q. Pomponius Musa of 66 BC. The Severan marble plan of Rome shows that the temple stood on the south-west side of the Circus Flaminius and north-west of the Portico of Octavia. It was restored in 29 BC by L. Marcius Philippus who surrounded it with a Porticus Philippi. The temple remained well known in the time of Cicero, who quoted it as an example of how a man of war had honoured the arts of peace. One could therefore imagine that on 30 June some literary men, together with the descendants of Fulvius Nobilior, might congregate there to offer their respects. If they did so, the solemnity of the occasion might have been lightened if their eyes happened to stray to some neighbouring barbers' shops, where according to Ovid ladies came to purchase their wigs.[191] (Pls 28, 4129).

July (MENSIS QUINCTILIS)

Until this month was renamed Julius in honour of Julius Caesar, it retained the name Quinctilis, the fifth month of the civil year that began in March. Whereas the names of the earlier months of the year from March (and indeed from January) to June were connected with the operations of nature or the deities that presided over these, Quinctilis was the first of the series to be named numerically, a practice which continued, with Sextilis, September, etc., until December marked the end of the natural year and the winter solstice. July saw the heat of the summer and was the period for harvesting: *'plerique messem faciunt'* says Varro (*Agr*.1.32.); also the rustic calendars, which indicate that the month was under the protection (*tutela*) of Jupiter and that sacrifice was due to Apollo and Neptune, draw attention to the need to harvest barley and beans. The festivals of the month marked in the calendars may have been important in very early days, but appear gradually to have lost much of their significance. At any rate details were not well known to Varro and Verrius, while unfortunately we are deprived of a wealth of information for the second half of the year through the fact that we do not have the last six books of Ovid's *Fasti* – whatever their precise fate may have been. However, a pleasure-seeking Roman of the late Republic would find better entertainment in the Games of Apollo than in many of the older festivals.

1 July   KAL. QUINCT.   **N**

[. . ., Iun]oni, [. . . , Felici]tati (Ant. mai.)
Felicitati in Capitolio (Ant. min.)

This cult of Juno, to whom the *Kalends* of each month were sacred, is not recorded elsewhere.

The temple of Felicitas may be that of Fausta Felicitas on the Capitol, which was attributed to 9 October by the Arval and Amiterne calendars, the differences of date perhaps referring to a restoration. The earliest reference to a sanctuary of Felicitas is to that erected by L. Licinius

Lucullus from booty taken in Spain in 151–150 BC. Felicitas was closely akin to Fortuna and was a deity whose help was particularly needed by generals: thus as early as 201 the Senate granted Scipio Africanus a triumph because he had defeated Hannibal through his *virtus* and *felicitas*; these two attributes, together with *auctoritas* and *scientia rei militaris*, were reckoned by Cicero as the requisites for a good general. Sulla went so far as to name himself 'Felix', and both Pompey and Caesar paid tribute to this abstraction which had become a deity.[191]

5 July	III NON. QUINCT.	NP

POPLIFUGIA
Feriae Iovi

The Poplifugia was the only festival in the whole year which was written in the calendars in large letters and yet was celebrated before the *Nones* of the month. But this is not the only puzzling feature. The form of the title appears to link it with the Regifugium in February, but later Romans seem to have been completely ignorant of what this Flight of the People was supposed to commemorate: so they invented two explanations, one mythological, the other historical. Either the people fled when Romulus disappeared from mortal sight during a tempest, or else it referred to the flight of the Romans when attacked by the people of Fidenae after the Gallic sack of Rome. Varro, in his *de lingua Latina*, says that traces (*vestigia*) of the rite appear in the sacrifices which he described in his (now lost) work on Antiquities. Modern speculations include the view that Jupiter was worshipped at the festival (but this does not appear to be supported) or that it was in some way expiatory and that some of the powers that were evoked were so terrifying as to require the people to flee – The Devil take the hindmost![193] What was done on 5 July in the later Republic may have been merely the formal maintenance of an old cult which no longer provoked much public interest.

6–13 July	PRID. NON. – III ID. QUINCT.

Ludi Apollinares

At a difficult period of the Hannibalic War the Sibylline Books and the oracles of a seer named Marcius prescribed Games in honour of Apollo, whose cult was one of the oldest and most important that the Romans took over from the Greek world. These were held, and four years later in 208 a plague persuaded the Romans to make them permanent and fix the date at 13 July. Thus Apollo was expected not only to help the Romans in their struggle against Hannibal but also to serve as a healing-god. These annual Games became so popular that the time devoted to them was gradually extended backwards from 13 July, so that by the end of the Republic they occupied no less than eight days (6–13) – thus in 190 BC they were being held at least as early as the 11 July, and in 44 BC they lasted seven days. Of the eight days two were given to Circus Games, the others to stage productions.

Livy describes the one-day celebration in 212. The praetor urbanus was put in charge; he received a monetary grant and two full-grown victims. The *decemviri sacris faciundis* saw to the sacrifices which were made according to the Greek rite; they comprised an ox for Apollo, a cow for Latona and two white she-goats probably for Diana (though Livy says for Apollo); all the animals had gilded horns. The people attending the festival wore garlands; matrons offered prayers and everyone feasted in the forecourt (of their own homes?) with open doors. As time went on, the Games became more elaborate. While horse-racing continued in the Circus Maximus, plays were produced in the theatres; Pliny says that in 60 BC cambric awnings were first provided in the theatre at the Games of Apollo. Ennius' tragedy *Thyestes* was staged shortly before his death in 169, and Cicero tells Atticus how at the Games in 59 BC the actor Diphilus attacked Pompeius Magnus in his line 'To our misfortune thou art Great' (*nostra miseria tu es magnus*) and was applauded to the skies. This is a reminder that the voice of the people could sometimes make itself heard at the Games, and indeed Cicero elsewhere actually equates the applause at the Games for Apollo with the witness and judgment of the Roman people (*testimonium et iudicia*). Cicero also referred to beast-hunts (*venatio*) at these Games, but they did not include gladiatorial combats. Later under the personal interest of Augustus the cult of Apollo became even more important in Roman life.[194]

6 July   PRID. NON. QUINCT.   N

(Fortunae Muliebri via Latina ad miliarium IV)

This temple of Fortuna Muliebris, which was dedicated on 6 July, is said to have been vowed on 1 December; this is recorded only in the literary sources and not in the calendars. It has been identified with the remains of a small temple found some four miles outside Rome on the Via Latina. It was linked, though not necessarily at first, with the story of Coriolanus: Dionysius of Halicarnassus relates that when the Senate wished to honour the women who had accompanied the wife and mother of Coriolanus and

had succeeded in dissuading him from his attack on Rome, they asked for
and received this temple to Fortuna Muliebris. Following 'the books of
the pontiffs', Dionysius adds that the women contributed a second statue
of the goddess at their own expense and that this statue on two occasions
uttered the words, 'you have conformed to the holy law, married women,
in giving me'. The women, at the advice of their priestess, then
established that no woman who had married a second time should touch
or garland the statue and that only newly married women or *univirae*
should pay worship to the goddess. The cult was confined to *univirae*
perhaps because widows and women who married twice were considered
unlucky (unworthy to approach Fortuna, whose help in fact they needed
all the more!). In view of the goddess' remark that the *matronae* had
'given' (but only the second statue?), it has been suggested that the temple
had been dedicated by, and not in honour of, *univirae* (and in early times
the right of married women to hold property was restricted).[195] The fact
that Dionysius wrote at length about the cult (though apologizing for the
digression) might suggest that interest in it was still lively in the Augustan
period, but on the other hand its dedication day is not recorded by any of
the calendars, not even by the pre-Caesarian Antiate calendar.

7 July   NON. QUINCT.   N

Palibus duobus (Ant. mai.)

As we have seen (p. 103), the Parilia on 21 April was held in honour of the
deity or deities Pales, who in 267 BC received a temple on the Palatine,
where they (or he or she) were worshipped as a deity of shepherds, *pastoria
Pales* in Florus, *Pales Matuta* in a scholiast.[196]

Ancillarum feriae (Silv.)
Nonae Caprotinae

The Feast of Serving Women is recorded in the late calendar of Silvius, but
not in the others. Silvius gives a brief resumé of the explanatory story
which Plutarch (*Cam.33, Rom.29ff.*) tells at much greater length. After
the capture of Rome by the Gauls, the Latins threatened the city and
demanded some of the Roman womenfolk. On the advice of a serving-
maid (*ancilla*), named Philotis or Tulola, the Romans sent out a number of
ancillae dressed in the finery of free women. At night, when the Latins
were asleep, they were disarmed by the women and Philotis gave the
Romans the signal to attack by lighting a fire-signal on a tall wild fig-tree
(*caprificus*). The Romans rushed out of their city, calling out each other by

name, and successfully fell on the Latins. Later they established a commemorative festival (*ancillarum feriae*), and named the *Nones*, on which the victory was won, the *Nonae Caprotinae*. At the festival, Plutarch tells us, booths of fig-tree boughs were erected outside the city. The Romans ran out, calling out many ordinary names, as Gaius, Marcius, and Lucius, and then feasted the women. Groups of gaily attired *ancillae* jested with the men and then had a mock battle among themselves. Plutarch also refers to another tradition, according to which this festival outside the city celebrated the death of Romulus, who disappeared from sight in a storm while he was addressing the people at Goats' Marsh; the people went out of the city, shouting the common names, to sacrifice at the Caprae Palus, which was in the lowest part of the Campus Martius near the later Pantheon. Plutarch confuses the issue by saying that this celebration in honour of Romulus was held on the day he vanished which was called Poplifugia and *Nonae Caprotinae*. But the calendars show that these festivals fell on different days, the 5th and 7th. It is tempting to connect the exodus of the people from Rome and the calling out of names with the Flight of the People, the Poplifugia, but in view of the evidence of the calendars for differing dates, a link seems implausible.

Varro, however states that the *Nones* of July were called *Caprotinae* because on that day, in Latium, women offered sacrifice to Juno Caprotina under a wild fig-tree; they also made some use of a branch from the tree. Macrobius specifically connects the sacrifice to Juno with the feast of the *ancillae*, whose legend he recounts. He also says that both *ancillae* and free women (*liberae*) attended the sacrifice to Juno Caprotina, to whom the milky juice of the fig-tree was offered in place of milk. The purpose of the stick cut from the tree, mentioned by Varro, is uncertain, but if the two ceremonies are parts of one, it is a plausible suggestion that the sticks were used by the *ancillae* in their mock battle and that the object may have been to stimulate fertility, as at the Lupercalia women were struck with strips of hide (p. 77). But behind the human aspect may lie the agricultural, and the fertility of the fig-trees themselves. Columella refers to this process which consisted of placing figs from a wild fig-tree among the branches of a cultivated tree (*ficus*) to encourage pollination, and this was best done in July. Thus the 'marriage' of a male *caprificus* with a female *ficus* might well have given rise to a festival of women.[197] At any rate Juno was a women's deity and the use of the 'milk' of the fig-tree was appropriate. Although it is scarcely possible to disentangle the threads, clearly 7 June was a day of celebration for *ancillae*, dressed in matron's clothing, perhaps in a ceremony of their own as well as in one which they shared with free women in honour of Juno.

(Conso in Circo)

Tertullian recorded that still in his day there was an underground altar to Consus at the first turning-point (*meta*) in the Circus, where sacrifice was offered on 7 July by the State-priests (*sacerdotibus publicis*), and on 20 August by the *flamen Quirinalis* and the Vestal Virgins. The accompanying inscription, 'Consus in counsel' (*Consus consilio, Mars duello, Lares Coillo potentes*) may be somewhat late since Consus is named in the nominative case, while the text of Tertullian's transcription of it is uncertain. The altar was at the south-east end of the *spina* of the Circus Maximus and was named by Tacitus as one of the corners of the Palatine *pomerium*. It was kept covered and was exposed only at the festival when sacrifices were offered on it. Consus was an old Roman god whose festivals (Consualia) were on 19 August and 15 December, perhaps representing the end of the harvest and of the autumn sowing. Though Tertullian was not alone in deriving his name from *consilium*, it much more probably derives from *condere*, to 'hide' or 'store', and thus Consus was the god of the store-bin of the harvested grain which was kept underground. For his worship at the Consualia see below under 19 August and 15 December.[198]

8 July   VIII ID. QUINCT.   N *Dies religiosus*

(Vitulatio)

Macrobius (3.2.11.ff.) says that after the Roman people had fled before the Etruscans on the *Nones* (hence the name Poplifugia), they won a victory on the following day (8 July) and established sacrifices for the goddess Vitula. Macrobius quotes various explanations of the name: Piso connected it with *victoria*, 'victory'; Fabius derived it from *vitulari* which meant *voce laetari*, perhaps 'to sing a paean', while a certain Hyllus said that Vitula was the goddess of joy; others connected her name with *vita*, 'life', since she received as offerings the first fruits of the earth which give life (cf. Virgil, *Geor*.3.77). Despite all this ingenuity, Roman scholars do not seem to have considered the possibility of *vitulus*, 'heifer', an animal which was used as a scapegoat in the rites at Iguvium (see p. 83). However, whatever the precise nature of the goddess, the ceremony on 8 July seems to have been an official one which was attended by the pontiffs.

These minor festivals held on 6–8 July, which we have just been reviewing, may not have commanded much interest in the late Republic, but they will have been still more overshadowed when the celebration of the Ludi Apollinares was gradually extended backwards to embrace first the 8th, then the 7th by Caesar's time, and finally the 6th as well.

13 July   III ID. QUINCT.   **C**

Apol[lini] (Ant. mai.)

On this, the chief day of the Ludi Apollinares, a sacrifice to Apollo is
mentioned by the Antiates maiores alone of the calendars. The reference
may be to the oldest temple of Apollo which was dedicated on account of a
plague in 431 BC and may have been preceded by a shrine to the god, an
Apollinare. It lay in the Campus Martius between the Circus Flaminius
and the Forum Holitorium, that is outside the *pomerium*, since it was a
foreign cult. If Asconius is right that there was only one temple of Apollo
in Rome before the Palatine temple vowed by Augustus, then this temple
was presumably the one restored by Sosius, consul in 32 BC (see p.188),
and was known as that of Apollo Medicus; this received a porticus in 179
and contained several famous works of art. The extant remains, including
three standing columns, belong to the restoration by Sosius. It was used
on occasion by the Senate for extra-pomerial meetings.[199] (Pl. 29).

14–19 July   PRID. ID. QUINCT. – XIV KAL. SEXT.

Mercatus

After the Apolline Games had finished, six days were set aside for markets
or fairs. Business could be combined with pleasure, and the crowds that
had come into the city from the countryside for the festival could make the
most of the opportunity to buy and sell. Similar markets (*mercatus*) are
marked in the calendars after the Ludi Romani and Plebeii.

15 July   ID. QUINCT.   **NP**

(Equitum Romanorum probatio (Phil.) or *transvectio)*

The 15th of July was a colourful day in the streets of Rome at certain
periods of her history. In order to celebrate the help received at the battle
of Lake Regillus from Castor and Pollux, who were believed to have
watered their horses in the Roman Forum after the victory, a cavalry
parade was established for 15 July by the censor Q. Fabius Rullianus in 304
BC. The celebration gradually lapsed in the course of time, but was revived
by Augustus, when it was a magnificent spectacle, as witnessed and
described by Dionysius of Halicarnassus:[200] 'the Roman knights whose
horses are supplied by the State (*equites equo publico*) ride in tribes and
centuries, as if coming from battle, crowned with olive branches and
wearing their purple robes with stripes of scarlet known as *trabeae*. They
begin their procession from a temple of Mars outside the walls, and going

through several parts of the city and the Forum, they pass by the temple of Castor and Pollux, sometimes to the number of 5,000, wearing whatever rewards for valour in battle they have received from their commanders, a fine sight and worthy of the greatness of the Roman dominion'. In origin this was an annual military parade, but it may well have become linked in some way to the census of the Equites which was conducted every five years by the censors (see p. 232). Their review was not a military pageant but a testing of qualification: as we have seen (p. 67), the whole corps of knights (of which the nucleus in early days was the 1,800 cavalrymen aged between 18 and 46) filed past the censors who were probably seated on the platform of the temple of Castor and Pollux in the Forum; each man then advanced individually and was either passed or discharged. While this review by the censors continued throughout the Republic until the censorship fell into disuse in the time of Sulla, the history of the military procession is unfortunately obscure: all that is known is that it had lapsed for a long time (*post longam intercapedinem*) when it was revived by Augustus who used it as a *probatio* or *recognitio* of the knights. We can only wonder how often it was celebrated in the mid-Republic: from being annual, it might have come to be held only in the years when censors were in office and somehow have been combined with this ceremony, but in its heyday this annual military parade of knights riding through the city, sacrificing presumably in the Forum at the temple of Castor and Pollux and then perhaps passing on up to the temple of Jupiter on the Capitol must have been a brave sight.

17 July   XVI KAL. SEXT.   C

Honori (Ant. mai.)

The history of the temple of Honos et Virtus just outside the Porta Capena is unusual. The first part was built by Q. Fabius Cunctator in 233 BC after his Ligurian campaign, and was dedicated to Honos. M. Claudius Marcellus vowed a temple to Honos and Virtus in 222, and after his capture of Syracuse in 211 he renewed his vow and wanted to rededicate the earlier temple of Honos to both deities in 208; forbidden by the pontiffs, he restored the old temple of Honos and built a new part for Virtus which was dedicated by his son in 205; in it he placed many of the artistic treasures that he had brought from Syracuse. It cannot have been the starting-place for the *transvectio equitum*, as stated in *de viris illustribus* 22, since it was not built until long after 304 BC (see above 15 July). There was another temple of Honos outside the Colline Gate, and yet another to Honos et Virtus built by Marius after his defeat of the Cimbri and

Teutones on the slope of a hill, probably the Capitol (in it the Senate met to recall Cicero from exile). In view of this there is slight uncertainty about which temple was dedicated on 17 July, but it most probably was the first mentioned. Honos and Virtus were regarded essentially as military qualities and their jugate heads are depicted on a *denarius* of 70 BC.[201] (Pl. 4130).

Victoriae in Capitolio (Viae Ardeat.)

A gold statue of Victory, sent by Hiero of Syracuse to encourage the Romans after Trasimene, was placed in the temple of Jupiter Optimus Maximus on the Capitol, while a Victory driving a *biga* was in the vestibule, but it is not known whether the sacrifice on 17 July was to one or other of these.[202] (Pl. 4131).

18 July	XV KAL. SEXT.	C Dies religiosus

Alliensis dies (Ant. mai.)
Dies Alliae et Fabiorum (Ant. min.)

On this black day (*dies ater*) traditionally the Fabii were defeated on the Cremera in 479 BC, and the Romans on the Allia by the Gauls who then captured the city in 390. Cicero, writing to Atticus (9.5.2.), says that 'our ancestors made the day of the battle of Allia of blacker memory than that of the capture of the city, because the second disaster arose from the first, so that the former is even now an ill-omened day (*dies religiosus*) while the other is commonly unknown'. How many educated Romans, like Cicero, recalled the day when it came round each year, we cannot tell.

19 & 21 July	XIV & XII KAL. SEXT.	NP

LUCARIA

Festus says the Romans celebrated the Lucaria festival in a large grove (*lucus*) between the Via Salaria and the Tiber (probably in the area of the Pincian Gardens), and provides a legendary explanation: the Romans, fleeing from the Gauls, had hidden in this grove, an idea doubtless engendered by the fact that the battle of Allia was fought on 18 July. According to Plutarch the money spent on public festivals was called *lucar* because it was derived from revenue from public groves (*luci*). That in fact *lucar* did originally mean a grove is shown by an early inscription from Luceria (*in hoc loucarid*), while another from Spoletium shows that an annual sacrifice (*res deina anua*) was performed in a *lucus*.[203] The Lucaria therefore probably goes back to primitive Rome when land was reclaimed from the forest in which lurked vague spirits that had to be propitiated before the trees were felled. Cato, as we have seen (p. 26), preserves a suitable prayer that should be used, together with the sacrifice of a pig, when a grove was to be thinned. The festival probably meant little in the late Republic.

| **20–30 July** | XIII – III KAL. SEXT. | |

Ludi Victoriae Caesaris

A temple to Venus Genetrix was vowed by Julius Caesar at Pharsalus and dedicated in his Forum on the last day of his triumph, 26 September 46 BC. The vow included Games which were repeated in 45 when (and thereafter) they were held from 20 to 30 of July and called Ludi Victoriae Caesaris (the festival of Venus Genetrix remained at 26 September) – whether or not Venus and Victoria are to be regarded as closely related or Victoria as created as a personal goddess of Caesar. The Games comprised seven days of scenic events, followed by four Circus celebrations. Cicero attended them in 45 and his comments are an interesting contrast to the disgust he showed at the ostentatious and cruel Games of Pompey in 55: he wrote to Atticus, 'It is something that the spirits are relieved by the spectacle and by the general feeling of religious associations' (*religionis opinione et fama*).[204] Since we are primarily concerned with the Republic, we need not consider these Games further, except to note that from 46 BC onwards more than half the month of July was given to Games, with eight days for Apollo and eleven for Caesar.

| **21 July** | XII KAL. SEXT. | NP |

LUCARIA (second day)

| **22 July** | XI KAL. SEXT | C |

Concordiae

A temple of Concordia stood in the Forum at the foot of the Capitol. The surviving remains belong mainly to a restoration by Tiberius in 7 BC, but the early history is uncertain. Camillus is said in 367 BC to have vowed a temple to Concord to celebrate the ending of the struggle between patricians and plebeians, a *concordia ordinum*, and Ovid and Plutarch imply that it was the temple restored by Tiberius and thus the one below the Capitol. However, in 121 after the death of Gaius Gracchus, L. Opimius was ordered by the Senate to build a temple to Concordia; he also built a Basilica nearby. But did he build a new temple or merely restore Camillus' work, and did in fact Camillus actually build (or only vow) a temple, or indeed was even his alleged intention to build, a later falsification (Livy assigns no temple to him)? Whatever the truth, it was almost certainly this temple that had its 'birthday' on 22 July.[205] Concordia was known as a goddess in Rome as early as 304 BC when Cn. Flavius dedicated a bronze shrine (*aedicula*) to her; thus, although appearing rather early for the adoption of a deified abstraction, the year 367 is by no means impossible. Another temple to Concordia stood on the Capitol (Pl. 4132).

If any Romans prayed to Concordia in the later Republic, it was no longer to bring patricians and plebeians together, but to achieve Cicero's dream of a *concordia ordinum* between senators and knights or perhaps between Optimates and Populares or between the constitution and military adventurers. There was no lack of *discordia*.

23 July	X KAL. SEXT.	NP

NEPTUNALIA

Neptune was probably an Italian god of water, whose domain was extended to the sea when he was equated with the Greek god Poseidon. He is first mentioned in Rome as one of the gods who shared in the first public *lectisternium* in 399 BC. Here he was paired with Mercury, possibly suggesting that the two gods were here regarded as guardians of trade and seafaring. Of his festival on 23 July we know only that arbours (*umbrae*) of leaves were made, presumably to protect the worshippers from the hot July sun. Its purpose may have been to seek security for the water-supply at this dry time of year. An altar of Neptune in the Circus Flaminius, which is first mentioned in 206 BC, was probably dedicated on 23 July. Neptune was the only god, except also Apollo and Mars, to whom a bull might be sacrificed.[206]

25 July	VIII KAL. SEXT.	NP

FURRINALIA

Even less is known of the Furrinalia than of the Neptunalia! According to Varro this festival was a state holiday (*feriae publicae*) for the goddess Furrina: 'honour was paid to her among the ancients, who established an annual sacrifice and assigned her a special priest (*flamen*), but her name is barely known, and even that to only a few.' Her nature remains obscure, though she has been thought to have presided over a spring or wells; later she was (probably wrongly) confused with the Furiae (Furies). One memorial remained: a *lucus Furrinae* on the Janiculum where Gaius Gracchus met his death and where today is the Villa Sciarra.[207]

30 July   III KAL. SEXT.   C

Fortunae Huiusque Diei in Campo

A temple to 'The Fortune of this Day', vowed by Q. Lutatius Catulus on the day of Vercellae, 30 July 101 BC, was dedicated by him on the anniversary of the battle. This Fortuna is the deity who presides over the happy issue of each day. The temple was in the Campus Martius and *may* be identified with Temple B in the Largo Argentina. L. Aemilius Paullus also built a shrine to this goddess on account of his victory at Pydna: this was probably on the Palatine, where there was a *vicus Huiusque Diei*. Both generals dedicated statues by Pheidias in the temples.[208] (Pl. 30).

August (MENSIS SEXTILIS)

For the farmer the harvest was about completed, and his tasks were according to Varro to cut straw, build stacks, harrow plough-land, collect leaf-fodder, and mow irrigated fields a second time. The rustic calendars order the preparing of stakes, the collecting of the harvest and wheat, and the burning of the coarse part of the flax; the month was under the protection of Ceres, and sacrifices were owing to Spes, Salus and Diana, and it was the month of the Volcanalia. Naturally several of the festivals had some connection with harvesting or storing the crops, while many of the rites were performed in the neighbourhood of the Aventine, Circus Maximus and the bank of the Tiber, which, as has been noted, was in earliest times part of the cultivated land nearest the city.[209]

1 August   KAL. SEXT.   F

Spes in Foro Holitorio

A temple of Spes (Hope) was built in the Forum Holitorium during the First Punic War by A. Atilius Calatinus (who also built a temple to Fides on the Capitol). It is probably to be identified with the middle of the three temples which now exist below the church of S. Nicola in Carcere. It is more recent than a temple of Spes on the Esquiline which became known as Spes Vetus.[210]

Victoris duabus in Palatio (Arv.)
Victoriae, Victoriae Virgini in Palatio (Praen.)

Two temples of Victoria stood on the Palatine. One was dedicated by L.
Postumius Megellus in 294 BC from the fines that he had exacted as curule
aedile; it seems to have been preceded by an ancient shrine of Victoria. The
other, to Victoria Virgo, was nearby and dedicated by M. Porcius Cato in
193.[211]

3 August   III NON. SEXT.   C

(Supplicia canum)

A remarkable procession took place annually on this day: one or more
dogs were crucified alive on a cross of elder-wood between the temples
Iuventus and Summanus, and were apparently carried round in procession. The alleged reason was that the temple dogs were asleep when the
Gauls tried to assault the Capitol. A goose (or geese), adorned with purple
and gold, was also carried round in a litter in token of its wakeful and alert
predecessors. Since the two temples were near the Circus Maximus, it is a
possible guess that this weird procession paraded in the Circus itself.[212]

5 August   NON. SEXT.   F

Saluti in Colle Quirinale sacrificium publicum (Vall.)

In 57 BC Cicero wrote to his friend Atticus, describing his triumphal
return to Italy and Rome from exile: 'I started from Dyrrachium and arrived at Brundisium on 5 August. There my little Tullia was waiting for
me, on her own birthday, which, as it happened, was the commemoration
day *(dies natalis)* of the colony of Brundisium and of the temple of Salus
near your house too'. It is interesting that Cicero knew and recalled the
date of the dedication of the temple of Salus. He referred to it again later in
45 when he made his famous quip that he would prefer to see Julius Caesar
(whose statue had been placed in the temple of Quirinus) sharing a temple
of Quirinus than of Salus.

Since part of the Quirinal was called collis Salutaris, an early cult of Salus
had probably been established there. Her temple however was dedicated in
302 BC by C. Iunius Bubulcus when dictator; it contained some well-
known paintings by C. Fabius Pictor (probably an ancestor of the annalist
Quintus Fabius Pictor). Salus was named Semonia according to
Macrobius; perhaps she shared a cult with Semo Sancus in early times (see
under 5 June). Under the Empire Salus became Salus Publica populi
Romani.[213]

9 August   V ID. SEXT.   C

Solis Indigitis in Colle Quirinale sacrificium publicum (Vall.)

King Tatius is said to have dedicated altars to Sol and Luna (Sun and Moon), and Quintilian refers to a Pulvinar Solis near the temple of Quirinus on the Quirinal. The sun was an obvious natural power to attract worship in the summer heat, and the cult of Sol Indiges appears to have been old (he also had a shrine at Lavinium). The meaning of Indiges remains doubtful, despite much controversial discussion: the Indigetes have been regarded as *di minores* (gods of limited function), as 'native' (as opposed to foreign) gods, or as ancestral gods. The sun (with the Moon) had another temple near the Circus Maximus, but his cult did not gain a major position until the third century AD.[214] (Pl. 4133).

12 August   PR. ID. SEXT.   C

Herculi Invicto ad Circum Maximum.

Hercules was one of the first foreign gods to be admitted into Rome and his earliest cult centre was the Ara Maxima in the Forum Boarium within the line of the Palatine *pomerium*. Thus placed within the Cattle Market and near the Tiber, his cult became popular with merchants, and it just possibly was introduced by Phoenician traders. He certainly was later equated with the Tyrian god Baal-Melkart and his worship, as we shall see, had some Semitic features: but his origin still remains uncertain. He was also identified with the Greek hero Heracles, who was recognized as 'a warder-off of evils' (*alexikakos*) as well as a traveller through his enforced Labours. At any rate he appeared in Rome early and his altar is said to have been dedicated by himself or by Evander after Hercules had killed the legendary Cacus. Near the altar was a round temple of Hercules Invictus (Victor), containing frescoes by the poet Pacuvius; its remains were destroyed by Pope Sixtus IV (1471-84), but an early drawing survives. Hercules Pompeianus had a temple (dedicated or restored by Pompey) near the Circus Maximus; it lies under part of the church of S. Maria in Cosmedin. It is not certain which of these three centres was honoured on 12 August, while on the 13th Hercules Invictus near the Porta Trigemina received its annual sacrifice. Finally, Hercules Victor was given a temple which was dedicated by L. Mummius in 142 BC and appears to have been on the Caelian hill.[215] (Pl. 31).

The cult at the Ara Maxima was at first in the control of two Roman *gentes*, the Potitii and Pinarii, until it was taken over by the State in 312 BC when public slaves were bought to attend the precincts (the earliest

Early 16th-century
drawing of the Temple of
Hercules Victor

attested State-cult of Hercules was at the *lectisternium* of 399). It was
celebrated in the Greek manner, with head uncovered, though crowned
with laurel. Women were excluded, though not at another altar of Hercules: Plutarch asks why, when there were two altars of Hercules, did
women receive neither share nor taste of the sacrifice offered at the larger
altar. Plutarch also mentions two further limitations: at the sacrifice to
Hercules there must be no reference to any other gods (no *generalis in-
vocatio*), and dogs were excluded from the precincts. Oaths were often
taken at the altar and business transactions agreed. Further, merchants
were accustomed to pay Hercules a tithe on the profit of a business deal (a
reminder of the tithe imposed in eastern markets for the benefit of
Melkart). But besides successful merchants, victorious generals also might
offer tithes of their booty. Individuals too made their offerings, but
perhaps none matched the millionaire Crassus who dedicated a tenth of his
whole fortune, perhaps in order to impress his fellow citizens with the extent of his wealth – and power. Such offerings would normally have
made the cult very rich, but since Hercules' temples are not recorded as
particularly well endowed with treasures and since the upkeep of the cult
cannot have been unduly expensive, it has been suggested that the tithes
may have been used in part to provide a free feast on the day of the festival:
this is made more probable because Hercules shared with Silvanus the
unusual distinction that no part of the sacrificial animals might be removed
from the precinct, and this would entail that what was not actually
burnt on the altar was eaten on the spot. Further, while other gods were

somewhat restricted in the foods they might receive as offerings, Hercules could eat and drink everything (*Herculi autem omnia esculenta, poculenta*); this was in line with his reputation for gluttony. When on 12 August the praetor urbanus sacrificed a heifer to Hercules and poured a libation from a special cup which was known as the *skyphos* of Hercules, this official offer- ing was no doubt supplemented from the tithes and contributions which private worshippers had made on that day as well as on other occasions throughout the year. Hercules gives the impression of having been rather a 'popular' deity with an appeal to the individual man, even apart from the likelihood that he provided a free meal on every 12th August.[216]

Veneri Victrici, Honori, Virtuti, V[. . .]Felicitati in theatro marmoreo
(Allif.)

Pompey built the first permanent stone theatre in Rome in 55 BC. To deflect criticism for building a permanent theatre, he built a temple of Venus Victrix at the top of the central section of the rows of seats in order that these might look like the temple steps, and so the whole structure could be dedicated as a temple and not as a theatre. Tiro, Cicero's freed- man, referred to it as Aedes Victoriae, perhaps a colloquial name (Aul. Gell. 10,1.7). The other nearby temples (or more probably altars) to Honos, Virtus, Felicitas and V (= Vesta, Valetudo??) are not known.

13 August   ID. SEXT.   NP

Dianae, Vortumno, Fortunae Equestri, Herculi Victori,
Castori, Polluci, Camenis (Ant. mai.)

This day was the occasion for the celebration of several cults, including that of Jupiter to whom all Ides were sacred, but the most important was that of Diana, since it involved a general day's holiday for all slaves.

Dianae in Aventino (Ant.mai., etc.)

Diana was an old Italian goddess, who was worshipped especially in groves, and was perhaps originally a 'wood-spirit' who gradually came to preside over the affairs of women. The most famous of her cult-centres was near Aricia, some sixteen miles south-east of Rome, where her temple stood on the shores of Lake Nemi in the grove whose 'king' (*rex nemoren- sis*, i.e. priest) became well known as 'the priest who slew the slayer and shall himself be slain' in the ritual involving the golden bough. To this grove in historical times women whose prayers had been answered used to come from Rome in processions with burning torches in gratitude to the goddess, as recorded by Ovid (*F.* 3.269) and Propertius (3.24.9f.). Considerable numbers of their votive offerings have been found, including models of reproductive organs and women with infants. Thus Diana's connection with women seems well established, but other offerings refer to her as goddess of the chase; they include statuettes of stags and indeed some domestic animals, suggesting that beside being the huntress goddess, she may well have been a goddess of fertility in general, both animal and human. Her wider links with the Greek goddess Artemis, with the moon, and with Ephesus and Massilia cannot be discussed here. (Pls 32, 4134).

Diana's earliest temple in Rome, probably preceded by an altar, was on the Aventine, a plebeian quarter of the city. It was founded in the sixth century by King Servius Tullius, possibly as a political move to transfer to Rome (or establish a rival to) the headquarters of the Latin League which had met at the religious centre near Aricia. But after the early Romans and the Latins had become united, any political aspect of the cult was soon forgotten and its social side was developed, although its original regulations, written in Greek letters, survived to be read by Dionysius of Halicarnassus. The temple became an asylum for runaway slaves and 13 August was a holiday for all slaves, male and female, perhaps after the toil of the harvest (this development was linked to the false connection between the word *servus*, 'slave' and King Servius). All Romans had to allow their slaves the day off, and Diana's cult was one of the few that slaves could attend. A more peculiar custom of the day was that Roman women made a particular practice of washing their hair: Plutarch surmises that the habit started with slave-women because of the holiday and that it spread to free-born women.[217] The site of the temple on the Aventine was probably just west of the church of S. Prisca on the clivus Publicius. It was an important building, so that the Aventine was sometimes known as the Collis Dianae. It contained a wooden statue of Diana of Ephesus and bronze copies of old laws; on its walls was one of the oldest sun-dials in Rome.

Vortumno in Aventino (Allif.; Amit.)
Vortumno in Loreto maiore (Vall.)

Vortumnus (Vertumnus) was an Etruscan god, worshipped at Volsinii, which was captured by M. Fulvius Flaccus who celebrated a triumph in 264 BC. It was probably he who built the temple on the north-west part of the Aventine in the Vicus Loreti Maioris (Loretum was an ancient laurel-grove); it contained a portrait of Flaccus in his triumphal robes. A statue of Vortumnus stood in the Vicus Tuscus, and Propertius describes the offerings made to him there. The origin of the name of this Etruscan god is uncertain: it may derive from a family name, though the Romans connected it with *vertere*, 'to turn'.[218]

Fortunae Equestri (Ant.mai. alone)

Vowed by Q. Fulvius Flaccus in 180 BC during his campaign against the Celtiberians, this temple was dedicated seven years later to Fortuna in her relation to the Equites. It was 'over against the stone theatre' (*ad theatrum lapideum*), probably the theatre of Pompey in the Circus Flaminius rather than the theatre of Marcellus. It clearly did not survive the Republic, because a problem arose in AD 22: in what temple were the knights to place the offerings they had vowed in connection with the empress Livia's health to Fortuna Equestris, since there was no longer any temple to Fortuna with this epithet.[219]

Herculi Victori (Ant. mai.)
Herculi Invicto ad Portam Trigeminam (Allif.)

Hercules had been honoured at the Circus Maximus the previous day. If the calendars give the festivals in order of their foundation, the temple of Hercules near the Porta Trigemina will have been founded after 173 BC, possibly by a victorious general.

Castori, Polluci in Circo Flaminio

This temple to Castor and Pollux could have been built by C. Flaminius, censor in 220 BC, only if the order in the calendars is not strictly chronological.

Camenis (Ant. mai.)

The Camenae were originally deities of springs and were later identified with the Muses. They gave their name to a district on the southern end of the Caelian Hill; it included a valley, a grove and a spring. Traditionally King Numa had built a small bronze shrine (*aedicula*) beside the spring. The Fasti Antiates make it clear that this temple was not the same as that dedicated to Hercules and the Muses by Nobilior in 189 BC (see 29 June).

Florae ad Circum Maximum (Allif.)

This probably refers to the temple of Flora whose *dies natalis* was 28 April (q.v.) and the 13 August to a restoration by Tiberius in AD 17 (Tac. *Ann.* 2.49).

17 August   XIV (Julian XVI) KAL. SEPT.   NP

PORTUNALIA (Ant. mai.) *Feriae Portuno ad Pontem Aemilium* (Allif)

Portunus was an ancient god, who had his special *flamen*. The latter's only recorded function was 'to put oil or grease (*persillum*) on the armour (*arma*) of Quirinus' (Festus, 238L). Originally Portunus was probably a god who protected doors, *portus* (the word is used with this meaning in the fifth century twelve Tables of law: 2.3). This is confirmed by the fact that he was depicted with a key in his hand, and it has been conjectured from a reference in a scholium to '*claves in focum*' that some ritual concerning keys was enacted on this day: perhaps old wooden keys were hardened (or purified) in the fire, and it may be that keys and doors were given attention at a time when the harvest was filling the barns and store-houses. An alternative explanation is that *portus* meant 'a means of carrying across' and that Portunus presided over a ferry across the Tiber in primitive times. But whether he was originally a ferryman or a doorkeeper, the meaning of *portus* later changed to 'harbour' and Portunus became the god of ports.[220]

The temple of Portunus is almost certainly to be identified with one of the two surviving temples (the so-called Fortuna Virilis and Vesta) in the Forum Boarium, more probably the former. The area around the temple was known as the Portunium and was frequented by flower-sellers, but Portunus himself was probably little regarded in the later Republic.[221] (Pl. 34).

Iano ad Theatrum Marcelli (Vall.; Allif.)

This temple of Janus was built by C. Duilius after his defeat of the Carthaginians at Mylae in 260 BC. It was dedicated on the day of the Portunalia (17 August) but after its restoration, begun by Augustus and completed by Tiberius in AD 17, its dedication day became 18 October. It stood in the Forum Holitorium by the theatre of Marcellus and may be identified with the (post-Republican) remains of a temple excavated in 1932/33 between the temple of Apollo and the church of S. Rita da Cascia.[222] (Pl. 4135).

Since Portunus probably had a connection with doors, as Janus certainly did, a link between the two gods has sometimes been assumed. Thus it has been argued that Portunus was an off-shoot of Janus; another view assumes that Duilius added Janus to Portunus in his building, and yet another that an original dedication to Portunus was changed to Janus in the Augustan age, but evidence for any link is not strong: coincidence of the dedication days and meanings of *portus/porta* may be sufficient explanation.[223]

19 August   XII (Julian XIV) KAL. SEPT.   F

VINALIA
VINALIA *Veneri ad Circum Maximum* (Vall.)
VINALIA *Feriae Iovi* (Allif.)

This was the second Festival of Wine, following the Vinalia Priora of 23 April. As we have seen (p. 106), they originally honoured Jupiter, but later Venus was associated with them. It seems that the wine of the previous harvest could first be brought to Rome on 23 April, while on 19 August the ceremonies of the Vinalia Rustica were designed to gain protection of the growing wines, and the *flamen Dialis* officially announced the vintage (*auspicatur vindemoniam*), a practice which continued in Varro's day.

The temple of Venus Obsequens near the Circus Maximus was built by Q. Fabius Maximus Gurges out of fines which he, as curule aedile, had imposed on women convicted of adultery; it was begun in 295 BC, possibly as a thank-offering for his father's victory over the Samites at Sentinum that year.[224]

Though not recorded in the Fasti Antiates, which refer to *Venere* and not to *Veneribus*, a temple to Venus Libitina was also dedicated on 19 August in the Lucus Libitinae on the Esquiline. This area was the headquarters of undertakers (*libitinarii*) where lists of the dead were kept and funerals arranged. Plutarch speculates on the curious connection: was it a philosophical device (instituted by Numa) to eliminate repugnance of funerals or a reminder that one goddess presides over births and deaths? Varro distinguishes between Venus Libitina and Venus Libentina, the goddess of sensual pleasure.[225]

21 August   X (Julian XII) KAL. SEPT.   NP

CONSUALIA (Ant. mai.)
CONSUALIA *Conso in Aventino sacrificium* (Vall.)

On 7 July, as we have seen (p. 163), the State-priests offered sacrifice at the underground altar of Consus, the god of the store-bin of the harvested grain, in the Circus Maximus. In addition Consus had two festivals, on 21 August and 15 December, the former celebrating the end of the harvest, the latter of the autumn sowing. On 21 August the *flamen Quirinalis* was in charge, with the Vestal Virgins in attendance (despite his antiquity, Consus had no *flamen* of his own). After the soil had been removed from the underground altar, Consus was honoured with sacrifice and burnt offering of first-fruits, and there were both horse and chariot races; further, horses and asses were garlanded and allowed to rest. A mutilated reference

to horses in the Praenestine calendar for 15 December, which includes the
tantalizing words '*itaque rex equo*', suggests that these games were held at
the winter Consualia, but the August harvest-home festival, when
flowers were in season and the animals needed rest after their work in the
fields, would be a more suitable time.[226] Hence it has sometimes been
argued that the Praenestine calendar is in error; more probably however, a
similiar ceremony and races were held on both occasions and the calendars
have omitted to give any detail for 21 August (under 15 December only
one of five calendars gives the detail noted). At any rate Dionysius of
Halicarnassus connects the horse-races with the Rape of the Sabine
Women, which Plutarch placed in August: Romulus is said to have at-
tracted the Sabines to Rome by the first celebration of the Consualia
which so engrossed the men that the Romans were enabled to steal their
women (but why Consus should have been connected with the Sabine
women remains unexplained). However, his connection with horses,
which probably was not primitive, may well have developed during the
Etruscan period at Rome, since the Etruscans were much given to horse-
races, and they may have associated his underground altar with the spirits
of the dead and the horse was regarded as a funerary animal.[227] Once
horse-racing had been added to the festival a link was established with the
Greek Poseidon, the god of horses (Hippios), and the Consualia were
wrongly considered to honour Neptune Equestris. However, the racing
made the Consualia an important day in the year for the ordinary Roman,
at least until Strabo's day (5.230) and probably much longer.

A temple to Consus was vowed or built on the Aventine by L. Papirius
Cursor, probably in 272 BC at the time of his victory in southern Italy: he
was depicted on the walls in his triumphal robes (as M. Fulvius Flaccus
was in the temple of Vortumnus nearby). The Fasti Vallenses give the
dedication day as 21 August, the Amiterni as 21 December: it has been
suggested that the latter may have marked a possible restoration by
Augustus.

23 August   VIII (Julian X) KAL. SEPT.   NP

VOLCANALIA

Volcano, Horae Quirini, Maiae supra Comitium (Ant. mai.) *Feriae
Volcano. Volcano in Circo Flaminio, Nymphis in Campo, Opi Opiferae
[in . . ., Horae] Quirini in Colle Volcano, Maiae supra Comitium* (Arval.)

The antiquity of Vulcan is attested by the existence of a *flamen Volcanalis*
who on 1 May sacrificed to Maia (see above, p. 116, 123), but the origin of
this Italian fire-god himself is uncertain. His name is not Latin, but despite

parallel Etruscan names he is unlikely to have been Etruscan since the Etruscan fire-god was named Sethlans; he had also been compared with the Cretan deity Velchanos. His temple always has to stand outside a city (because of his potential destructive force). At Rome his primitive altar, the Volcanal, lay in the Area Volcani, which had usually been located at the foot of the Capitol where a rock-hewn altar was found in the north-west corner of the Forum, but it now seems likely to be identified with the *area sacra* of the Lapis Niger. Before the Rostra was built, kings and magistrates used to address the people from this area which contained a bronze quadriga dedicated to Vulcan, and statues of Horatius and of Romulus with a tablet enumerating his exploits written in Greek letters. Also a lotus tree here, said to be as old as the city, was still growing in Pliny's time. Vulcan was given a temple sometime before 214 BC (when it was struck by lightning); it was ascribed to Romulus himself. According to Livy it was in the Circus Maximus, but it must be the same as that named in the Fasti Vallenses as being 'in Circo Flaminio'. The primary ceremonies of the Volcanalia, however, were presumably held at the altar in the Area Volcani.[228] (Pls 33, 38, 4123).

Of the cult virtually nothing is known except that 'the people (*populus*), drive animals into a fire as substitutes for themselves (*pro se*)',[229] while, as we have seen in reference to the Games of the fishermen on 7 July (see p. 148), live fish were offered to Vulcan as substitutes for human souls: fish might be particularly acceptable since when in the river they were beyond the god's reach. Whatever the priest may have done, the offering apparently came from individuals (*populus*). Vulcan's cult, at any rate in later times, does not seem to have been noticeably important in Rome: this is strange, since in nearby Ostia it was an outstanding feature of the city's religious life, and he was virtually its patron god.

Maiae, Nymphis in Campo, Opi Opiferae, Horae Quirini in Colle

When Vulcan was equated with the Greek god of fire, Hephaistos, he naturally became part of the Graeco-Roman mythological scene, but he was also given the titles of Quietus and Mulciber (*qui ignem mulcet*) and associated with Stata Mater: all of these names imply the power to halt fires. But he had other divine companions who also received worship on 23 August. Maia, his consort, who had received the sacrifice of a pregnant sow by the *flamen Volcanalis* on 1 May (p. 116) and (by confusion with Maia, the mother of Mercury) was also worshipped on 15 May (p. 122), now on 23 August received a sacrifice 'supra Comitium', that is in the Area Vulcani which rose above the Comitium. Nothing is known about the sacrifice to the Nymphs which is recorded only in the Fasti Arvales; the suggested identification with Juturna, who had a temple in the Campus Martius, is not very likely since here she was worshipped on 11 January (p. 64). Ops was a goddess who had two festivals: the Opiconsivia on 25 August and the Opalia on 19 December. She was associated with Consus, whose two festivals were held four days before those of Ops, and with Saturn, but her link with Vulcan is obscure. Her titles were Consiva and Opifera, and like Consus she probably had some connection with corn and the harvest. Her oldest place of worship was a small shrine in the Regia. Her later temple on the Capitol is first mentioned in 186 BC. L. Caecilius Metellus Delmeticus dedicated a temple to Opifera in the later second century; it probably lay in the Forum and is more likely to have been a new building rather than a re-dedication of the temple on the Capitol. Of Hora, the cult-partner of Vulcan, virtually nothing is known, though she was hailed by Ennius: *'teque Quirine pater veneror Horamque Quirini'.*[230]

| **24 August** | VII (Julian IX) KAL. SEPT. | C *Dies religiosus* |

Lunae in Graecostasi (Pinc.)

The moon-goddess (Luna) was worshipped on 31 March in her temple on the Aventine (p. 95). The Graecostasis was a tribunal or platform between the Comitium and Forum. It is first mentioned in 304 BC, but the sacrifices offered to Luna here may have been a late institution: they are mentioned only in the Fasti Pinciani.

(Mundus patet)

The *mundus* was a vaulted ritual pit, divided into two parts and with a cover (possibly called *lapis manalis*) which was removed three times each year, on 24 August, 5 October and 8 November. With the lifting of the lid, which was regarded as the Gate of Hell (*ostium Orci*: Festus, 115L), the spirits (*manes*) of the underworld emerged and could roam the streets of the city. The day was 'holy' (*religiosus*): no public business could be transacted, no battle fought, no army levied, no ships set sail, no marriage take place. So the sources, but the original purpose of the *mundus* remains uncertain. Warde Fowler suggested that it was a pit to store seed-corn at harvest (cf. *Cereris qui mundus appellatur*: Festus, 126L) and that later 'the Graeco-Etruscan doctrine of the underworld was engrafted on this simple Roman stem. Dis and Proserpina claim the mundus'. Though challenged, this view has been supported more recently by K. Latte. It is to be noted that no calendar includes the *'mundus patet'*, that 24 August was marked as a business day *(comitialis)* in the calendars and that the dead 'walked' during the Lemuria and Parentalia when the *mundus* was closed. So it may well be that the ghostly associations were later accretions to an earlier agricultural cult.[231]

A complication arises from the tradition that Romulus, when founding the city, is said to have put first-fruits into a pit in the Comitium, together with soil from the land from which each of his followers came. Apart from some discrepancies about the nature of this pit or trench, the possibility of identification or confusion with the *mundus Cereris* arises. Were there two *mundi*? If so, the second may well be identified with the remains of an archaic cistern, a chamber with a bee-hive roof, discovered in 1914 on the Palatine, but it is scarcely possible to disentangle the traditions satisfactorily.[232]

25 August	VI (Julian VIII) KAL. SEPT.	NP

OPICONSIVIA
Feriae Opi: Opi Consivae in Regia (Arv.)
Opi in Capitolio (Vall.)

Ops (Plenty), after receiving sacrifice in connection with the Volcanalia 23 August (see p. 178), had her own festival on 25 August. At her shrine in the Regia only the Vestal Virgins and the State-priest, who wore a white veil *(suffibulum)*, might enter; a special broad bronze vessel, called a *praefericulum*, was used. According to Festus she was regarded as the Earth *(terra)* and was worshipped in the Regia because she supplied the human race with all its resources *(omnes opes)*. As the cult is old, her *sacrarium* in the Regia may well correspond to the store-cupboard *(penus)* of the king (later the Rex Sacrorum); it housed the fruits of the earth and was tended by his 'daughters', the Vestal Virgins. Ops was also commemorated in her later temple on the Capitol.[233]

27 August	IV (Julian VI) KAL. SEPT.	NP

VOLTURNALIA
Volturno flumini sacrificium (Vall.)

The cult of Volturnus was very ancient, since he had his own *flamen* *(Voltumalis)*, but Roman antiquarians appear to have known little about him (he was regarded as the father of the fountain-deity, Juturna). If the name derives from *volvere*, 'to roll', it could suitably be applied to a river or wind: thus Volturnus was identified with Eurus, the south-east wind and it was also the name of a river in Campania. Or the name may be Etruscan, with a possible link with the Etruscan family name Velthuma. Thus Volturnus may have been a wind that might damage the growing vines and must be propitiated or a river god whose worship may or may not have spread from Etruria. Mommsen's suggestion that Volturnus was an early name of the Tiber involves the difficult question of the relationship between Volturnus and the deity Tiberinus to whom sacrifice was made on 8 December. Whatever solutions may be offered to this problem, the cult of Volturnus appears to have been little regarded in the later Republic.[234]

28 August   III (Julian V) KAL. SEPT.   C

Solis et Lunae Circenses (Phil.)

The Sun and the Moon had a temple near the Circus Maximus (see 9 August p. 171) which was dedicated on 28 August. Tacitus refers to it as *vetus aedem Solis ad Circum*, but it only became important when Games were added to its celebration in the later Empire. Tertullian says that the Circus was primarily dedicated to the Sun, whose temple was in the middle part of it; the statue of the Sun (probably driving a chariot) was on the top of the temple since it was not thought right to pay sacred honours under a roof to the god whom men have in the open above them.[235]

September

September, like November, was a month of Games rather than of the commemoration of individual deities. None of the festivals marked in large letters in the calendars occurs in this month, while about half of it was devoted to the Ludi Romani. In very early days the annual campaigning season was often over, and in the fields there was something of a lull between harvest and vintage. The rural Menologia merely prescribe painting the wine-jars with pitch, picking apples, and loosening the soil around the roots of trees ('*dolea picantur, pona leguntur, arborum oblaqueatio*'). Varro (*Agr.* 1.33) in his fifth period (between the Dogstar and the autumnal equinox) suggests a little more activity for the farmer who is to cut straw, build stacks, harrow ploughed land, gather leaf-fodder and mow irrigated meadows a second time. The rustic calendars say that the month was under the protection of Vulcan and that a feast (*epulum*) in honour of Minerva was held, but September was in fact very much Jupiter's month: the Ludi Romani, ultimately from the 5th until the 19th, derived from votive Games in his honour and reached their religious peak in the *epulum Iovis* on the 13th, while the late reference to Minerva's feast should probably be understood only as part of the *epulum* of Jupiter, Juno and Minerva.

1 September   KAL. SEPT.   F

Iovi Tonanti in Capitolio, Iovi Libero, Iunoni Reginae in Aventino (Arv.)

We are not here concerned with these two temples of Jupiter: the first was dedicated by Augustus in 22 BC and the latter (see 13 April, p. 102) was restored and dedicated by him on 1 September.

Before his capture of Veii in 396 BC Camillus vowed a temple to Juno Regina of Veii in order, by the ritual of *evocatio*, to persuade the goddess to abandon the city that she guarded and to come to Rome. After his victory he built the temple on the Aventine in 392; in it was the wooden statue of the goddess which he had brought from Veii. It lay close to the church of S. Sabina, and it too was restored by Augustus.[236]

5 September   NON. SEPT.   F

Iovi Statori (Ant. mai.)

Jupiter Stator, who had received a temple in 294 BC (see 27 June, p. 157), was given a second in 146 by Q. Caecilius Metellus Macedonicus, who also dedicated a temple to Juno Regina and the Porticus Metelli near the Circus Flaminius. It lies beneath the church of S. Maria in Campitelli. These two temples were probably the first to be made entirely of marble. In front of Jupiter's temple Metellus set up a row of equestrian statues of Alexander's generals, made by Lysippus.[237]

5–19 September   NON. SEPT. – XII (Julian XIII) KAL. OCT.

Ludi Romani

The oldest and most famous Games, the Ludi Romani or Magni, were held in honour of Jupiter Optimus Maximus whose temple on the Capitol was dedicated on 13 September 509 BC. From this single central date they were extended both ways and ultimately embraced about half the month (5th–19th); by the later Republic they had occupied ten days, and had reached fifteen before Caesar's death when a sixteenth was added in his honour (4 September).[238] Originally they had been votive Games, linked to the celebration of triumphal processions which had culminated at Jupiter's temple, but at least by 366 BC they had become annual; they were organized by the curule aediles and in 217 they cost a third of a million *asses*. How the days were distributed between the *ludi circenses* and *ludi scaenici* is not known in detail, but they started with a solemn procession to the Circus Maximus. This is described by Dionysius of Halicarnassus (7.72ff.). Led by the chief magistrates, it proceeded from the Capitol through the Forum to the Circus. Young men, either on horseback or on foot, were followed by charioteers, some of whom drove four horses abreast, some two, and others rode unyoked horses. The competing athletes came next, naked apart from loin-cloths. After them came groups of dancers, men, youths and boys, to the accompaniment of flute- and lyre-players. The dancers wore scarlet tunics with bronze belts, crested helmets of bronze, and swords; they carried short spears. Behind came others, impersonating satyrs in goatskins and Silenoi in shaggy tunics who mimicked and mocked the warrior dancers ahead of them. More flute- and lyre-players were followed by men who burnt incense along the route, and others carrying gold and silver vessels, both sacred and secular. Lastly images of the gods were borne shoulder-high on stretchers (*fercula*): they included not only the twelve Olympian deities, but Saturn, Ops, Themis, Latona, the Parcae, Mnemosyne and others such as the Muses, the Graces and the gods who once had been mortals, as Hercules, Aesculapius, Castor and Pollux. Finally came the sacrificial animals. With the consuls presiding, the priests after washing their hands purified the oxen with clear water and sprinkled them with *mola salsa*; they then ordered the assistants to sacrifice. The victim, still standing, was struck on the temple with a club and fell on the sacrifical knives held ready. After it had been flayed and cut up, a piece from each of the innards and of each limb was sprinkled with *mola salsa* and carried as a first-offering in baskets to the officiating priests, who put them on altars, kindled fires beneath, and poured wine over them as they were burning. 'I know about these rites', concluded Dionysius, 'since I have seen the Romans perform them even in my time'. (Pls 35, 36).

Dionysius, whose great interest in all this is to show that the Romans were not barbarians because in these ceremonies they followed Greek practice, then goes on to describe the Games themselves, which also reflect Greek custom. First came a race of four-horse and two-horse chariots and of unyoked horses. Dionysius also notes three-horse chariots, and two yoked horses with a third acting as a trace-horse. On occasion the driver had a companion, who as soon as the chariot crossed the winning post, leapt down and ran the length of the stadium in competition with his rivals; these runners determined the result of the whole race. Then followed running, boxing and wrestling, the winner of each event receiving a crown. Another form of racing, not mentioned by Dionysius but recorded as early as 169 BC, was for a rider (*desultor*) to have two horses reined together and to leap from one to the other, perhaps at the end of each lap of the Circus; this may have been socially more respectable than racing since it was indulged in by men of the upper class at Caesar's Games in 46 BC. It is curious that the Romans, unlike the Greeks on occasions, did not go in for events with jockey-ridden horses such as form the normal basis of horse-racing today.[239]

Another equestrian event may be noted, in parenthesis. On occasion a military tournament, called the *Ludus* (or *Lusus*) *Troiae*, was held in the Circus Maximus. Allegedly introduced by Aeneas, it may well have been of Etruscan origin, but if so, nothing is known about it until its celebration in Sulla's time (81 BC). Two squadrons of youths of good birth paraded in armour on horseback, carried out some complicated drill movements and then fought a sham battle. Such performances were given several times under Augustus, but how far citizens of the earlier Republic had a chance to see them we simply do not know.

To return to the normal horse-racing with chariots. These started from boxes (*carceres*) arranged in an arc of a circle at the end of the Circus in such a way as to equalize the distance of the course for each competitor. After the starting signal by the presiding magistrate, they then raced seven laps along and around the central *spina*, the turning-points (*metae*) involving most skill and danger. A race of seven laps covered some five miles and lasted a quarter of an hour; the Circus Maximus seated some 150,000 spectators. In Republic times the magistrates provided the chariots, horses and drivers (the last were generally slaves), but at least two 'factions' had developed, the Reds and Whites. The general view that the Greens and Blues were added only under the early Empire has recently been cogently challenged, and all the four Colours perhaps went back well into the days of the Republic, while chariot-racing itself was a legacy from Etruscan Rome.[240] The frenzied rivalry of the factions had developed well before the end of the Republic: in the 70s BC at the funeral of Felix, a charioteer of the Reds, one of his fans threw himself on the funeral pyre, while the opposing faction tried to rob Felix of this moving tribute of devoted support by claiming that the man had merely fainted at the smell of the spices burnt at the cremation. With the growing enthusiasm which matched that of modern football supporters at a Cup Final, went increasing betting as well as greater professionalism and organization. The Games also became social occasions when young men and women, smartly dressed, could meet and flirt, since the two sexes could sit together, which was not allowed in the theatre or amphitheatre.[241]

Not every Roman shared the crowd's delight in the Games. Cicero was no great lover of them, especially when they were vulgarly ostentatious, as were Pompey's Games in 55 BC, while in 54 Cicero took a holiday at Arpinum to avoid the heat at Rome during the Ludi Romani, and he describes how some leading young lawyers left Rome for Tusculum during the Games of 91 BC. Julius Caesar thought it politic to attend, but once he was criticized for dealing with his correspondence during the performance. Later on Pliny the Younger in a rather stuffy letter denounced the races as boring, childish and all the same with no novelty or variety. However this was not the view of the Roman crowd who spent the middle half of September enjoying free entertainment.[242]

13 September   ID. SEPT.   **NP**

Iovi Optimo Maximo (Ant. mai.)
Iovi epulum (Arv. Sab.)
Iovi, Iunoni, Minervae epulum (Vall.)
Epulum Minervae (Menol. mense Sept.)

On this day when the temple of Jupiter Optimus Maximus had tradi-tionally been dedicated by M. Horatius Pulvillus, the first consul of the Republic, Jupiter was honoured on the Capitol. At some time a feast (*epulum*) was established. This can hardly predate the dedication of the temple in 509, although it is just conceivable that it replaced an earlier common sacrificial meal of the primitive Romans at some other site, like that of the *feriae Latinae* (p. 111) or of the *curiae* at the Fordicidia (p. 102). However it is not specifically mentioned in the Republican Fasti Antiates maiores, while the late Menologia attribute a *epulum Minervae* to September; further, in his third decade Livy refers to the *epulum Iovis* only in connection with the Ludi Plebeii on 13 November, and not with the Ludi Romani. Mommsen therefore concluded that Jupiter's feast was celebrated on 13 September only under the Empire and that earlier Minerva alone received a feast in September. But, unlike the Menologia, the early imperial calendars mention a joint feast of Jupiter, Juno and Minerva, while the *epulum Iovis* is likely to be older than the institution of the Plebeian Games in *c*.220 BC and the building of the Circus Flaminius in which they were held. Thus, although we cannot be certain, a feast of Jupiter was not necessarily a feature only of the Plebeian Games, but may have been held on 13 September from early times.[243] (Pl. 404).

The increase in the number of public feasts led to the creation of a college of three *epulones* in 196 BC to organize the banquets; by the end of the Republic their members had increased to ten. The magistrates and

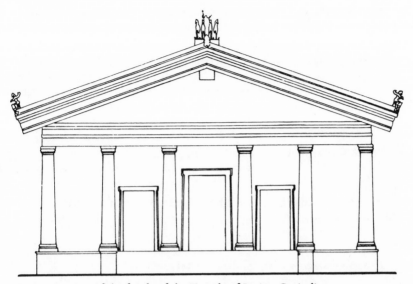

Reconstruction of the façade of the Temple of Jupiter Capitolinus

senators attended the *epulum Iovis*, which began with a sacrifice (perhaps a
white heifer). The second batch of *mola salsa*, which the Vestal Virgins had
prepared earlier in the year, was now used (the first had been offered at the
Vestalia, the third was reserved for the Lupercalia). At the banquet itself
images of the three deities presided, dressed for a feast: Jupiter, his face
reddened with *minium*, was placed on a couch (*lectulus*), while Juno and
Minerva had *sellae*. Tables with food were laid before them, and music was
probably played.[244] Unfortunately little detail is provided by the ancient
sources but clearly this gathering of all the senate in the visible presence of
the supreme divine guardians of the State must have been an impressive
spectacle and a fitting climax of the more solemn aspect of the Ludi
Romani.

A very important ritual in the early history of the Capitoline temple was
the driving of a nail each year on the *Ides* of September into a wall of the
temple by the praetor maximus or other magistrate. Whether this
ceremony was designed merely to record the passage of the years or had
some magical or apotropaic significance, it apparently did not outlast the
third century BC, and so need not need be considered here.[245]

14 September   XVII (Julian XVIII) KAL. OCT.   F *Dies religiosus*

Equorum probatio

The cavalry parade of 15 July (p. 164) had been a splendid spectacle in early days, but since this entry for 14 September does not appear in the Republican Fasti Antiates maiores, the references in the imperial calendars may apply only to the Empire.

20–23 September   XI (Julian XII–VIII) (Julian IX) KAL. OCT.

Mercatus

As after the Apolline Games of 13 July (p. 164), some days were now set aside for markets or fairs.

23 September   VIII (Julian IX) KAL. OCT.   C

Apollini, Latonae ad Theatrum Marcelli (Pal.)

The temple of Apollo had been dedicated in 431 BC. As a foreign cult it had been established outside the *pomerium* in the Campus Martius, and so the temple was often used for extra-pomerial meetings of the Senate. The day of its dedication is uncertain (13 July? See p. 164) but it was restored on 23 September (the birthday of Augustus) by a Sosius, probably C. Sosius, consul in 32 BC and governor of Syria, who enriched it with many famous works of art. It became known as the temple of Apollo Sosianus and was adjacent to the temple of Jupiter Stator. Its podium lies beneath the cloisters of S. Maria in Campitelli, and three of its columns were re-erected in 1940.[246]

26 September   V (Julian VI) KAL. OCT.   C

Veneri Genetrici in Foro Caesaris

At the battle of Pharsalus Julius Caesar vowed a temple to Venus Genetrix, the traditional ancestress of the Julian gens; it was built of solid marble in his new forum and dedicated on 26 September 46 BC on the last day of his triumph. Beside the statue of the goddess and two famous paintings, it contained a gilded statue of Cleopatra, a collection of engraved gems, and a breastplate decorated with British pearls.[247]

October

October was rather a lean month for festivals. Since it marked the end of the campaigning season, we find two ceremonies in honour of Mars, the October horse and Armilustrium, connected with purifying the army. It was also vintage time which was observed at the Meditrinalia. These two activities are recorded in the rustic calendars for the month: 'Tutela Martis. Vindemiae. Sacrum Libero'. After describing the preparations that should be made for the vintage Columella says that after the wine-cellar has been cleaned and fumigated, sacrifices must be offered with the greatest piety and purity to Liber and Libera and to the vessels of the wine-press (on the Liberalia of 17 March, see p. 91). Since the Codex Theodosianus made allowance for vintage holidays from 23 August to 15 October, Mommsen conjectured that 15 October was sacred to Liber and the vintage, but it is rather a far cry back to the Republic, and the precise date should perhaps be left uncertain.[248]

1 October   KAL. OCT.   N

Fidei in Capitolio

According to Livy King Numa established an annual worship of Fides (Good Faith) and ordained that the *flamines* should go to the shrine in a two-horse hooded carriage; before sacrificing they must wrap up their hands as far as the fingers as a sign that faith must be kept. The covering of the hands was designed to protect the shrine from human pollution: it may have been an eastern idea which reached Rome via the Greeks: at any rate Plautus refers to some submissive ambassadors coming with 'veiled hands' (*velatis manibus*). It is improbable that the cult of the personification of such an abstract idea can have been as primitive as Numa. Yet its introduction may not have been as late as is sometimes now suggested, since Fides was probably first regarded as an attitude of the gods to man rather than merely as loyalty between men: it embodied the belief in the reliability of the gods, if man did his part in maintaining the *pax deorum*: when a man prayed '*do ut des*', the *fides* of the god was thus engaged. Some confusion with the early cult of Dius Fidius (p. 146f.) may be involved, but neither Fides nor Dius Fidius had a *flamen*, and Livy's reference to *flamines* must merely mean 'priests' (*sacerdotes*). Apart from that, his description may apply to the later cult of Fides which was first introduced (unless it was preceded by a shrine) when A. Atilius Calatinus, consul in 258 and 254 BC, built her a temple, known as Fides Publica; it was dedicated on 1 October and stood on the Capitol, probably within the *area Capitolina*.

On occasion it was used for meetings of the Senate, and copies of international agreements were affixed to its walls. Horace seems to imply that the statue of the goddess had her right hand covered: 'rare Fidelity, her hand bound with cloth of white' (alba Fides velata panno).[249]

Tigillo Sororio ad Compitum Acili (Arv.)

In a story which is closely bound up with the early history of perduellio and provocatio (high treason and appeal), Livy tells how the hero Horatius was acquitted of having murdered his sister; in expiation his father erected a beam (tigillum) across a street and made his son pass under the 'yoke' with covered head. Dionysius tells of further expiation: before Horatius was sent under the yoke King Tullus Hostilius ordered the pontiffs to erect two altars to Juno Sororia and Janus Curiatius and offer sacrifice upon them. Here we have an example of false etymologies leading to primitive ceremonies being linked on to a legend, that of Horatius and the battle of the Horatii and Curiatii. Juno Sororia has nothing to do with sisters(sorores), but presided over the puberty of girls (sororiare: see p. 151), while Janus Curiatius probably presided over the passage to manhood of the boys of the curiae. The altars of these two deities thus formed the centre of 'rites of passage' in a primitive community and those who passed under the tigillum were purified. In later times after the abandonment of these early rites, Horatius was brought into the story because of the title Curiatius. Juno and Janus were associated with the Kalends of each month.[250]

The tigillum and the adjacent altars stood near the Compitum Acili in the south-west slope of the Oppian hill. It was probably a horizontal beam resting on two uprights, though Dionysius suggests a beam embedded in walls on the opposite sides of the street. It was kept in repair and still existed in the fourth century AD. The beam itself seems to have been a direct object of sacrifice, possibly regarded as a kind of janus or Janus. If an educated Roman, like Livy, had seen the priests sacrificing on 1 October, he might have thought of the story of Horatius, but scarcely of the adolescents of primitive Rome.

4 October   IV NON. OCT.   C

Ieiunium Cereris (Amit.)

In 191 BC the decemviri were ordered by the Senate to consult the Sibylline Books which prescribed that a fast (ieiunium) in honour of Ceres should be held every five years. Greek influence was probably at work, since on the second day of the Thesmophoria, an Athenian festival in honour of

Demeter (Ceres) in October, a fast (*nesteia*) was observed. In Augustus'
day the Ieiunium Cereris was held every year on 4 October.[251]

5 October   III NON. OCT.   C *Dies religiosus*

(*Mundus patet*)

For a second time in the year the *mundus* was opened: see 24 August,
(p. 180).

7 October   NON. OCT .   F

Iovi Fulguri, Iunoni Quiriti (Ant. mai.)
Iovi Fulguri, Iunoni Curriti in Campo (Arv.)

A shrine in the Campus Martius, open to the sky and probably ancient,
was dedicated to Jupiter Fulgur who hurled thunderbolts by day, while
Summanus was responsible for them at night (see 20 June, p. 153ff. and
Festus 254L).

Juno Curitis was worshipped at Falerii and could have been brought to
Rome by *evocatio* (like Juno Regina from Veii) when the Romans captured
the city in 241 BC, but if the epithet is to be connected with *curiae* her
origin may be much older. Her temple in the Campus Martius has
sometimes been thought to be Temple A in the Largo Argentina.[252]
(Pl. 30).

9 October   VII ID. OCT.   C

Genio Publico, Faustae Felicitati, Veneri Victrici in Capitolio

These sacred places on the Capitol are known only from the calendar
entries. The date of their construction is not known; indeed it is uncertain
whether there were three separate shrines, altars or temples. Genius
Publicus also had a temple or altar near the temple of Concord, mentioned
in 43 BC (Dio Cass.57.2.3). The temple of Fausta Felicitas might be
identifiable with that dedicated on 1 July (see p. 158), while Pompey had
built a temple to Venus Victrix (see 12 August, p. 173).

10 October   VI ID. OCT.   C

Iunoni Monetae (Ant. mai.)

This entry appears to refer to a ceremony commemorating a restoration of
the temple of Juno Moneta which had originally been dedicated in 1
June (see p. 127).

11 October   V ID. OCT.   NP

MEDITRINALIA
Feriae Iovi (Amit.)

Varro records that 'the Meditrinalia was named from *mederi* ["to be healed"], because Flaccus, a *flamen Martialis*, used to say that on this day it was the custom to pour an offering of new and old wine and to taste it in order to be healed. Many are accustomed to do this even now when they say "wine new and old I drink, of illness new and old I am cured".' Festus gives a similar quotation used on the day when the must was first tasted. Since it was clearly too early to start drinking the new wine and the real tasting and drinking took place at the Vinalia on 23 April (p. 106), the emphasis of the ceremony at the Meditrinalia was perhaps on the formal tasting after a libation (indeed, despite the lack of manuscript authority, some scholars would be read *libo* for *bibo* in the formula quoted by Varro). However that may be, this was clearly an important ceremony in early agricultural Rome, though the cultivation of the vine may not have antedated the Etruscan period. Meditrinalia may in fact derive from a non-Indo-European word, meaning the place of the ceremony, the wine-press. A goddess Meditrina is only a late Roman invention from the name of the festival, and the presiding deity was probably Jupiter, as the calendars suggest. Varro's remark that even in his day many people still 'toasted' the occasion is perhaps more likely to be true of the country rather than the town.[253]

13 October   III ID. OCT.   NP

FONTINALIA
Feriae Fonti extra Portam Fontinalem. (Viae dei Serpenti)

In this festival in honour of Fons, the god of Springs, garlands were thrown into springs and placed around the tops of wells. The sacredness of springs and wells was widespread in early times (and Rome is not the only place where even today coins are thrown into fountains). C. Papirius Maso, consul in 231 BC, whose army in Corsica had been saved by the timely discovery of a water-supply, dedicated a shrine (*delubrum*) to Fons and this may be the one outside the Forta Fontinalis, of which the site is not known.[254]

14 October   PR. ID. OCT.   EN

[. . .] *Penatibus in Velia* (Viae Ardeat.)

Mentioned in the *Sacrifices of the Argei*, by Livy and Obsequens, this temple of the Penates Dei on the Velia was in a poor state by the time of Augustus who restored (*fecit*) it. The date, 14 October, might refer to this restoration rather than the original dedication. It is uncertain whether it lay under the site of the church of SS. Cosma e Damiano.[255]

15 October   ID OCT.   NP

Feriae Iovi (Arv.)
(*Equus October*)

The entry of the feast of Jupiter, to whom all the *Ides* were sacred, has crowded out any reference to the 'October horse' which is given only in the late Calendar of Philocalus as '*Equus ad Nixas fit*' (the Ciconiae Nixae were post-Republican).

On 15 October a two-horse chariot-race took place in the Campus Martius and the right-hand horse of the victorious pair was sacrificed by the *flamen Martialis* on an altar to Mars in the Campus: according to Timaeus it was a war-horse and was killed with a spear. The horse's head was cut off and decorated with cakes. The inhabitants of the Via Sacra then fought with those of Suburra for possession of this grisly trophy; the winner, if the former, then nailed it to a wall of the Regia, but if the latter won, they fixed it to the Turris Mamilia. Meanwhile, the horse's tail, *cauda*, or genitals, still dripping with blood, were rushed to the Regia, where the blood was allowed to fall on the sacred hearth. The Vestal Virgins probably kept some congealed blood for use at the Parilia on 21 April (p. 105).

The original meaning of the rite has been much disputed: some believe in an agricultural genesis, others emphasize the military aspect. The former regard it as the last of a series of harvest festivals and believe that the horse represented a Corn-spirit. This view derives some support from Festus' statement, *id sacrificium fiebat ob frugum eventum* ('that sacrifice was made for the success of the crops'), but it is rejected by those who see in it a sacrifice to Mars connected with the purification of the army on its return from the summer campaign and linked with the Armilustrium on 19 October. Of course an element of truth might reside in both views: what was at first an agricultural rite could have developed into a military one, with a war-horse substituted for a farm-horse, especially if Mars himself started his divine career as an agricultural deity. However that may be, the military aspect prevailed and by the later Republic the October horse was regarded as a cleansing of the army: both Timaeus and Polybius set it in a military context (Polybius deriding Timaeus for linking it with the Trojan horse!).[256]

It may be that the struggle between the two factions had lapsed by the first century BC, but the rest of the ritual apparently continued, and Caesar may have had it in mind when in 44 BC he handed over two mutinous soldiers to the pontiffs and *flamen Martialis* who killed them in the Campus Martius and had their heads fixed on the Regia.[157]

(Ludi Capitolini)

The Capitoline Games are not recorded in the calendars because they were not public Games but were given by a College of Capitolini. This group of men were still active in the time of Cicero who in 56 BC wrote to his brother, telling him how they had expelled an unworthy member, an Eques named M. Furius Flaccus. The origin of the Games is uncertain, but was probably ancient since it was attributed to Romulus or to Camillus who had founded them to celebrate either the saving of the Capitol from the Gauls (Livy) or the conquest of Veii (Plutarch and Festus). The former perhaps derives from an attempt to explain the College of Capitolini, while the latter may be linked with a curious custom recorded by Plutarch: at these Games a proclamation was made that 'Sardians are for sale' and an old man, wearing a child's *bulla* round his neck, was led about in mockery; Plutarch identified this old man with the defeated king of Veii who was sold by auction along with other prisoners. Plutarch then explains that the Sardians were really Etruscans from Veii who had originally come from Sardis in Lydia. This explanation should be rejected since the Sardians must be Sardinians, but it is perhaps not necessary to follow Latte in arguing that since the Romans captured Sardinia only in 238 BC, the Capitoline Games must have been later than that. *Sardi venales* ('Sardinians for sale') became proverbial, but its connection with the Games remains obscure.[258]

If the Games in fact go back to pre-Republican times, they must have been held in honour of Jupiter Feretrius not Jupiter Optimus Maximus whose temple was dedicated only at the beginning of the Republic. Thus whereas Livy who attributes them to Camillus naturally names Jupiter Optimus Maximus, Tertullian and apparently Ennius, who believed in an earlier origin, refer them to Jupiter Feretrius; Tertullian calls them the Tarpeian Games, but says that Piso called them the Capitoline. The temple of Jupiter Feretrius, which was the oldest in Rome and was small, was traditionally built by Romulus to commemorate his winning the *spolia opima*, and it was here that those trophies which were won only twice in historical times (in 428 and 221 BC), were kept. It contained no statue of the god, but only a sceptre and a flint. The derivation of Feretrius is probably from *ferre*, 'to carry', rather than from *ferire*, 'to strike', both explanations being offered by the sources. If the former, it will refer to the carrying of weapons into the temple for dedication; if the latter, to the striking of agreements. The silex flint, originally probably a meteoric stone, was used by the Fetial priests in the ritual of treaty-making. The worship of Jupiter as a god of war is unusual, and is presumably due to the central position he had gained in seventh-century Rome, the time when the temple was probably dedicated.[259]

To return to the Games themselves, little is known beyond the story of the old man and the reference by a Scholiast on Virgil to Ennius' *Annals* which, he says, told how Romulus built a temple to Jupiter Feretrius and had greased hides spread out and held Games so that men fought with gauntlets (*caestibus*) and competed in running (*cursu*): the competitors were, in Ennius' line, 'rubbed down with oil, made supple and ready for taking arms' (*conque fricati oleo lentati adque arma parati*).[260]

19 October   XIV KAL. NOV.   NP *Dies religiosus*

ARMILUSTRIUM

The beginning of the campaigning season in March had been marked by the dancing of the Salii through the streets (p. 85), the Equirria (p. 89), the Quinquatrus and the Tubilustrium (p. 92), so its end in October saw the ceremonies of the October horse and Armilustrium when the army had to be purified from the dangerous infection that it may have incurred from contact with bloodshed and strangers. This was a festival in honour of Mars; his Salian priests probably once again danced and sang through the streets, during the sacrifices *tubae* were sounded, and the *arma* and *ancillia* were purified and then put away until the next year. It appears from Plutarch and Varro that the *lustratio* was performed on the Aventine 'ad *Circum Maximum*' in an open space called Armilustrium (it lay south of the church of S. Sabina), the Aventine possibly being the last point in the procession of the Salii.[261]

An entry in the Praenestine calendar seems to apply to 20 October, but it could be a note to the previous day's Armilustrium. It runs '[. . .] *sanguinem gustare antea frequenter solebant*' ('they frequently used to taste blood before'). This presumably refers to the tasting of blood from the sacrifice, a practice which had apparently ceased by the time of Augustus when the calendar was composed.

26 October – 1 November   VII KAL – KAL. NOV.

Ludi Victoriae Sullanae

These Games, at first known simply as Victoriae but later as Victoriae Sullanae to distinguish them from Caesar's Victory Games, were established in 81 BC to celebrate Sulla's victory over the Samnites at the Colline Gate. They culminated in the Circenses of 1 November, the day of the battle, and were staged by the praetors. They were first held in 81BC as indicated by a *denarius* of 59 BC: '*Sex. Nonius praetor* (in 81 BC) *ludos Victoriae primus fecit*'.[262] (Pl. 4137).

November

If October was a lean month for festivals, November was even leaner, but for those who had the time to attend there were plenty of Games, with the culmination of the Ludi Victoriae Sullanae on the 1st and the Ludi Plebeii from the 4th to 17th. But there was much work to be done in the fields, both ploughing and sowing. The rustic calendars prescribe *sementes triticariae et hordiariae* (sowing wheat and barley), and *scribatio* (trenching around trees): the month is under the care of Diana, and an *epulum Iovis* is mentioned.

1 November   KAL. NOV.   F

Ludi Victoriae Sullanae

4 – 17 November   PR. NON. NOV. – XIV (Julian XV) KAL. DEC.

Ludi Plebeii

These Games, first mentioned in 216 BC, were probably established in 220 when C. Flaminius was censor and built the Circus Flaminius in which they may have been held before probably being transferred to the Circus Maximus. They were second in importance only to the Ludi Romani, to which in a sense they were a counterpart: Flaminius was a popular leader and they were administered by the plebeian aediles, while the curule aediles were responsible for the Romani. Like the Romani, their central point was the Feast of Jupiter on the *Ides*, the *Equorum probatio* on the 14th and the first Circus Games on the 15th. It is not possible to trace their growth, but at their height the first nine days (4 – 12) were given to scenic performances and the last three (15 – 17) to the Circus Games. The procedure at both Plebeii and Romani appears to have been similar, and we have already seen Dionysius' description of the *pompa circensis* at the Games, with their solemnity, ribaldry and excitement, and their impact on Rome's social life (p. 184).

8 November   VI ID. NOV.   C *Dies religiosus*

(*Mundus patet*)

This was the third annual opening of the *mundus*: see 24 August (p. 180)

13 November   ID. NOV.   NP

Feriae Iovi. Iovi epulum

A feast of Jupiter, which may have been a feature of the Ludi Romani on 13 September (p. 186), was certainly held at the Plebeian Games, when the scenic days were divided from the Circus Games by the feast on 13 November; this is first mentioned for 213 BC when 'the Plebeian Games were repeated (*instaurati*) for two days, and on account of the Games a banquet for Jupiter was held' (Livy, 25.2.10). So once again the senators gathered for their solemn celebration of Jupiter.

Feroniae, Fortunae Primigeniae [Pie?]tati (Ant. mai.)
Feroniae in Campo, Fortunae Primigeniae in C[apitolio?]. (Arv.).

The name of the goddess Feronia *may* be Etruscan, though Varro regarded it as Sabine. Her cult was widespread in central Italy, but its chief centre was at *lucus Capenatis* which developed into a small town named Lucus Feroniae in Etruria near Mt Soracte; it was definitely identified with a site near Scorano in 1953. At Rome Feronia had a grove and later a temple in the Campus Martius; the latter is attested only in the calendars. Since her cult at Rome is curiously placed in the middle of the Plebeian Games, it was probably older than they were, and it could go back to a primitive fair, as at Lucus Feroniae. It is first mentioned at Rome when expiatory offerings were ordered by the Sibylline Books in 217 BC: they were extended even to the freedwomen (*libertinae*), who according to their ability had to contribute money for a gift to Feronia, while freewomen (*matronae*) contributed to Juno Regina on the Aventine. Though perhaps originally an agricultural goddess (she received an offering of the first-fruits of the season at Lucus Feroniae), she appears to have acquired a special association with freedmen and the granting of freedom to slaves. In explaining her name Varro called her Libertas, '*Libertatem deam dicit,*

Feroniam quasi Fidoniam', and an inscription on a seat in her temple at Terracina, where freedmen received the cap of freedom (*pilleus*) on their shaved heads, runs, 'Let the deserving sit down as slaves and rise as freemen' (*Bene meriti servi sedeant, surgant liberi*). It appears that at Terracina slaves could take sanctuary at her altar: this would be a Greek rather than a Roman custom. That her cult at Rome had a link with slaves and freedmen is suggested not only by the events of 217, but also by the fact that the only surviving dedication to her there was from an *ancilla*.[263]

Fortunae Primigeniae in C[. . .] (Arv.)

This temple is usually identified with that *'in Colle'*, but is more likely to be a different one on the Capitol, since the Colline temple was dedicated on 25 May (p. 123).[264]

[. . .]tati

The supplement *'Pietati'* is probable since Pietas is mentioned with Fortuna Primigenia in a inscription of the second century AD. Her temple in the Forum Holitorium was vowed by M',. Acilius Glabrio at Thermopylae (191) and dedicated by his son ten years later. In it was a gilded statue of the father, the first of its kind in Rome. The temple was destroyed in 44 BC to make room for the Theatre of Marcellus. One aspect of *pietas* was the relationship of parents and children, and this temple was connected with the (Greek) story of a daughter who supplied her imprisoned father or mother with her own milk. The connection may have arisen from the nearby Columna (Lactaria), where infants in need of milk were brought. It is interesting that at about the date of the foundation of the temple the personification of Pietas was attested by Plautus in his *Asinaria* and *Curculio*.[265]

14 November   XVII (Julian XVIII) KAL. DEC.   F *Dies Religiosus*

Equorum probatio (Ant. min.; Amit.)

See 15 July (p. 164f.)

18–20 November   XIII (Julian XIV) – XI (Julian XII) KAL. DEC.

Mercatus

December

Although no public Games were held in December, no less than six 'large-lettered' festivals appear in the calendar, though unfortunately we (like the later Romans) know little about them. Roman farmers could perhaps enjoy at least some of them, since work in the fields was less demanding during this month. The rustic calendars, which mark December as the beginning of winter, refer to the manuring of vineyards, the sowing of beans and the gathering of olives; the month was under Vesta's protection. Varro (*RR* 1.35) suggests some harder work (though not during the fifteen days on either side of the solstice): new ditches to be dug, old ones cleared, vineyards and orchards pruned; in addition lilies and crocuses were to be planted.

1 December   KAL. DEC.   **N**

Neptuno, Pietati ad Circum Flaminium (Amit.)

This entry probably refers to a restoration of an earlier altar or temple of Neptune, of which the *dies natalis* was 23 July (p. 168), by a Cn. Domitius (probably the consul of 32 BC). The temple contained a famous group of statutary by Scopas, representing Neptune, Thetis and others. Its identification with some remains in Via S. Salvatore in Campo is uncertain.[266]

The temple of Pietas by the Circus Flaminius was probably not the same as that in the nearby Forum Holitorium (p. 198) since there is no evidence that the latter was restored after its destruction by Caesar. It is first mentioned in 91 BC when it was struck by lightning.[267]

Lydus says that worship was also paid to Aphrodite (Venilia?), Amphitrite (Salacia?), Tyche Ephore (Fortuna Respiciens?), Sophrosyne (Prudentia?) and Eros (Cupid?), but this may be a later development.[268]

3 December   III NON. DEC.   **N**

(Bona Dea)

This women's festival to Bona Dea was not included in the calendars, since it fell into a category between private and public ceremonies and applied to only half the population. It was private in that it was not held in the temple of the goddess, it was not attended by the pontiffs or paid for by the State (*publico sumptu*). However, it was attended by the Vestal Virgins, was held *pro populo Romano*, and met in the house of a consul or praetor. Further its precise date was not fixed. In 63 BC it was held on the night of 3

December in the house of the consul Cicero, and in 62 sometime in December (probably the 3rd) in the house of the praetor Julius Caesar; in the compulsory absence of the men their wives presided.[269]

The annual sacrifice to Bona Dea was made in her temple on 1 May, as we have seen (p. 116). Its relationship to the December festival is not clear. The latter may have been the original ceremony. If it went back to regal times, with the king's wife and daughters (= Vestals) officiating, it retained its exclusive character because in the later Republic only a limited number of socially acceptable women are likely to have been allowed to attend. Alternatively, the cult may have arrived in Rome in the fourth or third centuries from Tarentum, whence Dania (= Bona Dea) is said to have come. In any case the foundation of her temple, presumably some time before 123 BC, will have provided wider scope for her worship, and the December celebration could remain more exclusive.

The goddess was, as we have seen, a somewhat vague earth-goddess who promoted fertility in women, and her cult was secret to the extent that neither the real name of the Good Goddess nor details of the sacred rites could be revealed. Though Cicero refers to her *mysteria* and Plutarch compares the cult with Orphic rites (accompanied by 'play' (*paidia*), much music and objects that could be revealed only to participants), the cult probably started as a solemn and seemly affair. Even if its repute suffered from the sacrilege committed by Clodius, it need not have degenerated under the Empire into the drunken orgy depicted by the moralist and satirist, Juvenal. As to the rite itself, which Cicero called *incredibilis caeremonia*, the room was decorated with vine-leaves, a pig was sacrificed, wine under the name of milk was offered to the goddess (and drunk by the worshippers?), there was music and dance. It is uncertain whether myrtle played any part in the ritual: according to Plutarch it was excluded from private use in the cult 'at home' (*oikoi*), because it was sacred to Venus and might suggest sexual impurity, and Macrobius said that it was banned from use in the temple, but the very emphasis on this negative aspect raises the possibility of its exceptional use in December (p. 117).[270]

The story of the desecration of the ceremony in 62 BC by P. Clodius is notorious. The rites were held in the house of Julius Caesar who was praetor; since his election as Pontifex Maximus he lived in the Domus Publica on the Via Sacra, his office being in the Regia. He himself, of course, and all males were excluded from the house, while his mother Aurelia and his wife Pompeia presided. Dressed as a woman and carrying a lute, young Clodius gained entry with the connivance of a maid-servant who ran on to tell Pompeia, with whom Clodius was alleged to be having an intrigue. But an attendant of Aurelia recognized his man's voice, and in horror Aurelia ended the rites and covered up what was not to be seen by men (*sunekalupsen*). Clodius was caught and driven out. The Vestal Virgins had to perform the rites anew, Caesar divorced Pompeia, and the affair led to Clodius' bitter hostility to Cicero who disproved an alibi which Clodius put forward at his later trial for sacrilege. The scandal will certainly have reminded men of the annual occurrence of this festival, but it remains a mystery why Cicero in Laodicea in 50 BC was so anxious to learn the exact date of the ceremony that he asked Atticus about it in two letters.[271]

5 December   NON. DEC.   F

(Fauno)

If on the *Nones* of December a Roman 'as one who long in populous city pent' had sought relief by a trip into the countryside, he might have encountered a pleasing sight, made famous by one of Horace's most attractive Odes (3.18). Here the poet calls on Faunus to pass through and bless his farmlands; in return the god will receive an offering of wine and a tender kid on the ancient altar smoking with incense. On December's *Nones* the countryfolk make peaceful holiday amid the fields and the farmer joyfully dances on the ground that he has dug with so much labour. Here we have the essence of true Roman country religion: the appeal to the vague and possibly dangerous spirit that guards the flocks to be present, but not to linger too long; the smoking altar of earth; the simple offering of wine and kid; the gambolling sheep; the quiet relaxation after the year's toil, and the dance on the hated land which had demanded so much labour. Horace knew the conventions of pastoral poetry, but here he is surely depicting what he himself had seen and perhaps shared in.

This annual festival was held in the *pagi* and not in Rome, so that it is not registered in the calendars, but it is included here because it must have played a significant part in the lives of many Romans, especially in early days. Faunus, whose name probably derives from *favere* and means 'the kindly one' but with a euphemistic connotation, remained essentially a spirit of the wild woodlands and though his cult was introduced into the city in the second century BC, it never seems to have made much appeal to the urban populace (p. 72).

8 December   VI ID. DEC.   C

Tiberino, Gaiae (Ant. mai.)
Tiberino in Insula (Amit.)

The discovery of the Fasti Antiates revealed that a deity named Gaia was worshipped along with the god Tiberinus whose temple was on the Tiber Island. Both deities are somewhat difficult to pin down. In times of drought prayers were offered to Tiberinus with the formula *'adesto Tiberine cum tuis undis'* ('mayest thou, O Tiberinus, be present with thy waves'), which is echoed in a line of Ennius, *'Teque pater Tiberine tuo cum flumine sancto'* ('And thee, father Tiberinus, with thy hallowed stream'). We are told by Servius that Tiberinus was customarily invoked) *indigitari solet*) by the pontiffs, while Cicero says he was invoked in the prayers of the augurs. He played an important part in the ritual of the pontiffs: thus Varro, who derived their name from *pons* (bridge), says that they had built and maintained the old bridge over the Tiber, and 'rites are prepared on both sides of the Tiber with no small ceremony' *(non mediocri ritu)*.[272]

The relationship of Tiberinus to Volturnus and the history of the name of the river Tiber need not be pursued here: Tiberinus Pater, which appears to be the later, may in fact be the older. At any rate the Varronian tradition in Augustine attributes the cult of Tiberinus to Romulus, and the date of his festival was on 8 December, which was the anniversary day of the dedication of his temple, whose site on the Tiber Island is not known. A reflection of this festival may survive in the words which Virgil, echoing Ennius, puts into the mouth of Aeneas who turned to the rising sun, duly raised water from the river in his hollow palms *('rite cavis undam de flumine palmis'*), and prayed *'tuqe, O Thybri tuo genitor cum flumine sancto'*.[273]

In the legends of early Rome two women named Gaia had links with the Tiber Island: a Vestal Virgin, Gaia Teracia of Fufetia, who gave the Campus Tiberinus or Martius to the Roman people, and Gaia Caecilia or Tanaquil, wife of Tarquinius Priscus, who was venerated in the temple of Semo Sancus (p. 147). Behind these legendary figures there lurks a deity; the word *gaius* means a magpie, and a theriomorphic origin for Gaia has been postulated.[274]

10 December   IV ID. DEC.   C

Tribuni [plebis magistratum ineunt] (Praen.)

This, and not the first day of the year, was the date for tribunes to assume the office to which they had been elected earlier.[275]

11 December   III ID. DEC.   NP

AGONALIA IN [DIGETI] (Ost.)

This is the fourth Agonalia of the year (see 9 January, p. 60) and, as confirmed by the Ostian Fasti, was held in honour of Indiges. Further, Lydus
ascribes it to the Sun, that is Sol Indiges, to whom offerings had been made
on 9 August at his altar on the Quirinal (p. 171). The significance of the
December festival may be that it was at the end of the sowing season (Columella says that the last sowing was called *septimontialis satio*, and the
festival of Septimontium fell on this day). Thus the sun's warming rays
were invoked for bringing all newly sown crops to fruition.[276]

Septimontium (Silv.)

This festival, which probably had no link with the Agonalia, is mentioned
only in the very late calendars; the early ones do not include it because it
was not a celebration of the whole people but only of a section, the *montani*
(*feriae non populi sed montanorum modo*: Varro, *LL.6.24*.). It goes back to a
very early stage in Rome's development in the seventh century BC when
the settlers of only seven hills were united, namely the Palatium, Velia,
Fagutal, Cermalus, Caelius, Oppius and Cispius (these were not, of
course, the later famed Seven Hills). This indicates an expansion of influence by an original settlement on the Palatine, but not yet one wide
enough to include the Quirinal and Viminal. Sacrifices were offered on
each of the seven hills according to Festus, though in another place he
refers, quoting Antistius Labeo, to *feriae* at them all but only mentions
sacrifices at two, namely the Palatuar (a sacrifice to the goddess Palatua) on
the Palatine, and the second on the Velia. An inscription of the Ciceronian
age refers to the *magistri et flamines* of the *montani* of Mount Oppius enclos-
ing and levelling a *sacellum* and planting trees at the expense of the *montani*
of Mount Oppius. Offerings appear to have been made on the same day at
sacred spots on each of the hills, and we might compared the activities of
the individual *curiae* at the Fornacalia (p. 73). However it is not easy to envisage the relationship of the parts to the whole, since the name Septimontium might seem to imply some degree of co-operation greater than merely separate actions on the same day. Despite the lack of evidence, it would
not be suprising if the ceremony involved a purification of all the relevant
districts by a primitive *amburbium* and ended in a common meal, as at the
Latin Festival. It should be stressed that this is pure hypothesis, but at any
rate centuries later the emperor Domitian celebrated the Septimontium
with a banquet (*epulum*) where senators and knights received better food

than the plebs and where he himself was the first to 'begin to eat', to initiate the ceremony.[277]

The most important celebration was presumably on the Palatine where Diva Palatua had her own *flamen Palatualis*. Beyond the sacrifice by the *flamen*, all we know of the celebration is that no carts or vehicles drawn by beasts of burden were allowed in the city. Plutarch surmises that the reason was either to allow a day of rest to beast as well as to man or else to ensure a good attendance by preventing people leaving the city. More importantly, he says that even in his day those who did not despise ancient customs still observed this provision. And we know that the festival was still flourishing in the time of Tertullian.[278]

| 12 December | PR. ID. DEC. | EN |

Conso in Aventino

The temple of Consus on the Aventine had been dedicated on 21 August or 12 December; a restoration by Augustus on 12 December remains uncertain (see p. 178). Consus was also honoured with Games three days later (see below).

| 13 December | ID. DEC. | NP |

Tellufri in Carinis?] (Ost.)
[Telluri. Lectisternium Cere]ri in Carinis (Praen.)

Tellus, the earth goddess, was a very ancient deity, so that a cult-centre probably preceded the templed which was vowed to her by P. Sempronius Sophus in 268 BC when an earthquake occurred during a battle with the Picentes. It was in Carinae, a district at the south-west end of the Esquiline on a site once occupied by the house of Sp. Cassius which was destroyed in 495 BC. In the disturbances in Rome in 56-55 BC and the alleged desecration of sacred places, the *magmentarium* (an archaic word meaning inner sanctuary) of the temple of Tellus had been exposed to public view; the temple was restored by Cicero's brother, Quintus, whose house was adjacent. The Senate sometimes met in this temple and on its walls was a map of Italy.[279]

Ceres was often linked with Tellus: so, for example, a pig was offered to both (*porca praecidanea suscipienda Telluri et Cereri*). Thus a restoration of *et Cereri* in the Ostian Fasti is quite possible. However the reading could be *in Carinis*, and there is no tradition that Ceres had a temple with Tellus in Carinae, though the father of Sp. Cassius is said to have consecrated to Ceres the property of his condemned son and a statue was made from the proceeds. But this statue is usually thought to have been placed in the temple of Ceres, Liber and Libera on the Aventine which Sp. Cassius dedicated in 493 BC (p. 102). However, Arnobius records a *lectisternium* of Ceres on the *Ides* which were the *natalis* of Tellus, and a note in the Praenestine Fasti also refers to a *lectisternium: aedi]les . . .] et lectisternium e lec[tis. . . faciunt quos] manceps praestat*. Thus whether or not Ceres shared in the temple of Tellus, she received her share of worship on the same day in a ceremony which is the only annual public *lectisternium* to be recorded in the Fasti.[280]

15 December   XVI (Julian XVIII) KAL. IAN.   EN (Ant.mai)
                                                      but probably NP

CONSUALIA
Feriae Conso (Praen.)

A note in the Praenestine Fasti runs, '*Equi et [muli flore coronantur] quod in eius tu[tela . . .]. Itaque rex equo [vectus . . .]* 'horses and (mules are crowned with flowers) because in his protection (. . .). And so the king on a horse (. . .)'.

This second festival of Consus probably repeated the horse-and chariot-racing and the garlanding of the horses that had marked the first celebration on 21 August (p.129f.)

17–23 December   XIV (Julian XVI) – VIII (Julian X) KAL. IAN.

SATURNALIA. Saturno (Ant.mai.)
Feriae Saturno. Saturno ad Forum (Amit.)
Feriae servorum (Silv.)

Saturnalia, one of the best known of Roman festivals, was perhaps the most popular: 'the best of days' (*optimus dierum*), said Catullus. From the strictly religious point of view it was celebrated only on 17 December, but in practice it extended to as many as seven days by Cicero's time, as is attested by Novius, a writer of Atellene farces ('*olim exspectata veniunt septem Saturnalia*'), and Cicero refers to *Saturnalibus secundis* and *tertiis*; later during the Empire the number fluctuated between three, five and seven days. The festival was held around the time of the winter solstice, a season when mankind in many places and at many periods has felt the need for rest and merry-making, not least at our own Christmas.[281]

Saturn, for whom the festival was held, has often been explained as a god of sowing or of seed-corn, deriving his name from *satus*; his celebration would thus come at the end of the last sowing of the year. This explanation does not lack difficulties, which include the fact that the letter *a* in Sāturnus is long, while that of *sătus* is short; some scholars therefore have looked to Etruria for the origin of his name. Further, sacrifices were offered to him in the Greek fashion (*Graeco ritu*) with uncovered heads, whereas Romans always covered their heads in order that they might not hear or see any ill omen during the sacrifice. This custom, however, may have arisen only after he was assimilated to the Greek god Kronos, the father of Zeus, who according to some legends was king of the Golden Age. Thus the Romans came to speak of the golden age of Saturn: *redeunt Saturnia regna*, cried Virgil in his longing that a child might be born to herald in a new golden age after decades of civil war.[282]

The temple of Saturn was dedicated on 17 December, probably in one of the early years of the Republic. It lay in the Forum at the foot of the Capitol; the imposing remains are quite late, but the existing podium belongs to a rebuilding by L. Munatius Plancus in 42 BC. It contained a statue of Saturn, which was filled with oil, apparently as a preservative. The statue was also bound with woollen bonds, which were undone on the day of the feast. Macrobius explains this as symbolizing the seed which had lain in the womb bursting into the light in the tenth month; perhaps an agricultural, rather than a human analogy might have been nearer to Saturn's original function, though in fact the custom may only represent an attempt to retain the presence and goodwill of the god. More significant for the ordinary citizen was the fact that the temple contained the State treasury.[283] (Pl. 37).

At this temple the Saturnalia opened with a great sacrifice, at which senators and knights wore their togas. Then followed a banquet, which apparently anyone could attend. This appears to have been established in 217 BC: Livy implies that the Saturnalia itself was first created then, but presumably we should understand that the *convivium publicum* was then first added to the sacrifice; he also adds that a *lectisternium* was ordered, but we do not know how often this ceremony accompanied the sacrifice. At the banquet less formal clothes (*synthesis*) and soft caps (*pilei*) were worn; it ended with a shout of '*Io Saturnalia*'. It was a time of general jollity: shops, law-courts and schools were shut, while gambling in public was allowed. Seneca refers – with disapproval – to the city resounding with merry-making, and few will have followed the unsocial Pliny who retired into a sound-proof room while the rest of his household was rejoicing.[284]

In the home all was relaxed, and (what was the best known feature of the holiday) masters waited at meal-time on their servants who briefly were treated as equals. This may reflect the customs of early times when master and man worked more closely together and the farmer relaxed among his hands. In a fragment by the old Latin poet Accius (born 170 BC) we read, 'when they celebrate the day they joyfully hold feasts throughout the countryside and towns, and each man waits upon his own slaves.' Within the family a mock king, *Saturnalicius princeps*, was chosen as a Master of Revels, a custom reflected more recently at Twelfth Night. Presents were given: little pottery dolls (*sigillaria*) to children, and wax-candles (*cerei*) to friends. Even the parsimonious Cato recommended an additional ration of 3½ *congii* of wine be given to his dependants (*vinum familiae*).[285]

The Saturnalia continued to be enjoyed throughout the days of the Empire, and Statius enthusiastically proclaims 'Time shall not destroy that holy day, so long as the hills of Latium endure and father Tiber, while your city of Rome and the Capitol remain'. Indeed some of its customs may well have been taken over and preserved via the Christian Church. The celebration of the Nativity of Christ on 25 December, just after the Saturnalia, is first attested in the calendar of Philocalus in AD 336, and the day may have been chosen in opposition to the festival held that day in honour of Sol Invictus, whose temple was dedicated in AD 274 by Aurelian. However that may be, the Christians celebrated a period of goodwill when families and friends feasted together, exchanged presents and even sometimes wore paper hats (*pilei?*).[286]

| **19 December** | XII (Julian XIV) KAL. IAN. | N(Ant.mai.) |
| | | NP (Amit) |

OPALIA
Feriae Opi. Opi ad Forum (Amit.)

December and August reveal a similar pattern: 21 August Consualia and 25 August Opiconsivia; 15 December Consualia, 19 December Opalia. The earlier celebrations of Ops on 23 and 25 August have been considered above (pp. 180, 181). Little more can be added about her cult, but the cult-centre *ad Forum*, celebrated on 19 December, is debated. Mommsen suggested that it was a *sacellum* attached to the temple of her 'husband' Saturn; more probably she had a separate temple, of unknown site, which was the one dedicated to Ops Opifera by L. Metellus (p. 180). Since Ops appears to have been linked to the earth and its fruits, the concatenation of 15 December (Consualia), 17 (Saturnalia) and 19 (Opalia) is probably indicative of the general thought behind these festivals.

Io [ventati?] (Ost.)

This sacrifice is more likely to have been in honour of Juventas (Youth) than of Jupiter (Io[vi]). Juventas had an old shrine (*aedicula*) on the Capitol within the *cella* of Minerva in the temple of Jupiter Optimus Maximus, traditionally because when the latter was built, Juventas, like Terminus, refused to be moved and so her shrine was incorporated in the later temple. When Roman youths assumed the gown of manhood (*toga virilis*) and became *iuvenes*, that is 'came of age', they made a payment to the temple treasury of Juventas (and perhaps also offered sacrifice to Jupiter). In the same way births were celebrated by monetary offerings to Juno Lucina on 1 March (p. 86f.) and deaths similarly to Libitina, whose Grove (Lucus) on the Esquiline was the headquarters of undertakers (Libitinarii) where deaths were registered and funerals arranged.[287]

In 207 BC at the battle of Metaurus M. Livius Salinator vowed a temple and Games to Juventas; its erection near the Circus Maximus was begun by him in 204 and it was dedicated by C. Licinius Lucullus in 191 when the Games which included the performance of plays, were held. The ceremony of the Roman *iuvenes* was probably transferred to this temple, where they gathered at the age of fourteen before they started on their military training three years later. Juventas was regarded as the goddess of young Roman manhood, and Salinator was probably viewing her in this light when he vowed the temple at a crisis in the Hannibalic War. True, she was also identified with the Greek goddess Hebe (adolescent beauty), the wife of Heracles, but when in 218 a *lectisternium* was appointed for Juventas and a *supplicatio* at the temple of Hercules, she and her Greek counterpart were already assimilated: at the beginning of the Hannibalic War her interest in the well-being of the *iuvenes* was probably paramount.[288]

This 'coming of age' ceremony could have been a private affair, held when each boy reached the requisite age, but more probably it was a public annual ceremony: at any rate Festus (92L) records that 'the sacred rites of Juventas were established for the young men' ('*Iuventutis sacra pro iuvenibus sunt instituta*'), and Cicero in a puzzling passage tells Atticus that in 60 BC the annual rites of Juventas (*anniversaria sacra Iuventatis*) had not been held; and it is just conceivable that the Ludi Iuventatis, vowed by Livius Salinator, had become annual. If then each year all the youths of Rome solemnly registered their attainment of manhood in a common ceremony (which is likely to have been arranged according to the census ratings of the families concerned), it must have been an impressive sight. Although the possibility that it took place on 19 December depends entirely on the restoration of the Ostian Fasti, yet this would have been a suitable date for preparing the *iuvenes* for their responsibilities in the coming year.[289]

21 December   x (Julian XII) KAL. IAN.   NP

DIVALIA ANGERONAE (Ost.)

Feriae divaſe Angeronae quae ab anginae morbo]appell ſatur, quod remedia eius quondam] prae [cepit. Statuerunt eam ore obligato] in ar [a Volupiae, ut moneret ne quis nomen] occul [tum Urbis enuntiaret . . .]m aiunt ob an[. . . . . .]m. (Note in Praen.)

'The festival of the goddess (Angerona who was) named (from the disease angina because she had once) prescribed (remedies for it. They set up a statue of her with the mouth bound) on the altar (of Volupia, in order to warn that no one should communicate) the secret (name of the city)'

This damaged note can be restored with reasonable confidence from the evidence supplied by Varro, Pliny, Macrobius and others.

The Divalia, held in honour of the goddess Angerona, was named Angeronalia by Varro and Festus. Pliny, in telling how Rome had another name which could be uttered only in secret ceremonies (*arcanis caeremoniis*), illustrates this ancient taboo (*exemplum religionis antiquae*) by quoting the fact that the statue of Diva Angerona was represented with a sealed bandage over her mouth (a finger on her lips, according to Macrobius). We cannot here go into the reason for this ritual name (to prevent enemies from calling on Rome's protecting deity by name and thus winning her over, as the Romans themselves had summoned Juno Regina from Veii by *evocatio*?) nor the nature of the name itself (John Lydus clearly believed it to be Amor, i.e. Roma spelt backwards, since he likened it to Eros). Whether or not Diva Angerona was the goddess of the secret name, the meaning of her own name and her nature are disputed. The Roman themselves connected her name with *angina* or *angor*: she gives relief from the disease *angina pectoris* for both man and beast (so Julius Modestus) or from pain (*angor*) and worry of mind (Verrius Flaccus). Mommsen and others have connected the name with the winter solstice (from *angere*, to 'raise up'), that is, to raise up the sun again. But it has been pointed out that before the Julian calendar the solstice did not coincide with 21 December but fell previously on varying dates. Another suggestion is to link Angerona with *angustissimo die anni* but this would encounter a similar objection.[290]

Angerona was worshipped either in the Curia Acculeia (Varro) or in the *sacellum* of Volupia where her statue stood on the altar (Macrobius), unless these were two names for the same place. The *sacellum* stood where the Nova Via entered the Velabrum. Volupia (from *voluptas*) was a minor deity of Pleasure according to Tertullian and Augustine who curiously name her in connection with children's deities.[291]

(Herculi, Cereri)

Nothing is known of this ceremony except that Hercules and Ceres received a sacrifice of a pregnant sow, loaves or cakes (*panes*) and a drink made from honey and wine (*mulsum*).[292]

22 December   IX (Julian XI) KAL. IAN.   C

Laribus Permarinis in Porticu Minucia (Praen.)

This temple of the Lares who guarded sailors was vowed by L. Aemilius Regillus while engaged with the navy of Antiochus the Great in 190 BC, and was dedicated in 179 by M. Aemilius Lepidus (who the next day dedicated temples to Diana and Juno: see below). A dedicatory inscription in Saturnian metre was placed on its walls. It stood in the Campus Martius, where it was later enclosed in the Porticus Minucia which was built in 110 BC (p. 146). The epithet Permarini may be the invention of Regillus, who also made a dedication to the Cabiri of Samothrace after his victory in terms similar to those used by Lepidus in his dedication.[293]

23 December   VIII (Julian X) KAL. IAN.   NP

LARENTALIA

*Accae Larentin[ae Parentalia fiunt]. Hanc alii Remi et Rom[uli
nutricem, alii] meretricem, Herculis scortum, [fuisse dic]unt. Parentari ei
publice, quod populum Romanum he[redem fece]rit magnae pecuniae,
quam accepe[rat testamen]to Tarutili amatoris sui.* (Note in Praen.)

'The Parentalia are held in honour of Acca Larentia. Some say that she was the nurse of Romulus and Remus, others that she was a courtesan, the mistress of Hercules. She received public funeral rites because she had left to the Roman people a large sum of money which she had received under the will of her lover Tarutilus.'

The Larentalia (later Larentinalia) consisted of the performance of the funeral rites (*parentatio*) at the supposed tomb of Acca Larentia (less correctly, Larentina). The myths about this obscure goddess vary: she was a

prostitute in the time of Romulus or of Ancus Martius, the mistress of
Hercules; she later married a wealthy man, Tarutilus, inherited his money
and left it to the Roman people. Alternatively, she was the wife of
Faustulus (probably a by-form of Faunus), the herdsman who found
Romulus and Remus being suckled by the wolf and brought them up; or
else she was Romulus' mother rather than foster-mother, the prostitute
(*lupa*) later being equated with the she-wolf (*lupa*). More important is the
origin of her name and of the Larentalia. A connection with Lares (deified
ancestors?) has been rejected on the ground of the quantity of the letter *a*
which is short in Lăres but long in Larentia; this objection however does
not appear to be valid. If her other name Acca is rightly compared with
Greek AKKO (akko) and Sanskrit *akka*, 'mother', she may well have
been Mater Larum, the Mother of the Lares: since after their deaths
Romulus and Remus became Lares, their foster-mother became Mater
Larum. But this is far from sure, as is her possible connection with the
Sabine goddess Larunda, who is equated with Lara whom Ovid said was
the Mother of the Lares (who was also called Mania). Equally uncertain is
any link between the Larentalia and the *feriae* of Jupiter which the
Praenestine calendar records.[294]

The festival was celebrated at the supposed tomb of Larentia in the
Velabrum, where it runs into the Nova Via, by the pontiffs and *flamen
Quirinalis*. Here, according to Varro, the priests made offerings to the Di
Manes of slaves.[295]

Plutarch asks why it is, while other Romans make offerings to the dead
in February, Decimus Brutus (consul in 138 BC) used to do this in
December; he ends his discussion by wondering whether the view that
Brutus was the only person to sacrifice in December was false, since 'it is in
December that they make offerings to Larentia and bring libations to her
tomb'. Plutarch here follows Cicero who explains that Brutus used
December as the last month of the year, as the ancients had used February,
that is, when the old year ending in February was superseded in 153 BC(?)
by a new year which ended in December, Brutus adapted to the new conditions. But admittedly the *parentatio* of Larentia in December is puzzling in
view of the Parentalia being held in February, but *if* the latter opened with
an offering to the dead Tarpeia (p. 75), a parallel might be drawn with the
sacrifice to Acca Larentia. Incidentally, it was another Brutus, namely
Decimus (designate consul for 42 BC), that Cicero wrote about to Marcus
Brutus, saying that he himself had carried a motion in the Senate that
Decimus' name be entered under the date in the State calendar, following
'the example of our forefathers, who bestowed this honour upon the lady
Larentia, at whose altar in the Velabrum you pontiffs are wont to make

sacrifice'. But this last quotation has been used to argue that, contrary to the drift of so much of the evidence, the Larentalia was not a festival of the dead: since it is alleged that such an offering could not have been made at an altar (*ara*.)[246]

Dianae, Iunoni Reginae in Campo, Tempestatibus (Ant.mai.)

During his campaign in 187 BC M. Aemilius Lepidus vowed a temple to Diana and, during the final battle, a second to Juno Regina. As censor in 179 he dedicated both these temples on 23 December, and received a grant of 20,000 *asses* from the Senate towards the cost of Games. He gave scenic Games for three days after the dedication of Juno's temple, and two days for Diana, and Games in the Circus for one day for each. Both temples lay in the Circus Flaminius. Diana's temple stood just west of the Circus. Juno's was described as *in Campo* (Fast. Ant.) or *in Circo Flaminio* (Livy). The hypothetical identification of either temple with temples A or B in the Largo Argentina is uncertain (see under 30 July, p. 169). The 23 December also saw a celebration of the Tempestates: whether this was at the same temple which Ovid describes under 1 June is obscure (see p. 127).[297]

25 December   VI (Julian VIII) KAL. IAN.   C

Before the establishment of the cult of the Unconquered Sun in AD 273, 25 December had no importance in the Roman civil calendar, but since it has been so significant in the Christian calendar, we may perhaps end the year by straying briefly from strict relevance. The day was notable in the Roman astronomical calendar, since in the Julian calendar it was the day of the winter solstice (*bruma*): Varro (*LL* 6.8) reckoned a year as the time which the sun took to pass from one shortest day (*bruma*) to the next. *Bruma* came to be used more loosely for 'midwinter', or for a space of time which began on 24 November and ended with the winter solstice on 25 December. In Byzantine days Brumalia was celebrated as a festival, and in Byzantium itself it lasted on until at least the tenth century.

Part Three

OTHER OCCASIONS

1 Triumphs and Ovations

Though not an annual ceremony, some one hundred triumphs were held in the one hundred and fifty years between 220 and 70 BC, so that a Roman would not have to wait many years to see one of the most spectacular displays ever staged in the city.

In origin the triumph was simply the king's return from a victorious campaign with his army and his thanksgiving offering to the god of the State. It thus had both a military and a religious aspect, and it may well have been a solemn procession designed to purify the general and his troops and also to offer spoils to Jupiter Feretrius: thus Festus (104L) says that the laurel-bedecked soldiers followed the chariot of the triumphator in order that they might, as it were, enter the city purged from human blood. Further, the procession around the city may also have been a kind of lustration of Rome itself, an *amburbium*.[298]

Under the Etruscan kings of the sixth century the triumph developed into a far more spectacular and splendid ceremony. Whatever it was called originally (possibly *ovatio*), its name 'triumph' reached Rome via Etruria: the Etruscan word **triumpe* appears to derive from Greek *thriambos* and may be equated with Latin *tripudium*, meaning a musical beat or dance and thus could well apply to a procession which marched to music. As they advanced, the soldiers used to shout 'Io triumphe'. Much of the pageantry also derives from the Etruscan period. The dress of the triumphing general was a purple toga (*toga purpurea*) and a tunic with a border the width of a hand-span, *palma* (*tunica palmata*). His face (or body) was reddened with minium; he wore a gold crown, carried an eagle-tipped sceptre and rode in a chariot. The dress appears to be the normal wear for Etruscan rulers and did not differ essentially from that either of the gods or more ordinary mortals; the Romans, however, differentiated the dress of gods, priests and men and believed that the triumphator used the *ornatus* of Jupiter Optimus Maximus. This has given rise to endless discussion on the status of the Roman triumphator: was his equipment regal or divine, and was he temporarily regarded as a god or did he remain a mortal, though a king? The idea of temporary deification does not accord well with what we know of early Roman ideas (though perhaps possible under Etruscan influences), and may have developed in Hellenistic times. However that may be, it was under the Etruscans that the Romans anthropomorphized their deities and provided Jupiter with a temple and statue, and it was to this new Capitoline temple that triumphs now made their way.

After the Etruscan period at Rome, the triumphs held by victorious Roman magistrates may have become more modest for a time, but with the growth of Roman power in the third and second centuries and under Hellenistic influences they became increasingly magnificent. Even the dress of the trumphator was improved: the *toga purpurea* was replaced by a *toga picta*, decorated with designs in gold thread, and the *tunica palmata* now was given elaborate palmette designs. The processions displayed ever more of the wealth of conquered peoples that was pouring into Rome, and attention was inevitably focussed more on the person of the general who had won this glory and wealth: if a Flamininus was hailed by the conquered Greeks as a god, might not even the more stolid Romans come to regard their victorious generals as approximating for a day to the god to whose temple the procession was marching in order to offer sacrifice? Jupiter might have granted the victory, but it had been achieved by the agent whom all could see and honour.

With this elaboration went closer definition of the terms on which triumphs might be granted to a Republican general. He must be a magistrate with *imperium* and his own auspices, but later the claims of pro-magistrates were conceded, while in the first century even *privati* with special *imperia*, like Pompey, were allowed the honour. The claimant must also have defeated a foreign enemy in a just war (*iustis hostilibusque bellis*): a victory in a civil war or against slaves would not qualify. He must have killed at least 5,000 men: this may be a later qualification, but in 62 BC it was enacted that a general must affirm his figures on oath. Further, the war must have been brought to an end (*debellatum*), so that the army could return to take part in the ceremony; but as overseas wars increased, this stipulation had to be relaxed and other forces could be substituted. On the day of his triumph the magistrate was allowed to exercise full *imperium* within the pomerium of the city, whereas normally he could not. Indeed when a general was claiming a triumph, the Senate met outside the city, usually in the temple of Bellona, to give him the opportunity to state his claims in person. It was the Senate who adjudicated such claims, though on occasion its decision was set aside by an appeal to the people or by violence, and it was the Senate that voted the grant of public money for the expenses. However, it could not always impose its will and some of the specific requirements (e.g. the 5,000 dead) may represent its attempt to keep control, especially after a flood of triumphs was held in the early decades of the second century.[299]

The procession was marshalled in the Campus Martius, where it was joined by the Senate and magistrates. Moving off in an anti-clockwise direction, as in a *lustratio* such as the Ambarvalia, it advanced through the Porta Triumphalis, probably a free-standing arch or gateway near the Circus Flaminius and the Porta Carmentalis. After sacrifice had been offered, it went by the Velabrum instead of going through the Forum Boarium, and passed along the Vicus Iugarius to return to the Velabrum by the Vicus Tuscus. Then on via the Circus Maximus and the road between the Palatine and the Caelian. This brought it to the Via Sacra which led through the Forum; after traversing this, it started to climb the Clivus Capitolinus.[300] Here the chief captives were led aside to the prison where they were killed, originally beheaded with an axe, but later strangled. The general then ascended to the Capitol and laid his laurel branch and the wreaths of his *fasces* in the lap of the statue of Jupiter. The victims were then sacrificed. A feast was provided for the Senate in the temple (except for the consuls, who though invited were asked to decline, in order that the triumphator might be the most distinguished person present), while the troops were entertained in the temple of Hercules. Pliny says (*NH*, 34.33) that on the occasion of triumphs the statue of Hercules Triumphalis in the Forum Boarium was dressed in triumphal clothing.

At the head of the procession came the magistrates and senators, followed by trumpeters and some of the spoils of victory on carts: arms and armour, artistic treasures, gold and silver, and paintings or models of some of the conquered countries, cities, mountains and rivers (one such tablet at Caesar's triumph over Pontus displayed the famous words, *veni, vidi, vici*). Then came the laurel (later golden) crowns presented to the general by defeated towns. The white oxen, soon to be sacrificed to Jupiter, followed, with gilded horns and garlanded, attended by the priests and young acolytes (*Camilli*), with the sacrificial implements and sacred vessels. The chief captives in chains, together with the hostages followed next. The climax was reached with the appearance of the general himself, followed by his army. First, his lictors in red tunics, their *fasces* wreathed in laurel (in later times without their axes), together with dancers and singers. Amid billowing incense, in a richly adorned chariot drawn by four horses, all wreathed in laurel, stood the general wearing his resplendent *tunica palmata* and *toga picta*. In his right hand he carried a laurel branch, in his left the eagle-topped ivory sceptre. In early times at least, his face was painted red, like the terracotta statue of Jupiter himself, and he wore a laurel wreath. Over his head a golden crown in the form of an oak-wreath was held by a slave whose duty it was to whisper occasionally a reminder at this moment of glory that the triumphator was mortal: 'look behind you and remember that you are a man' ('*respice post te, hominem te memento*'). His young children, boys and girls, rode either in the chariot or on the horses; his grown-up sons rode behind with his officers, who followed on horseback or on foot. Then might come any Roman citizens who had been rescued from slavery by the victory: they wore the cap of freedom. Behind marched the victorious army, their spears crowned with laurel, and shouting '*Io triumphe*' and singing songs of praise or ribald comments on their general, another method of limiting the pride of the triumphator whose glory might otherwise offend the gods.

Something of the splendour of the occasion may be gleaned from some of the details which Plutarch records (*Aemil.* 32ff.) in his description of the triumph of Aemilius Paullus over Perseus, king of Macedon, in 167 BC. By this time a triumph could not always be contained within one day: that of Paullus lasted three. 'The people occupied the parts of the city which offered a view of the procession and watched it wearing their white clothes. All the temples were open and filled with garlands and incense, while many attendants and lictors held back the disorderly crowds which were rushing about, and kept the streets clear and open. The first day was hardly sufficient for displaying the captured statues, paintings and colossal figures which were carried in 250 carts. On the second day the finest and richest of the Macedonian arms were paraded in many waggons, glittering with freshly polished bronze and steel. They were skilfully piled up in heaps . . . so that, as they were carried along they clashed against each other, with a harsh and terrifying sound . . . then followed 3,000 men carrying silver coins in 750 vessels, each of which contained 3 talents and was borne by four men, while others carried mixing bowls of silver, drinking horns, bowls and cups. On the third day at dawn trumpeters led the way, sounding a battle-cry, not a marching or processional tune. After them 120 stall-fed oxen with gilded horns, bedecked with fillets and garlands, were led to sacrifice by young men wearing aprons with hand-some borders; boys carried gold and silver libation vessels. Next came car-riers of gold coins which, like the silver, were divided out into 77 vessels containing three talents. After them came the bearers of the consecrated bowl, which Aemilius had ordered to be made of 10 talents of gold and adorned with precious stones, and then those who displayed the bowls known as Antigonids, Seleucids and Theracleian (named after a famous Corinthian artist), together with the gold plate of Perseus' table. These were followed by the chariot of Perseus, with his armour on which lay his diadem. Then at a little distance came the king's children, led along as

slaves, and with them a throng of weeping and supplicating foster-
parents, teachers and tutors . . . behind walked Perseus himself . . .
followed by a company of sorrowing friends . . . next came those who
carried 400 golden wreaths, which the cities had sent with their embassies
to Aemilius as prizes for his victory. Next, mounted in a magnificently
adorned chariot came Aemilius himself . . . wearing a purple robe inter-
woven with gold and holding in his right hand a branch of laurel. The
whole army also carried sprays of laurel, following the chariot . . . and
singing.' Unlike many other triumphing generals, Aemilius needed no
reminding of human mortality: one son, aged fourteen, had died five days
before the triumph, another, aged twelve, died three days after it.

For those who failed to obtain a full triumph, two lesser forms were
open: the *ovatio* or a triumph on the Alban Mount. An *ovatio* was granted
by the State to those whom it wished to honour but whose victories did
not include all the technical qualifications required for a triumph, or else to
men whom it did not favour but whose claim for a triumph could not be
completely refused: political intrigues often played a major part in
reaching a decision. At this so-called 'lesser triumph', the general entered
the city on foot (later on horseback), not in a chariot; he wore the *toga
praetexta* of a magistrate and a crown of myrtle, in place of the triumphator's robes and laurel crown; he held no sceptre, and he was accompanied by flute players instead of by trumpeters. He appears to have led
the procession which included the spoils of battle, but if he failed to bring
his army back (*exercitus non deportatus*), he seems to have been attended by
all the senators only and not by a full military parade; however,
presumably he must have been given at least a small military escort,
possibly of knights. The procession went to the Capitol where the general
is said to have sacrificed a sheep instead of a bull to Jupiter. In fact Plutarch
derived the word *ovatio* from *ovis*, 'a sheep', though more probably it
comes from the Greek shout *euoi*.[301]

An ovation was first granted by the Senate in 503 BC according to tradition, but its use was very sporadic: only one possible celebration is known
between 360 and 211, whereas there were seven between 200 and 174 BC;
then after a long gap, it reappears some forty years later when it was used
for victories over slave revolts in Italy and Sicily. Thus whereas in the late
Republic triumphs could be seen on average twice out of every three years,
an *ovatio* was a very much rarer sight.

A victorious general, who failed to win the Senate's approval for a
triumph or an ovation, could at his own expense celebrate a triumph on
the Alban Mount. This was first done by C.Papirius Maso in 231 BC during the *feriae Latinae*, the very old festival in honour of Jupiter Latiaris (p.

111), to which it was so to speak tacked on. The general acted on the authority of his consular power (*iure consularis impertii*) and the legality of his triumph was attested by its inclusion in the Fasti Triumphales which publicly displayed all the triumphs held in Rome. But though practised on occasion in the early second century, it was apparently not used in the late Republic, and in any case it centred on the temple of Jupiter on the Alban Mount and not in Rome itself.[302]

2 Funerals

The rites that accompanied birth, marriage and death naturally were generally private and domestic concerns, but when a Roman noble died the streets of Rome might witness an extraordinary scene, which made a deep impression on the Greek Polybius. His description (6.53) deserves full quotation: 'Whenever any famous man dies, at the funeral he is carried with all the funerary trappings to the Rostra in the Forum, sometimes sitting erect and conspicuous or more rarely reclining. Then with all the people standing around, an adult son if he has one left who happens to be in Rome, or if not some other relative, mounts the Rostra and speaks of the virtues and achievements of the dead man. Thus the people are reminded of what has been done and made to see it with their own eyes – not only those who took part in these achievements but also those who had not, and they are moved to such sympathy that the loss seems to be not confined to the mourners, but a public one affecting the whole people. After the burial and the performance of the usual ceremonies, they place the *imago* of the deceased in the most conspicuous position of the house, enclosed in a wooden shrine. This image is a mask, representing the dead man with remarkable fidelity both in the modelling and complexion. On the occasion of public sacrifices they display these likenesses and decorate them with much care, and when any distinguished member of the family dies, they take these masks to the funeral and put them on men who in their view bear the closest resemblance to the dead man in height and bearing. These substitutes wear clothes corresponding to the rank of the deceased: if he was a consul or praetor, a toga with purple stripes (*toga praetexta*), if a censor, a purple toga (*toga purpurea*), if a *triumphator*, a gold-embroidered toga (*toga picta*). They ride in chariots, preceded by the *fasces*, axes and other insignia according to the dignity of the offices of state held by each in his lifetime. When they reach the Rostra, they all sit in a row on ivory chairs. There could not be a more inspiring sight for a young man ambitious for fame and valour. For who would not be moved by the sight of the images of men renowned for their excellence, all together as if alive and breathing? What spectacle could be more glorious than this? Besides, the speaker who delivers the oration over the dead man about to be buried, when he has finished telling of him, recounts the successes and achievements of the others who are present, starting from the most ancient. Thus by the constant renewal of the good report of brave men, the celebrity of those who performed noble deeds is rendered immortal, while the fame of those who did good service to their country becomes known to the people and a heritage to future generations. But the most important result is that young men are thus inspired to endure every suffering for the common good in the hope of winning the glory that attends on brave men.'

This spectacle of the corpse and the masked figures representing his ancestors might have seemed grotesque, but it was apparently a moment of great solemnity and national union and fervour, when the traditions of older generations were passed on to the new. This right to display one's ancestral images (the so-called *ius imaginum*) was perhaps restricted, as was the title of *nobilitas* by the last century BC, to those families who had reached the consulship; if not, it may have been extended to the holding of any curule office. Since the consulship was a dual magistracy, an average of two consuls or ex-consuls must have died each year, so such ceremonial funerals were not an uncommon occurence in the Roman's year.

The masks (*imagines*) were probably not literally death-masks, but in early days, when they perhaps had some semi-magical aura, they were rough representations of the dead, which only became lifelike portraits with the introduction of the 'verism' of Hellenistic art about Polybius' own time. They were made of wax until late in the first century BC when other materials might be substituted. The description by Diodorus of the funeral of Aemilius Paullus, whose triumph we have already discussed, reveals a further point: not only were his ancestors portrayed, but apparently even Paullus himself: 'the nobles employ actors (*mimetai*) who through a man's whole life have carefully observed his carriage and the various peculiarities of his appearance'. Unless *mimetai* mean 'artists' or Diodorus has misunderstood his source, the dead man himself, at least on occasion, was impersonated; it is curious that Polybius does not mention this, but the custom seems confirmed by later usage since at the funeral of Vespasian a leading actor of mimes (*archimimus*) wore the emperor's mask and according to the usual custom (*ut est mos*) imitated the actions and words of the deceased. Diodorus also records that Paullus' funeral was attended by virtually the whole population of Rome, including the magistrates and senators who laid aside the affairs of state, as well as by many people from the towns around Rome. Another main feature of such funerals was the oration (*laudatio funebris*), which could be delivered over women as well as men, as for instance Popillia, the mother of Catulus (consul 102 BC) or later (in AD 23) the widow of C.Cassius, the tyrannicide, when twenty masks of her distinguished ancestors were displayed. These speeches, which were often preserved and sometimes published, emphasized the contribution made to the State by the individual, but above all exalted his *gens* which must have striven to outdo other *gentes* in honouring its dead.[303]

So far we have concentrated, with Polybius, on the climax, but the procession that led up to it must also have been an impressive sight. After a death, the body, clothed in magisterial robes, lay in state on a grand bed (*lectus funebris*) in the *atrium* of the house, with its feet towards the house-door; branches of cypress were placed outside. A herald (*praeco*) went around giving a public invitation to the funeral (thus called a *funus indicitivum*). The splendour of the procession was determined by the wealth of the family, though various sumptuary laws were passed (as early as in the Twelve Tables, 450 BC) to limit extravagance. Provision may sometimes have been made in the will of the deceased. Funerals were organized by professional undertakers whose business was situated, as we have seen (p. 177), at the temple or grove of Libitina, where deaths were registered. The attendants of the *designator*, who arranged the procession, were dressed in black. Musicians, playing *tubae*, *tibiae* and *cornua* led the way. Mourning women (*praeficae*), who sang dirges in honour of the dead man, came next. Dancers and mimers might follow, and then came the solemn line of chariots bearing the wearers of the *imagines*. The body of the deceased lay on a bier, which might be carried by relations or liberated slaves. Other relations, dressed in black, followed, sons with veiled heads, daughters uncovered and with dishevelled hair. When the procession reached the Forum it halted and the ceremony of the *laudatio* ensued. Thereafter the procession moved to the place of burial or cremation outside the city limits. By the late Republic cremation had largely replaced burial, though the latter was retained by certain families: thus the Cornelii Scipiones had a family tomb on the Appian Way, and Sulla was the first Cornelius to be cremated.

Funerals, even if public spectacles, were normally the responsibility of the family concerned, but on occasion the State did intervene to provide a public funeral (*funus publicum*). This was done even for some notable foreign prisoners: Syphax, the Numidian prince defeated by Scipio Africanus, after his death in Italy was so treated, as too was Perseus, the king of Macedon. Public funerals were also said to have been granted to some early Roman heroes, as Valerius Poplicola and Agrippa Menenius on account of their poverty. The first Roman recipient, however, may have been Sulla who was far from poor! The Senate voted the funds, the quaestors arranged the funeral through private undertakers, and the dead man and his descendants were granted a free burial place. Sulla's funeral probably outdid in splendour all previous funerals, and indeed a sumptuary law that he himself had passed had to be suspended. It was more like a triumph than a funeral. Women are said to have contributed such a quantity of spices that apart from what was carried in 210 litters, a large image of Sulla himself and another of a lictor were moulded out of costly frankincense and cinnamon wood. His corpse was carried on a golden litter 'with royal splendour', preceded by a large number of trumpeters who played dirges. No less than 2,000 golden crowns, hastily made gifts from cities, friends and soldiers, were displayed. All the priests and the Vestal Virgins escorted the body, together with the entire Senate, magistrates and a great number of Equites and legionaries who had served under him. In turn senators, knights, soldiers and the people raised loud cries of farewell. After the funeral oration had been delivered at the Rostra, senators carried the bier to the Campus Martius where the knights and army ran round the funeral pyre. The remains were buried in a tomb given by the State.[304]

Important funerals were sometimes enhanced by gladiatorial Games and scenic performances. The former, whose organizer wore a black robe (*praetexta pulla*), were known as *munera*, as services to the dead. Dramatic representations were less common, but the *Adelphi* of Terence was performed at the *ludi funebres* of Aemilius Paullus, and *ludi scenici* as well as gladiatorial combats were given at the death of Titus Flamininus in 174 BC. References are also made to the distribution of food and to public banquets. Thus in general important funerals, and their by-products, were a significant, if irregular, addition to public occasions in Rome.[305] (Pl. 39).

3 Meetings of the Senate

Attendance at meetings of the Senate was limited to senators and magistrates (and the *flamen Dialis*), and no one else, citizen or foreigner, was admitted unless introduced by a qualified magistrate. But although the public was denied entry to the Senate-house, the doors were left open and people could gather in the vestibule. Thus Livy describes a speaker referring to his kinsmen standing '*in vestibulo curiae*' and awaiting the Senate's decision, while later in his Second Philippic Cicero could indignantly exclaim 'why do the doors of Concord not lie open?' (the Senate was meeting in the temple of Concord). It was in the vestibule that sons of senators used to wait to escort their fathers home after a session, and no doubt people often congregated there to learn what was going on. If it wished, however, the Senate could go into secret session, when clerks (scribae) retired and the doors were shut. Further, the presiding magistrate could order senators to regard the deliberations as confidential: a senator was once reprimanded severely for inadvertently revealing details of the debate on the Third Punic War to a man whom he wrongly thought was a fellow senator. Thus in moments of crisis, just when people might be most eager to hear the debates, they might be debarred. But at these, as at other times, the people might disturb the meetings. Thus Cicero tells Atticus how in 57 BC on the day that he gave thanks for his return from exile in the Senate, crowds rushed to the Senate (homines ad senatum concurrissent) at the instigation of Clodius to demonstrate against a shortage of corn. When denouncing Catiline, Cicero referred to all the knights and other citizens who were standing around the Senate (qui circumstabant senatum) and a little later to those who were standing at the Senate-house (stare ad curiam). Thus although there was no Strangers' Gallery in the Roman Senate-house, the public could generally get some idea of its proceedings.[306].

The chief meeting-place of the Senate was the Curia Hostilia in the north-west corner of the Forum: since it was restored by Sulla (80 BC), burnt down and rebuilt in 52 and replaced by a new building in 44, naturally little is known about its early structure, except that it was approached by a flight of steps. But it was not the only meeting-place for the Senate, which could assemble in any inaugurated templum. Thus on occasion it met in the temple of Jupiter Capitolinus (when the consuls entered office and perhaps when a declaration of war was debated), of Castor, of Concord, and, less frequently, in those of Fides, Honos et Virtus, Jupiter Stator, Tellus, or even outside the pomerium to a distance of a mile, in the temples of Apollo or Bellona or in the theatre of Pompey (where Caesar was killed). The public could assemble on the steps of these temples and try to hear what was going on inside.

If a Roman citizen started early enough, he might see the senators gathering in the Forum and then waiting in a senaculum before entering the curia: this was perhaps originally an open area and later an assembly-hall (there were some others, e.g. at the temple of Bellona). In due season the senators were summoned by a herald (praeco) into the curia, where they might find that one or two had 'jumped the gun': Cato Uticensis was accustomed to sit reading in the curia while the others were assembling. The meeting was summoned by the magistrate (consul, praetor or tribune) who was to preside and its date and place would normally have been made public by an edict some days before. If our Roman citizen then looked in, he would have been seen a varying number of senators on different occasions. The post-Sullan Senate numbered 600 (or possibly 500), but the highest recorded attendance is 417, excluding magistrates; there may have been a quorum of 200 in certain circumstances, but our sources more often refer to a *senatus frequens* or *infrequens* than to any precise number. The senators wore a distinctive dress; curule and former curule magistrates wore a toga with a purple stripe, while ordinary senators wore a broad stripe on their tunics. All wore a gold ring and red leather shoes (*calceus mulleus*) of distinctive shape (details are uncertain, but a half-moon buckle was perhaps used only by curule magistrates). The Senators sat on benches (*subsellia*) ranged along the long sides of the rectangular building, perhaps raised on a low tier or two. They were not seated according to rank and had no fixed positions: in fact individuals sometimes moved closer to the speaker whom they wished to support, and the manner in which they left Catiline isolated is well known: '*simul atque assedisti, partem istam subselliorum nudam atque inanem reliquerunt*'. ('as soon as you took your place, they (sc. the ex-consuls) left all that area of seats vacant and empty'). The magistrates who had the right to preside sat on a tribunal (*tribunalia*), the consuls and praetors on their ivory curule chairs, the tribunes on a tribunician bench (*longum subsellium*); other magistrates do not seem to have sat in any special positions.[307]

Before entering the chamber the magistrate, who had summoned the meeting and was to preside over it, normally one of the consuls, sacrificed a victim and consulted the auspices, probably using the *pullarii* who kept the sacred chickens. We cannot consider details of procedure here, but roughly speaking, after he had made such report as he thought fit, other magistrates with the *ius referendi* (praetors or tribunes) could lay questions before the House. However, the presiding magistrate determined the order of business and submitted to the judgment of the senators whichever he liked of the opinions that had emerged in the course of debate. Senators, who rose to speak, were asked for their advice (*quid censes?*) in order of their official rank, while time would often not allow more junior members to speak. However, a senator, who had been granted the right to speak, could in fact discuss matters other than the proposal itself (*egredi relationem*), provided that he ended his remarks with his view on the motion. Voting was by a division (*discessio*), but often senators, without rising, might add a few words of assent to a speech and so the feeling of the House could be gauged without a formal count.

The presiding magistrate and the current magistrates, including the quaestors, could intervene in a debate: thus Cicero delivered his Fourth Catilinarian Oration in the middle of the *rogatio sententiarum* between the speeches of Caesar, a praetor designate, and Cato, a tribune designate. Such interruptions might lead to some sharp interchanges (*altercatio*): thus Suetonius refers to three days being wasted in useless wrangling (*triduoque per invitas altercationes absumpto*). Invective might be strong: '*eo die Cato* (trib.pl. 56 BC) *vehementer est in Pompeium invectus . . . respondit ei vehementer Pompeius*'. Marius, as tribune in 119 BC, even threatened to hale the consul Cotta off to prison unless he had a law rescinded: 'Cotta then turned to Metellus (his fellow consul) and asked him to express his opinion, and Metellus, rising in his place, agreed with the consul, but Marius ordered the court-officer to conduct Metellus himself to prison . . . so the Senate gave way and rescinded its vote'. Many lively scenes are recorded: thus in 54 BC Gabinius, under attack in the Senate, 'was wounded on every side and being assailed most bitterly by myself', wrote Cicero, 'the fellow could no longer stand it and in a voice trembling with rage, he called me an *exile*; at that the Senate rose to a man with a shout, and even made a move to attack him.' Again, Plancus, thanking Cicero for defending his interests in the Senate, refers to 'your unending altercations with my detractors' (*perpetua iugia cum obtrectationibus*).[308]. We do not know how often the Senate used to meet, since there was no fixed date (*senatus legitimus*) until it was introduced by Augustus, and magistrates summoned a meeting when they thought fit. However it was traditional for consuls to preside over a meeting on the day of their entry into office when religious matters were dealt with first, while it became customary (and legally binding by the lex Gabinia, probably in 61 BC) for the reception of foreign embassies by the Senate to take precedence over regular meetings in February. Further, it is not clear whether the holding of sessions was forbidden on certain days: it may be that tradition dictated that comitial days throughout the year should be avoided and that a lex Pupia, probably of 61 BC, forbade their use in January and February.[309]

If the more dignified Senate of 280 BC, which Pyrrhus' ambassador described as an 'assembly of kings' might be compared to the quieter at-mosphere of the British Upper House, the Senate of the later Republic often provided noisy scenes more reminiscent of the House of Commons. And since listening to a good quarrel may seem to many a form of enter-tainment, one may assume that the vestibule of the Senate-house was often thronged with idle crowds, as well as by the more seriously minded who may have wished to catch a glimpse of some of the great orators or hear the arguments for and against matters of national policy.

4 Meetings of the People

A more direct method by which the people of Rome could learn something of their affairs was a public meeting, a *contio* – and not only learn, but also to some extent express their feelings. Cicero says that the opinion and wish (*iudicium ac voluntas*) of the Roman people in public affairs could be most clearly expressed in three places: at a meeting (*contione*), at an Assembly (*comitia*), and at a gathering for plays and gladiatorial shows (*ludorum gladiatorumque concessu*). A *contio* was not a haphazard gathering, but a formally constituted meeting, summoned by a magistrate (or a priest), at which there was limited discussion but no voting. The meeting might be merely to convey information, but it might also serve as a preliminary to the calling of an Assembly (*comitia*) in which Roman citizens could vote on topics which had already been ventilated in the *contio*.[310]

An example of its general use is when Cicero, after denouncing Catiline in the Senate on 8 November 63 BC, held a public meeting on the next day to explain what had happened: Catiline had fled from Rome and measures were being taken to protect the city. Again, after presenting documentary evidence against the conspirators in the Senate, Cicero then went out to the people assembled in the Forum and told them what had occurred. This suggests a somewhat hurried informality, but a magistrate could in fact call such *contiones* to meet whenever he liked and either with or without any interval between the summons and the meeting. However his right to hold such a meeting could be overruled by a higher magistrate or vetoed by a tribune, while in the later Republic *contiones* were probably forbidden on *nundinae*. We hear of meetings in the Forum, on the Capitol and in the Circus Flaminius.[311]

Other meetings might be more formal. Although it is unlikely that the magistrate first took the auspices (except just possibly when a *contio* was designed to lead on to a *comitia*), he ordered the citizens to be summoned by a herald (*praeco*). He then invited any other magistrates or senators to attend and help him with their advice. After opening the meeting with prayer, he told the people what he had come to say, and allowed the other magistrates to express their views; the debate could, but need not, be extended to other citizens. The magistrate spoke from a platform (using the Rostra in the Forum at times), but private persons spoke from a lower position, perhaps from the steps. When allowing others to speak, he could indicate a maximum length for the speech. During the meeting all the crowd remained standing. Though, of course the meeting was designed for Roman citizens, non-citizens, who lacked the legal right to attend, and also women were apparently not turned away, though naturally they would not be called upon to speak. A well-known anecdote illustrates two aspects of a *contio*. Scipio Aemilianus, just back in Rome from his conquest of Numantia in Spain, was requested by a hostile tribune to say what he thought about the death of Ti.Gracchus, his brother-in-law. He replied that Tiberius had been justly killed (*iure caesum*), but when the whole meeting (*omnis contio*) shouted in protest, he asked, 'how could he, who so often had failed to be frightened by armed enemies, be frightened by men to whom Italy was only a step-mother?'. Thus a tribune had compelled one of Rome's most powerful men to express an opinion when he would have preferred to remain silent, while Aemilianus' disdainful reply shows that many present were freedmen or slaves of foreign extraction and not true Romans or Italians, some perhaps even a claque organized by his political enemies.[312] (Pl. 38).

In the later years of the Republic meetings became increasingly rowdy. In his defence of Sestius (56 BC) Cicero exclaims: 'what meeting has been held within these years – I mean one that has not been packed with hirelings, but a real one worthy of that name – in which the unanimous agreement of the Roman people could be clearly seen? Many meetings were summoned about me (i.e about Cicero's exile) by an accursed gladiator (i.e. P.Clodius), which were attended by no one who was not bribed nor by any honest citizen . . . these meetings of scoundrels could not be other than stormy (*illae contiones . . . necessario turbulentae*) . . . P. Lentulus, when consul, held a meeting about me; the Roman people came in crowds, men of all ranks, all Italy stood there (*omnes ordines, tota in illa contione Italia constitit*). He brought forward Cn.Pompeius . . . the rest of the leading men of the State (*principes civitatis*) spoke for me'. Cicero told Atticus of disorderly meetings held by Metellus, wild meetings by Appius, and raging mad meetings by Publius in 57 (*contiones turbulentae . . . temerariae . . . furiosissimae*). This was of course the period when politics were degenerating into violence with the gang warfare of Clodius and Milo, but if in earlier times actual violence was lacking, the people did not hesitate to voice their opinion strongly: thus when the tribune Baebius had been bribed to prevent Jugurtha replying in a *contio* summoned by Memmius, the people who were gathered in the meeting were greatly excited and tried to frighten the tribune by shouting, angry looks, often by threatening gestures (*clamore, vultu, saepe impetu*). What *contiones* were like during the struggle of the Orders in the early Republic we cannot tell, since the details given by Livy and other writers cannot be pressed. But in general, the *contio*, if scarcely an effective democratic organ, at least provided the State with a safety-valve which allowed the people to express their emotions and general feelings on some matters, and it often offered Rome a lively spectacle.[313]

The number of *contiones* held each year must have been considerable; only those that were preludes to meetings of the Comitia were confined to *dies comitiales*. When a *comitia* was to follow, the *contio* was dissolved and the citizens were ordered to go and vote (*ire in suffragium* or simply *discedere*) that is to form into their voting units in a *comitia*. Since, as Professor L.R.Taylor writes, 'voting was a major occupation of the citizens who lived in Republican Rome',[314] we must see briefly how it was organized for legislation, trials and elections in the rather complicated assemblies that had evolved in the course of the development of the Roman constitution, concentrating on the period after 287 BC when the resolutions of the plebeians (*plebiscita*) had the force of law.

First, the bare bones. There were three *comitia*. The earliest, the Comitia Curiata, by the late Republic had become a formal meeting in which the thirty *curiae* were represented by thirty lictors. It formally approved the appointment of magistrates and witnessed the inauguration of priests, adoptions and some kinds of wills; in it probably a pontiff each month announced the day on which the *Nones* would fall. The other *comitia* were the Comitia Centuriata and the Comitia Tributa. In the former the citizens gathered in 'centuries', groups each of which cast a corporate vote. But the centuries were so arranged in five *classes* that the wealthy could outvote the poor: the system was timocratic. In early days it had been the main law-making body, but after 218 BC it legislated but seldom, except in the declaration of war and peace. Similarly its early judicial functions in criminal trials decreased, but it continued its electoral function of electing the consuls, praetors and censors. The reason for its decline in these spheres was partly that its division into 193 centuries made the physical act of voting difficult to organize and control, and so the same people decided to meet sometimes on another basis, that of their local tribes, in a Comitia Populi Tributa, which had only 35 voting units, the tribes. This body enacted laws, held minor trials and elected quaestors, curule aediles, lower officers and special commissions. Finally, a Council of the Plebeians, Concilium Plebis, meeting on a basis of tribes and established in early days, by 287 BC had gained the right to legislate for the whole community. The exclusion of the patricians, who were relatively few in the later Republic, made little difference and this Concilium was in fact sometimes, confusingly, called a *comitia*. It carried the majority of laws passed in the last century BC, it held trials for non-capital offences and elected tribunes of the plebs and plebeian aediles, without auspices being taken first, unlike the two *comitia* which were presided over by a con-

sul or praetor, who enjoyed the *ius cum populo agendi* and the right of taking auspices. But the differences between this Concilium Plebis and the
Comitia Populi Tributa were not great.

A *comitia*, and the final preceding *contio*, could be held only on a *dies comitialis*, of which there were 195 in the year, the majority being in the second half of the month and often in immediate succession to one another.
Comitia were not necessarily held on every *dies comitialis*, and on some such
days they could not be held, namely on *nundinae* and days on which *feriae
conceptivae* or *imperativae* fell, while it would not be sensible to summon
them on days when Ludi provided a counter-attraction. The Comitia
Centuriata, which had a military origin in the citizens in arms, always met
outside the *pomerium*, normally in the Campus Martius, where an area was
set aside for a wooden enclosure. This Saepta, or *ovile* (sheepfold), comprised a number of 'pens' through which the voters could pass; it was uncovered and must have been very hot under the summer sun. Julius Caesar
planned a covered marble building with a high portico a mile in cir-
cumference, but it was not completed until after his death. This Saepta
Julia was near the Villa Publica, and probably on virtually the same site as
the earlier Republican construction. It enclosed an area of some 94 m.
wide and 286 m. long; it contained no seats (since *comitia* were primarily
held for voting, not for speaking) and was probably divided temporarily
(by ropes?) into a number (35?) of narrow parallel divisions running along
the length of the building.[315] The Saepta was also used by the Comitia
Tributa and the Concilium Plebis, at any rate in the late Republic, for
their meetings to hold elections, but for the passing of legislation and
judgments they met in the Forum. The reason for the difference was probably the question of numbers and space: in elections the tribes voted
simultaneously, so 35 divisions were needed at the same time, but in
legislative and judicial assemblies the tribes cast their votes one by one, so
that the actual voting area could be smaller and needed to accomodate only
one tribe at a time (with the other 34 awaiting their turn outside). For a
long while the Comitium in the Forum was used: this was an enclosed
stepped area. Between it and the Forum a new speaker's platform, the
Rostra, was erected in 338 BC, so that from it a speaker could face the
Forum and address the crowd in a *contio* and then turn round and face the
Comitium, as the tribes successively filed in. But in 145 BC a tribune led
the people from the Comitium to vote in the Forum, probably because the
Comitium was becoming too cramped. Another meeting place was the
temple of Castor, where, as we have seen (p. 67f.), there were sometimes
rowdy meetings. Yet another, but less spacious, meeting-place was on the
Capitol (the Area Capitolina) where most of the legislative and judicial

assemblies met from the time of the Hannibalic War to that of the Gracchi, but thereafter the Forum was mainly used.

The voting procedure in all the assemblies was in principle the same. Until 139 BC all voting was oral and public, with obvious possibilities for intimidation, but in that year a secret written ballot was introduced for elections and soon afterwards for legislative and judicial decisions. Votes were recorded on official tablets (*tabellae*) in set formulae: in legislation *Vti rogas* (V) and *antiquo* (A), namely for and against; in jurisdiction, *libero* (L) and *damno* or *condemno* (C) for acquittal or condemnation; at elections *dico* or *facio* for the (abbreviated?) name of a favoured candidate. The procedure was that the presiding magistrate presented the business in hand to the people in one or more *contiones*; the text of a proposed bill or a list of the candidates for office was read out. Thereafter the people went to the voting area, where they formed into groups of tribes or centuries. This must have been a confusing time, with much jostling, but also a social occasion as fellow-members of the units met each other again. Details of the voting procedure varied in the different assemblies, but it would be inappropriate to consider them here. In general, after a preliminary unit had been chosen by lot to vote first, the units filed into the enclosed space: in the Saepta members of each group advanced (in single file?) along one of the parallel divisions until each individual reached the end where a number of 'bridges' (*pontes*) led to the ballot-boxes, large urns (*cistae*). Here at the end of the hall was the raised tribunal on which the presiding magistrate sat, keeping a watchful eye on the proceedings. After tellers (*deribitores*) had counted the votes, he made an announcement of the results (*renuntiatio*).[316] (Pls 4138, 39).

Legislation and jurisdiction naturally took place as the occasion arose, but elections were annual events and involved a considerable number of people: after Sulla's time some seventy magistrates were chosen each year. Thus we might look briefly at what this entailed, and we happen to have a reasonable amount of evidence: Livy has shown the general pattern, since he describes seriatim all the elections from 218 to 167 BC, while Cicero throws much light on details, not to mention the pamphlet on electioneering which his brother Quintus wrote for him. In Rome there was no party system: men stood for election on a personal basis without necessarily being associated with any particular policy. In practice the candidates were drawn from a relatively small number of noble families, and few men outside these succeeded in reaching high office (Cicero was one of the outstanding exceptions). For support a candidate relied on his family, his *gens*, his clients, his freedmen, and all the help he could muster from other friendly families (sometimes aided by marriage connections) and from all social and economic groups. And so, with these *amici*, he struggled for success, in rivalry with members of other family groups, and with no party organization beyond the personal following that he could collect.

A prospective candidate made a preliminary notification of his intention (*professio*) to the presiding officer well before the election date, and if accepted he began canvassing (*petitio*). In the late Republic they might start nearly a year in advance (Cicero started to canvass on 17 July 65 BC for the consular elections in 64) and it would be a common sight to see a candidate in a specially whitened toga (*candidatus*) visiting the Forum with a large escort of friends and dependents and greeting the voters he met; he might be able to address many by name thanks to a slave with a good memory (*nomenclator*) who often accompanied him: 'as far as possible', wrote Quintus Cicero (*Pet*.36), 'go down to the Forum at fixed times; a large daily gathering escorting you to the Forum is a source of great honour and esteem'. He might perhaps persuade a friendly magistrate to hold a *contio* on his behalf where his merits could be aired and his rivals criticized. He might also employ election agents (*divisores*), each of whom was responsible for soliciting the votes of part of a tribe, while clubs (*sodalicia*) exercised an increasing political influence. Bribery was rife, and it is significant that *ambitus* which originally had meant 'canvassing' came to mean 'bribery': laws against it appear to have been ineffective. In his pamphlet Quintus Cicero wrote,' the chief fault in our State is that owing to bribery (*largitione interposita*) virtue and worth are forgotten', but he adds 'in all elections, however deeply stained with bribery, some centuries return candidates closely connected with them, without receiving bribes'. In a famous case in 54 BC Cicero conducted the defence of Cn. Plancius who was accused of bribery at the elections for aediles the previous year.

Electioneering propaganda, scrawled on the walls of Pompeii, shows the interest local elections generated there; enthusiasm in a larger city like Rome may have been less widespread, but on important occasions even voters from the Italian municipalities flocked to Rome in large numbers. We hear of many hotly contested struggles in the years described by Livy, while in Cicero's day the temperature was raised by increased bribery and violence. The elections took place in a hieratic order: first the consuls, and then, as soon as possible, praetors, curule aediles and quaestors. Their date was not precisely fixed and our knowledge is deficient, but when magistrates entered office on 15 March (i.e. until 153 BC?), January may have been the normal month, and when the official year started on 1 January, the elections may have been in November. After Sulla had differentiated more sharply between magistrates and promagistrates, they were transferred to July. Tribunician elections took place in July in the first century BC when tribunes entered office on 10 December. Thus, with the festivals and Games, July must have been a fairly busy month in Rome, despite the summer heat.

Legislation and trials in the popular assemblies were of course spread more throughout the year. In the early days of the Republic, the Comitia Centuriata had dealt with capital charges and appeal (*provocatio*), but although it heard one or two cases of treason (*perduellio*) in the late second century, by that time tribunes brought their main prosecutions before the Concilium Plebis. The first half of the second century in particular was the heyday of popular jurisdiction, when tribunes and aediles were active in exposing alleged abuses or merely bringing charges for political ends. Many of these trials involved some of the great men of the State, and when a Scipio or a Cato was charged, public interest must have been widespread. In fact Cato was said to have been prosecuted forty-four times, often before the *comitia*, but never condemned! The procedure was that notice of judicial action (as also of proposed legislation) had to be posted up at least a *trinum nundinum* before the final *contio* and the *comitia*. In the meantime other *contiones* (at least three before trials) were held and addressed by the president and often by other magistrates and perhaps by some private individuals. Then, if no unfavourable omens were reported, the trial could start on the appointed day after the last *contio*. But in 149 BC a permanent court was established to deal with extortion (*quaestio repetundarum*), and more such standing courts followed until Sulla formalized the whole system. These courts were in the hands of senators or Equites and they gradually overshadowed the jurisdiction of the tribunes who, though retaining the constitutional right, seldom brought prosecutions before the Tribes during the late Republic.

After 287 BC the people controlled legislation: the resolutions (*plebiscita*) of the Concilium Plebis became binding on the whole community; whereas the resolutions of the Senate (*senatus consulta*), which were strictly only advice to magistrates, were binding only in practice and not in law. But as the tribunes of the plebs came increasingly from the governing class, they carried much legislation that was generally acceptable. However, with the challenge of the Gracchi some tended to resume their earlier role of champions of the people, while others became tools in the hands of ambitious 'popular' politicians. The well-intentioned legislation of the Gracchi had led to bloodshed, and before very long tribunes were threatening the constitution by proposing 'extraordinary' commands for some of the *principes*. These, which were opposed by the Senate, gave rise to heated discussion and angry meetings, as when Gabinius and Manilius proposed commands against the pirates and against Mithridates for Pompey (67 and 66 BC) or when Vatinius moved that Caesar should be given a Gallic command.

In these various ways public meetings demanded not only the performance of civic duty but they also had their 'entertainment' value, especially when the fate of famous men or crucial issues were at stake. We can reach no real idea of how many voters attended regularly, but though Cicero might complain of low attendance at times, one can scarcely envisage a small turn out when Scipio Africanus, the conqueror of Hannibal, was arraigned, when Marius stood for the consulship or when Clodius proposed a law for the distribution of free corn, while at the election of Gaius Gracchus there was not sufficient room in the voting area of the Campus Martius for all the electors, some of whom had to shout their support from neighbouring house tops.[312]

5 The Census

A periodic census of Roman citizens was held, originally *quinto quoque anno*, every four years, but from 209 BC onwards the phrase was interpreted as every five years; the interval between two celebrations was named a *lustrum*. The duties of the censors included the revision of the list of citizens, the Equites and the Senate. Their scrutiny of the Senate (*lectio Senatus*) was mainly a private affair, since they only placed a mark (*nota*) in the register against the names of any senators whom they wished to expel and then added any new names. However, the revised list was apparently read aloud from the Rostra to the people assembled in a *contio*, and if a popular figure had been ejected, one can imagine that some demonstrations of public feeling might occur.[318] Thus when Cato in 184 BC expelled L.Flamininus, the brother of the victor of Cynoscephalae and of the liberator of the Greeks, a family as influential as the Flaminini could press for an explantion in the *contio*, and Cato was morally obliged to justify his action in a damning speech: not that the result did Lucius any good.

The review of the Equites, however, was a much more spectacular affair. It was held in the Forum, often at the temple of Castor and Pollux (see p. 64). Here the whole corps of the eighteen centuries of the Equites *equo publico* filed past the censor seated on a tribunal, each man leading his horse by the bridle when his name was called out. The censor then passed him (*traduc equum*) or discharged him (*vende equum*). A man could be discharged either *sine ignominia* or in disgrace; in the former case the reason would be the completion of the normal period of service, in the latter some moral weakness or failure to look after his horse properly. Here again, as with senators, censors might be activated by political as well as moral motives, as when Cato expelled L.Cornelius Scipio Asiaticus; though this was done without *ignominia* and perhaps on reasonable grounds it was a public insult to a leading member of a rival family. If and how this ceremony at any time was linked with the *transvectio* of the Roman Equites held on 15 July remains obscure (see p. 165); it was primarily a civil ceremony since the censors were not military commanders, while the *transvectio* appears to have been a military parade.

The census of the people was the first task of the censors who summoned them to meet in the Campus Martius. This was a reflection of the mustering of the army into its centuries, and it was these men, grouped in the five *classes*, that were the chief concern of the censors who had to register them in their tribes and assess their property in order to assign them to the correct *classes* for purposes of both taxation and military service. The head of each family had to answer questions about the property and age of all its members; the *capite censi*, whose property was less than the minimum qualification for enrolment in the *classes*, could be represented by the leaders of their tribes. Varro (*LL*,6.86) has preserved details of the preliminary procedure. After the censor had taken the auspices by night in a *templum*, he ordered a herald to issue a summons from the *templum* and then from the city walls to all citizen soldiers and to private citizens as spokesmen of their tribes (*curatores omnium tribuum*). At dawn the censors, the clerks and the magistrates were annointed with myrrh and ointments. At the meeting the two censors decided by lot which of them should conduct the *lustrum* and then after a *templum* had been established in the Campus Martius, the chosen censor held the meeting and continued what must have been a very long task. When he had finished this and all the other duties of the office, the end of the censorship was marked by a formal purification of the people (*lustratio*) who were again marshalled outside the *pomerium* in the Campus Martius. After a procession of the *suovetaurilia* had been led around them three times, the animals were sacrificed to Mars. The ceremony was known as *lustrum condere*, the precise meaning of the phrase having been much debated.[319] At this closing ceremony the censor in charge offered a conventional prayer to the gods to make the affairs of the Roman people better and greater (*ut populi Romani res meliores amplioresque facerent*) until in 142 BC according to the well-known anecdote the censor (Scipio Aemilianus?) changed the prayer to one that the gods would keep Rome safe for ever, since her affairs were already sufficiently good and great (*satis bonae et magnae sunt; itaque precor ut eas perpetuo incolumes servent*).[320]

Key to plans of Temples of Rome

The figures mark the position of (a) buildings whose sites are certain or approximately known, and (b) those, with a question mark added, of which the general area is known. The precise disposition of many of the lesser temples in some areas (e.g. the Capitol, Aventine or Campus Martius) remains uncertain, while even some existing temples (e.g. those in the Largo Argentina) cannot with certainty be attributed to the correct deities. The days and dates of their dedications, where known, are added (though cults on a site may often predate the dedication of a temple there).

PLAN 1

1? Temple of Flora
2? Temple of Quirinus. 17 Feb. 293
3? Temple of Sol Indiges. 9 Aug.
4? Temple of Salus. 5 Aug. 302
5? Temple of Tres Fortunae. 5 April
6 Temple of Semo Sancus. 5 June 466
7? Shrine of Fons. 13 Oct. 231
8 Temple of Juno Lucina. 1 March c.375?
9? Temple of Venus Libitina. 19 Aug.
10? Trigarium
11? Caprae palus
12? Temple of Juturna. 11 Jan.
13? Grove of Anna Perenna. Festival 14 March
14 Saepta
15 Diribitorium
16–90 See plan 2
91? Tigillum Sororium. 11 Oct
92? Temple of Tellus. 13 Dec.268

93? Shrine of Vica Pota. 5 Jan.
94? Temple of the Lares. 27 June
95? Temple of Jupiter Stator. 27 June
96? Temple of Fors Fortuna. 24 June
97 Lucus Furrinae. 25 July
98? Temple of Hercules Invictus ad Portam Geminam. 13 Aug.
99? Temple of Luna. 31 March
100? Temple of Vortumnus. 13 Aug.c.264?
101? Temple of Jupiter Libertas. 13 April
102? Temple of Juno Regina. 1 Sept.392
103? Armilustrium. 19 Oct.
104? Temple of Consus. 21 Aug. 272
105? Temple of Minerva. 19 March
106? Temple of Diana, 13 Aug.
107? Temple of Flora. 28 April 241 or 238
108? Temple of Mercury. 15 May 495

109? Temple of Summanus. 20 June c.278
110? Temple of Iuventas. 19 Dec. (?), 191
111? Temple of Venus Verticordia, 1 April 114
112? Temple of Venus Obsequens. 19 Aug.
113 Circus Maximus
114? Temple of Bona Dea. 1 May
115? Temple of Honos and Virtus. 17 July 205
116? Temple of Honos. 17 July 233
117? Temple of the Tempestates. 1 June or 23 Dec.c.259
118? Mars. 1 June
119? Temple of Minerva Medica
120? Shrine of Minerva Capta. 19 March c.241
121? Temple of Hercules Victor. 142
122? Temple of Carna. 1 June
123? Grove of the Camenae. 13 Aug.

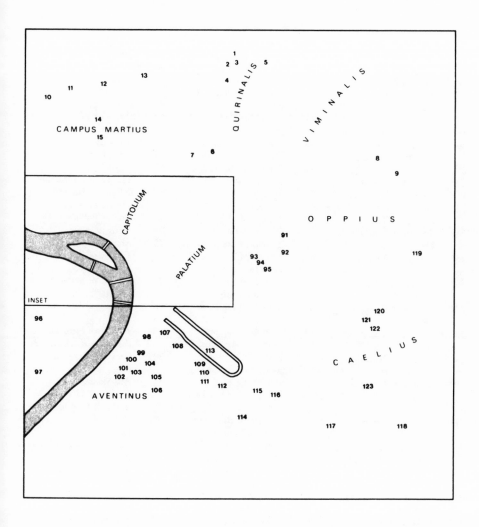

CAMPUS MARTIUS

QUIRINALIS

VIMINALIS

CAPITOLIUM

PALATIUM

OPPIUS

INSET

AVENTINUS

CAELIUS

1
2 3 5
4
13
11 12
10
14
15
7 6
8
9
91
92
119
93
94
95
96
120
121
122
98 107
99 108
100 104 113
101 103 109
102 105 110
106 111 112
115 116
123
114
97
117 118

PLAN 2

16	Temples in Largo Argentina	39?	Temple of Juno Sospita. 1 Feb. 194	62	Rostra
17?	Temple of Juno Curitis. 7 Oct.	40?	Shrine of Carmentis. 15 Jan.	63?	Temple of Ops. 19 Dec.
18?	Temple of Fortuna Huiusce Diei. 30 July c.101	41?	Temple of Faunus. 13 Feb. 194	64	Curia
				65	Lapis Niger
		42?	Temple of Vediovis. 3 Jan.194	66	Comitium
19?	Grove of Feronia			67	Shrine of Venus Cloacina
20?	Temple of Lares Permarini. 22 Dec.179	43?	Shrine of Tiberinus. 8 Dec.	68	Volcanal
21	Theatre of Pompey	44	Temple of Aesculapius. 1 Jan.c.291	69	Lacus Curtius
22?	Temple of Fortuna Equestris. 13 Aug.173			70	Regia
		45	Temple of Juno Moneta. 1 June 344	71	Temple of Castor and Pollux. 27 Jan.484
23?	Shrine of Jupiter Fulgur. 7 Oct.	46?	Temple of Venus Erucina. 215	72	Temple of Vesta
24?	Temple of Neptune. 1 Dec.			73	Domus Publica
		47?	Temple of Mens. 215	74	Lacus Juturnae
25?	Temple of Vulcan. 23 Aug.	48?	Temple of Concord. 5 Feb.216	75	Area of S.Omobono
26?	Temple of Hercules Custos. 4 June			76	Temple of Fortuna. 11 June
		49?	Temple of Fausta Felicitas. 1 July	77	Temple of Mater Matuta. 11 June
27?	Temple of Pietas. 1 Dec.	50?	Temple of Jupiter Feretrius	78	Temple of Portunus. 17 Aug.
28?	Temple of Castor. 13 Aug.	51	Temple of Jupiter Optimus Maximus. 13 Sept. 509	79?	Temple of Hercules Pompeianus. 12 Aug.?
29?	Temple of Mars. 14 May 135 (?)	52?	Temple of Fortuna Primigenia	80	Grove of Helernus. 1 Feb.
30?	Temple of Hercules Musarum. 30 June c. 189	53?	Temple of Fides. 1 Oct 254 or 250	81?	Ara Maxima
				82?	Temple of Hercules Invictus. 12 Aug.?
31?	Temple of Diana. 23 Dec. 179	54?	Temple of Honos and Virtus 17 July 233	83?	Shrine of Volupia. 21 Dec.
32?	Temple of Juno Regina. 23 Dec. 179	55?	Temple of Ops. 25 Aug.	84?	Tomb of Acca Larentia. 23 Dec.
33?	Temple of Jupiter Stator. 5 Sept. c. 146	56?	Shrine of Genius Publicus.	85?	Temple of Lares. 1 May
34?	Temple of Apollo. 13 July 431	57	Temple of Vediovis. 7 March 192	86?	Shrine of Victoria Virgo. 1 Aug.193
35?	Temple of Bellona. 3 June c.296	58	Tabularium	87?	Temple of Victoria. 1 Aug.
		59	Temple of Saturn. 17 Dec.c.509(?)	88?	The Lupercal
36?	Temple of Pietas. 13 Nov.181	60	Temple of Concord. 22 July c. 367 (?)	89	Temple of Magna Mater. 11 April 191
37?	Temple of Janus. 17 Aug.c.260	61?	Shrine of Genius Publicus, etc. 9 Oct.	90?	Temple of Juno Sospita. 1 Feb.?
38?	Temple of Spes. 1 Aug.				

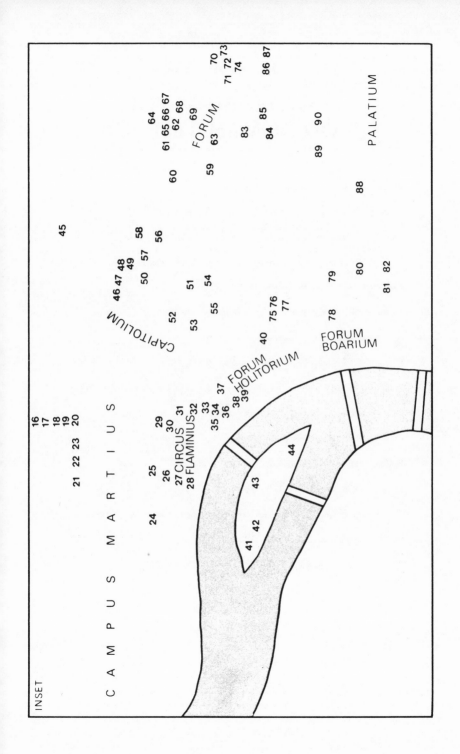

GENERAL WORKS
ON ROMAN RELIGION

More detailed works are quoted in the Notes

Altheim, F., *A History of Roman Religion* (London, 1938)

Bailey, C., *Phases in the Religion of Ancient Rome* (Oxford, 1932)

Bayet, J., *Histoire politique et psychologique de la religion romaine*² (Paris, 1969)

De Sanctis, G., *Storia dei Romani,* IV.2.1. (Florence, 1953)

Dumézil, G., *Archaic Roman Religion* (Chicago, 1965)

— *Fêtes romaines d'été et d'automne* (Paris, 1975)

Grenier, A., *Les religions étrusques et romaines* (Paris, 1948)

Halliday, W.R., *Lectures on the History of Roman Religion* (Liverpool, 1922)

Latte, K., *Römische Religionsgeschichte* (Munich, 1960)

Ogilvie, R.M., *The Romans and their Gods* (London, 1969)

Radke, G., *Die Götter Altitaliens* (Münster, 1949)

Rose, H.J., *Ancient Roman Religion* (London, 1949)

Warde Fowler, W., *The Religious Experience of the Roman People* (London, 1922)

— *The Roman Festivals* (London, 1889)

Wissowa, G., *Religion und Kultus der Römer*² (Munich, 1911)

ABBREVIATIONS

Aelian, *NH* — Aelian, *De Natura Animalium*

App. *BC* — Appian, *Bella Civilia*

Arnobius, *Adv. Nat.* — Arnobius, *Adversus Nationes*

Augustine, *Civ.D.* — Augustine, *De Civitate Dei*

Aul.Gell — Aulus Gellius, *Noctes Atticae*

Caesar, *BC* — Caesar, *Bellum Civile*

Cato, *Agr.* — Cato, *De Agricultura*

Censorinus, *DN* — Censorinus, *De Die Natali*

Cic. *Arch.* — Cicero, *Pro Archia*

  Att. — *Epistulae ad Atticum*

  Cael. — *Pro Caelio*

  Cat. — *In Catilinam*

  Div. — *De Divinatione*

  Dom. — *De Domo Sua*

  Fam. — *Epistulae ad Familiares*

  Fin. — *De Finibus*

  Har.Resp. — *De Haruspicum Responso*

  Leg. Agr. — *De Lege Agraria*

  Leg. — *De Legibus*

  Leg.Man. — *De Lege Manilia*

  Mil. — *Pro Milone*

  Mur. — *Pro Murena*

  Nat.Deor. — *De Natura Deorum*

  Phil. — *Orationes Philippicae*

  Pis. — *In Pisonem*

  QFr. — *Epistulae ad Quintum Fratrem*

  Rep. — *De Republica*

  Sen. — *De Senectute*

  Sest. — *Pro Sestio*

  Tusc.Disp. — *Tusculanae Disputationes*

Columella — Columella, *De Re Rustica*

De Vir Ill — *De Viris Illustribus*

Dio Cass. — Dio Cassius

Dion. H. — Dionysius Halicarnassus

Festus — Festus (edited by W.M.Lindsay)

Grom. *Vet.* — *Gromatici Veteres*

Lactantius, *Div. Inst.* — Lactantius, *Divinae Institutiones*

Lydus, *Mens.* — Lydus, *De Mensibus*

Macrob. — Macrobius, *Saturnalia*

Minucius Felix, *Oct.* — Minucius Felix, *Octavius*

Ovid, *AA* — Ovid, *Ars Amatoria*

  F. — *Fasti*

  Pont. — *Epistulae ex Ponto*

Petron. *Sat.* — Petronius, *Satura*

Pliny, *NH* — Pliny, *Naturalis Historia*

Plut.*Qu.Rom.* — Plutarch, *Quaestiones Romanae*

Suet. — Suetonius

Tac. *Ann.* — Tacitus, *Annales*

  Hist. — *Historiae*

Tertullian, *Nat.* — Tertullian, *Ad Nationes*

  Apol — *Apologeticus*

  Spect. — *De Spectaculis*

Val. Max. — Valerius Maximus

Varro, *LL* — Varro, *De Lingua Latina*

  Rust. — *De Re Rustica*

Virg.*Georg* — Virgil, *Georgics*

Altheim, *HRR* — F.Altheim, *A History of Roman Religion* (1938)

Bömer — F.Bömer, *P.Ovidius Naso: Die Fasten*, 2 vols (1958)

CAH — *Cambridge Ancient History*

CIL — *Corpus Inscriptionum Latinarum* (1863–)

CQ — *Classical Quarterly*

CR — *Classical Review*

Crawford, *RRC* — M.Crawford, *Roman Republican Coinage* (1974)

Dar.Sag. — Ch. Daremberg, and E. Saglio, *Dictionnaire des Antiquités grecques et romaines* (1877–1919)

Degrassi, A.Degrassi, *Inscriptiones*
 ILLRP *Latinae Liberae Rei*
 Publicae, (1957–63)

 In.It. *Inscriptiones Italiae* XIII, ii,
 Fasti Anni Numani et
 Iuliani (1963)

De Sanctis, G.De Sanctis, *Storia dei*
Stor.Rom. *Romani* (1907–66)

Dessau, *ILS* H.Dessau, *Inscriptiones*
 Latinae Selectae (1892–1916)

Dial.Arch. *Dialoghi di Archeologia*

ERE J.Hastings, *Encyclopaedia of*
 Religion and Ethics
 (1908–21)

Frazer, *Fasti* J.G.Frazer, P.*Ovidii Nasonis*
 Fastorum Libri Sex, i–v
 (1929, repr. 1973)

ILS H.Dessau, *Inscriptiones*
 Latinae Selectae (1892–1916)

JDAI *Jahrbuch der deutschen*
 archäologischen Instituts

JRS *Journal of Roman Studies*

Latte, RR K.Latte, *Römische*
 Religionsgeschichte (1960)

Mem.Amer. *Memoirs of the American*
Acad.Rome. *Academy in Rome*

MERF *Mélanges d'archéologie . . . de*
 l'École française de Rome

Michels, A.K.Michels, *The*
Calendar *Calendar of the Roman*
 Republic (1967)

Momigliano, A.Momigliano, *Primo*

Contributi (*Secondo, etc.*) *Contributi alla*
 storia degli Studi classici
 (1955–)

Mommsen, Th. Mommsen, *Le Droit*
Dr.publ. *publique romain* (1887)

Nash, *Pict.Dict.* E.Nash, *Pictorial*
 Dictionary of Ancient Rome
 (1961–62)

Not.Scav. *Notizie degli scavi di antichità*
Num.Chr. *Numismatic Chronicle*

OCD *Oxford Classical Dictionary*[2]
 (1970)

Ogilvie, Livy R.Ogilvie, *A Commentary*
 on Livy, Books 1–5 (1965)

PBSR *Papers of the British School at*
 Rome

Platner-Ashby, A.B.Platner and T. Ashby,
Top.Dict. *A Topographical Dictionary*
 of Ancient Rome (1929)

PW A.Pauly,G.Wissowa and
 W.Kroll, *Real-Encyclopaedie*
 d. klassichen
 Altertumswissenschaft
 (1893–)

Rose, ARR H.J.Rose, *Ancient Roman*
 Religion (1949)

TAPA *Transactions of the American*
 Philological Association

Warde Fowler, W.Warde Fowler, *The*
Festivals *Roman Festivals*, (1889)

Wissowa, RKR G.Wissowa, *Religion und*
 Kultus der Römer[2] (1911)

NOTES

Part One
RELIGION AND FESTIVALS

1 H.J. Rose, *The Year's Work in Classical Studies, 1939-1945* (1948), 123.

2 Early Roman primitivism is naturally discussed in all the standard books on Roman religion, and only a few books can be mentioned here. *Mana*: see especially H. Wagenvoort, *Roman Dynamism* (1947); H.J. Rose *ARR* (1949).

Myth: F. Altheim, *A History of Roman Religion* (1938), 200ff.; M. Grant, *Roman Mythology* (1971); in general: G.S. Kirk, *Myth, its Meaning and Functions in Ancient and Other Cultures* (1970), and *Greek Myths* (1974).

Altheim and Dumézil: among their numerous writings Altheim's *History of Roman Religion* and Dumézil's *Archaic Roman Religion*, 2 vols (1974), may be singled out. For criticism of Altheim, see H.J. Rose, *Harvard Theological Review*, 1934, 33ff., of Dumézil see Rose, *JRS*, 1947, 183ff.

For further details and other works published in the last thirty years or so, see A.K. Michels' valuable survey in *Classical Weekly*, 1955, 25ff., and surveys by Rose, *Year's Work in Class. Studies, 1939-1945*, 85ff., and *1945-1947*, 85ff., and *JRS*, 1960, 161ff.

P. Boyancé has collected his reviews on early Roman religion (including reviews of Wagenvoort, Dumézil and J. Bayet's *Histoire politique et psychologique de la religion romaine*², 1969) in his *Études sur la religion romaine* (1972). Quotation from Momigliano, see *Terzo Contributo*, 583.

3 A.D. Nock, *Essays on Religion and the Ancient World* (ed. Z. Stewart, 1972), ii, 603, i, 333.

4 On the word *numen* see F. Pfister, *PW*, s.v. It is important to remember that we have virtually no Latin literature earlier than the third century BC and so nothing like contemporary evidence for what the ancestors of the Romans called these vague powers whose existence is presupposed in the ritual of such ceremonies as the Terminalia. S. Weinstock argued (*JRS*, 1949, 166f.) against H.J. Rose that *numen* did not mean 'divinity' by itself (contrast, e.g., *numen Iovis*) until the Augustan period. Rose (*Harvard Theol. Rev.*, 1951, 109ff.) replied in detail to this criticism and concludes that whether *numen* was an old or a comparatively new word, the early Romans did have such a conception, whatever they may have called it – and that is the more important aspect. For continued rejection of *mana/numen* of G. Dumézil, *Archaic Roman Religion* (1974), 18ff.

5 Fetiales: see Livy, 1.24.4ff.; 32.4ff. (Cf. Ogilvie, *Livy*, 110ff., 127ff.). Details of the procedure and formulae, given by Livy, reflect more of what the second-century antiquarians reported than the original wording. See also J.W. Rich, *Declaring War in the Roman Republic in the Period of Transmarine Expansion* (1976), and compare some doubts expressed by E. Rawson, *JRS*, 1973, 166ff.

6 On the apparent clash between conservatism and innovation, see J. North, *PBSR*, 1976, 1ff.; A.J. Toynbee, *Hannibal's Legacy* (1965), ii, ch. XII. Yoked oxen: Cic. *Div.* 2.77; Festus 226L. Caesar: Pliny, *NH*, 28.76.

7 E. Rawson, *JRS*, 1973, 162. For further discussion, see this article, 'Scipio, Laelius and Furius and the Ancestral Religion'. On the impact of rationalism on religion

in the late Republic, see now J.H.W.G. Liebeschuetz, *Continuity and Change in Roman Religion* (1979), 29ff.

8 For a criticism of B. Farrington's view of 'popular' Epicureanism (*Science and Politics in the Ancient World*, 1939), see A. Momigliano, *JRS*, 1941, 149ff. = *Secondo Contrib.* 375ff.

9 For a translation of this work, see H.C.P. McGregor and J.M. Ross, *Cicero, The Nature of the Gods* (Penguin, 1972); it contains a good introduction by Ross who sketches the intellectual background.

10 On the continuing belief in divination (though not to the same extent belief in augury) in the late Republic, see J.H.W.G. Liebeschuetz, *Continuity and Change in Roman Religion* (1979), 7ff.

11 On Varro's theology, see especially Augustine, *Civ.D.*6. 2–9, and, briefly, Latte, *RR*, 291ff., A.D. Nock, *CAH*, x, 470f. and Liebeschuetz, *Continuity and Change in Roman Religion*, 36f. *Civilis rel.* and *naturalis*: Aug. 6.6 God and universe: Aug. 7.6. Correct deity: Aug. 4.22. One and other gods: Aug. 4.11.

12 Distraction of writing: Cic. *Nat. deor.* 1.9. Tullia's *fanum*: Cic. *Att.* 12.36.1. Cf. 12.18. *Consolatio: Tusc. Disp.* 1.66. Cf. Lactantius, *Div. Inst.* 1.15.18.

13 On Roman morality and religion, see Liebeschuetz, *Continuity and Change in Roman Religion*, 39ff.

14 *Feriae*: see Macrob. 1.16.2ff.; Varro, *LL*, 6.12–26.

15 192 BC: Livy, 35.40.7.

16 Cf. also Servius, ad Virg. *Georg.* 1.268; Festus, 292L. Scaevola: Macrob. 1.16.9ff.

17 *Vilicus*: Cato, *Agr.* 5.1; 5.4 *Vilica*: ibid.143. Cf. A.D. Nock, *Harvard Theol. Rev.*, 1952, 190 (= *Essays on Religion and the Ancient World*, 1972), 738.

18 On chronology in the time of the Roman Republic see above all A.K. Michels, *The Calendar of the Roman Republic* (1967), to which I owe much in this section of this book. On wider matters, see E.J. Bickerman, *Chronology of the Ancient World*[2] (1979), and A.E. Samuel, *Greek and Roman Chronology* (1972). Michels (97ff.) argues that the new calendar was not in-troduced until the *Decemviri* established it in 451/0 BC and that they made January the first calendar month. Without necessarily accepting these dates, it may well be that 153, the traditional date for starting the year, is far too late. For discussion of Michels' main theses, see R.M. Ogilvie, *CR*, 1969, 330ff. and A. Drummond, *JRS*, 1971, 282f.

19 *Calata plebe*: Macrob.1.15.10. *Calantur Nonae*: Varro, *LL*, 6,27. *Feriae* proclaimed by rex: Macrob. 1.15.12 implies all the festivals, but Varro, *LL*, 6.20 says only the first: perhaps an announcement of all in early times had become merely a token announcement of the first by Varro's time: cf. Michels, *Calendar*, 20, n. 30.

20 On *nundinae* see especially Michels, *Calendar*, 84ff. A *trinundinum* was a period of time which had to elapse between, for instance, the promulgation of a bill and the vote on it, or between the publication of the names of candidates for election and the actual voting. Its length is uncertain: between 17 and 24 days, see A.W. Lintott, *CQ*, 1965, 281ff. and Michels, 194ff. Seven-day calendar, the Fasti Sabini, see Degrassi, *In. It.* 51ff.

21 FP occurs on 21 Feb.(Feralia) on two calendars (Caer. and Verul.), while two others (Ant. mai. and Maff.) give F; it is marked by only one (Caer.) on 23 April (Vinalia) where two others (Ant.mai. and Praen.) give F, and one (Maff.) gives NP, and on 19 Aug (Vinalia) by three (Ant. mai., Maff. and Amitern.) where two (Allif. and Ant. min.) give F and one (Vall.) gives NP. The F appears to stand for Fasti, but the meaning of the P is quite uncertain: Mommsen suggested *fastus principio*, i.e. *fastus* at the beginning of the day only, a divided day (*fissus*), and he is followed by Degrassi (*In.It.*334f.), but this is not entirely satisfactory, as pointed out by Michels (182), since by analogy NP should mean *nefastus principio* which it certainly does not.

22 So Michels, *Calendar*, 50ff.

23 Michels, *Calendar*, 106ff. argues that before the lex Hortensia of 287 BC there was no distinction in the calendars bet-

ween *dies comitiales* and *dies fasti*. But as Ogilvie points out (*CR*, 1969, 330f.) a quotation from the pontifical records of 389 BC (in Macrob. 1.16.24) refers to *dies comitiales*.

24 Michels, *Calendar*, 68ff. But contra, see Degrassi, *Latomus*, 1969, 464; 467.

25 *Dies religiosi*: see Aul. Gell. 5.17.2, 16.18; Festus, 348L; Plut., *Qu.Rom.* 25; Ovid, *F*.5. 485ff.; Livy, 6.1.12. See Wissowa, *RKR*, 443ff.; Michels, *Calendar*, 62ff. Cicero's letter: *Att.* 9.5.2. Latin Festival: Cic. *QFr.* 2.4.2; see Michels, *Calendar*, 64, n.12.

26 Varro, *LL*, 6.29.

27 Cannae: Aul. Gell.5.7.3. Trasimene: Ovid, *F.* 6.763f. Arausio: Plut. *Lucull.* 27.8f. *Nundinae* and *Nones*: Macrob. 1.13.16–19; Dio Cass. 40.47 (52 BC). According to Dio (48.33.4) a day was intercalated into 41 BC to avoid such coincidences, but he is probably confused by some adjustment of the recently introduced Julian calendar, and the intercalation of single days was not practised. See Michels, *Calendar*, 164ff., who thinks that the superstition was not an early Roman one, but spread into Rome under the influence of Hellenistic astrology. Trimalchio: Petron. *Sat.*, 30.

28 The standard edition of these Fasti is A. Degrassi, *Inscriptiones Italiae*, XIII, *Fasti et Elogia*. Fasc. ii, *Fasti Anni Numani et Iuliani* (1963), which essentially replaces Mommsen's great edition, *CIL*, I² (1893). The Fasti Antiates maiores are also printed in Degrassi, *Inscriptiones Latinae Liberae Rei Publicae* (1963), 23ff.

29 Nobilior: Macrob. 1.12.16. Verrius Flaccus: Suet. *de gram.* 12.

30 On the dating of the calendar and modern views see Michels, *Calendar*, 207ff.

Part Two
THE ROMAN YEAR

January

31 Varro, *Rust.* 1.36. Columella, 11.98; 6–14. Menologia: *CIL*, I², 280.

32 Ovid, *F*.1, 79ff. Cf.*Pont.* 4.4.9. On

various aspects and for fuller documentation see Mommsen, *Dr. publ.* i, 116ff. (auspices); ii, 286ff. (procedure).

33 Dion.H. 2.6. (camp out: Epaulizontai); Cic. *Div*.2.34.71. The agent was not a member of the College since he was paid: Dion. H. 2. 6. 2.

34 Bibulus: Dio Cass. 38. 6. 5. The elder Cato also auspicated at home: *'domi cum auspicamus'*, Festus, 268L (though this could refer to *auspicia privata*).

35 Flaminius: Livy, 21.63.10. Equites in front: Ovid, *Pont.* 4.9, 18. Crowds: *Pont.* 4.4. 28. Aequimelium: Cic. *Div.* 2.39.

36 Ovid, *Pont.* 4.4.41.

37 Maior consul: L.R. Taylor and T.R.S. Broughton, *Historia*, 1968, 166ff. On the constitutional problems involved, see Mommsen, *Dr. publ.* i, 41ff.

38 Oath: App. *BC.*, 1.31. Contio: Suet. *Tib.* 32, Cic. *Leg. Agr.* 2.1, Plut. *Aem. Paul.* 12.

39 Snake on Island: Livy, 10.47, *Epit.* xi; Ovid, *Metam.* 15. 622–745 (quotation from 744). 180 BC: Livy, 40.37.2. On Aesculapius, see E.J. and L. Edelstein, *Aesculapius* (1945).

40 Varro, *LL*, 7.57. He refers to *'Aesculapi aedes vetus'*, but this probably applies to the island temple and not to an earlier one: so Latte, *RR*, 225n2. Photo in Nash, *Pict. Dict.* 1, 508f.

41 Inscriptions: Degrassi, *ILLRP*, nos 35–39; *ILS*, 3833–37, 3840, 3821, *CIL*, vi.7–20. Claudius: Suet. *Claud.* 25.

42 Degrassi, *In.It.* 338.

43 The two temples: the sources are confused. The Calendars refer the temple on the Tiber Island to Vediovis, but Livy (31.21.12; 34.53.7) refers Purpureo's dedication to Jupiter. However in the first passage the text is probably corrupt and Merkel's old emendation of *Vediovi* for *deo Iovi* should be accepted. In the second passage the reading should probably be retained and an error attributed to Livy. If the temples in these two passages were in fact dedicated to Jupiter, why are they not so recorded in the Calendars? Livy also says (35.41.8) that in 192 two temples, vowed by Purpureo, were dedicated to

Jupiter on the Capitol. He is probably in error here, and one temple must be that of Vediovis (the second could be an error for that of Vediovis on the island, or it *might* be a temple of Jupiter on the Capitol, though this is improbable, or it might be simply an erroneous duplication by Livy or his source). The confusion of Vediovis and Jupiter is found also in Ovid, *F*.1.293f., and Vitruvius, *Arch.* 3.2.3. A cult of Jupiter Iurarius on the island is attested by an inscription (*ILS*, 3038), but it is not recorded in the Calendars or anywhere else. Despite all these difficulties a temple to Vediovis on the island is accepted by most scholars. On the confused issue, see further Degrassi, *In. It.* 388 and J. Briscoe, *Comment. on Livy xxxi-xxxiii* (1973), ad Liv. 31.21.12 (p.112ff.).

44 Cicero, *Nat. deor.* 3.62. Vediovis: Etruscan, e.g. Preller-Jordan, *Röm. Mythologie*, I³ (1881), 263. Ve- = stem: L.A. Holland, *Janus and the Bridge* (1961), 188. Apollo: Aul. Gell. 5.12.12. *Iuvare:* Aul. Gell. 5.12.8. *Di manes:* Macrob. 3.9.10, Wissowa, *RKR*, 237, Lucilius: frg. 631. Latte, *RR*, 81. Little Jupiter: Festus 519L, cf. Ovid, *F*.3.437, C. Koch, *Der römische Juppiter* (1937), 68. Vesca: Ovid, *F.* 3.445f. Mediterranean: E. Gjerstad, *Opuscula Romana*, ix, 1973, 35ff., *Early Rome*, v (1973), 32ff.

45 Tatius: Varro, *LL*, 5. 74. Pottery: Gjerstad, *Early Rome*, v, 32. Altar, *ILS*, 2988; Degrassi, *ILLRP*, 270 (*Vediovei patrei genteiles Iuliei/Vedi (ovei) aara/leege Albana dicata*). Alban cults at Bovillae: Cic. *Mil.* 85, Strabo, 5.231. Albani: *ILS* 6188. Julii at Bovillae: Tac. *Ann.* 15. 22, 3; 2.2.41. C. Koch (*Der römische Juppiter* (1937), 39ff., 61ff., 661) argues that Jupiter Indiges is another name for Vediovis who was identified with Aeneas, the ancestor of the Julian gens. S. Weinstock (*Divus Julius*, 1971, 5ff.) would identify Vediovis, a youthful Jupiter, with Iulus, the son of Jupiter-Aeneas (there were two traditions: that Iulus was or was not identifed with Ascanius, Aeneas' son).

46 Pliny, *NH*, 16.216. Excavation: Nash,

Pict. Dict. 2, 450ff., with bibliography, and photos; statue, 495. Aul. Gell. 5. 12.12; cf. Latte, *RR*, 82, n.1. Goat sacrificed to Apollo; Livy, 25.12.13 (*Apollini bove aurato et capris duabus albis auratis*).

47 Macrob. 1.16.6. 1 Jan. 59 and 58 BC: Cic. *Att.* 2.2.3, *Pis.* 4.8. 2 Jan. 50 BC: *Att.* 7.7.3. 31 Dec. 67 BC: Dio Cassius, 36.24.2. Dion. H. 4.14.4.

48 *Turres; finita agricultura; iugum:* Schol. Persius 4, 28. Another interpretation of the *iugum* in Persius (*quandoque iugum pertusa ad compita figit*) is given by L.A. Holland (*TAPA*, 1937, 425ff. and *Janus and the Bridge* (1961), 66ff.)

49 Woollen balls: Festus, 272, 15L. *Caput*: Rose, *ARR*, 34. Macrob. 1.7.34. Lustration, Latte, *RR*, 91. *Numen*, Rose, *ARR*, 39.

50 Aul. Gell. 10.24.3. Propertius, 5.3.37. Dion. H.4.14.3. Bailiff; Cato, *Agr.* 5, 3. Extra wine: Cato, *Agr.* 57.

51 Cic. Att. 2.3.4; 7.7.3. That it was Pompey's Alban villa and not Cicero's (as is sometimes said, e.g. Latte, *RR*, 91) is made clear by *Att.* 7.5.2: *unde in Albani Pompeii*. Banning and restoration: Cic. *Pis.* 81; Asconius, Clark p. 7, 1. 15; Suet. *Caes.* 42. Augustus: Suet. *Aug.* 30, 31: Dio Cassius, 55.8.6.

52 Temple: Livy 2.7.12. Derivation: Cic. *Leg.* 2.28; Asconius, *In Pis.* 52, p.13C. Arnobius, 3.25, gives 'Victa et Potua'.

53 Ovid, *F.* 1.317: Festus, 9L; Varro, *LL*, 6.14.

54 Ram: Varro, *LL*, 6. 12; Arval Brethren, Henzen, 1.144, *ILS*, 5047.

55 Prayer: Livy, 8.9.6. Salii, apud Varro, *LL*, 7.27. Sky-god: so also Varro, apud Augustine, *Civ. D.* 7.27 (cf. John Lydus, *de mensibus*, 4, 2).

56 Two communities: Plutarch, *Romulus*, 21 1. Romulus?: the name is missing in the inscription, and various supplements have been suggested; for Romulus, see Degrassi, *In. It.* 398. Alternatively the entry might be linked to the capture of Fidenae in 426 by the dictator Man. Aemilius (Livy, 4.31–4). No firm connection can be established with the story that the Fabii left Rome by the Porta Carmentalis on their ill-fated expedition to the Cremera in 478. Carpentum: Ovid, *F.* 1. 619ff.

57 Ovid, *F.* 1, 585. Virgil. *Aen.* 8. 336. Temple: Plutarch, *Qu. Rom.* 56. cf. *Romulus*, 21. Altar: in S. Omobono area, see Nash, *Pict. Dict.* 2, 415. Varro: apud Aul. Gell. 16.16.4. Postverta: Ovid, *F.* 1. 633ff, refers to Postverta and Porrima, sisters or companions of Carmentis, of whom one sings about what was long ago (*porro*), the other of the future (*venturum postmodo*); Macrob. (*Sat.* 1.7.20) follows Ovid, though he calls them Antevorta and Postvorta. Child-birth first: Ogilvie, *Livy*, 59. Augustine, *Civ. D.* 4.11. Moon-goddess: R. Pattazzoni, *Stud. Mat.* 1941 = *Studies in Hist. of Religion* (1954), i, 110ff., based on coinage. Goddess of beginnings: A. von Domaszewski, *Abhandlungen zur röm. Religion* (1919). Water-nymph: Wissowa, *RKR*, 220.

58 Flamen: Cicero, *Brut.* 56. *Sacrum pontificale*: Ovid, *F.* 1. 462. *Scortea*: Ovid, *F.* 1. 629; Varro, *LL*, 7. 84. *Flaminica*: Festus, s.v. Mortuae (152L).

59 Cicero, *Brut.* 57. Schultze, *Zur Gesch.lat. Eigennamen* (1904), 530, n.3, however, regards Laenas as an Etruscan-Latin name: cf. Maecenas, Asprenas.

60 Juturna. The form Diuturna is also found (e.g. *CIL* 6, 30951 and in the older MSS of Cicero, *pro Cluentio*, 101). It is uncertain which is the older. Some (e.g. Latte, *RR*, 77n.3) suppose Iuturna to be later, others (e.g. Wissowa, *RKR*, 222n.9 and Altheim, *HRR*, 243f.) consider it to be the earlier. Altheim connects the first part of the name with the Latin root *div-* (cf. Diana, Iov-) and the second part with an Etruscan suffix (-tur, -thur), i.e. 'daughter of Jupiter'; he further believes that this suggests a close connection with Castor and Pollux, the Dioscuri, or Sons of Zeus.

Numicus: B. Tilly, *Virgil's Latium* (1947), 76. Sacrificial water: Servius, *ad Aen.* 12.139.

61 Lacus Juturnae: see Nash, *Pict. Dict.* 2, 9ff, for illustrations of the surviving remains.

Varro, *LL*, 5.71.

62 Campus Martius temple: Ovid, *F.* 1.463f. *Qui artificum*: Servius, *ad Aen.* 12.139.

63 Ovid, *F.* 1.705. Livy, 2.42.5.

64 Velia temple: Varro ap. Non. 531, Donat. ad Ter. *Eun.* 256. Archaic statues: Dion. H. 1.68. Inscription: see S. Weinstock, *JRS*, 1960, 112ff. Penates at Lavinium: Timaeus, as reported by Dion. H. 1.67.4.

65 Temple of Castor: illustrations in Nash, *Pict. Dict.* 1 210ff., and L.R. Taylor, *Roman Voting Assemblies* (1966). Discussion of steps and political uses: Taylor, *op. cit.* 25ff., 41ff., 108f. (122 for discussion of *pro aede Castoris* in the lex Bantina of late 2nd century). The steps were all destroyed in the late 19th century: see illustrations in Nash and Taylor.

66 Cato: Plutarch, *Cato min.* 27-29. Caesar: Dio Cass. 38.6.2. Clodius: Cicero, *Sest.* 34, *Dom.* 110, *Pis.* 23. Sestius: Cicero, *Sest.* 79.

67 Ovid, *F.* 1.657ff. Varro, *LL.* 6, 26. Sowing: Pliny, *NH*, 18. 50. Cf. K.D. White, *Roman Farming* (1970), 180.

68 Varro, *Rust.* 1.2.1. On the Sementivae see J. Bayet, *Revue de l'histoire des religions* 1950, 172 ff.

February

69 Last month: Ovid, *F.* 1.49. Spring: Varro, *Rust.* 1.28. *Purguntur*: Columella, 11.2.15.

70 *Februa*: Varro, *LL* 6.13; Ovid, *F.* 2.19.

71 Everriator: Festus, 68L. Lictor: Ovid, *F.*2.23 (cf. Bömer, *ad loc.*)

72 Cethegus: Livy, 32.30.10; 34.53.3. Caecilia: Cicero, *Div.* 4.99.

73 Juno Sospita: Livy, 32.30.10. See in general A.E. Gordon, *The Cults of Lanuvium* (1938), E.M. Douglas, *JRS*, 1913, 61ff., G. Hafner, *JDAL*, 1966, 186ff. Consuls at Lanuvium: Cic. *Mur.* 41. 90. Attributes: Cic. *Nat. deor.* 1.82. On the Republican coinage, see M. Crawford, *RRC*, nos 316, 379, 384, 412, 472/2a, 509 (the moneyers derived from Lanuvium). Sospita appears frequently on the coinage of Antoninus Pius and Com-

modus, who were born near Lanuvium. For the snake cult see Propertius, *Eleg.* 4.8, 3ff., Aelian, *NH* 11.16. The link between Sospita and the girl with the snake is almost certain, since both are depicted on the same coin (Crawford, 412).

74 Ovid, *F*.2.67, 6.105. Festus 83L. Dumézil (*Fêtes romaines*, 225ff.) regards Helernus as a protector of vegetables (cf. *holus*, 'vegetable') and links him with Carna who was worshipped on the *Kalends* of June (q.v.) which were called *Kalendae Fabariae* (beans): cf.Ovid, *F*.6.105ff.

75 Concordia in Capitolio: Livy, 22.33.7; 23.21.7.

76 Faunus in Insula: Livy, 33.42.10; 34.53.3. Cf. Ovid, *F*. 2.193.

77 FP: see Michels, *Calendar*, 182f. Antiquity: Degrassi, *In. It.* 408f, defends Mommsen's view of the later emergence of the Parentalia against Latte's argument (*RR* 99n.2) for its antiquity.

78 Cornelia's letter: quoted by Nepos, frg. 1.

79 Tarpeia: Dion. H.2,40, quoting the annalist Piso. The conjecture was made by Mommsen, but rejected by Latte, *RR*, 111 n.2 (Tarpeia could not have had a grave on the Capitol and was not a *parens*. The offering made to her was not an offering to the dead and was not made by a Vestal). Degrassi (*In. It.* 409) however is not convinced by Latte.

80 Varro, *LL*. 6.13. Festus, 75L. Ovid, *F*. 2.565ff. Cicero makes a casual reference to the Feralia: writing from Formiae on 3 March 49 BC to Atticus he says that 'Caesar left Corfinium on the afternoon of the same day, namely the Feralia, on which Pompey left Canusium at dawn' (*ad Att.* 8.14.1. Cf. 9.1.1).

81 Caristia: Ovid, *F*.2. 617ff., Val. Max. 2.1.8. For a late development see Latte, *RR*, 274 no.3, 339 n.2. Tibullus: 1.10.17ff.

82 Lupercalia: see especially Plut. *Romul.* 21; other references include Ovid, *F*.2. 267ff. (esp. 282–4, 377–81, 425–30); Livy, 1.5.1–2; Val. Max. 2.2.9; Suet. *Aug.* 31.4; Dion. H. 1.32.3–5 and 80.1; Varro, *LL* 6.13; Festus, 75L; Plut. *Numa*, 19;

J.Caes. 61; *Qu. Rom.* 68, 111; August. *Civ. D.* 18, 12; Serv. *ad Verg. Ecl.* 8.82; Censor, *DN* 22, 15; Cic. (*Caelio*, 11, 26) refers to the Luperci as 'a sort of wild and thoroughly pastoral and rustic brotherhood of regular Luperci, which was formed in the woods before the institution of civilized life and law (*fera quaedam sodalitas et plane pastoricia atque agrestis*). Modern discussions include Wissowa, *RKR*, 209f.; Latte, *RR*, 84ff.; Frazer, *Fasti*, 2, 328ff.; A.K. Michels, *TAPA*, 1953, 35ff., E. Gjerstad, *Early Rome*, v, 26ff.; D.P. Harmon, *Aufstieg und Niedergang der röm. Welt*, I, 2, 1441ff.

Much remains uncertain, e.g. the supposed presence of the *flamen Dialis*; the popular naming of the Luperci as *creppi* (meaning goats?); the naming of the goat-hide thongs as Juno's cloak (*amiculum Junonis*; Juno Sospita at Lanuvium wore a goat-skin); the significance of the forehead blooding and cleaning; a possible connection of the *praenomen* Kaeso (held by some Fabii and Quinctii) with the ritual *striking* with thongs (*februis caedere*, Servius, *ad. Aen.* 8, 343) or indeed with the Julii *Caesares*; wolves as the dead (cf. Michels, *op. cit.*); women struck on the palms of their hands or on the back; not to mention any possible analogies with the rite of 'being born of a goat', practised by the Kikuyu of Kenya (cf. Frazer, *op. cit.* 341ff.).

83 Less probable derivations, mentioned by Ovid (*F*.2.477ff.), are from the Sabine town of Cures or from the Sabine word *curis*, a spear. On sacred spears see Frazer, *Fasti*, 2, 399ff. Cf. also Festus, 304L; Varro, *LL*, 6.13; Plut. *Qu. Rom.* 89.

84 The bearded head of Quirinus is shown on a *denarius* of 56 BC (Crawford, *CRR*. n.427). On that of N. Fabius Pictor, issued in 126 (Crawford, n.268), Q. Fabius Pictor is depicted with helmet, cuirass, spear and shield, and also with a priestly *apex*. He is the praetor of 189 who was forbidden to go to his province of Sardinia since he was also *flamen Quirinalis*. That he was shown with armour does not necessarily suggest their Quirinus was a

war-god, but merely perhaps emphasizes Pictor's claim to a military office. (Pl. 4015).

85 The temple was dedicated on 17 Feb.: the reference in the Venusine calendar under 29 June to *Quirino in Colle* probably refers to a reconstruction by Augustus in 16 BC.

86 The precise site of the temple is uncertain; inscriptions suggest that it was on the north side of the Alta Semita near the east part of the gardens. Its appearance, as restored by Augustus, is described by Vitruvius (3.2.7) and depicted on a 2nd-century relief found beside the baths of Diocletian: see P. Hartwig, *Mitteil.* 1904. 27ff., 157ff., Taf. iv. A fairly early inscription was 'Quirinio L. Aimilius L. f. praitor' (*CIL*, 1².803, Degrassi, n.251). probably the praetor of 205 or 191.

87 Wissowa, Roscher, *Lexikon . . . Mythologie*, 5,381.

88 *Grom. Vet.* 1.141.

89 Ovid, *F.* 2.635ff. Plut. *Qu. Rom.* 15, *Numa*, 16, 1. Cf. Varro, *LL* 6.13.

90 *Liber Coloniarum*, 1, 221ff., Lachmann.

91 See *Not. Scav.* 1921, 122ff.; Michels, *Calendar*, 160ff.

92 Festus, 310L; cf. 346L.

93 Plut. *Qu. Rom.* 63. See H.W. Parke, *Festivals of the Athenians* (1977), 162ff.

94 Frazer, *Fasti*, 2, 500ff.

95 Ovid, *F.* 2.838 implies chariots, but *F.* 3.522, Varro, *LL.* 6.13 and Festus, 71L mention only horses. For the Trigarium as a possible site see T.P. Wiseman, *Liverpool Classical Monthly*, 1979, 132. The position of the Trigarium was established by F. Coarelli, *MEFR*, 1977, 839ff., just south-east of the Tarentum temples.

96 See J.W. Poultney, *The Bronze Tablets of Iguvium* (1959). On the Ceri, see R.S. Conway, *Ancient Italy and Modern Religion* (1933), 2ff.

March

97 On Mars, see U.W. Scholz, *Studien zum altitalischen und altrömischen Marskult und Marsmythos* (1970).

98 Ovid, *F.3.* 137ff, (cf. Bömer, *ad loc.*); Macrob. 1.12.6.

99 Dress of Salii: Dion. H. 2.70.2f.

100 Frazer, *Fasti*, 3, 65ff.

101 Ovid, *F.* 3.245ff. (cf. Bömer, at 257); Pliny, *NH*, 16.235; Servius, *ad Aen.* 4.518.

102 Plautus, *Miles Glor.* 691. Tibullus, 3.1.2f; 8.1. Tertullian, *De Idolatria*, 14. Horace (*Od.* 3.8.1) shows that bachelors did not give presents. See also Juven. 9.51ff. Macrob. (6.4.13) preserves a fragment of an Atellan farce entitled *Kalendae Martiae* by Pomponius (later Republic): *vocem deducas oportet, ut mulieres videantur verba.* This suggests that men were excluded from the rites of Juno Lucina: apparently, as in Aristophanes' *Thesmophoriazusae*, a man had dressed up as a woman in order to attend a women's festival. But there is evidence (see S. Weinstock, PW, *RE*, s.v. Matronalia, 2308) that in the late Empire men dressed up as women on 1 Jan. and 1 March. Weinstock suggests the possibility that Pomponius may be reflecting an early Roman practice connected with Juno Lucina on 1 March rather than following Aristophanes. If this was so, there would be a precedent for Clodius' escapade at the Bona Dea festival, and 1 March will have been an even more riotous day than is usually supposed.

103 Ovid, *F.* 3.430. Dion. H. 2.15.4. Excavation: Nash, *Pict. Dict.* 2, 490ff., with bibliography, reconstruction and photographs.

104 For this and further arguments see Warde Fowler, *Festivals*, 44f. Equirria: Ovid, *F.* 3. 517ff. Cf. J. Loicq, *Latomus*, 1964, 491ff.

105 Mamurius: Lydus, 4.49; Serv. *ad Aen.* 7.188; Minucius, *Octavius*, 24. 3; Propertius, 5.2.61. Cf. also Varro, *LL*, 6. 59; Festus, 117L: Plut, *Num.* 13.6. Cf. also A. Illuminati, *Studi e Documenti di Storia delle Religioni* (1961), 41ff.; J. Loicq, *Hommages à J. Bayet* (1964), 401ff; H. Stern, *Rev. des Études Latines*, 1974, 70ff.

106 Anna Perenna: Ovid, *F.* 5.523ff. (Cf. Bömer, *ad loc.*): Macrob. 1.12.6: Martial, 4.64.16f; Lydus, 4.49. Various other interpretations of Anna have been offered, e.g., by F. Altheim (*Terra Mater* (1931),

91ff.) who turned her into 'Mother Perna', a form of Ceres. Two more recent articles are R. Lamacchia, *Parola del Passato* (1958), 384ff. and D. Porte, *Rev. Phil.* (1971), 282ff.

107 Women selling cakes: Ovid, *F.* 3.713ff., esp. 725f.: Varro, *LL*, 6.14: Augustine, *Civ. D.* 4.11.6, 6.9: 7.21. On Liber see A. Bruhl, *Liber Pater* (1953).

108 Ovid, *F.* 3.785f. Festus, 103L. Ausonius, 7.24.29.

109 Macrob. 1.4.15. Varro, *LL*, 6.14.

110 Cic. *Att.* 6.1.12. Cf. Ovid, *F.* 3.771ff.; Propertius, 4.1. 132; Catullus 68.15; Cic. *Att.* 9.17.1.

111 Varro, *LL*, 6.14 and Festus 304L.

112 Varro, *LL*, 5.85. Charisius, apud Keil, *Gromatici Latini*, 1, 81.

113 Dion. H. 2.64.3.

114 Minerva and Mars: the myth-makers and poets found a link between these two deities in the mysterious figure of Nerio or Neriene. Nerio originally was probably a characteristic of Mars, his *vis et potentia et maiestas quaedam*', as explained by Aulus Gellius (13.23), who goes on to quote the remark in Plautus (*Truculentus*, 515) that Nerio was the wife of Mars. Apparently the vague Nerio was gradually personalized as a goddess, who became the wife of Mars and was later identified with Minerva. Hence stories arose, such as how Mars was tricked by Anna Perenna: he fell in love with Minerva, but Anna tricked him by arranging a bridal ceremony after which Mars lifted the bridal veil only to discover old Anna, and not Minerva as Anna had promised (see e.g. Ovid, *F.*3.675ff.) Cf. Warde Fowler, *Festivals*, 59ff., but Frazer, *Fasti*, 3, 121ff. rejects Gellius' explanation of Nerio as the 'power' of Mars and thinks that a marriage between Mars and Nerio may be an early idea and not the result of later Greek mythologizing.

115 Tertullian, *de idolat.* 10; Juvenal, 10.114.

116 Ovid, *F.* 3.835ff; Varro, *LL*, 5.47.

117 The note in the Praenestine calendar is confirmed by Varro, *LL*, 6.14 and by Festus (480L) who adds the item about the lamb. Ovid, *F.* 3.850. Lydus, 4, 60.

The Praenestine note adds that a certain Lutatius (the consul of 102?) recorded that among the ruins on the Palatine after the Gallic sack of Rome in 390 a *clava* was found with which Romulus had inaugurated the city, while Cicero (*Div.* 1.17.30) says that the priestly *lituus* used by Romulus survived the Gallic sack and was preserved in the *curia* of the Salii on the Palatine. Since Cicero also says that *lituus* meant both the curved staff of the augurs and the trumpet used to sound a battle-charge, some confusion is possible and the *clava* might be a trumphet (*tuba*) rather than a priestly *lituus* (cf. Mommsen, *Röm. Staatsrecht*, III, 386 n.6)

118 Ovid, *F.* 5.726. See W. Ehrlers, PW, *RE* sv. Tubilustrium, 757.

119 Servius: Tac. *Ann.* 15.41. Damage 182: Livy, 40.2.2. Mummius: Vitruvius, 5.5.8. Gracchus: Orosius, 5.12.8. 84 BC: Appian, BC, 1.78. Luna Noctiluna on Palatine: Varro, *LL*, 5.68; cf. Horace *Od.* 4.6.38. Titus Tatius: Varro, *LL*, 5.74; Dion. H. 2.50.3. Varro's invocation: *Rust.* 1.4–5. Late introduction of cult of Luna: Wissowa, *RKR*, 315; early: G. De Sanctis, *Stor. Rom.* IV, 2, 235f.

April

120 Cincius and Varro, quoted by Macrob. 1.12.12f. Ovid, *F.* 4.88.

121 For an attempted explanation of the development of the ritual and a discussion of the temples, with full references, see G. Radke, PW, *RE* s.v. Verticordia. On the Veneralia see R. Schilling, *La religion romaine de Vénus* (1954), 389ff.; C. Floratos, *Hermes*, 1960, 197ff.

122 Livy, 29.10 and 14; 34.54.3; 36.36.3. Ovid, *F*, 4.259ff.

123 *Moretum*: Ovid, *F.* 4.367. Praetor: Dion. H. 2.19.4. Temple: Cic. *Har. Resp.* 2.25.

124 Temple of Magna Mater: see Nash, *Pict. Dict.* 2, 26ff; Arch.Laziale, ii (1978), 67ff.

125 Cic. *Har. Resp.* 2.22ff.

126 Lucretius, 2.600ff. Cicero, *Leg.* 2.9.22; 16.40. Ovid, *F.* 4.179ff.

127 Dion. H. 2.19.4. *Mutitationes*: Aul. Gell. 2.24. *Sodalitates*: Cic. *Sen.* 13.45.

128 Praeneste   inscription: Degrassi,
     ILLRP, 101. Cicero, *Div.* 2.87.
129 See T.P. Wiseman, *PBSR*, 1974, 3ff, and
     1976, 44ff. See the former also for discus-
     sion of the identification of the temples in
     the Circus Flaminius area which has been
     much debated in recent years, not least by
     F. Coarelli.
130 Ovid, *F.*4.621ff. Rullianus and Gracchus:
     Livy, 10.29.14; 24.16.19.
131 Ovid, *F.* 4.692ff. *Forda*: thus Ovid; others,
     e.g., Varro, *Rust.* 2.5.6, gives *hordae*. Cf.
     Varro, *LL*, 6.15; Festus, 91L; Lydus,
     4.72.
132 Cerialia and peace: Ovid, *F.* 407ff.; Virg.
     Georg. 1. 344ff. White robes: Ovid, *F.*
     4.619f. Foxes: Ovid, *F.* 681ff. (text cor-
     rupt at 709: cf. Bömer, *ad loc.*). Plebeian
     meetings: Aul. Gell. 18.2.11; Plaut. *Men.*
     102. On Ceres see H. Le Bonniec, *Le
     Culte de Cérès à Rome* (1958).
133 See Cicero, *Att.* 14.14.1, 19.3. Cf.
     Degrassi, *In. It.* 444; S. Weinstock, *Divus
     Julius* (1971), 184f. 367.
134 Varro, ap. Schol. in Persium, 1.75. H.J.
     Rose, *ARR*, 75, thinks the offering was
     eked out to all, while R.M. Ogilvie,
     Romans and their Gods, 81f., thinks
     celebrations were organized by and
     throughout the thirty *curiae*. Dumézil
     (*Arch. Rom. Rel*; 229ff.; *Fêtes romaines*,
     188ff.) denies the use of the blood of the
     October horse. Other references to the
     Parilia, beside those quoted in the text, in-
     clude Varro, *LL*, 6.15; Cic. *Div.* 2.98;
     Dion. H. 1.88.3; Vell. 1.8.4; Plut. *Rom.*
     12.1; Athenaeus, 8.361. On Parilia and
     Rome's birthday see Bömer at *F.* 4.721.
135 Festus, Paul. Excerpta, 323L. Varro, *LL*.
     6.16: '*vinum novum ne vehatur in urbem ante
     quam vinalia kalentur*'. On the Vinalia see
     R. Schilling, *La religion romaine de Vénus*
     (1954), and *Rev. des Etudes Anciennes*,
     1959, 108ff.
136 Numa: Pliny, *NH*, 18.285; Tert. *Spect.* 5.
     Robigalia: Ovid, *F.* 4.905ff. Cf. also
     Varro, *Rust.* 1.1.6; Festus, 325L; Col-
     umella, 10.342.
137 Ovid, *F.* 4.905ff. Ovid's garden: Ovid,
     Pont. 1.8.43ff. On the problems see
     Bömer at *F.* 907.

138 Temple. 241 BC: Velleius, 1.14.8; 238BC:
     Pliny, *NH* 18.286. Annual games: a dena-
     rius of C. Servilius of 57 BC, which shows
     the head of Flora with the legend FLORA
     PRIMUS, is generally thought to refer to
     the first annual games in 173 (with a
     putative ancestor of Servilius as aedile in
     charge), but Crawford (*CRR*, 1, no.423)
     interprets the legend as (*flamen*) *Floralis
     primus* and not as *Floralia primus fecit*.
139 Floralia: Ovid, *F.* 4.943ff.; 5.183ff.,
     277ff., 327ff. Juvenal, 6.249f. Cic. *Verr.*
     2.5.36. Persius, 5.177. Cf. also Pliny, *NH*
     18.286; Vell. 1.14.8; August. *Civ.D.* 2.27;
     Lactant. *Div. Inst.* 20.10. For Tiberius see
     Dio Cassius 56.19.1. A rite named Florifer-
     tum was so called according to Festus (81L)
     because on that day ears of wheat (*spicae*)
     were carried into the sanctuary (*sacrarium*).
     It is uncertain whether this offering was
     made to Flora or Ceres, and, if to Flora,
     whether on 27 April or 3 May.
140 *Feriae Latinae*: Dion. H. 4.45. Cf. Dar.
     Sag.s.v; Wissowa, *RKR*, 24ff; Latte, *RR*,
     144ff.
141 *Cabenses sacerdotes*: *CIL* VI, 2173–75; *ILS*
     5009.
142 *Carmen petere*: Cic. *Planco*, 23, Varro, *LL*,
     6.25. According to the Fasti the first
     triumph *in monte Albano* was held in 231BC:
     Degrassi, *In. It.* 78.
143 Oscilla: Plut. *Qu. Rom.* 86; Dion H. 1.38;
     Schol. Bob. *ad Cic. Planco* 23.
144 Cic. *Fam.* 8.6.3. Caesar, *BC.* 3.2. This
     festival was held in Dec. 49, and was ap-
     parently a second celebration (Dio Cass.
     41.14; Lucan, 1.550), so either it was
     repeated because faulty the first time or
     Caesar was granted the honour of special
     feriae. See S. Weinstock, *Divus Julius*
     (1971), 322f. Fasti: Degrassi, *In. It.* 143ff.
145 176 BC: Livy, 41.16. 199 BC: Livy, 32.1.9.
146 Cic. *QFr.* 2.4.2; *Rep.* 1.14. Pliny, *NH*,
     27.45. Lucan, *Phars.* 5.403.

May

147 Maius: Macrob. 1.12.16ff.; Ovid, *F.*
     5.110; Aul. Gell. 13.23.2.
148 Maia: Cornelius Labeo, ap. Macrob.
     1.12.18, 20.

149 Bona Dea Subsaxana: Ovid, *F.* 5.147ff.;
Macrob. 1.12.21f., 25f. Licinia: Cic.
Dom. 136. Damium: Festus, 60L. Bona
Dea: see also G. Piccaluga, *Studi e Mat. di
Storia d. Relig.* (1964), 195ff.

150 Lares Praestites: Ovid, *F.* 5.129ff.
Sacellum: Tac. *Ann.* 12.24. Dog-skins:
Plut. *Qu. Rom.* 51. Coin: Crawford,
RRC, 312, no. 298.

151 Lemuria: Ovid, *F.* 5.421ff., 479ff.

152 Porpyrio, *ad Hor. Epist.* 2.2.209. Nonius,
197L.

153 Manes paterni: Ovid, *F.* 5.444f. See H.J.
Rose, *Univ. California Publicat. Clas. Phil.*
12. 1941. Ogilvie, *Romans and their Gods*,
85.

154 See Macrob. 1.7.34f.; Varro, *LL*, 9.61;
Festus, 114L. E. Tabeling, *Mater Larum*
(1932).

155 Temple: Nepos ap. Priscian. 8.17; Schol.
Bob. in Cic. *Arch.* 27; Val. Max. 8.14.2;
Pliny, *NH*, 36.26.

156 Dion. H. 1.38; Aul. Gell. 10.15.30;
Varro, *LL*, 7.44; Festus, 14L; Ovid, *F.*
5.621ff.; Cic. *Sex. Amer.* 100 (cf. Festus
450L); Plut. *Qu. Rom.* 32, 86; Macrob.
1.11.46. Cf. Bömer at Ovid, *F.* 5.621ff.

157 See Wissowa, *Gesammelte Abhandlungen*,
211ff. and in *PW* s.v. Argei; generally
now rejected, e.g. more recently by Latte,
RR, 412ff. For further discussion of
modern views see D.P. Harmon, *Aufstieg
und Niedergang der röm. Welt*, I,2 (1974),
1446ff.

158 Temple: Livy, 2.21.7, 27.5f.: Val. Max.
9.3.6.. Aqua Mercurii: Ovid, *F.* 5.673ff.

159 Cf. Latte, *RR*, 118. Tubilustrium: Ovid,
*F.*5.725f.

June

160 Ovid, *F.* 6.1ff. Brutus: Macrob. 1.12.31.

161 Macrob. 1.15.19.

162 Ovid, *F.* 6.183ff. Cult centre: Plut. *Cam.*
27. Voice: Cic. *Div.* 1.101.

163 Ovid, *F.* 6.191f. 388 BC: Livy, 6.5.8.
Assembly: Livy, 7.23.3.

164 Cic. *Nat. Deor.* 3.51. Ovid, *F.* 6.193f.

165 Macrob. 1.12.31. Ovid, *F.* 6.101.

166 Macrob. 1.12.32–3. Ovid, *F.* 6.170.
Varro, ap. Non. Marcell., s.v Mactare,

p.539L. Inscription: *CIL.* 111, 3893.
Wissowa, *RKR*, 236; R. Pettazzoni,
Studi Etruschi, xiv, 1940, 163ff. Both re-
jected by Latte, *RR*, 71 n.3, who thinks
the name could be connected with Oscan
Karn–, 'part' or 'portion'.

167 Ovid, *F.* 6.199ff. Livy, 10.19.17. On the
temples in the area of the Circus Flaminius
see T.P. Wiseman, *PBSR*, 1974, 3ff.

168 See esp. Varro, *LL*, 5.66. Semo and Dius
Fidius: the same (Wissowa, *RKR*, 130;
Warde Fowler, *Festivals*, 135ff.), different
(Latte, *RR*, 127).

169 Tanaquil: Festus, 276L. Vitruvius: Livy,
8.20. Inscriptions: Quirinal, *ILS*, 3472;
Tiber Island, *ILS*, 3474. Justin Martyr,
Apol. 1.26; Tertullian, *Apol.* 13. See also
Ovid, *F.* 6, 213ff.; Dion. H.9.60.8;
Varro, *LL*, 5.66.

170 Ovid, *F.* 6.235ff; Festus, 274L; Varro,
LL, 6.20. Cf. H.J. Rose, *JRS*, 1933,
46ff.

171 Romulus: Augustine, *Civ.D.* 4.23. Pontiffs: Serv. *ad Aen.* 8.330, *a pontificibus indigitari solet.* Augurs: Cic. *Nat.Deor.*3.52,
in augurum precatione.

172 Ovid, *F.* 6.241ff.; Livy, 22.9.10,
23.30.13: Cic, *Nat. Deor.* 2.61.

173 Ovid, *F.* 6.249f. 309ff.; Serv. *ad Ecl.*
8.82. Cf. M.Beard, *JRS* 1980, 12ff.

174 Ovid, *F.* 6.311ff., 469; Propertius,
4.1.21; Lactant. *Div. Inst.* 1.21.26; Lydus,
4.94. Paintings: see Rostovtzeff, *Soc. Econ
Hist Rom. Empire*, Pl xv, 4; Wissowa,
Ges. Abhandlungen (1904), 69.

175 Lucretius, 5. 656f. Varro, apud Augustine,
Civ.D. 4.8. Ovid, *F.* 6.545 (in general
473ff).

176 Excavations at S. Omobono, A. Som-
mella, *Parola del Passato*, clxxii–clxxiii,
1977. Terracottas: Q.E. Maule and
H.R.W. Smith, *Votive Religion at Caere*
(1959), 74ff. (and for Mater Matuta in
general).

177 Slaves: Plutarch, *Qu. Rom.* 16. *Testuacia*:
Varro, *LL* 5.106. *Liba tosta*: Ovid, *F.*
6.482. Nephews and nieces: Ovid, *F.*
6.559, Plut. *Qu. Rom.* 17. Adolescents:
Festus, 380L. See H.J. Rose, *CQ*, 1934,
156; accepted by Latte, *RR*, 87, but not
by S. Weinstock, *JRS*, 1961, 212.

178 Virgo: Varro apud Nonium, 278L, Arnobius, *Adv. nat.* 2. 67. Statue: Ovid, *F.*
6.569ff.; Pliny, *NH*, 8. 194 and 197;
Varro, ap. Non. s.v. *undulatum* 178L. Sejanus' statue: Dio Cass., 58.7. Dionysius'
view: Dion. H. 4.40.7. Pudicitia: Festus,
282, 3L, cf. Livy, 10.23.3.

179 Ovid, *F.* 6.650. See De Sanctis, *SR*,
IV,2,i, 132 n.24.

180 Livy, 9.30, 5ff. Varro, *LL*, 6.17. Festus,
134L. Val. Max. 2.5.6.

181 See Varro, *LL*, 6.32. Festus, 310L. Ovid,
F. 6.713.

182 Quotation: Ovid, *F.* 6.731f. Statue
struck: Cic. *Div.* 1.10; Livy, *Per.*·14, 197
BC: Livy, 32.29.1. Varro, *LL*, 5.74.

183 Augustine, *Civ. D.* 4.23. Pliny, *NH*,
2.53, cf. Festus, 254L. Inscriptions: *CIL*,
vi, 206, 30979, 30880.

184 Warde Fowler, *Festivals*, 161. Latte.*RR*,
209. H.J. Rose, *OCD*², s.v. Summanus.
S. Weinstock, PW, s.v. Plautus, *Bacch.*
895, *Curc.* 415. Lucretius, 5.521.

185 Arval Br.: *ILS* 5048, Henzen, 146.
Cakes: Festus 474L; on cakes in religion in
general, see 'Cakes and Loaves', *ERE*. A
rare bronze coin of Domitian depicts the
Capitoline temple of Jupiter: in the pediment is an anguipede monster which has
been identified as a representation of Summanus: see H.A. Cahn, *Num. Chr.* 1946,
18. This is somewhat speculative, but if
true it might be regarded as supporting an
Etruscan origin for the god, since the
Etruscans were rather fond of monsters.

186 See Ovid, *F.* 6.771ff.; Varro, *LL*, 6.17.
Dion. H. (4.27.7) assigns two temples to
Servius, one in the Forum Boarium (see p.
150), the other, which he wrongly names
as Fortuna Virilis, on the banks of the
Tiber. Carvilius: Livy, 10.46.14. Inscriptions: *ILS*, 3682, 3682a, 9253; Degrassi,
ILLRP, 96–99. A fourth temple:
dedicated in the Gardens of Julius Caesar
near the Tiber in AD 17 (Tac. *Ann.* 2.41);
it is not likely to have been merely a
restoration of Carvilius' temple. See also
S.M. Savage, 'The Cults of Trastevere'
Mem. Amer. Acad. Rome. xvii, 1940, 35ff.

187 Cicero, *Fin.* 5.70. Columella, 10, 311ff.
Inscriptions: see previous note.

188 Festus, 479, 9 (with supplement *ex li (bris*
fatalibus). Circus Flaminius: *CIL*, xiv,
4541 = *Insc. It.* viii, i, 205). Horse-racing:
Varro, *LL*, 5.154. Altheim: *HRR*, 71ff.
186 BC: Livy, 39, 22.

189 See Ovid, *F.* 6.791f. Latte, *RR*, 93 n.4.
Weinstock, *JRS*, 1961, 212. Temple:
Obsequens, 41, Augustus, *Res Gestae* 19.

190 Foundation: Livy, 10. 37, 15; 36,11.;
Ovid, *F.* 6.793f.; Nash, *Pict. Dict.* I.534,
with photograph. Hymn: Livy, 27.37.7.

191 See Ovid, *F.* 6.797ff. Eumenius, *Pro in-*
staurandis scholis (Paneg. ix, 7.). Coins:
Crawford, *RRC*, n.410. Cicero, *Arch.*
27. Wigs: Ovid, *Ars Amat.* 3.161ff.

July

192 Scipio: Cic. *Fin.* 4.22. Cicero: *Leg. Man.*
28. On Felicitas see S. Weinstock, *Divus*
Julius (1971), 112ff.

193 Romulus: Dion. H. 2.57, Plut. *Pomp.*
29. Flight of Romans: Varro, *LL*, 6.18.
Jupiter: Wissowa, *RKR*, 116. Cf. H.J.
Rose, *CQ*, 1934, who supposes a Jupiter
Poplifugus who *fugat exercitum*, 'puts the
army to flight'. Fear: Latte, *RR*, 128.

194 Games in 212: Livy, 25.12, 27, 23.5;
Festus, 23L; Macrob. 1.17.25ff. Awnings: Pliny, *NH*, 19.23. 59 BC: Cic. *Att.*
2.19. Applause: Cic. *Phil.* 1.36. cf. 2.13.
Venatio: Cic. *Att.* 16.4.

195 Fortuna Muliebris: Dion. H. 8.55f.;
Festus, 282L; Val. Max. 1.8.4. Augustine, *Civ. D.* 4.19. Position: T. Ashby,
PBSR, 1907, 79. Dion. H. 8.55.6. Fortuna's remark: cf. Val. Max. 1.8.4. *'rite,*
me, matronae, dedistis riteque dedicastis'.
Univirae: Latte, *RR*, 181.

196 Florus, 1.15.5. Schol. Veron. Virg.
Georg. 3.1.

197 Varro, *LL*, 6.18. Macrob. 1.11.36ff.
Columella, 11.2.50. Cf. Frazer, *Fasti*, II,
343ff. and Dumézil, *Fêtes romaines*,
271ff.

198 Tertullian, *Spect.* 5.7. On Consus see A.
Piganiol, *Scripta Varia* (1973), 175ff.

199 Dedication: Livy, 4.25.3, 29.7.
Apollinare: Livy, 3.63.7. Asconius: *In or,*
in toga cand. p.90 Cl. Portico: Livy,

40.5.6. Photo of temple: Nash, *Pict. Dict.*
I, 29.

200 Livy, 9.46.15; *De Vir. III.* 32.33 Dion.
H. 6.13.4; Val. Max. 2.2.9; Pliny, *NH*,
15.19; Sueton, *Aug.* 38.3.

201 Colline Gate temple: Cic. *Leg.* 2.23.58;
cf. Degrassi, *ILLRP*, n.157, Denarius:
Crawford, *RRC*, n.403.

202 Hiero's statue: Livy, 22.37. 5–12. Victory in *biga*: Tacit. *Hist.* 1.86.

203 Lucaria. Festus 106L: Plutarch, *Qu. Rom.*
88. Inscriptions: Luceria and Spoletium:
Degrassi, *ILLRP*, 504 & 506 respectively.

204 Venus and Victoria virtually identical:
Wissowa, *RKR*, 292. Caesar's goddess,
S. Weinstock, *Divus Julius*, 91. 55 BC:
Cic. *Fam.* 7.1.5. 45 BC: Cic. *Att.* 13.44.2.

205 Ovid, *F.* 1.641. Plut. *Camil.* 42. For
sources and full discussion, see A.
Momigliano, 'Camillus and Concord',
CQ, 1942, 111ff. (= *Secondo Contrib.*
89ff. (doubting Camillus' temple of 367).

206 Lectisternium: Livy, 5.13.6. Umbrae:
Festus 519L. Altar: Livy, 28.11.4. Bull:
Macrob. 3.10.4. quoting Labeo.

207 Furrina: Varro, *LL*, 6.19. Springs: A.W.
Van Burren, *OCD²*, s.v. Furrina. Cicero,
(*QFr*, 3.1.4) mentions a *ponticulus qui est ad
Furrinam* near Arpinum; this might suggest a water-course or spring. Altheim
(*HRR*, 116ff.) argues for an Etruscan
origin of Furrina and a connection with
the Furies (as Cicero believed: *Nat. Deor.*
3.46.) Janiculum grove and shrine, where
finds are not earlier than *c.* AD 200: see
S.M. Savage, *Mem. Amer. Ac. Rome*,
1940, 35.

208 Fortuna Huiusque Diei: Cf. Cicero, *Leg.*
2; 28. Catulus: Plut. *Mar.* 26 Statues;
Pliny, *NH*, 34.54, 60. Dumézil (*Fêtes romaines*, 32 ff.) argues that Furrina presided
over wells, but was later overshadowed
when Neptune extended his domain to include underground as well as surface
water. He also sees a pattern linking the
Neptunalia and Furrinalia (23 + 25 July)
and the double Lucaria (19 + 21), the
former dealing with surface and underground water, the latter first with clearing forests by felling trees but then by uprooting (*exstirpatio*). Thus the early

Roman farmers prepared their land towards the end of July.

August

209 Varro, *Rust.* 1.33. See Warde Fowler,
Festivals, 190.

210 Cic. *Leg.* 2.11.28. See Nash, *Pict. Dict.*
1,418ff.

211 Livy, 10.33.9; 35.9.6.

212 Dogs and geese: Pliny, *NH*, 29.57; Plut.
de fort. Rom. 12; Servius, *ad Aen.* 8.652;
and for the date, Lydus, *de mens.* 4.114.

213 Cicero, *Att.* 4.1.4; 12.45.3. Macrob.
1.16.8. Salutaris: Varro, *LL*, 5.52.
Bubulco: Livy, 9.43.25.

214 Tatius: Varro, *LL*, 5.74. Lavinium:
Pliny, *NH*, 3.56.

215 Phoenicians: see e.g. R. Rebuffat,
MEFR, 1966, 7ff.; J. Heurgon, *The
Rise of Rome* (1973), 73f. Round temple:
Nash, *Pict. Dict.* I, 472ff. The topographical and historical relations between
the temples of Hercules around the Forum Boarium are not entirely clear: see
Platner-Ashby, *Top. Dict.* 253ff. (The
Fasti Vallenses confuse the temple of Hercules Invictus with the temple of Hercules
Magnus Custos in the Circus Flaminius).

216 Uncovered head: Macrob. 3.6.17,
quoting Varro. Laurel: *ibid* and 3.12.2.
Plutarch, *Qu. Rom.* 60 and 90. Oaths:
Dion. H. 1.40.6. *Esculenta*: Festus 298L.
Public feast: Varro, *LL*, 6.54; Festus,
240L. Cf. Latte, *RR*, 216f.; Ogilvie,
Romans and their Gods. 93

217 6th-century date (Festus, 460L): see A.
Momigliano, *Terzo Contrib.* 641ff. against
the attempt by A. Alföldi, *Early Rome and
the Latins*, 85ff. to assign the temple to a
date after 500 BC. Cf. Ogilvie, *Livy*,
182ff. Slaves; Festus, 460L. Hair: Plut.
Qu. Rom. 100.

218 Portrait: Festus, 288L. Statue: Propertius,
4.2.13ff.

219 Flaccus: Livy, 40.40.10, 42.10.5. Stone
theatre: Vitruvius, 3.3.2. Livia: Tac.
Ann. 3.7.

220 Key: Festus, *Epit.* 48L. Scholiast: Veron.
ad Verg. Aen. 5.24.Cf, S. Weinstock,

JRS, 1961, 211. Ferryman: see L.A. Holland, *Janus and the Bridge* (1961), ch. 9, who thinks that the key (*clavis*) attributed to Portunus was originally a tiller (*clavus*); she also interprets the corrupt passage of Festus to mean '*Persillum* is the name the priests give to a wooden implement which has been dropped into pitch and which the flamen Quirinalis uses to daub the tackle (*arma*) of Portunus'. Thus the *flamen* of Portunus would disappear.

221 Temples in Forum Boarium; see Nash, *Pict. Dict.* 1, 411ff. Flowersellers: Fronto, *Ep.* 1.7.

222 Tac. *Ann.* 2.49. See L.A. Holland, *Janus and the Bridge*, ch. 12, for full discussion: she believes that the building was not a full *aedes*, a closed and roofed building, such as was used nowhere else in the cult of Janus.

223 Off-shot of Janus: Wissowa, *RKR*, 112. Later addition: P. Grimal, *Lettres d'humanité*, 1945, 15ff. Change: Latte, *RR*, 416 n.4.

224 *Flamen Dialis*: Varro, *LL*, 6.16. Dedication: Livy, 10.31.9.

225 Venus Libitina: Festus, 322L. Undertakers: Plut. *Qu. Rom.* 22. Libentina: Varro, *LL*, 6.47.

226 Consualia: Dion. H. 1.33.2; 2.31.3: Plut. *Qu. Rom.* 48; Varro, *LL*, 6.20; Festus, 36L; Tertullian, *Spect.* 5.5. Praenestine calendar, s.v. 15 December: '*Equi et [muli Flore coronantur], quod in eius tu [tela . . .]. Itaque rex equo (vectus . . .).* The rex was of course the Rex Sacrorum.

227 Cf. R. Ogilvie, *Livy.* 66.

228 Volcanal site: F. Coarelli, *Parola del Passato* xxxii (1977), 166ff. Quadriga: Dion. H. 2.54.2. Lotus: Pliny, *NH*, 16.236. Altar: see Nash, *Pict. Dict.* 2, 517ff; Circus: Livy, 24.10.9.

229 Varro, *LL*, 6.20.

230 Ops. Pliny, *NH*, 11.174. Cic. *Att.* 6.1.17 refers to a statue of Scipio Nasica near the temple of Ops (cf. Tyrrell and Purser, *Correspondence of Cicero* (1914), iii, 344ff. Hora: Ennius, *Ann.* 117V.

231 Festus, 126L, 144f.L, 115L. Macrob. 1.16.16. Ostia Orci: Festus, 115L. Ceres: Festus, 126L. Cf. Warde Fowler,

Festivals, 211f. Latte, *RR*, 141ff.

232 Romulus: Ovid, *F.* 4.821ff. (Cf. Frazer, *Fasti*, iii, 384ff.); Plut. *Rom.* 11. Palatine mundus: Nash, *Pict. Dict.* 2, 166.

233 Varro, *LL*, 6.21; the text, *Sacrarium quod adeo actum*, is corrupt: *adeo artum* or *ideo sanctum* have been suggested. *[Praefericulum . . .]:* Festus, 292L. Terra: Festus, 202L. Temple: Livy, 39.22.4.

234 Juturna: Arnobius, 3.29. Tiber/Vulturnus: Varro, *LL*, 6.21; 7.45; Festus, 519L. See *PW*, s.v. Tiberinus and Volturnus; A. Momigliano, 'Thybris pater', *Terzo Contrib.* 609ff, esp. 632ff; and (rejecting Mommsen), Latte, *RR*, 37, 131f. Wind: Dumézil, *Fêtes romaines*, 78ff.

235 Tacitus, *Ann.* 15.74. Tertullian, *Spect.* 8. It is uncertain whether a fragment of the Praenestine calendar (*Solis et Lunae . . . Martem*) belongs here. Accepted by Wissowa, *RKK*, 316n.3 and by Degrassi, *In. It.* p.503, it is rejected by Latte, *RR*, 232 n.4: the reference to Mars creates difficulties.

September

236 Livy, 5.21ff. Dion. H. 13.3. Val. Max. 1.8.3.

237 Velleius, 1.11.3; Vitruvius, 3.2.5; Pliny, *NH*, 36.40.

238 See Degrassi, *In. It.* 507. Ten days: Livy, 36.2.4. In the Fasti Antiates maiores (compiled before 55 BC) the Games are recorded as M[agni] on 8–10 Sept. and presumably (orginally) on 7, 11–12 (not on 13 because of the *epulum Iovis*) and on 14–19, but they were probably omitted for 4–6. They were called Romani in contrast with the *feriae Latinae*, and Magni as compared with other Ludi at Rome.

239 *Desultor*: Livy, 44.9.3.

240 See Alan Cameron, *Circus Factions* (1976), 53ff. On Circus Games in general see H.A. Harris, *Sport in Greece and Rome* (1972), 184ff.

241 Felix: Pliny, *NH*, 7.186. Men and women: Ovid, *AA*, 1.167; *Am.* 3.2.

242 Cicero: *QFr.* 3.1.1; *de orat.* 1.24. Caesar: Suet. *Aug.* 45.1 Pliny: *Ep.* 9.6.

243 See Mommsen, RF, 2.45.4. His view was
     rejected by Warde Fowler, Festivals,
     216ff., Wissowa, RKR, 127 n.11, De
     Sanctis, SR, IV. 2.1.317, Degrassi, In. It.
     509, and Habel, PW, Suppl. V, 621, but
     accepted by Latte, RR, 377ff. For epulum
     Iovis at Plebeian Games, see e.g. Livy,
     29.38.8; 33.42.11.

244 Lectisternium: Valer. Max. 2.1.2. Music:
     Cicero, Tusc. 4.4: et deorum pulvinaribus et
     epulis magistratuum fides praecinunt.

245 Clavus annalis: see Livy, 7.3.5; Fest. Epit.
     49L. This key (or keys, if there were two
     types) has provoked much discussion, but
     is important for the earlier rather than the
     later centuries of the Republic. See
     Beloch, Röm. Gesch. 36ff.; Momigliano,
     Quarto Contrib. 273ff., 403ff.; K. Han-
     nell, Das altrömisch.Amt (1926), 125ff.; E.
     Gjerstad, Early Rome, 5. 100ff.; Les
     Origines de la republique romaine (Entretiens
     13, 1966), 186ff., 192ff. The practice was
     revived in different form and cir-
     cumstances by Augustus (Dio Cass.
     55.10.4.)

246 Livy, 4.25.3; 29.7; Pliny, NH, 13.53;
     35.99; 36,28 & 34. Senate meetings: e.g.
     Livy, 39.4.1; Cic. Att. 15.3.1. See Nash,
     Pict. Dict. 1, 28f.

247 See Nash, Pict. Dict. 1, 424ff. Appian, BC,
     2.68, 102; Dio Cass. 41.22.3; 43.22.2.

October

248 Columella, 12, 18.4. Codex Theod.
     2.8.19. Mommsen: see Degrassi, In. It.
     531ff.

249 See Livy, 1.21.4: cf. Dion. H. 2.75.2.
     Plautus: Amph. 256. Hor. Odes, 1.35.1.
     On the cult see De Sanctis, SR, IV,ii,1.
     295f.; Latte, RR, 327; Ogilvie, Livy,
     103f.

250 Tigillum Sororium: see Livy, 1.26; Dion.
     H. 3.22; Festus, 380L; Schol Bob. ad Cic.
     Mil. 3.7. L.A. Holland, Janus and the
     Bridge (1961), 77ff.; Latte, RR, 132;
     Ogilvie, Livy, 117

251 Ieiunium Cereris: see Livy, 36.37.4.

252 Juno Curitis: cf. Festus 56L: curiales men-
     sae, in quibus immolanatur Iunoni, quae Curis
     appellata est.

253 Meditrinalia: Varro, LL, 6.21; Festus,
     110L. Reading libo: Degrassi, In. It. 519;
     G. Radke, Kleine PW, s.v. Meditrina.
     Derivation: Latte, RR, 74, n.3. Latte's
     denial that the presiding deity was Jupiter
     is rejected by S. Weinstock, JRS, 1961,
     212.

254 Garlands: Varro, LL, 6.22. Corsica:
     Zonaras, 8.18.14. Fontinalis Porta:
     Festus, 75L.

255 Argei: apud Varro, LL, 5.54. Livy,
     45.16.5. Obsequens ad 165 BC. Augustus,
     Res Gestae, 19. Dion. H. 1.68.1. Cf.
     Degrassi, In. It. 520.

256 October horse: Timaeus, apud Polyb.
     12.4bl; Festus, 190L, 246L: Plut. Qu.
     Rom. 97; Dio Cass. 43.24.4. Agricultural
     origin: Warde Fowler, Festivals, 241ff.;
     Frazer, Golden Bough v.2.42ff.; H.J.
     Rose, Roman. Quest. of Plut. (1924), 208.
     Military: Wissowa, Dumézil, Arch. Rom.
     Rel. 215ff; Fêtes romaines, 145ff. (Strongly
     anti-agrarian) RKR, 144ff. See also
     U.W. Scholz, Studien zum altitalischen und
     altrömischen Marskult und Marsmythos
     (1970). Site of race in Campus Martius: F.
     Coarelli has suggested the Trigarium on
     the west side: Guida archeologica di Roma
     (1974), 239.

257 Caesar: Dio Cass. 43.24.4. Story denied
     by J.S. Reid, JRS, 1912, 41. For Dumézil
     (Fêtes romaines, 99ff) Meditranalia was a
     festival of the mixing of the new must
     with the boiled down wine of the
     previous year (cf. Columella, 12.21).

258 Capitolini: Cic. QFr. 2.5.2. Romulus:
     Schol. Bern, ad Verg. Georg. 2.384.
     Camillus: Livy, 5.50 (cf. Ogilvie, Livy,
     740f.); Festus, 430L. Plutarch: Rom. 25.6
     Latte, RR, 442 n.1.

259 Jupiter Feretrius: Livy, 1.10.6f. (cf.
     Ogilvie. Livy, 70); Dion. H. 2.34.4;
     Latte, RR, 136.

260 Ennius: Schol. Bern, ad Verg. Georg.
     2.384.

261 Armilustrium: see Varro, LL, 5.15.3;
     6.22; Festus, 17L; Plut. Rom. 23.3;
     Lydus, de mens. 4.34. The participation of
     the Salii is not directly attested, but pro-
     bably rightly assumed. (The argument
     that the Salii were active in October

FESTIVALS AS RECORDED IN THE CALENDARS

(Where they are certain, abbreviations are expanded and missing letters restored, and very minor differences in spelling, as found in the fragments of the individual calendars, are not recorded here. For these details see Degrassi, *In.It.*).

1 January	*Aesculapio, Co [r]p [nidi?],*		(Ant.mai.)
	Vediove (Ant. mai.)	5 February	*Concordiae in Capitolio*
	Aesculapio, [Vediovi] (Mag.)		(Ant.mai.)
	Aesulapio, Vediove in Insula		*Concordiae in Arce* (Praen.)
	(Praen.)	13 February	*[Parentatio incipit e]x h [ora*
5 January	*Vicae Potae* (Ant.mai.)		*VI?]* (Praen.)
9 January	AGONALIA (Maff., Praen.)		*Virgo Vestalis parentat* (Phil.)
	Agonia [. . .] aut quia [. . .]		*Parentatio tumulorum in [cipit],*
	(Note in Praen.)		*quo die Roma liberata est de*
11 January	CARMENTALIA		*obsidione Gallorum* (Silv.)
	(Ant.mai., Maff., Praen.)		*Parentalia* (Menol.Col.and
	Dies Carmentariorum (Phil.)		Vall.)
	Carmentalia de nomine matris		*Favon. (pro Fauno).* (Ant.mai.)
	Euandri (Silv.)		*Favno in Insula* (Viae Princ.,
	Iuturnae (Ant.mai.)		Amedeo.)
	[. . .] Carmentis partus curat	15 February	LUPERCALIA (Ant.mai.,
	omnia que futura, ob quam		Caer., Opp., Farn., Phil.,
	caussam in aede eius cavetur ab		Silv.)
	scorteis omnique omine morticino	17 February	QUIRINALIA *Quirino*
	(Note in Praen.)		(Ant.mai.)
15 January	CARMENTALIA *Carmenti*		QUIRINALIA *Quirino in*
	(Ant.mai.)		*Colle* (Caer.,Farn.)
	CARMENTALIA (Caer.,		QUIRINALIA
	Maff., Verul. Opp., Praen.,		(Maff.,Verul.)
	Phil.)		*Quirinalia, quo die Romulus,*
	Feriae Carmenti ob eandem		*occisus a suis, Quirinus ab hasta,*
	caussa [m quod] III idus. Hic		*quae a Sabinis curis vocatur, non*
	dies dicitur institutu [s a		*apparuisse confictus est.* (Silv).
	Romulo], si Fidenas eo die		*[. . .] Quiritis [. . .] rum idem*
	cepisset. (Note in Praen.)		*(. . . Sabino nom) ine hasta curis*
27 January	*Aedis Castoris et Pollucis*		*[Martem Sabin] i dicant*
	dedicata est (Praen.)		*Quirinum [. . .]um. Feriae*
	Castori, Polluci ad Forum		*[stultorum].* (Note in Praen.)
	(Verul.)	21 February	FERALIA (Ant.mai., Caer.,
	Ludi Castorum Ostiis, quae		Maff., Verul.)
	prima colonia facta est (Silv.)		FERALIA. *Dis inferis* (Farn.)
1 February	*Iunoni Sospitae Matri Reginae*	22 February	*Caristia* (Phil.)

22 February	*Cara Cognatio ideo dicta quia* *tunc, etsi fuerint vivorum* *parentum odia, tempore obitus* *deponantur* (Silv.) Caro Cognatio (Menol. Col. and Vall.)		*Capitolio* (Farn.) *Liberalici. C.(ircenses), m(issus)* *xxiiii* (Phil.)
23 February	TERMINALIA (Ant.mai., Caer., Maff., Verul., Phil., Silv.Menol. Col. and Vall.)	19 March	QVINQVATRUS. *Minervae* (Ant.mai., Farn.) QVINQVATRUS (Caer., Maff., Verul.)
24 February	REGIFVGIVM (Caer., Maff., Verul., Phil.) *Regifugium, cum Tarquinius* *Superbus fertur ab urbe expulsus* (Silv.)		QVINQVATRUS *Feriae* *Marti* (Vat.) *Quinquatria* (Phil. Silv., Menol. Col. and Vall.) [. . . *rectius tamen alii putarunt*
27 February	EQVIRRIA (Ant.mai., Caer., Maff., Mag., Verul.)		*dictum ab eo quod hic dies est* *post V idus, quo*] *d in Latio*
1 March	*Feriae Marti* (Praen.) *N(atalis) Martis. (Circenses),* *m(issus) xxviii* (Phil.) *Iunoni.* (Ant.mai.) *Iunoni Lucinae Exquiliis, quod* *eo die aedis ei dedicata est per* *matronas, quam voverat Albin* *[i filia] vel uxor, si puerum* *[parientem] que ipsa (m fovisset).* (Praen.)		[*post idus dies simili fere ratione* *decli*] *narentur. Artificum dies,* *[quod Minervae] aedis in* *Aventino eo die est [dedicata.* *Sali] faciunt in Comitio saltu* *[adstantibus po] ntificibus et* *tribunis Celerum* (Note in Praen.)
		23 March	TVBILVSTRIVM (Ant.mai., Caer., Maff., Viae Lanza, Verul., Vat., Farn., Phil.)
7 March	*Vediove in Capitolio* (Ant.mai.) *Vediovi, Artis Vediovis inter* *duos lucos* (Praen).		TVBILVSTRIVM *Feriae* *Marti* (Ost.,Praen.) *Hic dies appellatur ita, quod in*
9 March	*Arma ancilia moventur* (Phil.)		*atrio Sutorio tubi lustrantur,*
14 March	EQVIRRIA (Ant.mai., Maff., Verul., Farn., Viae Princ., Amed.) EQVIRRIA *Feriae Marti* (Vat.)		*quibus in sacris utuntur. Lutatius* *quidem clavam eam ait esse in* *ruina Palati incensi a Gallis* *repertam, qua Romulus Urbem* *inauguraverit* (Note in Praen.)
	Mamuralia (Phil.) *Sacrum Mamurio* (Menol. Col. and Vall.)	24 March	*Q[uando] R[ex] C[omitiavit]* *F[as]* (Maff., Viae Lanza).
		31 March	*Lunae* (Caer.)
15 March	*Feriae Iovi* (Verul.) *Annae Perennae* (Ant.mai., Farn.) *Feriae Annae Perennae via* *Flaminia ad lapidem primum* (Vat.)	1 April	*Lunae in Aventino* (Praen.) *Veneralia* (Phil.) *Frequenter mulieres supplicant* *Fortunae Virili; humiliores etiam* *in balneis, quod in eis ea parte* *corporis utique viri nudantur,* *qua feminarum gratia*

17 March	LIBERALIA (Ant.mai.,
	Maff., Menol.Col, and Vall.)
	LIBERALIA. AGONALIA
	Libero, Liberae (Caer.)
	LIBERALIA. AGONALIA
	(Vat., Verul.)
	LIBERALIA *Libero in*
		4 – 10 April	*desideratur* (Note in Praen.)
			4 *Ludi Matri Magnae* (Maff.)
			   Ludi Matri d(eum)
			   Magnae I(daeae).
			   (Praen).
			   Ludi Megalesiaci (Phil.)

Nobilium mutitationes cenarum
solitae sunt frequenter fieri, quod
Mater Magna ex libris Sibullinis
arcessita locum mutavit ex
Phrygia Roman (Note in
Praen.)
5-9 *Ludi* (Maff.etc)
8 *Natalis Castoris et Pollucis.*
Circenses m(issus) xxiii (Phil.)
9 *Ludi.* (Maff., etc.)
10 *Ludi in Circo* (Maff.,
Ost.,Praen.,Vat.)
Megalesiaci.Circenses m (issus)
xxiv (Phil.)

5 April   *Fortunae Publicae* (Ant.mai.)
Fortunae Publicae Citeriori in
Colle (Praen.)

10 April   *Matri deum Magnae Idaeae*
(Ant.mai. on 11 Apr.)
Matri deum Magnae Idaeae in
Palatio, quod eo die aedis ei
dedicata est (Praen.)
Matri deum Magnae in Palatio
(Quir.)

12-19 April   *Ludi Cereri* (Caer., etc.)
19 *Loedi Cereri in Circo*
(Caer.)

13 April   *Iovi Victori, Iovi Libertati*
(Ant.mai.)

15 April   FORDICIDIA (Ant.mai.,
Caer.,Maff., Vat., Ost.,
Tusc., Praen.) *[. . . vocabulum]*
Oscum et Sa [binum . . .]
(Note in Praen.)

19 April   CERIALIA (Caer., Maff.,
Ost., Praen.)
CERIALIA *Cereri, Libero,*
Liberae (Ant.mai., Esq.)

21 April   PARILIA *Roma condita*
(Ant.mai.)
PARILIA (Praen., Via
Lanza)
PARILIA *Roma condita.*
Feriae coronatis omnibus
(Caer.)
PARILIA *Roma condita.*
Feriae coronatis omnibus. Annus
pastoricius incipit (Esq.)
Natalis Urbis. Parilia dicta de
partu Iliae (Silv.)
Oves lustrantur (Menol.Col.

and Vall.)
[. . .] est [. . .] dae qu [. . .]
ignes transiliunt . . .] principio
anni pastorici . . .] redigitur.
(Note in Praen.)

23 April   VINALIA *Veneri Erucinae*
(Ant.mai.)
VINALIA (Maff., Ost.,
Praen.)
VINALIA *Veneri* (Caer.)
VINALIA *[Veneri Erucinae]*
e[xtra portam Collinam] (Esq.)
Io[vi . . .]m[. . .] ded[. . . vini
omnis novi libamentum Iovi]
consecratum [est, cum Latini
bello preme] rentur ab Rutulis,
quia Mezentius rex Etruscorum
paciscebatur, si subsidio venisset,
omnium annorum vini fructum
(Note in Praen.)

25 April   ROBIGALIA (Ant.mai.,
Caer., Maff., Esq., Praen.,
Ost.)
Feriae Robigo Via Claudia ad
milliarium V, ne robigo
frumentis noceat. Sacrificium et
ludi cursoribus maioribus
minoribusque fiunt. Festus est
puerorum lenoniorum, quia
proximus superior meretricum
est (Note in Praen.)

27 April–   *Ludi Florae* (Caer., etc.)
3 May   *Eodem die aedis Florae, quae*
rebus florescendis praeest,
dedicata est propter sterilitatem
frugum. (Note in Praen.)
Ludi in Circo (Caer. etc)
Floralici. Circenses, m(issus)
xxiiii (Phil.) *Florae* (Ven.)

1 May   *Laribus* (Ven.,Esq.)
9 May   LEMURIA (Ant.mai.,Ven.,
Maff.)
11 May   LEMURIA (Ant.mai.,Ven.,
Maff.,Tusc.)
Ma[niae] (Ant.mai.)
13 May   LEMURIA (Ant.mai.,
Ven., Maff., Tusc,)
14 May   *Marti Invicto* (Ven.)
15 May   *Feriae Iovi* (Ven.)
[Mercurio] Maiae, [. . .] Invicto
(Ant.mai.)

15 May	*Mercurio, Maiae* (Ven.)
	[Mercurio], Maiae ad Circum
	Maximum (Caer.)
	Mercurio (Tusc.)
	Natalis Mercurii (Phil.)
	Sacrum Mercurio (Menol.Col.)
	Sacrum Mercurii (Menol.Vall.)
21 May	AGONALIA (Ant.mai.,
	Caer., Esq.)
	AGONALIA *Vediovi* (Ven.)
23 May	TVBILVSTRIVM (Ant.mai.,
	Caer., Esq.,Mag.,Maff.)
	TVBILVSTRIVM *Feriae*
	Volcano (Ven., Amit.)
24 May	*Q[uando] Rex C[omitiavit].*
	F(as) (Maff., Viae Lanza)
25 May	*Fortunae populi Romani*
	Quiritium (Ant.mai. on 24)
	Fortunae Primigeniae in Colle
	(Ven.)
	Fortunae Publicae Populi
	Romani Quiritium in Colle
	Quirinali (Caer.)
	Fortunae Publicae Populi
	Romani in Colle (Esq.)
	Fortunae Publicae Populi
	Romani Quiritium in Colle
	(Mag.)
	[. . .] ri [. . .] in Velia [. . .] m
	(Note in Amit.)
1 June	*Marti in Clivo. [Iunoni] in*
	[Arce] (Ant.mai.)
	Iunoni Monetae (Ven.)
3 June	*Bellonae in Circo Flaminio*
	(Ven.)
4 June	*Herculi Magno Custodi* (Ven.)
	Ludi in Minicia (Phil.)
	Sacrum Herculi (Menol.Col.
	and Vall.)
5 June	*Dio Fidio* (Ant.mai.)
	Dio Fidio in Colle. (Ven.)
7 June	*Vesta aperitur* (Phil.)
8 June	*Menti in Capitolio* (Ven.,
	Maff., Viae Graziosa)
	Menti (Tusc.)
9 June	VESTALIA *Vestae*
	(Ant.mai., Ven.)
	VESTALIA *Feriae Vestae*
	(Maff.)
	VESTALIA (Tusc., Phil.)
	VESTALIA *Feriae Vestae ad*

	Ianum (Viae Graziosa)
11 June	MATRALIA *Matri Matutae*
	(Ant.mai., Ven.)
	MATRALIA (Maff., Tusc.,
	Phil.)
	Fortunae (Ant.mai.)
13 June	*Feriae Iovi* (Ven.)
	Iovi (Tusc.)
15 June	*Vesta clauditur* (Phil.)
19 June	*Minervae* (Ant.mai.)
	Minervae in Aventino (Esq.,
	Amit.)
20 June	*Summano ad Circum*
	Maximum (Ven., Esq.,
	Amit.)
24 June	*Forti Fortunae trans Tiberim ad*
	milliarium I et VI (Esq.,
	Amit.)
	Forti Fortunae trans Tiberim ad
	lapidem I et VI (Mag.)
	Sacrum Herculi, Fortis Fortunae
	(Menol.Col. and Vall.)
27 June	*Lar[ibus], V[. . .]* (Ant.mai.)
1 July	*[. . ., Iun]oni, [. . ., Felici]*
	tati (Ant.mai.)
	Felicitati in Capitolio
	(Ant.min.)
5 July	POPLIFVGIA (Maff., Ant.
	min.)
	POPLIFVGIA *Feriae Iovi*
	(Amit.)
6–13 July	*Ludi Apollini*
	5 *Ludi Apollinares* (Phil.)
	6–12 *Ludi Apollini* (Maff. etc)
	13 *Ludi Apollini* (Ant.mai.)
	Ludi in Circo (Maff., etc.)
	Apollinaria (Guidizz.,
	Menol.)
7 July	*Palibus [duobus].* (Ant.mai.)
	Ancillarum feriae, quorum
	celebritas instituta est ideo, quia
	capta Urbe a Gallis, cum
	finitimi prius victi tradi sibi
	Romanorum procerum coniuges
	postularent et consilio Philotidis
	ancillae famulae dominarum
	vestibus adornatae datae illis
	fuissent, his nuntiantibus
	praedictos somno sopitos et ebrios
	posse superari, facta victoria sic.
	(Silv.)

13 July   *Apol[lini]* (Ant.mai.)

14-19 July   *Mercatus* (Maff., Later.).
15-19 (Viae Ardet., Amit.)

15 July   *Equitum Romanorum probatio* (Phil.)

17 July   *Honori* (Ant.mai.)
Victoriae in Capitolio (Viae Ardeat.)

18 July   *Alliensis dies* (Ant.mai.,Amit.)
Dies Alliae et Fabiorum (Ant. min)

19 July   LVCARIA (Ant.mai., Maff., Amit.)

20-30 July   *Ludi Victoriae Caesaris*
20-26 *Ludi* (Pinc.,Maff.,etc.)
27-30 *Ludi in Circo* (Pinc., Maff. etc)

21 July   LVCARIA (Ant.mai., Maff., Amit.)

22 July   *Concordiae* (Ant.mai., Princ.)

23 July   NEPTVNALIA (Ant.mai., Maff.Mag., Guidizz., Menol.Col, and Vall.)
NEPTVNALIA *Feriae Neptuno* (Pinc., Allif.)

25 July   FVRRINALIA (Ant.mai., Maff., Mag.)
FVRRINALIA *Feriae Furrinae* (Pinc.,Allif.)

30 July   *Fortunae Huiusque Diei* (Pinc.)
Fortunae Huiusque Diei in Campo (Allif.)

1 August   *Spei, Victoris (duabus)* (Ant. mai.)
[Victoris duabus in Palatio, Spei] in foro Holitorio (addit.Arv.)
Victoriae, Victoriae Virgini in Palatio, Spei in Foro Holitorio (Praen.) *Spei ad Forum Holitorium* (Vall.)
Spei (Ant.min.) *Sacrum Spei.* (Menol. Col and Vall.)

5 August   *Saluti* (Ant.mai.)
Saluti in Colle (Later., Amit., Ant.min.)
Saluti in Colle Quirinale sacrificium publicum (Vall.)
Natalis Salutis. Circenses, m [issus] xxiiii (Phil.)

9 August   *Solis Indigitis in Colle Quirinale sacrificium publicum* (8 Aug.Vall.)

    Soli Indigeti in Colle (Allif.)
Soli Indigeti in Colle Quirinale (Amit.)

12 August   *Herculi Magno Custodi in Circo Flaminio* (Vall.)
Herculi Invicto ad Circum Maximum, Veneri Victrici, Honori Virtuti, V[. . .] Felicitate in theatro marmoreo (Allif.)
Herculi Invicto ad Circum Maximum, Veneri Victrici, Honori, Virtuti, Felicitati in theatro marmoreo (Amit.)

13 August   *Dianae, Vortumno, Fortunae Equestri, Herculi Victori, Castori, Polluci, Camenis* (Ant.mai.)
Dianae in Aventino et Vortumno in Loreto maiore (Vall.)
Feriae Iovi, Dianae, Vortumno in Aventino, Herculi Invicto ad Portam Trigeminam, Castori, Polluci in Circo Flaminio, Florae ad Circum Maximum (Allif.)
Feriae Iovi. Dianae, Vortumno in Aventino, Castori, Polluci in Circo Flaminio (Amit.)
Dianae in Aventino (Ant.min.)
Dianae (Guidizz.) *Natalis Dianes* (Phil.)

17 August   PORTVNALIA (Ant.mai., Maff.,Fandozz.)
PORTVNALIA *Portuno ad Pontem Aemilii* (Vall.)
PORTVNALIA *Feriae Portuno ad Pontem Aemilium* (Allif.,Amit.)
PORTVNALIA *Feriae Portuno* (Ant.min.)
Tiberinalia (Phil.)
Iano ad Theatrum Marcelli (Vall., Allif.)

19 August   VINALIA *Venere* (Ant.mai.)
VINALIA (Maff., Amit., Ant.min., Fandozz.)
VINALIA *Veneri ad Circum Maximum* (Vall.)
VINALIA *Feriae Iovi* (Allif.)

21 August	CONSUALIA (Ant.mai., Pinc.,Maff.,Fandozz.)		Ludi Romani (Maff., Vall., Amit.Ant.min.)
21 August	CONSUALIA Conso in Aventino sacrificium (Vall.)		5–12 Ludi (all preserved calendars, except Ant.mai.) 13 and 14: see these dates below.
23 August	VOLCANALIA Volcano, Horae Quirini, Maiae supra Comitium (Ant.mai.) VOLCANALIA Feriae Volcano. Volcano in Circo Flaminio, Nymphis in Campo, Opi Opiferae [in . . . Horae] Quirini in Colle, Volcano, Maiae supra Comitium (Arv.) VOLCANALIA Volcano (Pinc.) VOLCANALIA (Maff., Menol.Col.) VOLCANALIA Volcano in Circo Flaminio (Vall.) Volcanalici. Circenses, m(issus) xxiiii (Phil.)	5 September 13 September	15–19 Ludi in Circo (Vall., Amit.,V.dei Serp.) In Circo (Sab., Maff.,Ant.min.) Iovi Statori (Ant.mai.) Iovi Optimo Maximo (Ant. mai.) Iovi epulum (Arv.,Sab.) Iovi, Iunoni, Minervae epulum (Vall.) Epuli indictio (Ant.min.) Epulum indicitur Iovi, Iunoni, Minervae in Capitolio (V dei Serp.) Epulum Minervae (Menol. Col. and Vall.)
24 August	Lunae in Graecostasi (Pinc.)		
25 August	OPICONSIVIA (Ant.mai., Pinc., Maff.) OPICONSIVIA Feriae Opi: [Opi Consivae] in Regia (Arv.) OPICONSIVIA Opi in Capitolio (Vall.) OPICONSIVIA Feriae Opi Consivae (Allif.)	14 September 20–23 September 23 September	Equorum probatio (Sab.,Maff., Admit.,Vall.,Ant.min.V.dei Serp.) Mercatus (Pinc.,Maff.,Vall., V.dei Serp.) Apollini, Latonae ad Theatrum Marcelli, Felicitati in campo Martio, Iovi Statori, Iunoni Reginae ad circum Flaminium (Pal.Urbin.)
27 August	VOLTVRNALIA (Ant.mai., Pinc.,Maff.,Allif., Mag.) VOLTVRNALIA Feriae Volturno (Arv.) VOLTVRNALIA Volturno flumini sacrificium (Vall.)	26 September 1 October	Veneri Genetrici in Foro Caesaris (Pinc.,Praen., Vall.) Fidei (Ant.mai.) Fidei in Capitolio, Tigillo Sororio ad Compitum Acili (Arv.) Fidei in Capitolio (Amit.)
28 August	Solis et Lunae Circenses missus xxiiii (Phil.) [. . .] it subin [de . . . So] lis et Lun [ae . . . o] Martem [. . .] (Praen.)	4 October 7 October	Ieiunium Cereris (Amit.) Iovi Fulguri, Iunoni Quiriti (Ant.mai.) Iovi Fulguri. Iunoni Curriti in Campo (Arv.) Iovi Fulguri. Iunoni Quiriti in Campo (Paul)
1 September	Iovi Tonanti in Capitolio, Iovi Libero, Iunoni Reginae in Aventino (Arv.) Iovi Tonanti in Capitolio (Amit.) Feriae Iovi (Ant.min.)	9 October	Genio publico, Faustae Felicitati, Veneri Victrici in Capitolio, Apollini in Palatio (Amit., Arv.)
4–19 September	Ludi Romani 7–19 Magni (Ant.mai.) 4 Ludi Magni in honorem Iovis O.M. (Arv.)	10 October	Iunoni Monetae (Ant.mai.,

Sab.)

11 October   MEDITRINALIA
              (Ant.mai.,Pl.Fanti., Sab.,
              Maff.)
              MEDITRINALIA *Feriae Iovi*
              (Arv., Amit.)

13 October   FONTINALIA (Ant.mai.,
              Pl.Fanti.Sab.,Maff.,Tarent.)
              FONTINALIA *Fonti extra*
              Portam Fontinalem (Viae
              Ardeat.)
              FONTINALIA *Feriae Fonti*
              (Amit.)
              FONTINALIA *Feriae Fonti*
              extra Portam Fontinalem
              (V.dei Serp.)

14 October   [. . .] *Penatibus in Velia* (Viae
              Ardent.)

15 October   *Feriae Iovi* (Arv.)
              Equus ad Nixas (Phil.)

19 October   ARMILVSTRIVM (Arv.,
              Sab.,Maff.,Amit.,Ant.min.)

20 October   [. . .] *sanguinem gustare antea*
              frequenter solebant (Note in
              Praen.)

26 October–   *Ludi Victoriae Sullanae*
1 November   26 *Ludi Victoriae Sullanae*
              (Arv.,Sab.,Maff.)
              27–31 *Ludi* (Arv.,Sab.,
              Maff.)
              1 November *Ludi in Circo*
              (Arv.,Opp.,Ant.min.,V.dei
              Serp.)

1 November   *Ludi in Circo* (Arv.etc)

4–17   *Ludi Plebei*
November   4–12 *Ludi or Ludi Plebei*
              (Arv.,Maff.,Amit.,
              Ant.min.)
              13 *Iovi epulum:* see 13th.
              14 *Equorum probatio:* see 14th
              15–17 *In Circo or Ludi in*
              Circo (Arv.,Naff.,Amit.,
              Ant.min., Phil.)

13 November   *Feriae Iovi. Iovi epulum* (Arv.)
              Epuli indictio (Maff.)
              Epulum indicitur (Ant.min.)
              Iovi epulum. Circenses, missus
              xxx (Phil.)
              Feroniae, Fortunae Primigeniae,
              [Pie?]tati (Ant.mai.)
              Feroniae in [Ca]mpo, Fortunae

Primigeniae in C (apitolio?)
(Arv.)

14 November   *Equorum probatio* (Arv.,
              Maff.,Ant.min.,Amit.)

18–20   *Mercatus* (Arv.,Maff.,Amit.,
November   Ant.min.)

1 December   *Neptuno, Pietati* (Mag.,Opp.)
              Neptuno, Pietati ad Circum
              Flaminium (Amit.)

8 December   *Tiberino, Gaiae.* (Ant.mai.)
              Tiberino in Insula. (Amit.)

10 December   *Tribuni [plebis magistratum*
              ineunt] (Praen.)

11 December   AGONALIA (Maff.,Praen.,
              Ant.min.)
              AGONALIA INDIGETI
              (Ost., Amit.)
              Septimontium (Guidizz.; Silv.
              wrongly at 12 Dec.)
              Septimontia (Phil.)

12 December   *Conso in Aventino* (Ost.,
              Amit.)

13 December   *Tellur [i in Carinis?]* (Ost.)
              [Telluri. Lectisternium Cere?] ri
              in Carinis (Praen.)
              Telluri (Ant.min.)

15 December   CONSVALIA (Ant.mai.)
              CONSVALIA *Feriae Conso*
              (Praen., Amit.)
              Equi et [muli flore coronantur],
              quod in eius tu [tela. . .]. Itaque
              rex equo [vectus. . .] (Note in
              Praen.)

17–23   SATVRNALIA *Saturno*
December   (Ant.mai.)
              SATVRNALIA *Feriae*
              Saturno (Maff.)
              SATVRNALIA *Feriae*
              Saturno Saturno ad Forum
              (Amit.)
              SATVRNALIA (Ost.
              Guidizz., Phil.,Menol.Col.
              and Vall.)
              Feriae servorum (Silv.)

19 December   OPALIA *Opi* (Ant.mai.)
              OPALIA (Maff.,Ost.)
              OPALIA *Feriae Opi. Opi ad*
              Forum (Amit.)
              Io[ventati?] (Ost.)

21 December   DIVALIA (Ant.mai.,Maff.,
              Praen.)

21 December   DIVALIA ANGERONAE
               (Ost.)
               Feriae divaſe Angeronae quae
               ab anginae morbo] appellſatur,
               quod remedia eius quondam]
               praeſcipit. Statuerunt eam ore
               obligato] in arſa Volupiae, ut
               moneret ne quis nomen]
               occulſtum Urbis enuntiaret
               . . . ſn aiunt ob an [. . . ſn
               (Note in Praen.)

22 December   *Laribus Permarinis* (Ant.mai.
               ad 21 Dec; Ost.)
               Laribus Permarinis in Porticu
               Minucia (Praen.)

23 December   LARENTALIA (Ant.mai.,

Maff.,Ost.)
LARENTALIA *Feriae Iovi*
(Praen.)
Accae Larentin ſae Parentalia
fiunt] Hanc alii Remi et Rom
ſuli nutricem, alii] meretricem,
Herculis scortum, [ſuisse dicJunt.
Parentari ei publice, quod
populum Romanuḿ heſredem
feceJ rit magnae pecuniae, quam
accepe ſrat testaman] to Tarutili
amatoris sui (Note in Praen.)
Dianae, Iunoni Reginae in
Campo, Tempestatibus
(Ant.mai.)

THE ANNUAL CALENDAR

(The character letter quoted for each day is, in doubtful cases that which seems probable for the Republic, see A.K. Michels, *op. cit.* (Appendix 2).

January

1	A	F	KAL.	*Aesculapio, Vediovi in insula, Co [ronidi?]*
2	B	F		
3	C	C		
4	D	C		
5	E	F	NON.	*Vicae Potae*
6	F	F		
7	G	C		
8	H	C		
9	A	NP		AGONALIA
10	B	EN		
11	C	NP		CARMENTALIA. *Iuturnae*
12	D	C		
13	E	NP	EID.	*(ovis idulis)*
14	F	EN		
15	G	NP		CARMENTALIA
16	H	C		
17	A	C		
18	B	C		
19	C	C		
20	D	C		
21	E	C		
22	F	C		
23	G	C		
24	H	C		
25	A	C		
26	B	C		
27	C	C		*Castori et Polluci*
28	D	C		
29	E	C		

Feriae Conceptivae
c.3–5   Compitalia
c.24–26?   Sementivae or Paganalia

February

1	F	N	KAL.	*Iunoni Sospitae Matri Reginae,. Helerno*
2	G	N		
3	H	N		
4	A	N		
5	B	N	NON.	*Concordiae in Capitolio*
6	C	N		
7	D	N		
8	E	N		
9	F	N		
10	G	N		
11	H	N		
12	A	N		
13	B	NP	EID.	*Fauno in Insula. (ovis idulis)*
				13–21 *Parentalia*
14	C	N		
15	D	NP		LUPERCALIA
16	E	EN		
17	F	NP		QUIRINALIA
18	G	C		
19	H	C		
20	A	C		
21	B	F		FERALIA
22	C	C		*(Caristia)*
23	D	NP		TERMINALIA
24	E	N		REGIFUGIUM
25	F	C		
26	G	EN		
27	H	NP		EQUIRRIA
28	A	C		

Feriae Conceptivae
Fornacalia (ending 17 February)
Amburbium

March

1	B	NP	KAL.	*Feriae Marti. (Ancilia movent.)*
				Iunoni Lucinae. (Matronalia)
2	C	F		
3	D	C		
4	E	C		
5	F	C		
6	G	C		
7	H	F	NON.	*Vediovi*
8	A	F		
9	B	C		*(Ancilia movent.)*
10	C	C		
11	D	C		

(March)

12	E	C		
13	F	EN		
14	G	NP		EQUIRRIA. *Mamuralia*
15	H	NP	EID.	*Feriae Iovi. (ovis idulis). Annae Perennae*
16	A	F		*(Itur ad Argeos)*
17	B	NP		LIBERALIA. AGONALIA
18	C	C		
19	D	NP		QUINQUATRUS. *Minervae. Feriae Marti*
20	E	C		
21	F	C		
22	G	N		
23	H	NP		TUBILUSTRIUM
24	A	F		Q.R.C.F.
25	B	C		
26	C	C		
27	D	C		
28	E	C		
29	F	C		
30	G	C		
31	H	C		*Lunae in Aventino*

April

					Games
1	A	F	KAL.	*Veneralia. Veneri Verticordiae. Fortunae Virili*	
2	B	F			
3	C	C			
4	D	C		*Matri Magnae*	Ludi Megalenses
5	E	N	NON.	*Fortunae Publicae*	,, ,,
6	F	N			,, ,,
7	G	N			,, ,,
8	H	N			,, ,,
9	A	N			,, ,,
10	B	N		*Matri Magnae*	,, ,,
11	C	N			
12	D	N			Ludi Cereri
13	E	NP	EID	*Iovi Victori, Iovi Libertati. (ovis idulis)*	,, ,,
14	F	N			,, ,,
15	G	NP		FORDICIDIA	,, ,,
16	H	N			,, ,,
17	A	N			,, ,,
18	B	N			,, ,,
19	C	NP		CERIALIA. *Cereri, Libero, Liberae*	,, ,,
20	D	N			
21	E	NP		PARILIA. *Roma condita*	
22	F	N			

(April)   *Games*

23	G	F	VINALIA. *Veneri Erucinae*	
24	H	C		
25	A	NP	ROBIGALIA	
26	B	C		
27	C	C		
28	D	C		Ludi Florae
29	E	C		,, ,,

Feriae Conceptivae
Feriae Latinae (sometime between January and April)

May   *Games*

1	F	F	KAL.	*Bonae Deae. Maiae. Laribus Praestitibus*	Ludi Floraes
2	G	F			,, ,,
3	H	C		*Florae*	,, ,,
4	A	C			
5	B	C			
6	C	C			
7	D	F	NON.		
8	E	F			
9	F	N		LEMURIA	
10	G	C			
11	H	N		LEMURIA. *Ma[niae]*	
12	A	C			
13	B	N		LEMURIA	
14	C	C		*Marti Invicto. (Argeis)*	
15	D	NP	EID.	*Feriae Iovi, Mercurio, Maiae, [. . .] Invicto. (ovis idulis)*	
16	E	F			
17	F	C			
18	G	C			
19	H	C			
20	A	C			
21	B	NP		AGONALIA. *Vediovi*	
22	C	N			
23	D	NP		TUBILUSTRIUM. *Volcano*	
24	E	F		Q.R.C.F	
25	F	C		*Fortunae Publicae Populi Romani Quiritium*	
26	G	C			
27	H	C			
28	A	C			
29	B	C			
30	C	C			
31	D	C			

Feriae Conceptivae
c.29?   Ambarvalia

June

Games

1	E	N	KAL.	Marti in Clivo. Iunoni Monetae. (Tempestatibus). (Carnae)	
2	F	F			
3	G	C		Bellonae	
4	H	C		Herculi Magno	
5	A	N	NON.	Dio Fidio	
6	B	N			
7	C	N		(Vesta aperitur)	(Piscatorii Ludi)
8	D	N		Menti	
9	E	N		VESTALIA	
10	F	N			
11	G	NP(?)		MATRALIA. Matri Matutae. Fortunae	
12	H	N			
13	A	NP	EID.	Feriae Iovi. (ovis idulis). (Quinquatrus minusculae)	
14	B	N			
15	C	F		(Vesta clauditur)	
16	D	C			
17	E	C			
18	F	C			
19	G	C		Minervae	
20	H	C		Summano	
21	A	C			
22	B	C			
23	C	C			
24	D	C		Forti Fortunae	
25	E	C			(Ludi Taurei quinquennales)
26	F	C			,, ,,
27	G	C		Laribus V(. . .). Iovi Statori	
28	H	C			
29	A	C (day added by J.Caesar)			
30	A	C		Herculi Musarum	

July (MENSIS QUINCTILIS)

Games

1	B	N	KAL.	Iunoni. Felicitati	
2	C	N			
3	D	N			
4	E	N			
5	F	NP		POPLIFUGIA. Feriae Iovi	
6	G	N		(Fortunae Muliebri)	Ludi Apollinares
7	H	N	NON.	Palibus, (Nonae Caprotinae). (Conso).	,, ,,
8	A	N		(Vitulatio)	,, ,,
9	B	N			,, ,,
10	C	C			,, ,,

(July (MENSIS QUINCTILIS))   *Games*

11	D	C			Ludi Apollinares
12	E	C			,, ,,
13	F	C		*Apollini*	,, ,,
14	G	C			Mercatus
15	H	NP	EID	*(Equitum Rom. transvectio) (ovis idulis)*	,,
16	A	F			,,
17	B	C		*Honori. Victoriae in Capitolio*	,,
18	C	C		*Alliensis dies*	,,
19	D	NP		LUCARIA	,,
20	E	C			Ludi Victoriae Caesaris
21	F	NP		LUCARIA	,, ,, ,,
22	G	C		*Concordiae*	,, ,, ,,
23	H	NP		NEPTUNALIA	,, ,, ,,
24	A	N			,, ,, ,,
25	B	NP		FURRINALIA	,, ,, ,,
26	C	C			,, ,, ,,
27	D	C			,, ,, ,,
28	E	C			,, ,, ,,
29	F	C			,, ,, ,,
30	G	C		*Fortunae Huiusque Diei*	,, ,, ,,
31	H	C			

August (MENSIS SEXTILIS)

1	A	F	KAL.	*Spei. Victoriae*
2	B	F		
3	C	C		*(Supplicia canum)*
4	D	C		
5	E	F		*Saluti*
6	F	F		
7	G	C	NON.	
8	H	C		
9	A	C		*Soli Indigiti*
10	B	C		
11	C	C		
12	D	C		*Herculi Invicto. Veneri Victrici. Honori, Virtuti.* *V[estae?]. Felicitati*
13	E	NP	EID.	*Dianae. Vortumno. Fortunae Equestri. Herculi Victori.* *Castori, Polluci. Camenis. Florae. (ovis idulis)*
14	F	F		
15	G	C		
16	H	C		
17	A	NP		PORTUNALIA. *Jano*
18	B	C		

(August (MENSIS SEXTILIS))

19	C	F	VINALIA. *Veneri*
20	D	C	
21	E	NP	CONSUALIA. *Conso*
22	F	EN	
23	G	NP	VOLCANALIA. *Volcano. Horae Quirini. Maiae.*
			Nymphis. Opi
24	H	C	*Lunae. (Mundus patet)*
25	A	NP	OPICONSIVIA. *Opi*
26	B	C	
27	C	NP	VOLTURNALIA
28	D	C	*Solis et Lunae*
29	E	C	

September   *Games*

1	F	F	KAL.	*Iunoni Reginae*	
2	G	F			
3	H	C			
4	A	C			Ludi Romani
5	B	F	NON.	*Iovi Statori*	,, ,,
6	C	F			,, ,,
7	D	C			,, ,,
8	E	C			,, ,,
9	F	C			,, ,,
10	G	C			,, ,,
11	H	C			,, ,,
12	A	N			,, ,,
13	B	NP	EID.	*Iovi Optimo Maximo. (ovis idulis).*	,, ,,
				Epulum Iovi, Iunoni, Minervae	
14	C	F		*Equorum probatio(?)*	,, ,,
15	D	N			,, ,,
16	E	C			,, ,,
17	F	C			,, ,,
18	G	C			,, ,,
19	H	C			,, ,,
20	A	C			Mercatus
21	B	C			,,
22	C	C			,,
23	D	C		*Apollini. Latonae*	,,
24	E	C			
25	F	C			
26	G	C		*Veneri Genetrici*	
27	H	C			
28	A	C			
29	B	C			

October   *Games*

1	C	N	KAL.	*Fidei. Tigillo Sororio*	
2	D	F			
3	E	C			
4	F	C		*Ieiunium Cereris*	
5	G	C		*(Mundus patet)*	
6	H	C			
7	A	F	NON.	*Iovi Fulguri. Iunoni Curriti*	
8	B	F			
9	C	C		*Genio Publico. Faustae Felicitati. Veneri Victrici*	
10	D	C		*Iunoni Monetae*	
11	E	NP		MEDITRINALIA. *Feriae Iovi*	
12	F	C			
13	G	NP		FONTINALIA. *Fonti*	
14	H	EN		*Penatibus in Velia*	
15	A	NP	EID.	*Feriae Iovi. (Equus October). (ovis idulis).*	Ludi Capitolini
16	B	F			
17	C	C			
18	D	C			
19	E	NP		ARMILUSTRIUM	
20	F	C			
21	G	C			
22	H	C			
23	A	C			
24	B	C			
25	C	C			
26	D	C			Ludi Victoriae Sullanae
27	E	C			,, ,, ,,
28	F	C			,, ,, ,,
29	G	C			,, ,, ,,
30	H	C			,, ,, ,,
31	A	C			,, ,, ,,

November   *Games*

1	B	F	KAL.		Ludi Victoriae Sullanae
2	C	F			
3	D	C			
4	E	C			Ludi Plebeii
5	F	F	NON.		,, ,,
6	G	F			,, ,,
7	H	C			,, ,,
8	A	C		*(Mundus patet)*	,, ,,
9	B	C			,, ,,
10	C	C			,, ,,
11	D	C			,, ,,
12	E	C			,, ,,

(November)

					Games
13	F	NP	EID.	*Feriae Iovi. Iovi epulum. (ovis idulis).*	Ludi Plebeii
				Feroniae. Fortunae Primigeniae. [Pie?] tati	,, ,,
14	G	F		*Equorum probatio*	,, ,,
15	H	C			,, ,,
16	A	C			,, ,,
17	B	C			
18	C	C			Mercatus
19	D	C			,,
20	E	C			,,
21	F	C			
22	G	C			
23	H	C			
24	A	C			
25	B	C			
26	C	C			
27	D	C			
28	E	C			
29	F	C			

December

1	G	N	KAL.	*Neptuno. Pietati*
2	H	N		
3	A	N		
4	B	C		
5	C	F	NON.	*(Fauno)*
6	D	F		
7	E	C		
8	F	C		*Tiberino*
9	G	C		
10	H	C		
11	A	NP		AGONALIA. *Septimontium*
12	B	EN		*Conso*
13	C	NP	EID.	*Telluri [Cere?]ri. (ovis idulis)*
14	D	F		
15	E	NP		CONSUALIA. *Conso*
16	F	C		
17	G	NP		SATURNALIA (continuing some years till 23rd).
				Saturno. Feriae servorum
18	H	C		
19	A	NP		OPALIA. *Feriae Opi. Io[ventati?]*
20	B	C		
21	C	NP		DIVALIA. *(Herculi. Cereri)*

(December)

22	D	C	*Laribus Permarinis*
23	E	NP	LARENTALIA. *Dianae. Iunoni Reginae.*
			Tempestatibus
24	F	C	
25	G	C	
26	H	C	
27	A	C	
28	B	C	
29	C	C	

Feriae Conceptivae
Early December: *Bona Dea*

CHRONOLOGICAL LIST OF
TEMPLES, ETC.

The dates given are those of the dedication. When only the year in which a temple was vowed is known, this date is given, marked with an asterisk. For the early period some of the dates are traditional and uncertain, and many temples may have been preceded by altars or shrines to the deities concerned.

Before 509	?	Jupiter Feretrius in Capitolio
	?	Terminus in Capitolio
	?	Iuventas in Capitolio
	11 June	Mater Matuta in Foro Boario
	11 June	Fortuna in Foro Boario
	13 August	Diana in Aventino
509	13 September	Jupiter Optimus Maximus in Capitolio
495	15 May	Mercurius ad Circum Maximum
493	19 April	Ceres, Liber, Liber ad Circum Maximum
?	19 March	Minerva in Aventino
484	27 January	Castor in Foro
466	5 June	Dius Fidius in Colle
Between 432 & 381	17 December	Saturnus in Foro
431	13 July	Apollo in pratis Flaminiis
392	1 September	Juno Regina in Aventino
388(?)	1 June	Mars in Clivo
?	1 March	Juno Lucina Esquiliis
367(?)*	22 July(?)	Concordia in Foro
344	1 June	Juno Moneta in Arce
302	5 August	Salus in Colle Quirinali
4th century	5 January	Vica Pota
	6 July	Fortuna Muliebris Via Latina ad milliarium IV
	24 June	Fors Fortuna trans Tiberim ad milliarium I
296*	3 June	Bellona in Circo Flaminio
295*	13 April	Jupiter Victor
295*	19 August	Venus ad Circum Maximum
294	1 August	Victoria in Palatio
294*	27 June	Jupiter Stator in Palatio
293	17 February	Quirinus in Colle
293	24 June	Fors Fortuna trans Tiberim ad milliarium VI
291	1 January	Aesculapius in Insula
278	20 June	Summanus ad Circum Maximum
273(?)*	21 August or 12 December	Consus in Aventino
268*	13 December	Tellus in Carinis
267*	7 July	Pales Duo
264*	13 August	Vortumnus in Aventino

260(?)*	17 August	Janus ad Theatrum Marcelli
260(?)*	17 August	Portunus in Foro Holitorio
259*	1 June or	Tempestates ad Portam Capenam
	23 December	
258*	1 August	Spes in Foro Holitorio
c.250	1 October	Fides in Capitolio
241*	19 March(?)	Minerva in Caeliolo
238(?)	27 April	Flora ad Circum Maximum
233*	17 July(?)	Honos ante Portam Capenam
231*	13 October	Fons extra Portam Fontinalem
3rd century	4 June	Hercules Magnus Custos in Circo Flaminio
	13 November	Feronia in Campo
	23 August	Volcanus in Circo Flaminio
	1 December	Neptunus ad Circum Flaminium
	25 August	Ops in Capitolio
		Libertas in Aventino
	19 August	Venus in Luco Libitinae
	12 August	Hercules Invictus ad Circum Maximum
	13 August	Castor and Pollux in Circo Flaminio
	28 August	Sol ad Circum Maximum
	8 December	Tiberinus in Insula
	27 June	Lares V[. . .] in Sacra Via
	14 October	Penates in Velia
	7 October	Jupiter Fulgur in Campo
		Minerva Medica
	31 March	Luna in Aventino
	9 August	Sol Indiges in Quirinale
		Venus Cloacina
216	5 February	Concordia in Capitolio
215	8 June	Mens in Capitolio
215		Venus Erucina in Capitolio
205	17 July	Honos et Virtus ante Portam Capenam
194	1 January	Vediovis in Insula
194	1 February	Juno Sospes ad Forum Holitorium
194	13 February	Faunus in Insula
194(?)	25 May	Fortuna Pop.Rom.Quirit. in Colle
193	1 August	Victoria Virgo in Palatio
192	7 March	Vediovis inter duos lucos
191	10 April	Magna Mater in Palatio
191	19 December (?)	Iuventas ad Circum Maximum
189 (or later)	30 June (?)	Hercules Musarum in Circo Flaminio
181	23 April	Venus Erucina ad Portam Collinam
181	13 November (?)	Pietas in Foro Holitorio
179	22 December	Lares Permarini in Porticu Minucia
179	23 December	Diana ad Circum Flaminium
179	23 December	Juno Regina ad Circum Flaminium
173	13 August	Fortuna Equestria ad theatrum lapideum
		Felicitas in Velabro
146	5 September	Jupiter Stator in Circo Flaminio
142		Hercules Victor
117–104		Ops Opifera in Foro

114	1 April	Venus Verticordia
101	30 July	Fortuna Huiusce Diei in Campo
Soon after 101		Honos et Virtus
End of 2nd or 1st century	1 December	Pietas ad Circum Flaminium
55	12 August	Venus Victrix, Honos, Virtus, V[. . .], Felicitas in theatro marmoreo
46	26 September	Venus Genetrix in Foro Caesaris

INDEX